Forbidden Revelation

Forbidden Revelation

Secret Teachings to My

Exclusive Inner Circle

Mark Hamilton

NEOTHINK® BOOKS

Published by The Neothink® Society
850 S. Boulder Highway, Henderson, Nevada 89015, U.S.A
First published in the United States of America by
Integrated Management Associates
8 6 5 7 9
1st Printing
Copyright ©Mark Hamilton, 2012
All rights preserved
LIBRARY OF CONGRESS
CATALOGING-PUBLICATION DATA
Hamilton, Mark

ISBN # 0-911752-00-5

Printed in the United States of America

August 2012 [FR] [7,250]
June 2013 [FR] [4,861]
April 2014 [FR] [5,176]
November 2014 [FR] [5,796]
March 2016 [FR] [5,000]

Table of Contents

Introduction

One of the greatest benefits of membership in The Neothink® Society is The Journey with Mark Hamilton. These essence meetings have been transcribed from Mr. Hamilton's web-based Mentor Program. Here he describes each level of your twelve-level journey:

Level One opens the door to the person you were meant to be as you learn how to play as an adult. By discovering value creation, stagnation quickly gets replaced with exhilaration, and the child of the past returns. Your life leaps to a new level as you tap your deepest motivational root through discovering your Friday-Night Essence.

Level Two reveals the highly-guarded Neothink® hidden secret, the coveted Ten-Second Miracle. The Ten-Second Miracle provides you with another powerful path to value creation – to the life you were meant to live. Indeed, the creation-driven life is what the human mind is supposed to experience; value creation brings values to society and pride and happiness to oneself . . . and is the answer to the often-asked question, "What is the meaning of life?" Your Friday-Night Essence and the Ten-Second Miracle are two powerful secrets to value creation.

Level Three unveils how and why you were chosen to join the Neothink® Society. You also learn our highly-guarded Neothink® Marketing Secret. That meeting teaches you about the Forces of Nature and the Forces of Neothink®...and the powerful marketing forces of both. It also explains how common denominators can be used to pull forth those powerful marketing forces. Our highly-guarded Neothink® Marketing Secret prepares you for the next leg of the journey where wealthy living awaits!

Level Four introduces the concept of taking the secret society, for the first time, to the public. The ideas of local Neothink® Clubhouses, local meetings, even a local political movement are introduced. The approach is to still keep our secrets within our society, but to now invite quality people at large into our newly named Society of Secrets. We are transitioning from a Secret Society to a Society of Secrets.

Level Five goes through, in detail, the three meetings to be held in the newly forming Neothink® Clubhouses, as follows: the Introduction Meetings, the Workshop Meetings, and the Clubhouse Meetings. Level Five also goes into detail about the development of a new political movement now named the Twelve Visions Party.

Level Six solidifies the structure of the new entities, the newly forming local Neothink® Chapters (Clubhouse Congregations), the internal workings, the applications. In this meeting, the "marketing machine is complete" and is ready to move forward.

Level Seven identifies the two pillars holding up the anticivilization – politics and religion. This historic meeting delivers a plan to trump those two pillars through our Society of Secrets in order to peacefully take down the anticivilization.

Level Eight presents the big picture. In your eighth month, you will see the major movements that will come out of the Society of Secrets. You will see the coming Twelve-Visions World. In this world, people live with great wealth, health, and peace. They are happy, exhilarated, in love, and looking for eternal life.

Level Nine releases the specifics on the first of several major movements to come out of the burgeoning Society of Secrets. This first major movement is the political movement designed to trump politics and begin to take down the anticivilization. The Society of Secrets, from within its Tier Two, will spread its first major movement across the country, and then the world.

Level Ten prepares apprentices for mentoring lower-level apprentices. Level-Ten Apprentices are now ready to put priceless values back into the Society of Secrets, including mentoring and helping lower-level apprentices. Level-Ten Apprentices are now openly invited, during the last leg of the journey, to bring their talents and skills into the Neothink® Society to make it stronger. Becoming a value creator in the Neothink® Society, living one's Friday-Night Essence, is exhilarating beyond description. Just imagine seeing one's own value creation moving forward the SOS Goal, the Superpuzzle . . . you making a difference in the course of mankind. Level Ten also digs deeply into the new Twelve-Visions Government structure. For the first time, Mark Hamilton reveals integrated specifics behind a never-before-known government based on service rather than power, bringing to our planet a never-before-seen freedom paradigm and unprecedented wealth, health, and peace.

Level Eleven opens its arms to these high-level apprentices who finally experience their full human potential, unburied during this journey. Upon finally knowing their hidden abilities, these special apprentices in their final leg of the journey can finally know and access the persons they were meant to be.

Level Twelve points the world-wide Neothink® juggernaut straight toward the future Twelve Visions World as the high-level apprentices' transition to mentors. These new mentors experienced emotions not felt before — the euphoria of lifting others, too, into the life they were meant to live. As mentors, they lift loved ones into a better life, a new world, the Twelve Visions World.

Level-One Essence Meeting
Introduction

Look at the front page of most any newspaper today. You're looking at an anticivilization full of irrationality and mediocrity in which live the masses. Your journey is one that leaves that anitcivilization to come into a new world. To come into an exclusive civilization here within our exclusive Secret Society. The Neothink® civilization full of rationality in both financial and emotional wealth.

As your mentor during your new year long journey into this new world I ask you to let go of your preconceived notions of what these meetings are. The format here is tried and true for your best benefit. These meetings work in concert with your heirloom packages. Together with these tools and techniques in your heirloom packages combined with these meetings, well, your life will turn into an incredible journey as you evolve, with my help, into the exclusive society of the happiest, wealthiest people alive.

That being said, you must put aside your pie-in-the-sky expectations. It's all going to happen, but not today, this instant.

This brings me to an article I once read by a leading Neothink® Society member which I adopted for my own journey. The article about wealth and success described a foot traveler who steadily moves forward. He's not covering a lot of ground all at once, but he is always moving forward. So over a year the amount of ground he covers amounts to a lot.

Well, I applied that analogy to myself which saved me from my own pie-in-the-sky expectations and kept me steadily moving forward. I knew that after a year I would have covered a lot of ground and I did. My journey became a journey of no return; one that led me to wealth and happiness.

I want to take you on that same journey of no return, one that leads you to wealth and happiness. You are now the foot traveler as I once was.

Now, let me back up to what I said earlier about the front page of most any newspaper. I have a broad base portfolio of media I look at, all the while knowing that although I live in that world I'm reading about, in that anticivilization, it's not my world.

Although I have to deal with the irrationalities of that world, my world is free from purposeful irrationality which is why I'm wealthy and happy and am surrounded by amazing, brilliant friends.

We're not naive to the ways of the world; in fact, we're increasingly controlling the ways of the world, steadily pulling that big iron ball toward our world, a rational world of wealth, health, pride and happiness. The world in which human beings were meant to live.

I'm talking about the Neothink® World which you've come to learn through your heirloom packages. You really are entering that world. With me as your mentor, you and your family will be living in that Neothink® World with us, prosperous and happy.

You have enormous potential. I honestly plan to bring out your human potential. That is not hype as you'll soon discover.

So, welcome to the Neothink® Secret Meetings. As you know, I am Mark Hamilton, author of many of your Neothink® manuscripts.

Among the leading members, I've been selected as your mentor at the Neothink Society. I'll conduct today's secret meeting by taking your questions and providing answers.

The subject of today's Level One Meeting is Wealth and Happiness. I want to make it clear that these Secret Meetings are absolutely not designed to teach what has already been taught in your heirloom packages. I'm going to assume here that you already know the information thoroughly in your heirloom packages which is why we allowed substantial time to pass before your debut level meeting today. I'll reference specific places in the heirloom packages where I want you to go back and take a deeper look relative to today's meeting.

Ok, let's dive into today's subject of wealth and happiness.

Q) What is the Neothink® Core Secret to Wealth & Happiness?

MH) A perfect question to start today's secret meeting. You know from your Second Heirloom Package, in Vision One, the answer to *both* wealth and happiness is discovering and then making your living through your Friday-Night Essence. Your Friday-Night Essence, as you know from Visions One, is the *productive activity* (not entertainment, sports, or hanging out) that you would actually enjoy doing on a Friday Night (our long-embedded "shut down night"). Whatever productive activity we *want* to do when our system otherwise says "shut down" gives us the clue to the person we were meant to be. I have to assume our members here read Vision One and understand what that means. If not, then you must revisit Vision One. Today, right now, I will give you a catalyst to this secret of happiness and wealth:

When we were young children, we played a lot and we were happy. Play and happiness went hand-in-hand. In fact, playing filled us with euphoria. We need to define what PLAYING is for adults. Playing and happiness go hand-in-hand, even in adults.

When adults are *creating values*, they are playing. In fact, creating values fills us with euphoria. If you have been so fortunate as to have experienced creating values, you will relate: Creating values is how adults play.

Imagine filling your day with play time, with euphoria. That is exactly what happens when you create values. Vacations are not really our play time; creating values is our play time. The great value I have discovered in vacations, by the way, is spending time with and getting close to my children, wife and close friends.

Q) How will playing make me wealthy?

MH)   Excellent   question.   Those   who   become independently wealthy do so by playing – it's the only way. In fact, my use of the word "playing" is NOT a metaphor. Creating values is how adults really do play, feel stimulated, happy, and, ultimately, become wealthy. Adults do not become wealthy by begrudgingly dragging themselves out of bed, shuffling themselves to work, waiting intolerably for the work day to pass. Those poor souls – the majority of the working class – never get rich. The reason it is that way, as explained in Book Two, Vision Two is: they're stuck in a stagnant routine-rut. They're stuck in value ***production***, not value ***creation***.

On the other hand, imagine those who open their eyes in the morning excited to get up and ***play***, those who get ready quickly to get to their creations. They ***play*** all day long at taking their creations to new levels. And, they eventually, get rich.

Playing is the mental makeup of the rich. ***Playing*** at our Friday-Night Essences is perhaps the longest-held secret of the ultra rich.

Q)   I'm having trouble identifying my Friday-Night Essence. Can you help?

MH) Here is what I say to my Level-One apprentices: You do not need to worry if you cannot put your finger on your Friday-Night Essence right now. What is more important is to work toward ***creating values***. When you rise past producing values to creating values as explained in Vision Two, you will experience such an infusion of exhilaration that you will begin to PLAY. Go through the step-by-step process called The Self-Leader System in the Vision Climax inside your Second Heirloom Package. It will help lift you from value production to value creation. That's when you will begin *to play* in life. When you begin *to play*, your creations will become your Friday-Night Essence. Moreover, you will acquire the power and money to identify and pursue deeper dreams/Friday-Night Essences. Playing as an adult will bring you success, wealth, and happiness…playing via creating values.

Q) I have just broken through to value creation at my place of work. Is this euphoria I feel in a place that I previously dreaded a normal reaction?

MH) Yes, euphoria is a typical reaction. You have just experienced the sudden shift from what higher-level Neothink® members recognize as the life of the living dead into the life of an immortal. When you live by playing, creating values, building pride, happiness, love and wealth, then you can and *want to* live forever, which is what creative human beings are meant for. You feel euphoria because you are becoming the person you were meant to be. As you progress from a Level-One member into the higher levels, you will learn what we are doing to eradicate aging and death for Earth's First Immortals on our planet – i.e., the Neothink® Society members. By the way, the euphoria is NOT temporary. As a value creator, it is immortal. You could live forever with limitless happiness. You become immune to the burden of life, as identified in Heirloom Package Two, Vision Two. The underlying burden of life in the anitcivilization is the reason a desperate drive to eradicate aging and death does not exist. But that drive will rise from our secret society.

Q) I feel a little depressed and a little afraid to meet other Neothink® members because I have not improved. Why not?

MH) As your mentor, I must confess that I (not one of you) composed and injected that question. I did this not to be negative, but to address a large number of you who perhaps are fascinated with the discussion, but are not getting immediate results. My answer to you is: absorb these meetings with me. I will take you on an amazing journey over the next year, starting with today's teaching. The material in these meetings is specifically selected by me. I plant the right seeds of knowledge into your minds, which will root and grow. For example, you will be surprised at how learning our secret today of *playing at life*…how that psychological perspective – that seed of knowledge watered and nourished by the tools in your heirloom packages – will grow from today's seed into a tree of knowledge and direction bearing delicious and nutritious fruit. You cannot see the eventual harvest when looking at the little seed. But I can, and I do see that harvest every single day among members who started one year ago just as you are starting today. I was precisely accurate when I originally told you that a year from now, you will be a different person living a different life. Over the next week, I want you to go back into Vision One, Two and through the Vision Climax in your Second Heirloom Package. Let me repeat: go through Vision One, Two, and the Vision Climax. Study the specific tools again. Let those tools clear your path to what I revealed today – your tools to begin *playing* at life. I promise you, this exercise of marrying the tools in your heirloom package to the secret knowledge in these meetings will be huge.

Level-One Essence Meeting
Part One

Q) I have a mundane job and I'm sick of it. How do I start to play?

MH) Remember, creating value is **playing** for adults. You must dig back into the eternally valuable tools in your heirloom packages to make it happen. You need to study Vision One about your Friday-Night Essence. You need to study the Vision Climax that will ultimately lift you from boring routine rut of **value production** that comes from specialized thinking in a following mode…into exhilarating **value creation** that comes from integrated thinking in a self-leader mode. There is no shortcut around those disciplines in the Vision Climax. However, by applying those techniques — **they are the shortcut** — you will rise from value production to value creation and experience the psychological shift from a job you are sick of to a job you cannot wait to go and play.

Q) I have studied and applied the techniques in The Neothink® System in my First Heirloom Package and the techniques of all Twelve Visions in my Second Heirloom Package. The results have blown me away. I am no longer helplessly stuck as a follower in life. I am now an integrated thinker and am excelling and excited. This whole idea of PLAYING seems mind-blowing to me. It's like…I can really get totally into what I'm doing every day and not get dragged down by anything. Why do I feel so jazzed about it?

MH) I can tell you exactly why. But first, I want to point out that you are a perfect example of marrying the tools in your heirloom packages to the lessons in these meetings-with-your-mentor. Through the techniques in your packages, you have lifted yourself from silently suffering in your routine rut into excelling through exciting integrated thinking, which means you are now or soon will be breaking into value creation. Now realize, breaking into integrated thinking and moving onto value creation is how human beings were supposed to live for the past 3000 years. That means, you are discovering the person you were supposed to be — the self-leader. That is why you are feeling so good about yourself and about life.

Now, to answer why the whole idea of PLAYING seems mind-blowing to you and why you feel so jazzed about it — all conscious and unconscious guilt from this anticivilization fades away and drop off of you when you realize you are PLAYING as an adult. What guilt? Guilt poured into you at every turn. For instance, the villain in just about every movie you have watched since you were a child is the businessman, the job creator, that value creator. You innocently watch a movie and absorb guilt without even knowing it. The idea of PLAYING releases you from the years and years of absorbing guilt. PLAYING releases you from bondage to this guilt-ridden anticivilization. PLAYING like a kid — it brings you back to the long-forgotten child of the past deep inside your soul. PLAYING returns you to happiness — limitless, eternal happiness like the child, which is the true nature of human beings.

Finally, in harmony with your true nature, with the eternal happiness now within you, both the child and now you (having reunited with your child of the past) want to live forever. We are going to get into the whole idea of immortality as you steadily evolve to higher levels in the coming months. You are joining the force in society — a parallel society — that will ultimately eradicate aging and death. But for now, since you have broken through to integrated thinking and value creation and are obviously discovering the financial leaps — imagine how the value creator's wealth would compile if there were no death! There would be eternal wealth and happiness for us. Wealth itself would become so abundant for us that our drive would center on creating values that significantly benefited others, which is the very definition of happiness. Indeed, human beings are designed to live forever with great wealth and happiness.

Q) I was drawn like a magnet to the Three Insights in my Second Heirloom Package and to Earth's First Immortals in my Third Heirloom Package. I think and feel so strongly along those same lines. What is going on now to arrest aging?

MH) You have to wait for specifics until you get to higher levels in the coming months. But this I will say now: For human beings to die is NOT how we are supposed to be. Our minds are designed to create forever and to enjoy the eternal happiness and wealth our creative minds will bring us. It is too soon to go into specifics, but that will happen soon. By the way, those of you involved in the scientific/medical realm of antiaging research, feel free to send me background about yourself and what you are doing.

Q) Mark Hamilton, first let me say I love your works and am honored to "speak" with you and feel "blessed" that you are my mentor.

MH) Thank you.

Q) My question to you is: how can I also "speak" to all the other Neothink® members on a daily basis to share in their thoughts and experiences?

MH) There exists an exclusive, secret web site that no one but inside-members can access, where members "speak" to each other about endless topics and share worthy experiences. Only those who own the three heirloom packages as you do can join this exclusive web site. There is a monthly maintenance charge to support its costs/existence. I believe the charge is a dollar a day or thirty dollars per month. But people gain priceless values and make lucrative contacts, including physical contacts through this restricted web site consisting of open discussions 24/7. In fact, because most people who send in questions to me are so far back in the queue, their important questions do not make it into this meeting, so they go to the secret web site to ask their questions and get many solid answers from other members including high-level members such as myself and other leading members who power/think your future. The web site is probably worth millions of dollars to you in the long run. Moreover, there are about two-thousand pages of secret knowledge on the web site that you have never seen before. The URL is www.activeneothinkmember.com.

I've met many very successful people, not one of them is ever laboring at work. Instead every one of them is playing. They are happy, eternally happy. Learning how to play as an adult is *the* secret to wealth and happiness.

We'll pause here for you to send in your questions and comments. You must send them in. I'm watching them here on my computer. I do require that you send me comments either now or sometime during the other breaks. I need to see your individual progress in order for you to move up to Level Two next month. I am right here, right now reading all questions and comments.

If you have questions, I will not directly answer your questions through email. But I need to know your questions to track your progress. Many of your questions will be addressed in future meetings.

Also, to get your questions answered today, go to the secret web site after today's meeting and ask those same questions. The secret website is interactive with inside members here to answer your questions. That secret web site URL is www.activeneothinkmember.com.

After you send me your questions and comments, move on to Part 2.

To send me your questions and comments you will be prompted, after I'm done talking here, exactly how to do that and you will be prompted how to continue in Part Two.

Level-One Essence Meeting
Part Two

Q) I have begun making a lot more money using the techniques in The Neothink® System in my first book and The Self-Leader System in my second book. First, I want to thank you for that. Second, I want to ask you why I now have an obsession to make enough money to build a large custom home for myself, my wife and two children.

MH) The desire to build is inherent in human beings. Pyramids in Ancient Egypt, city-states in Ancient Greece, castles of ancient monarchs, palaces in the Middle East, skyscrapers in American and Asia, celebrity mansions: you name it. When you build a structure, you are creating something that did not exist before, which is a form of value creation (as long as the structure is built from the builder's EARNED money). It is also a form of value reflection, for you concretize, see, and enjoy your wealth-earning competence in your structure. Your desire to build a beautiful custom home is very understandable. You should use that desire as inspiration and a source of energy to push further into integrated thinking and value creation. We all need to identify such desires that motivate us and use those as energy toward our evolution from followers to self-leaders, from value producers to value creators (Vision Two in Heirloom Two).

Q) Hello. I am a female member. In the Second Heirloom Package, Vision Seven, you write about the dual essences of a woman as opposed to the single essence of a man. How exactly would a woman, who is a mom and housekeeper, PLAY in the way described here?

MH) Very good question. First, let me clarify that both females and males as human beings, get their source of happiness from value creation. The difference is that women can get their source of happiness through her husband's value creation, in a supportive role and as mom of their children. His value creation becomes hers, too. I won't go into why that is so in today's meeting, for that is explained, as you said, in Vision Seven. Instead, I will answer how you can experience PLAYING as described here. PLAYING is an adult's state of mind in tending to and experiencing his or her value creation. A supportive wife/mom's role, say, of taking care of and taking time with the children is all part of her dynamic of value creation, as explained in Vision Seven. Therefore, she can experience the PLAYING state of mind while with her children, for instance. Like her husband who shifts his mindset to happy, guilt-free PLAYING at life, so can she. Both husband and wife will experience a leap of happiness and emotional freedom. The children, too, who pattern their emotional dispositions after their parents, will benefit enormously with happier childhoods and teenage years. PLAYING at life as adults lifts husband, wife, and children into an exclusive society of the happiest (and wealthiest) families on Earth. These families will go on to join the great dynasties.

Q) I feel very lucky to have been selected to join the Neothink® Society at such a young age — I'm a twenty-one-year-old man. I'm also single and interested in meeting some nice women. Is that possible?

MH) You can and will meet nice, attractive women, even among those NOT in our secret society. Let me start by saying that single men who acquire our secrets are indeed very lucky. You see, they do not have to apply the same sorting standards that women do (as explained in Vision Seven). The man who goes through the evolution from follower to self-leader only needs the woman who responds to his character. It can be ANY woman, so to speak. So his pool of prospects is large and all around him. Now, here is when it gets exciting: Women perceive a sexual energy and a magnetic draw to men who rise above others, from followers to self-leaders. That fact has to do with both the Forces of Nature (Vision Three) in this anticivilization (which is why you will attract women from the general society around you) and with the forces of the supersociety (Vision Three) in tomorrow's Civilization of the Universe (which is why you will attract women from the secret society). As you apply the techniques in your heirloom packages to rise from a specialized thinker (i.e., a follower) to an integrated thinker (i.e., a self-leader), women of all backgrounds will be drawn to you. You will be able to feel and use that sexual energy to motivate your drive into value creation and playing at life. It is very rewarding for a man — even a happily married man who would never consider intimacy with another woman — to perceive women's attraction to him. But to a single young man such as yourself, women's growing attraction to you will fuel your efforts. Women's attraction to you becomes a highly motivating cycle as you evolve into the self-leader and into value creation while witnessing women's interest in you grow. When your increased income allows, do not feel guilty about purchasing some concrete signs of your success such as expensive shoes, watch, car. Those purchases from a self-made self-leader are real signs of your success, competence, and strength — all aphrodisiacs to women. Those purchases, combined with your growing confidence and self-assured demeanor, will make you an increasingly irresistible man. Of course, as you will eventually discover, perhaps several years from now, the greatest reward of all is when you settle down with the love of your life and discover the immense joy of children.

Q) After reading Earth's First Immortals, I woke up to the rare and precious love for my four children. I sometimes get paralyzed with the realization of how my kids are flying by their wonderful childhoods, and then it will be over. I guess life itself is flying by. Is there something I can do to stop their childhoods from flying by?

MH) You cannot stop it, but you can slow it down and always feel good that you did not miss out on their precious time as children. Go into Vision Twelve and read The Preciousness and feel it; experience the preciousness with your children. PLAYING (i.e., children's games) with your children is critical to be a fulfilled parent who did not miss out. PLAYING is an important part of your children's source of development and happiness. (Of course, teaching them responsibility and good study/work ethics is always important.) Playing WITH YOU is precious to your children, and they will NEVER forget it. Soon you will discover, once you make the transition to playing their games (it is a transition), you will discover that your play time together is also precious TO YOU, and YOU will NEVER forget it. You cannot get so close to them any other way. Moreover, playing their games with them will slow down their fleeting childhoods because you, in a sense, soak it in. You will not, as they pass their irreversible stages, ever feel that you missed out, which makes their transition into adulthood easier to accept, no longer something sad that you almost dread…but something good that you can embrace with excitement when the time comes. Furthermore, by having been so involved and so close during their childhoods, they will naturally want you to be close and involved during their adulthoods. Life is transitory, my friend, which engages the Neothink® Society's ultimate mission: eradicate aging and death.

Now, we have time for one more question. Before I take that question, however, I want to point out that in our hour together, I have selected and answered fourteen questions. There are HUNDREDS of questions in the queue. Granted, I selected the fourteen questions as those most beneficial to my group of "apprentices" at Level One. However, the hundreds of questions are, frankly, extremely important questions that can be answered with great value to you by other Neothink® members, especially by those at the higher levels. The Neothink® Secret Society has a secret web site that no one can get into but our members who attend these secret meetings. In that secret web site is a discussion board where you can take your questions at any time and be helped by other advanced members. Honestly, their help is priceless. Moreover, on this secret web site are over two thousand pages of very high-level Neothink® secrets that do not appear in your three heirloom packages. The web site is where the activity of the secret society takes place, too, and you need to be there. There is a maintenance fee to you of thirty dollars per month (a dollar a day), which the secret society charges to keep itself financially sound to be there for your children and grandchildren. However, your access to the action of the secret society, just the guidance you receive alone, will be worth a personal fortune to you over time. Everything comes out of this secret web site, including our future summits (i.e., get-togethers), organized goals (as seen in Earth's First Immortals), social events and more. To get into the secret web site, go to www.activeneothinkmember.com

As you know, Neothink® is fully integrated knowledge. Whenever Neothink® engages wealth and happiness we'll also engage self-esteem, romantic love and family love as we did in Part Two and we'll engage aging and mortality which we will in Part Three to come.

Before we go to Part Three however, I pause here to urge you to send me your questions and comments. I'm sitting here reading and expecting your questions or remarks. I must catch your thoughts and feelings right now during the moment. That's why we pause here; to give you time to do this. Take a moment and communicate directly with me. Right now, during the moment, during the break.

When I finish speaking the screen will prompt you as to how to send in your questions and comments to me and then how to continue with Part Three of the meeting.

Level-One Essence Meeting
Part Three

Now, let me select the final questions for today's session. Here they are:

Q) Hi Mr. Hamilton. I am 76 years old and have "achieved it all". Speaking from a position of power and wisdom, I must say your material truly opens the world of power and wealth to the ordinary person stuck in powerlessness. Just as you teach others, I have created values for the past fifty years, and as you say, I have played at life and still do, each and every day! After being brought into the Neothink® Society, I now want to shift my creative efforts, wealth, and ability to get things done into the most important mission for mankind: curing aging and death. Mark, I am an eternally happy immortal who wants to escape the mortal anticivilization. I'm too happy to die! Where can I pour my enormous assets and energy to overcome the unfathomable tragedy of death?

MH) Magnificent question, which I will address after I post the second final question:

Q) I have read all my heirloom packages, Mr. Hamilton. Amazing stuff. Oh, how I wish I were young again to use it all! I am 85 years old, and I silently suffered in frustration all my life. Now, I finally know why. There **always was** something more — much more. But now, Mr. Hamilton, I'm physically not able to start from nothing and rise up. Do you have any suggestions for someone with just a little time left?

MH) Reading your question (i.e., the second question directly above) made me very sad on several levels. Although I am a middle-age man myself, I have experienced the "end game" dynamic in life through others I loved. My most honest and sincere answer to you (which also begins to answer the first of the final two questions above) is to get directly involved in the growing efforts of the secret society to cure man's worst

18

physical disease, human aging, and to eradicate civilization's worst natural disaster, death itself. You suddenly become involved in creating the greatest value in mankind's history. That alone makes you feel good. You saw in your Third Heirloom Package, Earth's First Immortals; actions necessary to break through the mortal anticivilization into the immortal Civilization of the Universe. Those actions are in motion in the Neothink® Society, from the political dynamics to the scientific dynamics. These are very exciting, very stimulating actions just waiting for your participation and passion. Moreover, these actions become increasingly social, involving more and more grassroots efforts, both secret-society gatherings and general-populous gatherings. Addressing both gentlemen, this is where I suggest you pouring yourselves into. The stimulation and excitement is unmatched by any other goal or mission on Earth. This is the second gentlemen's one chance, one shining moment to experience exciting value creation… and not just value creation, but value creation of the greatest value in the Universe — rescuing human life by eradicating death. Believe me, this is really PLAYING for people in your situation, for *anyone*, for you are working toward creating the greatest value. And the payoff when successful is giving you your life back — the greatest gift in existence to the immortal value creator, whom you will become. The actions for this goal will come out during the course of these monthly meetings and on the secret web site www.activeneothinkmember.com.

Now, I normally would not bring this up to my Level-One class, but because these final two questions touched me so deeply, I will let you in on this, for this could be something of enormous excitement particularly to my 85-year-old apprentice: In your Third Heirloom Package, Earth's First Immortals, in Books Two and Three of the trilogy, you read about The Church of God-Man. Neothink® members seriously interested in starting a monthly congregation in their local neighborhoods contact me now. (Those congregations, of course, will be limited to Neothink® members only. And because of the potential misunderstandings of the word "church", we will call those congregations your local Neothink® Secret Society meetings.) You will meet, interact with, and develop presentations for those local members. I will help you develop those presentations and provide you with materials to run your local Neothink® Secret Society meetings successfully. From your congregations can also come the ideas for other local movements such as a local Neothink® Party political movement, a local business-alliance networking as explained in Earth's First Immortals, a local infusion of knowledge and support for the Association for Curing Aging and Death. The emotional rewards for creating these congregations that move us toward the immortal Civilization of the Universe could be unmatched by anything else. What an amazing thing for anyone to embark upon, what amazing play time for adults, including my 85-year-old apprentice. There could be financial incentives as well. To be current on the details on how to become a local Neothink® Secret Society organizer (or how to attend existing local meetings), send a letter of interest to me at the same e-mail address where you send your questions. I will post your letters on our secret web site www.activeneothinkmember.com.

Moreover, the organization of the Neothink® Secret Society meetings along with the organization of the grassroots Neothink® Party, the business alliance, and the Association for Curing Aging and Death will occur through that secret web site. That is where our future actions and developing secrets are revealed. I mentioned before that the society collects a dollar-a-day to pay for the web site to maintain it and keep it available for the next generation. I myself, upon leaving today's meeting, am going straight into our secret web site to read the discussion board for the amazing aftermath following this meeting. There will be advanced members there, including me, to offer feedback, guidance, and help for you Level-One apprentices.

I want to take a moment here to add that the hundreds of questions in my queue, many of which I have skimmed over during this hour, reflect the talent and human potential of this Level-One class. You are, in all sincerity, a very special class with hidden talents, exactly as I had planned when selecting you. I want all of you to feel free to participate in the discussion board, give input and help other members wherever you can. I think highly of this Level-One class. That is why I requested to be your mentor. Use the discussion board to learn, teach, and evolve. That mind-opening exercise will serve you well. Over the next month reading and participating on the discussion board, you will most easily evolve into Level-Two.

It's been a rewarding time for me bringing you through your debut meeting. Now you can begin to perceive a separation between our hidden world we see and the exposed world almost everyone else sees. You're moving into a different world, into an exclusive society that rises above the rest.

With me working with you over the next year, you will complete your journey into that Neothink® Society of the wealthy and happy few on this planet. A crucial part of your journey where you can gain enormously between our meetings is the Neothink® Secret Society's hidden web site where all the action is. Where only our members can go. I strongly urge you to go there right now to register. There are many secrets there you must see. Over two thousand pages of Neothink® secrets yet unseen by your eyes.

I am there frequently and I personally read all your comments on the discussion board. The leading members go there daily to read your insights and to often participate in the discussion board. We read everything you post and we track your progress.

When we feel it's needed, we enter your discussions on the discussion boards. You are simply moving into another society, another civilization described in your heirloom packages as the "Civilization of the Universe."

In our civilization, intentional irrationality doesn't exist. So our people flourish as will you.

I'm just really happy you're finally becoming an active part of this prosperous secret society. I look forward to my Level Two secret meeting.

Until then, I'll see you where the action is, at our Neothink® Society's meeting place www.activeneothinkmember.com.

Oh, and one final point that you learned in your Third Heirloom Package. Deep, deep in the Neothink® Society reside Earth's First Immortals.

You are my handpicked apprentice group and you have the special traits to join them.

You can only get to know and understand them deep in the secret society at the secret web site. There, we literally give you the secret formula that will make you an immortal. The secret web site contains the secret Neothink® formula to immortality, biological immortality.

You will join the few first immortals on earth and become part of the greatest kept secret of all time.

The secret formula is your one and only secret shot at living much younger for much, much longer.

Go to www.activeneothinkmember.com. Do that now to be best prepared for your next secret meeting. I'm going to talk to you directly and interact with you directly as one of Earth's first immortals. You'll never have been talked to or interacted with in that way ever before.

So get ready for your next meeting by learning the secret formula to biological immortality and transforming into an immortal, joining the first immortals on earth. Go to www.activeneothinkmember.com right now.

Next month you'll experience the most exciting hour in your life.

Until then, I'll see you at www.activeneothinkmember.com. I'm going there right now. See you there.

Secret Teachings to My Exclusive Inner Circle

Level-Two Essence Meeting
Introduction

Today you will learn the Ten-Second Miracle. You've waited a long time for this I know. I had to be sure you were showing signs of integrated thinking, which you have. I follow the secret web site very closely and I'm happy with the progress I've seen.

You've waited so long, let's not waste any time, let's get right to it.

To get to the Ten-Second Miracle I must first address those apprentices who are still having a problem finding their Friday-Night Essence. Let's get to it.

Q) I am having a hard time finding my Friday-Night Essence. Can you help?

MH) First let us understand why this can be a tough experience for people. You are trying to go through a leap of the mind into a new mentality. You are trying to leap from the following mode into the integrating mode. Finding your Friday-Night Essence opens your taproot to deep motivation. That motivation brings downstream focus into your efforts. Downstream focus will eventually carry you through the leap from the following mode (i.e., value production) into the integrating mode (i.e., value creation).

Only one time before did the human mind go through a leap into a new mentality. As you know, that first leap happened between two thousand and three thousand years ago when man leapt from the bicameral mentality to human consciousness. As revealed in the Second Insight of the Second Heirloom Package, the stories throughout the Bible and the struggles of Jesus document man's amazing multi-millennial journey out of the bicameral mentality into human consciousness. Now you, my apprentices, will attempt to make mankind's only other

25

leap ever into a new mentality…in a year! What a remarkable journey we are on!

The struggle to find your Friday-Night Essence is understandable — your mind simply does not work that way. This is a huge shift, and I am going to help you make that shift over the next year. The payoff is a new world of exhilaration, happiness, wealth, and love.

Imagine the explosion of prosperity from the first shift of the mind, from the bicameral mind to the conscious mind, as seen with the rise of the great philosophers, artists, and scientists in Ancient Greece. You will go through a similar explosion of prosperity from the second shift of the mind, from the mysticism-plagued conscious mind to the mysticism-free Neothink mind.

Q) I understand the Friday-Night Essence, and I want to become the person I was meant to be. I just cannot seem to find my FNE. I know others are getting it, I see their posts on the secret web site. Some members on the secret web site have really helped me. The special chat session really helped. With their help, I am getting close, but I am not quite there yet. Can you help me discover the person I was meant to be?

MH) Yes I can help you, but let us transcend you for a moment and ask your same question to all of my apprentices who cannot seem to find their Friday-Night Essences: Who is the person you were meant to be?

To answer that universal question, we must ask what we were meant to be, as human beings. What is the essence of a human being? What is the essence of the human mind? Let me ask you, what does the human mind do that no other brain or computer or robot can do on our planet? The answer is: we can CREATE. Our essence as human beings is: CREATION — VALUE CREATION.

We human beings are meant to create — to be value creators. Creating, for humans, is the opposite of stagnating. Remember last month, I told you that value creating is how adults PLAY, how adults make happiness? So, where does that lead us?

Well, let us get back to you now and your Friday-Night Essence. Your FNE taps into your deepest root of motivation inside you. That deep-rooted motivation becomes the relentless force — the downstream focus — that will eventually pull your mind free from its snag in stagnant value production; downstream focus will eventually release your mind and allow it to finally flow forward into exhilarating value creation.

Remember, the person you, me, all human beings are meant to be…are creators…value creators. Your Friday-Night Essence with its downstream focus is A TOOL for you to pull free from value production and flow into value creation. Your FNE with its downstream focus is a TOOL to release your potential and bring you forward into the person you were meant to be — the value creator.

Q) A tool?

MH) Yes, a tool…not necessarily an end in itself, but a means to an end. To what end? To becoming the person every human being was meant to be — a value creator.

I have received many emails from members who have found and pursued their Friday-Night Essences, which brought them a rush of downstream focus and exhilaration. They are on their way toward value creation — toward the person they were meant to be.

I have received as many emails from members who have NOT found their Friday-Night Essences. In the last meeting, I told you not to be overly concerned if you could not find your FNE.

Today, you are learning why I told you not to be overly concerned. Your FNE is a TOOL to lift you out of your stagnant routine rut into exhilarating value creation. FNE is a means to an end — that end result being value creation.

For those of you who cannot find their Friday-Night Essences, today I am going to give you another way to value creation. Today, I am going to give you another powerful TOOL to lift you out of your stagnant routine rut into exhilarating value creation.

That tool is called: THE TEN-SECOND MIRACLE.

Level-Two Essence Meeting
Part One

The 10 Second Miracles. Are you ready? I believe you are.

The next section is what you have waited so long for. So let's go right back to it.

Q) I have been searching unsuccessfully through all your Heirloom Packages to find the Ten-Second Miracles. Can you reveal them to me?

MH) Yes I can. The Ten-Second Miracles are not in the Heirloom Packages because you have to reach Level Two before they are revealed. You are now ready — now that I m moving you up to Level Two — ready for me to reveal the Ten-Second Miracles. You have waited a long time, I know. I watch you on the web site, in the forums and the chat rooms, and I see you integrating now. I see the integrated thinking beginning to flow. That is where you need to be — graduated into a Level-Two Apprentice showing signs of integrated thinking — to be able to utilize this great tool called the Ten-Second Miracle. So, here we go:

Ten-Second Miracles come from the next mentality. They are the insights, visions, and breakthroughs…the insights through appearances to what is, the visions into the future, and the breakthroughs into new knowledge. The Three Insights and the Insight Climax in the Second Heirloom Package are classic examples. The Visions and the new techniques throughout all three Heirloom Packages came from Ten-Second Miracles. They are so difficult because they are a function of Neothink — our next mentality. All three Heirloom Packages are Neothink creations coming at you from the next mentality.

We waited until you were at Level Two to introduce you to Ten-Second Miracles. They occur through integrating knowledge, snapping together knowledge, like snapping together puzzle pieces. When the pieces are in place, sometimes after years of integrating as in the case of Neothink®, suddenly in about ten seconds, you see the whole puzzle picture in your mind. It seems like an incredible miracle. You now see past conventional wisdom or whatever is put out there for you to see. It is an amazingly indescribable moment to see something no one else has seen before you, throughout history. The power of your mind awes you at that point of experiencing a Ten-Second Miracle.

It is powerful. From integrating existing knowledge you break through illusions and nearly unbreakable appearances to what is — often never-before-seen new knowledge. That process, by the way, defines how the self-leader functions and why he or she becomes so stunningly successful.

I am going to give you an example of a Ten-Second Miracle at even the lowest entry-level job. I did not know what to call it at the time, but as a fifteen-year-old boy hired as a dishwasher in my first official job, I saved the restaurant from going under through a Ten-Second Miracle. By seeing my story at this low-level job, it becomes easier to see how practical Ten-Second Miracles can be:

I worked the night shift that summer washing dishes and cleaning the restaurant after it closed. When the restaurant closed for the day, and I went out front to clean, the owner would sit in one of the booths. Night after night I would hear him telling the manager that the restaurant was not going to make it. There were not enough customers. He would say how he had trouble meeting payroll. As I heard this night after night, I started to look at the business differently. I started looking at it through numbers and income instead of through the stagnant tasks I performed. For instance, I would look out front during the day periodically to see how many customers were eating. As I did my routine rut, my mind started working differently, always thinking how the number of customers could increase. I started to think about everything: what was on the menu, how the food was prepared, how the waitresses dressed and looked. I started looking at the customers and soon realized the customers were not locals. They were passing through on their way to major destination points. I started thinking about everything. I even walked out front before work one day and studied the sign and the curb appeal. Here I was in my first official job, a fifteen-year-old kid, quietly looking at all these things and thinking about them in terms of numbers of customers and income. I was not trying to save the restaurant. My mind just started working differently.

One night after closing, I carried the bags of garbage out back. I had to lug the heavy bags across a very dark patch of desert dirt to the trash bin. This particular night, after weeks of seeing the restaurant not through my dead-end tasks, not through my routine rut, but through all the areas of the business where the money could be, where the power was, I experienced my first Ten-Second Miracle. On my way up the back stairs after taking out the trash, I turned around and looked at the black patch of dirt I had just walked over on my way back from the trash bin. Suddenly, in about ten seconds, the answer to the restaurant's problems unfolded in my mind in the most unsuspecting way. Everything I had been seeing came snapping together into a puzzle picture.

In my mind, I saw the customers as not locals, most were just passing through. I saw the curb appeal out front was nice, but only the width of the restaurant with a hotel on the south side and a side street on the north side with a gas station on the north side of that side street. The front of the restaurant was on a major federal highway going north and south, so people did not want to park across the street. In ten seconds, I saw THE PROBLEM WAS LACK OF PARKING. The space in front of the restaurant could handle two or three cars at the most and was always full. Once cars passed that spot, they could not

31

park because of the hotel on one side and the side street and gas station on the other side. Past the hotel or gas station, the distance became too far, and there were new restaurants with easier parking up ahead; at that point, those potential customers were forever lost. I looked back at the patch of dirt where the trash bin sat. That was the missing piece. Although it was too small to handle more than just a few cars, that was not the point. The breakthrough, I realized, was to get the passersby to turn onto the side street by placing a sign out front that said FREE PARKING around back. (Parking meters lined the few spots in the front.) The dirt patch could be paved and offer customers free parking. Even if that little parking lot were constantly full, ample free parking awaited customers on both sides of the quiet side street. By seeing the FREE PARKING sign up front, cars would turn onto the side street to get to the parking lot. Full or not, they could find plenty of parking. Moreover, they were now committed to park and eat. We would now capture all those potential customers!

I stood there on the steps to the back entrance and shook my head in awe of the whole puzzle picture in my head. I knew it would work. I walked in and, for the first time since I started working there, I talked to the owner. I said I knew how to save his restaurant. He looked at me for an awkward moment, and then told me to sit down in his booth. Instead of just telling him, I instinctively grabbed a napkin and asked for a pen. I drew out my whole vision on that napkin. Without realizing what I was doing, I drew out the puzzle picture that was in my head, including the front curb appeal, the problem with parking, the proposed free-parking sign, the paved parking lot out back, the side street...I even draw out the fifteen to twenty cars I envisioned parked around the little restaurant!

The owner sat there in awe. He knew I was right. The first thing that finally came out of his mouth was, "You ought to be the owner of this restaurant, not me."

That summer I worked there, the restaurant was going out of business. But thanks to my Ten-Second Miracle, that restaurant is still in business today, over thirty years later. It still operates with the same name (named after the owner) and the same sign.

What happened to me was rare. Perhaps because of my young age and my constant exposure to the woes of the owner, I was able to suddenly see differently everything around me at work. I was able to see things from the perspective of the ESSENCE of the business (i.e., how to increase profits)...not from the blind and dead perspective of my routine rut. Because of seeing the business from the perspective of its ESSENCE, the things I saw stayed in me and began, unbeknownst to me, to quietly integrate together into a puzzle of how to increase the business. Suddenly, unbeknownst to me, the missing piece snapped into place when I walked through the dark patch of desert to the trash bin. The Ten-Second Miracle occurred in my consciousness as the missing piece snapped into place and the puzzle-picture filled my head. I did not know it then, but that was Neothink in action. (I even drew my explanation for the owner on a napkin because Neothink works beyond words...in pictures.) As a fifteen-year-old boy, I experienced integrated thinking coming together into a puzzle. When the pieces all came together, a puzzle picture was revealed, and I experienced my first Ten-Second Miracle. That Ten-Second Miracle saved the business and kept it going profitably for another entire generation.

In the years that followed, I learned just how rare that experience was. The mind just does not work that way. We are held back because of mysticism...because of the old bicameral-like way of viewing the world. For instance, the dishwasher views his job by what is directly before his eyes, his boring repetitive tasks. He does not view his place of work beyond that rut, by its essence, it's exciting money-making essence.

The mind just does not go there. Learning how to do this, how to see the essence of things around you, starting right at work, is going to bring out the hidden talents and potential we see in you.

This is what Miss Annabelle was teaching Teddy's dad. Remember in the Miss Annabelle story, starting on page 35, she left the school for the day and ran into Teddy and his dad outside playing football. Go back and read that three-page story. Miss Annabelle tells Teddy's dad to see past the appearance of his routine-rut job...to see the essence of his business. She tells him to see past his stagnant tasks, to the money-making essences of the business he works for. She tells him to see the money-making responsibilities and possibilities. In short, she is telling him to look at his place of work differently than before, from a different viewpoint...from the viewpoint where our minds do not naturally go.

Our minds do not naturally go there because our minds do not naturally integrate knowledge. Our minds merely react to our routine tasks. The Second Insight in the Second Heirloom Package explains how the bicameral mutation occurred through the Plato/St. Augustine combination during and after the breakdown of the bicameral mind.

I want to get your minds working this different way. However, we do not want to fool ourselves. This goes beyond willing your mind to do this. Because of the bicameral mutation in our minds also called mysticism, our minds need to develop and have the tools to make the shift.

Level-Two Essence Meeting
Part Two

All right. I'm going to get your minds working this different way that will lead you into making Ten-Second Miracles.

It's time for me to give you the tools to make the shift. So here we go.

Q) How do I get started making Ten-Second Miracles?

MH) I will teach you how. Let us start revisiting a story you read as part of your homework from the first meeting. In the Vision Climax that I asked you to read, there is a story about Charles Nash. Remember? He was a young man hired to do the most boring, routine rut-job imaginable: pounding iron. He stepped into that stagnant job and quickly made a Ten-Second Miracle. He suggested a power hammer that saved the company a lot of money and permanently changed the way that job was done. Nash was then moved to the drill press. When the owner of the company came by his station a few days later, Nash had accomplished another Ten-Second Miracle. Remember how his station looked different than all the others? He had designed a treadle and an overhead spring that left both hands free for faster production. The company permanently adopted Nash's breakthrough and moved him to yet another routine-rut job, but this time to see what Ten-Second Miracle he would bring the company. Nash quickly developed another Ten-Second Miracle in the trimming department. He told management to buy a better grade of tacks so the men, who held them in their mouths, would not spit them out on the floor from cut lips and tongues, wasting the company's money. Nash saw his place of work through different eyes than his working-man peers. He saw through to the essence of the business…to the money-making essence. Needless to say, he rose as a self-leader to the top of General Motors and eventually started his own company that put out the famous Nash Rambler.

I wanted you to read that story in the Vision Climax before today's meeting because we are going to find a key to the Ten-Second Miracles in that story and in the story I told you today about my first job. My mind, Nash's mind, worked differently than others in order to make our Ten-Second Miracles.

Consider, the other dishwashers' minds did not work the way my mind worked, nor did the other working men's minds work the way Nash's mind worked: Most human minds just do not work the Ten-Second Miracle way.

Because our minds do not naturally work that way, you need certain tools to make these Ten-Second Miracles. To grasp those tools, let us look back now at the stories of Nash and of me as a dishwasher. How did Nash come through with all those Ten-Second Miracles on his way to the top? How did I as a fifteen-year-old dishwasher come through with such a business-saving Ten-Second Miracle? Both Nash and I were looking at business differently — from a different viewpoint. We both saw the business through different eyes — through the eyes of numbers. I kept looking at the business around me as to how to improve the number of customers and, therefore, increase the profits. Nash kept looking at the business around him as to how to make things more cost-saving efficient and, therefore increase the profits. As a result of our different viewpoint of the businesses we worked for, we both experienced invaluable Ten-Second Miracles.

Looking at the business around us through the eyes of numbers opens up a whole new world. John D. Rockefeller frequently talked about that whole new world of numbers. NUMBERS ARE YOUR TOOLS TO MAKE TEN-SECOND MIRALCES YOURSELF.

Here's how it happens. Seeing through the eyes of numbers drags your routine-stuck mind out of its perceive-and-react prison and pulls your mind into the perceive-and-integrate self-leader world. When Rockefeller discovered that new world, he had a hard time leaving work and went on to become the richest man alive. All superachievers discovered this new world. Today, you will too.

Numbers pull you out of the routine way your mind always works now and into creativity. Numbers are your tools to shake up your routine thinking patterns — to see things differently, spark creativity, integrate knowledge in never-before-thought-of ways to see new ways of doing things, just like Nash and me.

Whereas your Friday-Night Essence uses your deeply driven motivation to pull your mind out of the stagnant following mode into the exhilarating creating mode, the Ten-Second Miracles use numbers to do that. Numbers and subsequent Ten-Second Miracles is how Rockefeller and Nash and all superachievers got so successful and wealthy. For, those numbers are how the superachievers pried their minds loose from the old following mode and rolled ahead into creativity — value creation at all levels...starting small with efficiencies such as the younger Nash suggesting a power hammer all the way up to major contributions to the world such as the older Nash bringing us Nash Motors and his beloved Nash Rambler.

Now, it is your turn to pry your mind from the old following mode routine rut. To do this, I want you to start looking through the eyes of numbers all around you at work. Start a numbers mini-day, if possible. Start small, just with improving the efficiencies of your own tasks. That first step gets your mind looking at things differently — looking at the numbers, even on a small scale. Improve your efficiency; notice the improvement in terms of the numbers. What do you save the company in time and costs? Now, you are making a difference in your company, and that is rewarding. That is inspiring. Let your awareness of numbers grow within you. Exert Project Curiosity (Vision Climax, Heirloom Two) and broaden your world of numbers.

You need to spend a month focused on numbers; working hard observing the essence of the company you work for, just as Charles Nash did, just as I did, just as every superachiever did. I am not asking you to make a Ten-Second Miracle by next month, although some of you will. However, I am trying to get your minds to work in a way they have not worked before. I am getting your minds to make a leap into another way of thinking — integrated thinking and then Neothink. It is a dramatic leap from the specialized following mind into the creative integrating mind. It is a huge leap. But you now have the tools to make that leap.

So there you go, the Ten-Second Miracles. We're going to come back in a little bit to cover more on Ten-Second Miracles. But first I want us to ponder. Where am I taking you? Where are we headed in the next year? Let's take a moment to answer that.

MH) Now that I have revealed the Ten-Second Miracle and given you the tools to go for it, I am going to take this opportunity to give you an idea of your year-long journey with me.

It is a two-fold journey:

1) I will help your mind make the leap into the new Neothink mentality with all its personal, financial, emotional rewards. Imagine making Ten-Second Miracles routinely. Imagine making major marketing breakthroughs, which I am going to teach you next month.

2) When you make the leap forward into creation, value creation, the person you were meant to be, you will discover

exhilaration, happiness, eventually wealth. You will discover the deeper love for life that is eternal. In short, you will become an immortal trapped in a mortal anticivilization, just like the students of Miss Annabelle. At that point, you will pursue with a passion the superpuzzle laid out in that Heirloom Package. A growing number of you will essentially become "The Group" from that Heirloom Package. That Heirloom Package is actually the Neothink Vision of what is ahead. Together, we will pursue the superpuzzle to leap beyond this anticivilization into the Neothink® World and onto the immortal Civilization of the Universe.

This brings me to what I left off with in our first meeting. I asked you to go into the secret web site and read The Formula to Biological Immortality by Dr. Frank R. Wallace.

It is by and far the most integrated piece of writing in the history of mankind. That is why you will gain enormously from each subsequent reading. The underlying point of Wallace's eternal Pax Neo-Tech is: the shift to becoming an immortal civilization is a psychological shift.

The tools I am teaching you (such as your Friday-Night Essence and Ten-Second Miracles that move you into value creators) cause that psychological shift to happen in you. You will join the value creators here over the next year. Value creators experience eternal exhilaration and eternal happiness and are immortal by nature. They are immortals trapped in a mortal anitcivilization. We can change that.

As an immortal, you will become the manifestation of The Group of Miss Annabelle and her students. The map is there, in the Heirloom Package. The journey is here, in our Neothink® Secret Society.

You will start the grassroots political movement, for instance. Whenever I bring this up, I must qualify that anyone running for office under the Neothink® name would have to remain true to the Neothink® Constitution found throughout the Neothink® literature.

You will and are currently organizing local Neothink® Secret Meetings.

"Wow," you might say, "it's up to me?" Yes. The basis of Neothink® is self-responsibility. There is no higher authority to do it for you. It is up to you. You are The Group. Continue to get organized. The secret web site is the home base for organizing, communicating, and feedback. Meetings are organizing now through the web site and are now taking place around the country. I want to state here that I would like feedback from each meeting that takes place. I track the Neothink® movement closely. You need my essence input, which will come through these Monthly Essence Meetings.

I have made the decision that the organizing of the local meetings around the country must take place through the www.activeneothinkmember.com web site. That web site does come with a dollar-a-day maintenance fee to keep the society in place and strong. I have determined that logistically, for now, this is the only way for me to track the evolvement of the local meetings in order for me to develop the proper essence guidance. I do encourage all Neothink® members wishing to attend or host those secret meetings to get on the www.activeneothinkmember.com web site. The ability to interact with hundreds of others like you on that web site is priceless. The ability to meet people like you in person through that web site is priceless. Moreover, the thousands of pages of Neothink® literature on that web site are priceless. The secret web site www.activeneothinkmember.com will increasingly become our catalyst to get out of boring stagnation and into exciting creation and emotional exhilaration.

All of you have been chosen to take this journey with me and with your fellow secret society members. As those already in the secret web site can agree, this is going to turn into, quite likely, the most exciting year of your life. One thing is for sure: Your future will never be the same again!

Level-Two Essence Meeting
Part Three

Now that you know about your journey and where you're headed, let's get back to your lesson today.

Now, let us go back and complete our revelation on the two most sought-after questions by Level-One Apprentices. Those two most pressing questions were:

1) I cannot find my Friday-Night Essence; what can it be?

2) I cannot find the Ten-Second Miracles; what can they be?

Everyone does have a taproot that goes right down into his or her essence. Tapping into one's essence, one's deepest motivation is what you have been seeking — a Friday-Night Essence. To some, finding your Friday-Night Essence is not happening right now. That is okay.

Whereas you do have a deepest taproot, you also have a very deep root system that ties into your essence as a human being. Remember your essence as a human being? Creation, value creation, is our essence as human beings. Value creation in itself — ANY value creation — is a deeply rooted source of motivation and exhilaration in every human being. As a human being, the person you were meant to be is: a creator — a value creator.

So now, if we broaden your downstream-focus search from beyond your one, deepest taproot to your deep root system — value creation in general — the search (for what to some feels like finding a needle in a haystack) suddenly can be found right before you, wherever you are, even right where you work now. But, you must break through into that value creation. The major new tool I gave you to do that today is The Ten-Second Miracle (with your new mindset for numbers).

Forbidden Revelation

Your Friday-Night Essence taps your deepest root of motivation. That internal drive, that burning passion, eventually breaks you through into value creation. Remember, a major reason you are searching for your FNE: it is the tool that will bring you past your boring routine rut into value creation and into your essence as a human being. Creativity is the essence of human beings. One's FNE is a major tool to leap into value creation. Remember last week I said VALUE CREATION for an adult is PLAYING. Now for those who cannot find their FNE, there is another way to get to value creation... to their essence as a human being. That other way, of course, is through Ten-Second Miracles.

This brings us back to my assignment to you. Spend this month looking at everything around you at work from the mindset of NUMBERS. Ask yourself, where can I improve those numbers? Even the smallest improvement is a sparkle of value creation. You will be on your way!

I want you to really do this and exert the effort. Do not just go to the discussion boards and say, "I'm not able to do this, help me." By Level-Two you know this is another way of using the mind that does not come easily. You know this is hard for human beings to do right now. But you have some real tools given to you today in this Essence Meeting. Come back into this meeting as often as you need to thoroughly absorb my lesson. This is the real deal, and I only give this attention and direction to my apprentices and no one else. Study this lesson over and over again. Today you were given the key to break through into value creation. There is no other key. This is it. This is what every major successful person used to rise to the top of the world. None of the inspirational books or positive thinking books will lift you there. Today's lesson will. Do not just think, "Oh, I got it." Come back here several times and re-digest this information.

You need to spend a month focused on numbers and working hard observing the essence for the company you work for just a Charles Nash did, just as I did, just as every superachiever did. Again, apply Project Curiosity and get to know your business while looking at it differently, at its essence, through the eyes of numbers. Indeed, seeing the numbers in business is the way to cut through powerless appearances such as your stagnant set tasks down to the powerful essence — to the money-making essence that will lead you to Ten-Second Miracles.

Now, I will leave you with a rhapsody of thoughts…

Once you experience playing at life as an adult, as I taught in your debut meeting last month, then you will rediscover your child of the past, the thrill of living, and the desire for eternal life.

You will begin playing at life, remember, the moment you uncover your Friday-Night Essence. Experiencing your Friday-Night Essence, even if for a few hours per week, will eventually lead you into value creation. The conscious mind is the only living and nonliving thing on Earth and throughout the Universe that can create. Creation is your human essence, which separates you from all the other living things.

Without creation, you increasingly fall into the Forces of Nature, down into stagnation. Stagnation will eventually — has to eventually — kill the conscious mind. That is WHY we die today, in the 21st Century.

Discovering and pursuing your Friday-Night Essence will lead you eventually into value creation and eventually into wealth creation and onto the life you were meant to live. That life — the creative life — experiences new exhilaration each new day and never wants to end.

You learned today, your Friday-Night Essence is one of two major TOOLS to pull your mind from stagnant value production into exhilarating value creation. You learned today your second major tool to pull your mind from the non-integrating mode into integrating value creation: The Ten-Second Miracles. You learned to see your place of work differently — through the eyes of numbers — to make creative Ten-Second Miracle breakthroughs.

When you live the creative life, you become the life that never wants to end. You become an immortal trapped in a mortal civilization, an anticivilization. You learned in the Miss Annabelle story the deepest secret of the Neothink® Society...its secret mission underneath everything else. That secret mission is to bring the first immortals on Earth — those here in the Neothink® Society who discover the creative life — an immortal civilization, the Civilization of the Universe.

Over the next year, you will become one of Earth's first immortals trapped in Earth's mortal anticivilization. Over the next year, perhaps unbeknownst to you now, as you evolve into the creative life you will naturally embark upon new actions in life that directly contribute to shifting the mortal anticivilization toward an immortal civilization. You will pursue those actions not out of obligation, rather out of desire. Many of the actions are concretized in your Miss Annabelle story.

For example, are you politically motivated? Consider a grassroots Neothink® political movement in your community. See the Heirloom Packages as your guide.

Are you interested in finally meeting other like-minded people in your local area? Starting and conducting local secret society meetings can bring enormous rewards. Those meetings will grow as we continually bring in fresh, promising new members in your area to join your local secret meetings.

Are you an educator? Consider the Miss Annabelle approach to education. Communicate with us about participating in a Neothink® School patterned after the Miss Annabelle Schools of Geniuses.

Are you a real-estate investor? Consider a master planned community with the concepts found in those beautiful Paradise Cities in the Miss Annabelle story.

Are you in the film industry? Consider the Miss Annabelle story as a Hollywood movie either through a production studio or produced through an indie or through the Neothink® Society itself.

Are you a journalist or work in the media? Consider the impact you could have as a Jake Catchings, an Al Patterson in newspaper and television, a Natasha Stokov Kemp in talk radio. Even novices will have a potential outlet right here at our Neothinksociety.com web site when we release our news and opinion page. That Neothink® News Outlet could expand into something major. Be sure to get your articles and by-lines established from the beginning.

Are you an investor? Consider investing in a scientist who is leading a valid research project toward curing aging, perhaps someone overseas deep into stem-cell research. The Neothink® leading members are looking into such approaches and scientists right now.

Are you a musician? Consider breathing the Neothink® sense of life into your music and lyrics. The unique value of your music could be stunning. Let us know your progress. Post it on the web site! Start a Neothink® band!

You will be evolving into a value creator with immense power throughout this year. The above suggestions may seem realistic before this year is over. I want you to continue to study and actualize Neothink® in your life using your Heirloom Packages, these secret meetings, and the secret web site.

Whether or not any of those examples above apply to you, over the next year you will evolve into value creation. As you experience growing exhilaration in your daily life, you will eventually contribute to the secret mission out of your growing desire to preserve your creative life.

In conclusion, let me ask: Who are you? Ask yourself that directly: Who am I? Say it out loud: WHO AM I?

The answer is; you are what you create. Think about that — you are what you create. You might create a warm, loving, and nurturing home and learning environment for your family. You might create a major empire. Adults are what they create. Conscious beings are what they create!

Yet so many adults never learn how to create. If the adult conscious mind does not create as it is designed to do, then it stagnates. The fact that so many — the majority — of adults create nothing, means they increasingly with age feel they have done nothing meaningful with their lives as they increasingly suffer in stagnation. The internal feelings as adults grow older should be the direct opposite. They should feel they have done meaningful things with their lives as they enjoy increasing exhilaration and happiness. Over the next year, that will come true for you personally, with my help and the help of others here. You will evolve into the creative life. You will increasingly discover real happiness, love, and wealth as a value creator.

Bringing about the Neothink® World is a long, Neothink Journey. Generations of members exist at different capacities. You are the generation of Neothink® Members who can pursue the roadmap laid out in the Miss Annabelle story. Eventually you will desire to contribute to the Secret Mission just as the twelve students did. You, my apprentice group, embody the twelve students.

I want to see you promise fulfilled. Eventually, I want to see mankind's promise fulfilled, which is the Miss Annabelle story.

Exciting, isn't it. It all grows from here. For example, if I see you looking at your place of work, down at the money making essence of business, looking through the eyes of numbers, looking through this new viewpoint, then next month I'm going to give you something big.

If I go to the secret web site and see my Level Two apprentices advancing, then next month I'm going to give you the Neothink Secret to making major marketing breakthroughs.

Think about this, an ordinary guy on the Neothink® discussion board, not unlike your discussion boards at the secret web site, went out and started one of the major Internet services that we all know and use. Today, he's now worth billions...Just an ordinary guy. He used the Neothink® approach to marketing breakthroughs

I'm giving it to you, if you're ready.

Until then, have a miracle month. I'll track your progress at www.activeneothinkmember.com.

Level-Three Essence Meeting
Introduction

Welcome to your Level Three Marketing Meeting, where today I'm going to reveal the Neothink® secret to making major marketing breakthroughs.

Before I do that, I'm going to answer your most frequently asked question which is, how did The Neothink® Society select me for this journey?

I'll give you a clue; apprentices meeting around the country have unanimously written me letting me know of the friendship, the harmony and the love in their meetings. I'm going to tell you why that is and how The Neothink® Society selected you for this journey.

Q: Why was I chosen for this journey in the Neothink® Society? Why me? How did The Society chose me?

MH: The Neothink® Society discovered you. Each and every one of you is a chosen one for this journey. Why? You are all searchers. The Neothink® Society discovered you while you were searching…unknowingly for the Civilization of the Universe and the life you were meant to live. You were searching, unlike most other adults, because your child of the past never resigned to the irrational anticivilziation. Whether you realized it or not, your child of past, deep inside was searching for the person he or she was meant to be. And we reached your child of the past through our unique, secret-message marketing, as you will learn later today.

You were searching, and we found you. Whether you are young or old, rich or poor, not one of you resigned to the anticivilization. And that bond, as you will learn, our group constitutes one of the most powerful bonds in existence. On the secret web site, apprentices refer to each other as a family. The apprentices did that on their own because, as they organize and meet each other in person, they feel a unique closeness they never felt with others before. When you meet in person, your child of the past, your infant Zon buried deep inside, is greeting another's infant Zon. That explains the harmony and closeness and love during these congregations, as I fully knew you would experience. How did I know? The answer is the same as why you are here: Your child of the past is alive and reaching for the Civilization of the Universe. That is why we chose you and why you are here. You are very rare. So are the others you meet during your congregations. Those people will become your lifelong friends. They are your soul mates.

I have seen feedback on the secret web site that when you get together, you notice a wide range of differences exists among you, but the closeness and harmony is a unique, unmatched experience. We comb society far and wide to select out the very few persons in whom the child of the past is alive and searching. You apprentices make up that selection. That common denominator that bonds you all together into a family is the same common denominator that bonds the students together in the Miss Annabelle Story. Although you might not realize it yet, it is the most powerful bond on Earth today.

Indeed, this is a very diverse group. But what pulls us all together is the child of the past within. If you felt alone before coming into The Neothink® Society and before meeting others in your local area (many have emailed me telling me how they felt alone, even lonely, before joining us), the reason is: among those around you, the child of the past has resigned to the anticivilization life. But not the child of the past in any of you. Now, finally, like finding your family of loved ones, you have met people who are like you: people with their child of the past alive and searching. Like you, they are searching for something more than this anticivilization life; they are searching for the C of U life they were supposed to live. Your diversity is going to add strength to our common goal of bringing the C of U to Earth.

Forbidden Revelation

Let me enlighten you to something just below the surface of your mind: Bringing Neothink® into the world just might be your long-lost Friday-Night Essence. In fact, it may be many if not most of your FNEs; for the child of the past made you a searcher, searching for something more than the anticivilization…searching for the life you were meant to live. After all, that is what Neothink® is. You searched your whole life for Neothink®, and now spreading Neothink® to bring about the Neothink® World for you and your children to live in could very well be your FNE. Neothink® and living the Neothink® life was what you were out there alone searching for ever since you were a young child. You refused to lie down and play dead in this anticivilization. You wanted to LIVE. And you never gave up. Now you are here. Later, I am going to give you a way to pursue your Friday-Night Essence of bringing about a Neothink® World. I am talking about joining me in living a life of changing the world!

Is it all starting to make sense now? We spend more time and money in operations on finding the rare searchers of the world than on anything else. Moreover, we spend more time in operations on finding YOU — the searchers — than on anything else the past two years. Senior staff members meet, and we apply our decades of experience and wisdom; we generate reports on you and others. It is true those reports are computer generated, for that is the technology that allows us to most effectively do this. Do you realize that anyone can, through a computer, learn all about someone else? I am not saying that we ran a background report on you, which we did not. But we did use the computer for extensive cross-referencing, using custom-written programs unique to The Neothink® Society that we have perfected over the years with the sole purpose to help us find the select few searchers of the world. After time-consuming meetings and very extensive and expensive human and computer research and further extensive review of confidential reports, we felt convinced that you were a searcher with the child of the past reaching out for us. Moreover, we hurried to contact you during the Cycle Two phase of your life. That is the phase when you are ready to take action and break bondage. We wanted you ready to take action when you were invited into The Neothink® Society.

Let me tell you, Level-Three Apprentices and rare searchers, your journey is just beginning! You are finally here, all together, with me! Make no mistake about it: we DISCOVERED you. We WANTED you. You are the chosen ones because you have a fire inside, perhaps only a pilot light right now, but your flame never went out. Just like Miss Annabelle's students, the infant Zon is alive within you. During your one-year journey here together with me, that infant ZON will grow. Your pilot light inside will combust into a burning passion for your previously unknown Friday-Night Essence...your essence to change the world! YOU are going to CHANGE THE WORLD.

Okay, let us all take a deep breath and just take a moment. Go ahead...breathe in...hold it...hold it...okay...release. What you just read about yourself — your past and your future — is powerful and profound. I am your mentor, and I feel deep emotions every time I talk about how we discovered you, who you were, who you are, and who you will become.

Are you ready to move on? Let us move on to the next topic.

Q: I am a truck driver, and I feel I am stuck. How can I break out of my routine rut?

MH: I will take a moment before getting into the Neothink® Marketing Secret to address the person trapped in a job of labor. The problem with a job of labor is dealt with extensively in the Neothink® System, found within the Heirlooms. In short, the division of labor was a major development responsible for the extraordinary ascent of man's standard of living. The division of labor led to the Industrial Revolution and the invention of the assembly line.

However, the division of labor comes from the old, nature-based, bicameral-like mentality — use the body, not the mind. Labor traps us in the following mode, the mode of stagnation. I do say in The Neothink® System that you ARE trapped when you work a job of labor. Those jobs of labor will someday go to computers, robots, laser technologies, and other technologies.

If you cannot assemble a mini-company at your place of work as described in The Neothink® System and in the Vision Climax in your Second Heirloom Package, then you must consider your job as your income mini-day. You may have to work your FNE and TSM around your income mini-day.

The division of essence, which I created in the mid-1980s, is developed for the next mentality and has been kept secret here in The Neothink® Society. It divides business not by dead-end physical routine-rut labor, but by open-ended mental money-making essence. Every job has money-making purpose. And that money-making purpose stimulates and motivates THE MIND!

Every business can be divided by essence into creative jobs instead of by labor into stagnant ruts as demonstrated in The Neothink® System. Doesn't that sound right? When you know that is right (look in The Neothink® System), then you can know there is an entire world outside of your job of labor. If you cannot turn your job of labor into a job of the mind...into a money-making essence (after all, we are talking about a world-wide shift in business structures), then you can look outside your job. You can look outside your job in two basic ways.

1) For a more monetarily prosperous livelihood with these Neothink® tools,

OR

2) For a more emotionally fulfilling adventure.

Sometimes, in time, those two can merge. For example, if you pursue the second approach above, keep your job of labor for your income, but start something you really enjoy for a hobby. Remember Maslow's hierarchy of needs? If you have your income, your job of labor, that allows your mind to focus on creativity. So, with your income mini-day, you can have a hobby that does not make money but makes you happy.

Let us say you like painting on canvas. Start painting as a hobby. Do it outside your income mini-day and enjoy yourself. Perhaps someday you will be able to sell your art, perhaps even open a gallery and make a living from your FNE.

There are other examples I could give you, but time dictates we now must get into this month's primary lesson: the Neothink Marketing Secret. I hope I helped those stuck in jobs of labor.

One final point before we move into the Neothink Marketing Secret, THIS NEOTHINK® ADVENTURE can be and IS many of your FNEs, which may be largely overlooked. This journey and its outcome is more than a hobby. This is the movement that will change the world, which I will talk more about later today. EMBRACE IT! See it as a FNE even if there is not money in it. Voluntary movements can become people's FNE, such as political movements.

As per my choice, I am losing major money by taking my apprentices through this journey. It consumes my time, every day. I have little time for the other crucial activities that demand my attention. Other areas of progress and profits must be sacrificed as I go through this year-long journey with my new apprentices. But in the long run, I know it will be worth it. Your dollar-a-day maintenance fee on the secret web site barely covers my direct programming costs. Most of all, other critical Neothink® programs and major projects are held back because of my devotion to this group. My loyalty to this group takes top priority this year at some heavy costs to The Neothink® Society. In fact, remember in the Miss Annabelle Story the superachievers putting the goal of the superpuzzle above their own profits and ventures? Both in the Miss Annabelle Story and here in The Neothink® Society, people sacrifice time and money in view of the larger picture. If we do not, we will never enjoy the new world of peace, wealth, health, happiness, and immortality. It comes down to how badly you want that new world and what you will do to bring it about. No one else outside of The Neothink® Society will do this. It is up to us.

I embrace this journey. I invest this time in you at a financial loss. You, too, can embrace this journey. You can make this your FNE. Making money or not, this is value creation. This is historically essential value creation at a time when our anticivilization is most vulnerable. Next month, for those who *feel* this, awaits a whole new opportunity opening up to Level-Four Apprentices. But I do not want to jump ahead yet. You must first absorb and learn the Neothink® Marketing Secret, which will enable you to successfully bring Neothink® to the public if you chose this opportunity.

Okay, enough foreshadowing, let's roll into the Neothink® Marketing Secret (NMS). It is a three-piece Neothink® puzzle. We will dissect each piece along the way so you can use the separate pieces until the time comes when the pieces can come together and emit the synergy of Neothink. So, let's go now to our primary lesson today. Go now to Part One of this Level-Three Meeting.

Level-Three Essence Meeting
Part One

In Part One, I'm going to reveal the first two pieces to the Neothink® Marketing Secret.

Whether you're an entrepreneur, a laborer, a retiree, a housewife — I'm going to give you the tools to open up a whole new life; that elusive Civilization of the Universe life.

So let's dig in.

Q: Ever since last month's meeting, I could barely wait to find out: what is the Neothink Secret to making major marking breakthroughs?

MH: Today you will learn the highly-guarded Neothink® Marketing Secret. You, my Level-Three Apprentices, know my ultimate goal to bring about the conditions that will lead to biological immortality, which goes well beyond the realm of money. Nevertheless, these secrets I will teach you today are my Neothink® marketing secrets that have made me a wealthy man in the most unlikely field of writing and disseminating literature that will ultimately change the world. This is information you will get nowhere else; it is homegrown Neothink®. The following Neothink® Marketing Secret — a Neothink® Puzzle — has never been told outside our secret society. Many insiders have benefited enormously from what you are about to learn.

Even if you are not in a position to market anything right now, someday you could be, perhaps as soon as next month. Moreover, as I will demonstrate later, each piece of the Neothink® Marketing puzzle can be used for advantages beyond the business world. I will show you in Part Three of this Level-Three meeting that FNEs, TSMs, and now the three components to the Neothink® Marketing Secret (NMS) extend beyond business.

Now, let us roll into the Neothink® secret to making major marketing breakthroughs. As you know, Neothink creates a new mind space through forming puzzle pictures. I will now apply that new way of using the mind to marketing.

Three major puzzle pieces form the NMS puzzle picture. This three-piece Neothink® Puzzle delivers powerful marketing synergy when snapped together. I will dissect each piece of the puzzle along the way of revealing the NMS. As with any Neothink® puzzle, you can use each piece independently until that Neothink leap comes when you snap the pieces together into a locked puzzle that emits the synergy of Neothink®. Now, for the first puzzle piece:

The First Puzzle Piece to the Neothink®
Marketing Secrets
COMMON DENOMINATORS

I see you talking about common denominators on the secret web site. That pleases me. You are getting started, for common denominators are the building blocks of integrated thinking.

Great marketing ideas come from identifying needs that are large common denominators among large segments of the population. An example is the giant Internet service that we all know and use. The founder, as I mentioned last month, was an ordinary person who became increasingly familiar with Neothink® business, particularly integrated thinking, through the Neothink® Library and the Neothink® Discussion Board on the Internet, just as you are. He soon broke through to an amazing common denominator for the Internet. He started that Internet service, and today he is worth many billions of dollars. I cannot mention his name for privacy reasons, but those who had access to the Neothink® Discussion Board a decade ago know who he is. An interesting point is: he initially came into

Neothink® despising it. (I must say here that I do not know the details surrounding his particular evolvement, and the person who did know the intimate details is no longer living.)

That founder of the major Internet service used integrated thinking; he identified and then integrated a large common need with an effective, practical service. He used the first puzzle piece of the Neothink® Marketing Secret: he identified a large common-denominator need for a product/service.

That success story demonstrates the enormous riches that can come from leaping beyond the normal way of using the mind, beyond the non-integrating, automatically-reacting bicameral-like mode, leaping ahead into the new way of using the mind: integrating percepts into concepts into puzzles as shown in Vision Nine in your Second Heirloom Package. The Internet billionaire looked into the business world and integrated a large common need for a product/service.

Yet, there is much more still to know about common denominators in the world of marketing. For instance, to find a large common need for a product or service, as our Internet billionaire did, is the most sought-after dream of would-be entrepreneurs and, therefore, the most mined common denominators. So *many* people look for a product or service that will "catch on"; they look for that common-denominator need first and foremost, making the product idea often too competitive and difficult to find a winner.

There are other places in business to find common denominators. Henry Ford found his big common denominator in manufacturing. That common denominator, of course, was: bring the work to the people instead of the people to the work. Ford had his production line manage the people instead of the people manage production. That common denominator captured his entire manufacturing process through his creation of the assembly line, which turned out to be the biggest manufacturing breakthrough of all time. In turn, that comprehensive manufacturing common denominator gave way to one of the greatest marketing breakthroughs of the twentieth century, Ford's original vision: making the car affordable to the average American.

Making the car affordable to the average American was a huge marketing common denominator, of course, but Ford could not start with that. He had to look through his business to find his common denominator elsewhere — in manufacturing — to bring the marketing breakthrough to the people.

Now, let us look here at making Neothink® a household word as common as the car and the light bulb. We all know that widespread Neothink® is ultimately needed to cause mankind to take the leap out of this anticivilization into the Civilization of the Universe. Those of us in this secret society know that Neothink® is the greatest common-denominator need/product on our planet. However, people outside this secret society do not know this. And they will not know this just by being introduced to Neothink®. (They will not know the need for Neothink® in their lives until they feel emotionally drawn to Neothink®). Like Ford and the car, we must look in different areas of the business of Neothink® until we find a common denominator elsewhere beyond the product itself. Ford found his common denominator in manufacturing. Neothink® will find its common denominator in personnel – *in you.*

Let us stop and realize this group, as diverse and different as you are, has come together through one extraordinary powerful common denominator. You are the rare people of the world whose child of the past is alive and searching. Deep inside, you did not resign to the anticivilization. You are soul mates. You really are the chosen ones who will bring mankind out of the anticivilization and bring mankind into the Civilization of the Universe.

Before I go on, let us pause here to take in what this means. You are part of a moment in history that will forever change the world. This moment in time is so big that, ironically, it is hard to see. Indeed, it can be hard to comprehend that you are actually part of something so big: a moment in time that will change the course of mankind for eternity…right here, right now, with you and me. For some, this event will be just too big to come into focus and see. I understand that. For others, you will see, through wide-scope integrating, the whole picture. You will "get it", and this will become your drive in life, your Friday-Night Essence responding to your child of the past, within.

Let us move on: We are learning the full range of common denominators. Yes, we can look for that common need for a product or service such as the Internet billionaire did. However, that is the toughest place to break through with the common-denominator advantage since most people look there first and foremost. So, we are looking for other areas in the business where common denominators can be identified and then used to ultimately achieve huge marketing success. Ford found his common denominator in manufacturing. Neothink® will find its common denominator in personnel.

In the Heirlooms, I break down business into four fundamental components:

1) Values/Product
2) Numbers/Marketing
3) Operations (includes manufacturing)
4) Personnel

Again, the Internet billionaire found his common denominator in his product/service. Ford found his common denominator in his operations/manufacturing. The Neothink® Society will find its common denominator in its personnel/this group. The magnitude of Neothink®'s common denominator will unfold next month when, for the first time, I will deliver the plan to take Neothink® public.

You are the first generation of Neothink® that will be allowed to go public! For two generations, senior Neothink® Society members have talked about this next move. It finally materializes with you.

So, we saw examples of powerful common denominators for the product, the operations, and the personnel. The other fundamental component of business above is numbers/marketing. Let us now focus on finding powerful common denominators for numbers/marketing. That focus leads us straight into the second puzzle piece of the Neothink Marketing Secret:

The Second Piece to the
Neothink® Marketing Secret
FORCES OF NATURE

The Forces of Nature, as presented in Vision Three in your Second Heirloom, are huge common denominators. Understanding Forces of Nature can make the difference between failure and success. Forces of Nature are the stimulations everyone seeks. Your marketing and advertising must capture those huge common denominators, even if they tie into the anticivilization. (You will capture Forces of Nature in your advertising honestly.) As I go through the Forces of Nature, the subject matter may seem immature to you, even ridiculous. If you feel that way, here is the reason: We leapt into human consciousness after the breakdown of the bicameral mind between two thousand and three thousand years ago.

We are no longer animals of nature; we are conscious beings, a manmade leap beyond nature. However, we still crave those animalistic stimulations, those Forces of Nature. Because we are no longer animals of nature, rather we are conscious beings, those Forces of Nature amount to under-evolved stimulations, particularly to highly evolved Neothink® men and women. As I go through how to use Forces of Nature in marketing, keep a couple of things in mind: First, we are in an anticivilzation of bicameral-like reactions and must reach people at their level. Second, there is a third puzzle piece to the Neothink® Marketing Secret that is unique to The Neothink® Society. That third puzzle piece will come in later and nullify all the nonsense of the Forces of Nature.

All right, some examples of the Forces of Nature are:

1) Fastest and easiest prosperity and wealth — desire for instant gratification, for low-effort, get-rich-quick opportunities.

2) Attraction to most beautiful and sexy beings — desire for beach babes and hunks

3) Conserving energy via path of least resistance — desire for lazy way to get paid

4) Seeking power and prestige over others — desire for social and political advantages

5) Highest consumption for least energy spent — desire for least work for most money.

6) Looking for adulation and applause — desire for popularity and its advantages

7) Maximum caloric intake for survival — desire for sweets and overeating

8) Propagate genes, maximize offspring — desire for promiscuous sex

The Forces of Nature have such influence over us because they offer the stimulation modern needed and desired for survival for 200,000 years. By getting down to the Forces of Nature — the raw stimulations that influence every living adult — you tap into some of the largest common denominators in existence. To most people, Forces of Nature are irresistible.

The Forces of Nature give you the most powerful marketing and advertising tools. When you advertise something, tap into the Forces of Nature. Wrap the Forces of Nature around your selling points to reach people's underlying desires. For example, you have heard the expression "sex sells". Desire for beauty and random sex is a powerful and universal Force of Nature.

Prostitution is called the world's oldest profession. It comes solely from a Force of Nature working on human beings. Pornography comes from that same Force of Nature. The numbers on the pornography industry are staggering. Those staggering numbers reflect the marketing power in Forces of Nature.

Gambling has its roots in the Forces of Nature: get something for the least energy spent (i.e., get something for nothing). The numbers on the gambling industry are staggering, too.

Underneath it all, Forces of Nature are always working on you, trying to influence your every move, urging you to get things automatically, without human thinking or decision making. After all, the bicameral mind automatically reacts to external stimuli. The bicameral mind does not integrate, think, and make decisions. The bicameral mind does not work for its gains. It just reacts automatically, as in the case of prostitution and gambling. That desire for automatic, instant gratification is the state of most people's minds today. Instead of integrating and prospering, the mind today does not do that. But it jumps at the "opportunity" to get something for nothing. That is why the leap into integrated thinking and Neothink is so difficult.

One of our Neothink® Society apprentices owns a gym. What I say may or may not apply in his situation, for I have not met him or seen his gym. But to illustrate the point, let us say he plans to advertise. Would he want to advertise the hard work it takes to lose a few pounds? No. Instead he would want to engage the powerful Forces of Nature. He would want to show images of beautiful and sexy people and imply that his gym offers the easy way to look like those beauties. Whereas that approach might seem offensive to a hard worker as I know he is; Part Three of this three-piece Neothink® puzzle will help this all make sense.

Understand the Forces of Nature at work, such as: sex appeal, beauty, prestige, prosperity, wealth, power, popularity, health, social advantages for self and children. Appeal to the Forces of Nature and not to the hard work. That goes for any ad. Forces of Nature are automatic, stimulating, and satisfying. They tie back to the bicameral-like anticivilization, and we are in an anticivilization. People do not want to hear about hard work. Whereas I know nothing about marketing for a gym, I understand Forces of Nature. A fundamental Force of Nature is: wherever women are, men will come. Offer deep discounts to women; perhaps let them in for free. Of course, that decision would require the gym's owner to get into the numbers to make the proper ten-second miracles here. Remember, marketing and advertising demand constant studying of the numbers, as you learned in our last meeting, in order to make the invaluable ten-second miracles.

When The Neothink® Society finally found you, we knew you were a searcher. Yet, what nerves did we first touch in you to get your immediate attention? Let me pause here to say: I am giving you our proprietary marketing secrets here. Again, this is for your eyes and ears only. You may pass those secrets on to your children and spouse only. Okay, what nerves did we touch in you? Indeed, we used the Forces of Nature in our marketing to get your attention! And so do the other best marketers in the country. Even if they do not explicitly understand the Forces of Nature, the invisible hand (Adam

Smith) brings the country's most successful marketers into secretly using the Forces of Nature.

Although The Neothink® Society uses the Forces of Nature to get your attention, we do something unique that even the world's best marketers do not understand and will not understand for some time to come. That secret is what brought all of you together into the strongest modern-day common bond among human beings. That secret is what caused the child of the past inside this group to select Neothink® not just once but **three times** over the many other offers in your mail. That third puzzle piece of the Neothink Marketing Secret takes Neothink® marketing into another dimension altogether. That third and final piece to the NMS puzzle brings indestructible longevity to Neothink® as it would to any business. Indeed, that third piece to the Neothink Marketing Secret is why, whereas other companies come and go, Neothink® has been around for so long and will be around for as long as it takes to put ourselves out of business...that is, Neothink® will be around for as long as it takes to achieve biological immortality.

Let us move on now to the third secret puzzle piece that is unique to The Neothink® Society, for only we understand the leap of the mind into the next mentality.

Level-Three Essence Meeting
Part Two

When I reveal the third puzzle piece, it will solve the mystery of why you are here at The Neothink® Secret Society. The third puzzle piece surpasses all marketing approaches the world has ever known. It is unique to Neothink® for it comes from the Civilization of the Universe.

Q: What is the mysterious secret to Neothink®'s marketing longevity? I have seen other offers come and go, but Neothink® has been around since before my time.

MH: That mystery is answered within the third puzzle piece of the Neothink® Marketing Secret:

The Third Puzzle Piece to the Neothink®
Marketing Secret
FORCES OF NEOTHINK®

Most people do have the child of the past inside, but the child is in a state of complete resignation. Even if your consciousness does not know this, YOUR child of the past unlike others was reaching up with both arms — what we here at The Neothink® Society call the Cycle Two stage of your life. You were a searcher, and when we contacted you, your mind was in the active searching mode. ...It is all making sense now, isn't it?

That buried little Zon within people, if *reached*, will respond. In fact, every person was once a little mysticism-free Zon, a very, very long time ago before the child absorbed the mysticism, the mind-virus from the adult world around him. That little Zon, that child of the past buried deep inside, is THE largest common denominator in existence...even larger than the Forces of Nature. That is why the product Neothink® has the greatest potential of any product on Earth. And YOU are at the ground floor of that potential, as you will learn next month!

By understanding the Forces of Neothink® (Visions Three and Four in the Second Heirloom), we at The Neothink® Society send a secret message to that child of the past within. Through a secret code that I will reveal in a moment, we speak his or her language. Again, we have to do so in code, for the anticivilization-infected conscious mind will block any direct communication from the Civilization of the Universe. For instance, remember how The Group in Miss Annabelle's Secrets could not communicate to the masses their goal of biological immortality? That would have destroyed the presidential campaign. Instead, Daniel and Jeremiah had to "shift" the platform from the Forces of Neothink® back to the familiar, anticivilization-based Forces of Nature.

Now, think back to your first correspondence from The Neothink® Society, that 56-page pamphlet, your original Neothink® Orientation Booklet. That Neothink® Orientation Booklet says that inside its pages is a secret message your subconscious will absorb. Remember that? Remember that repeated mention of a secret code, a secret message? That secret message, written in secret code for your inner child of the past, is what Neothink® marketers spend their entire lives perfecting. To rescue your child of the past and bring searchers like you into the secret society, Neothink® marketers spend their lives learning how to get past your anticivilization-infected mind to reach through to that C of U child of the past deep inside, that infant Zon deep inside.

As I am going to teach you, Neothink® marketers must learn to communicate in code — a secret code. Again, the mysticism-infected conscious mind will shut off any talk from the mysticism-free C of U. For example, if you talk to most adults about biological immortality and living forever, their eyes glaze over. An entire generation ago, after years and years of numbers and ten-second miracles, Neothink® marketers learned to reach the child inside through a secret code, a secret message for the buried child who wants to live forever. I will give you specific examples of our secret code, how it works, and how YOU can do this, too. I will show you how this will bring about an indestructible strength to your business that other businesses do not have. Why? In the end, the child of the past within is THE LARGEST COMMON DENOMINATOR among the human race!

Before I go into specifics, I want to take this opportunity to explain that this secret-message marketing is completely different and new. No one outside The Neothink® Secret Society understands secret-message marketing because it is coming from the next mentality. When people do not understand something, they can lash out in fear or in misunderstanding. That explains why, on some Internet forums, people lash out at Neothink® Marketing. Not understanding this secret-message marketing, some people misunderstand our statements as gimmicks. Let me say right now: there are NO gimmicks in Neothink® marketing. There have NEVER been gimmicks in Neothink® Marketing. Everything is real — as real as our products — everything. But only those inside the Secret Society and three levels into these secret meetings, as you are now, know this. During this Level-Three Monthly Essence Meeting, your own eyes are opening to just how real Neothink® marketing really is.

I sometimes compare what we are doing (i.e., secret-message marketing from the next mentality) to another era during the only other leap in mankind's mentality: Conscious Jesus tried to communicate his message of human consciousness, of God-Man, to bicameral peasants. He could not communicate that next mentality directly. He had to talk in a secret code that the bicameral man could respond to. Jesus had to talk in allegories and parables, which he knew could reach into the bicameral mind and help it undergo the leap into the decision-making God-Man. Jesus gained enemies from both those in power who clearly understood what Jesus was doing and who wanted him gone, and form those not in power who just could not understand Jesus, his new mentality, or his secret-message "marketing". Of course, today Neothink® works around those same enemies.

Before I teach you how to write this secret code to the infant Zon within, let me say that this entire lesson applies to the arts as well. Many contemporary songs appeal to the Forces of Nature, from tribal beats to sex-starved lyrics. (Let me say, for the record, I am not passing judgment. In fact, recent studies have shown that different music stimulates different parts of the brain. During one specific stage of my writing process, I have introduced music of all genres to "turn on" certain parts of my creative and emotional brain.)

The few complex compositions as well as simple songs that enjoy longevity tend to have an emotional message from beyond the anticivilization...unknowingly from the C of U. *What a Wonderful World* performed by Louis Armstrong comes to mind. Enduring classical music comes from a C of U sense of life.

...Imagine the several artists and songwriters in this apprentice group applying the NMS to their art.

I will first teach you how to create and send a C of U secret message to mankind's largest common denominator: the child of the past, the infant Zon within, the person we were ALL once when we were very young, the person we were ALL meant to be. Before I do this, I must remind you again that these puzzle pieces are highly-guarded, proprietary Neothink® trade secrets. This is for your ears and your eyes only. And you may pass these secrets to your children and spouse. Here we go...

Let us start with the ultimate C of U accomplishment, the greatest Forces of Neothink®, our goal at The Neothink® Society, The Group's goal in the Miss Annabelle Story, this group's goal in The Neothink® Society, the greatest of all supersociety stimulations:

Biological Immortality…

Now with this example, I am going to show you how to snap together all three pieces to the NMS puzzle. Remember in the Heirlooms, straight-out talk of biological immortality brings empty responses from adults. Because of their bicameral-like existence, they just are not interested in eternal stagnation. As The Neothink® Society learned a generation ago, it is a fool's journey to attempt to communicate the possibilities of the next mentality to the current mentality. Instead, through numbers and many ten-second miracles, we made the discovery of secret-message marketing.

By keeping the concept of immortality in the marketing piece while bringing in one of the most powerful Forces of Nature — procreation — we developed the expression: sexual immortality. Here we have shifted the Forces of Neothink® back to a Force of Nature while, at the same time, sending a secret message to the infant Zon — the world's largest yet most difficult common denominator to tap. Through this "shifting" technique explained by Jeremiah in the Miss Annabelle's Story, one's child of the past deep in the right-hemisphere brain hears the C of U talking to him. One's adult self in the left-hemisphere brain hears the Forces of Nature talking to him. The adult will experience an impulse to purchase the product in response to the irresistible Force of Nature, SEXUAL immortality. The child of the past will absorb a residual that will keep him coming back and looking again and again at the ad in response to his long-sought Force of Neothink®, sexual IMMORTALITY. The three-way combination of tapping large common denominators, pushing forces-of-nature impulses, and planting Forces-of-Neothink® residuals result in enduring, indestructible marketing power.

Let us examine more closely this "shifting" technique, shifting residual-capturing Forces of Neothink® toward impulse-capturing Forces of Nature to gain the synergy of both. We saw in the expression "sexual immortality" the secret code reaching out to the buried Zon within while, at the same time, capturing the impulsive Force of Nature for the adult mentality, this capturing two very large common denominators. That is vivid example of the three-piece Neothink® Marketing puzzle snapping together.

Let us look further at the greatest Force of Neothink®: biological immortality. Whereas we will not come out and advertise that C of U concept, we will talk about "looking young and living young much, much longer" or "staying young, virulent, and sexually active indefinitely." We are sending the secret message to the child of the past while appealing strongly to the adult's Forces of Nature.

Let us look further at another great Force of Neothink®: a living job of value creation. One cannot market that concept; it is just not strong enough. But we can shift it. Forces of Nature push us toward prosperity wherever we can get it for survival…the more abundance, the better. Now, remember that a living job with essence, a value-creating job, has money-making essence, a money-making purpose. You learned that in your Heirloom Packages. A living job of essence (value creation) in contrast to a dead job of labor (value production) is the only job in which one can generate money without limits. Therefore, to shift the Force of Neothink® — a living job of value creation — to bring in the Forces of Nature, we emphasize the remarkable money-making possibilities of Neothink®. The Forces of Nature give the adult a strong impulse to get this real route to big money. The Forces of Neothink® give the child of the past a residual to keep coming back to Neothink®. For, we blend together the possibilities of making big money with creating values that did not exist before. Indeed, we blend together the Forces of Nature with the secret message to the infant Zon within. As you now know, that secret message is *value creation*.

Let us look at yet another Force of Neothink®: eternal romantic love. Eternal romantic love is one of the many values often gained while living a Neothink® life. The C of U concept of eternal romantic love is not strong enough to successfully market in this anticivilization. So, we shift and present the C of U concept *through* the Forces of Nature. For example, "lovemaking" in nature generally amounts to random, purely physical mating. So, Neothink® wraps that powerful Force of Nature around the secret message. If marketing to men, for instance, Neothink® Marketing will emphasize the beautiful and sexy women a Neothink® man will often find himself interacting with. Neothink® Marketing further emphasizes that a number of those gorgeous women will want his attention and even his love…and when he finally settles down and selects his spouse, he will love her forever, and she will love him forever. He will never leave her, and she will never leave him.

Do you see both the Forces of Nature speaking to the adult and the secret message speaking to the child of the past, the infant Zon within? Raw, animalistic, automatic physical intimacy is, indeed, available to Neothink® men and is emphasized in the marketing. However, within that message resides the secret code: when you settle down, you will love your spouse forever, and she will love you forever. Although blended into the Forces of Nature, the infant Zon hears that secret message deep inside your mind. The person you were meant to be hears our secret message calling out: come live the life you were meant to live!

Another Force of Neothink® is: legitimate power and prestige from one's value creations for society. In other words, one who provides major values to society has natural respect from others, natural power and prestige. Neothink® contains the tools and the program to lift people into a new life of value creation and, therefore, legitimate power and prestige. Yet that C of U concept could not be marketed successfully in this anticivilization. A generation ago, we learned that lesson after years and years of trying with millions of dollars draining from our efforts. After the long battle, we finally discovered how to shift the C of U concept and present it through the Forces of Nature while putting our secret message in the presentation. For example, we might emphasize the adulation and social advantages and favors you will receive as the wealthy and powerful man-on-the-hill. That superior-than-your-peers Force of Nature sparks the adult's anticivilization impulse to purchase the product. However, in that message, we will name-drop; we will reveal some money/power giants or renowned scientists who rose through Neothink®. Realize those money/power/prestige giants are value creators and enormous values to society. And that sends the secret message that the infant Zon inside recognizes through all the Forces of Nature...about the C of U life he or she was supposed to live.

Do you see what Neothink® Marketing is doing here?

Go back to your situation. Why did you respond to Neothink® amid all the other solicitations bombarding your mailbox? Not just once, but NINE times? That is how many back-and-forth correspondences we had (includes you reading your three Heirlooms) before you could finally enter your debut meeting. Your child of the past reached out and grabbed hold of and would not let go of the C of U, which was being secretly communicated to you within the Forces of Nature.

If this third puzzle piece seems daunting, you do not need to pursue it in your marketing yet. To get started, concentrate on the first two puzzle pieces for now. Concentrate on identifying common denominators. Look in all four fundamental components of business for common denominators. Also, particularly in the marketing component, recognize and engage the Forces of Nature. That is your focus for now. Just spend time on those first two puzzle pieces for now.

Like the Neothink® System (i.e., the mini-day/power-thinking team, mini-companies, division of essence, etc.), any one of these three puzzle pieces can substantially advance your efforts, even cause a major marketing breakthrough. You can use each puzzle piece independently for substantial gains. As you eventually learn how to start integrating them — snapping them together — you will gain increasing synergy and soaring success.

Throughout this whole process, keep your mind focused on the numbers in order to break through with those priceless ten-second miracles. As time goes on and you experience financial gains from identifying and formatting common denominators and advertising the Forces of Nature, then you can begin to bring in the missing piece to the Neothink® puzzle. The third puzzle piece, the final piece, when done right, will bring a synergy to your business that will make it enduring and indestructible. Someday the history of Neothink® will be told. That untold story will show how indestructible Neothink® is, as reflected in the Miss Annabelle's Story.

Now, before we leave the three-piece Neothink® Marketing Secret, let me revisit the first piece — common denominators. When you identify a common denominator as the Internet billionaire did in product, as Ford did in operations, as Neothink® did in personnel, you must then implement that common denominator. The key here lies in formatting. Ford formatted his common denominator through the assembly line. The Internet billionaire formatted his common denominator through a remarkable community-created/community-curator concept. And next month, I am going to format you — that is, those of you with a burning passion to bring about the C of U on our planet. I will be watching the secret web site to see who has passion burning within to lift mankind into the C of U. (Those of you who are not subscribed to the secret web site really need to subscribe in order to be part of the ground-floor opportunities coming next month. You are already missing all the many local meetings, the business opportunities, the licensing opportunities, the political movement, and now the ground-floor opportunity next month. All activities and opportunities come out of the secret web site. It is "the brain" of the Neothink® Movement.)

One concluding point on implementing and formatting common denominators: When you find your own common denominators for your own business, your best formatting tools are found in the Heirlooms' business techniques. You do not need any miracle breakthrough such as an assembly line. All the techniques you need to format and implement your common denominators can be found in the business techniques inside your Heirlooms.

That completes the Neothink® Marketing Secret. In Part Three of this meeting coming up next, I will show you how to use these techniques beyond business. I will also tell you a little more about what's coming to you, next month. Go now to Part Three of this Level-Three Meeting.

Level-Three Essence Meeting
Part Three

Now that you know how we found you, how we reached down and took the hand of your child of the past and lifted you toward the Civilization of the Universe, let me say welcome, welcome home.

Your child of the past and mine, together, we will continue ahead on the most important journey of our lives.

Q: How can I use all your great secrets if I am retired?

MH: Let us come down a notch or two from the high-powered Neothink® Marketing Secret and ask what about the truck driver, the dishwasher, the retiree, the housewife? Does the NMS apply to entrepreneurs only?

Actually, today's three puzzle pieces do apply beyond business. I mentioned the arts briefly earlier today. I will expand on that a little further in a moment.

First, let me back up and say that all three lessons thus far may seem directed to entrepreneurs only, but that is where I am honing my examples. All three lessons apply beyond business.

Let me back up to last month, the Ten-Second Miracles. Remember, I said the Heirlooms came from making many of those Ten-Second Miracles. The Heirlooms, of course, have nothing to do with business per se. The Heirlooms came from writing, philosophy, psychology, and art. The Ten-Second Miracles come from the new puzzle-building way of using the mind. Numbers help you see the puzzle pieces and snap together those Ten-Second Miracles at work.

Again, the essence of TSMs is pulling together puzzle pictures. Numbers are tools at work that help you do that. The TSM is the new way of using the mind that can apply anywhere, in any circumstance. Pushing the mind to absorb knowledge, to see *what is*, and to integrate something better causes this new way of thinking in whatever you do. Our minds do not do that naturally.

In life in general, you can pull together these remarkable Neothink® Puzzle Pictures. But our minds just do not go there, for our minds are infected with a virus, with the bicameral mode known as mysticism. Many of you at the secret web site are seeing through the eyes of numbers at work, and many of you have begun making Ten-Second Miracles. That really pleases me.

Now, revisiting the first meeting, the FNE also applies to everyone, even those who cannot make their FNEs their livelihoods. At least they can find it and inject that joy and happiness and that PLAY into their lives. The FNE applies to the truck driver, retiree, dishwasher, it does not matter. And, those having trouble finding their FNE should take a closer look at spreading Neothink® to bring about the world they have always sought, especially next month as you gain the opportunity to be among the first generation of Neothink® Society members to take Neothink® public.

This month's lesson, the Neothink® Marketing Secret, also applies beyond the business world. Teaching your mind and your children to always seek common denominators, for instance, simply makes you a more evolved, integrated thinker. Vision Nine in your Second Heirloom Package goes into detail on this exercise to becoming a genius. Moreover, imagine how valuable it is to understand the Forces of Nature for raising your children, for example, or for understanding your spouse, your friends, or yourself for that matter. Those forces are always at work on all of you. Also, imagine how valuable it is to understand the Forces of Neothink to guide yourself and your loved ones toward the C of U life.

Indeed, your FNEs, the TSMs, and the three puzzle pieces to the NMS — all three lessons so far — reach beyond the entrepreneur. Those three lessons are the tools you need to make the leap into the next evolution of man — into the mysticism-free Neothink® man or woman.

As of today, your three most pressing questions have been answered in the first three lessons:

1) What is my FNE?
2) What is the Ten-Second Miracle?
3) How did The Neothink® Society chose me?

Let us look more closely at #3, how did we choose you? In choosing you to come into The Neothink® Society, we have created perhaps the most powerful common denominator in recent history. You are all here because your child of the past directed you here! Some of you will dispute that statement: "I'm here to make big money!" the Forces of Nature in you will scream! That is your left-brain "awareness" speaking, however. Consider you got here only after ordering and reading all THREE Heirlooms. After receiving and reading the first Heirloom, if you were only seeking the Forces of Nature, say instant monetary gratification, you would not have kept coming back for the other two Heirlooms. The Forces of Neothink talking to your child of the past kept you coming back. ...You might have seen astute apprentices on the secret web site make this same observation. (This is not to say, however, that you will not make a lot of money.)

So, here we are, together, the group with such diversity, such very different financial statuses, job statuses, power levels. Yet, underneath all our differences the child of the past inside each of us survived the anticivilization and brought us together: you, all of you, with me. We all intellectually recognize and emotionally desire the rational Neothink® World, the super-prosperous supersociety, the immortal C of U on Earth. WHAT, I ask you, are we going to do with this amazing common denominator? Are you ready to do what I see so many of you hoping for? Are you ready to go outside the society? Are you ready to go public and change the world? The lesson today has given you the tools — the power to do that. After all, changing the world will be every bit a Neothink®-Marketing dynamic as it is a Neothink®-Living dynamic. Yes, we have the business dynamic and the product dynamic to do this. I ask you again, are you ready to go out there and change the world? Think about it: YOU are now part of this SUPERPUZZLE!

Stop to think for a moment — who else, what else can effectively change this world? Libertarians? Objectivists? Republicans? Democrats? There is no one and nothing beyond us. Why us? The answer is: no one else knows the next mentality. Only we do. Moreover, we are not a powerless think tank. We have the engine of business and marketing driving this forward.

The next phase is the EXCITING PHASE. What if I tell you I am going to turn those of you who are interested into marketers bringing Neothink® to the public? Does that touch a nerve of being your FNE? Let me add that Neothink® is truly the only product on Earth that EVERYONE needs. The marketing could go much deeper and far longer than any other royalty-based marketing program for any product or service. And you apprentices here in the Secret Society, on the secret web site (where Neothink® movements are organized and orchestrated), you come in on the ground floor of all that royalty-marketing potential! You are among the first generation of taking Neothink® public. You are in a rare moment in Neothink® history. The opportunity will bring emotional and financial rewards. That journey begins next month. Learn, learn, learn the Neothink® Marketing Secret this month. View this meeting more than once to master the three NMS puzzle pieces and to prepare yourselves for next month's opportunity.

Let me make myself clear: Taking Neothink® public begins in our next meeting, with Level-Four Apprentices leading the charge through my mentorship. This offers an enormous opportunity to you. In that meeting, I will release the plan to take Neothink® public on two fronts:

1) A royalty-based marketing program that goes several layers deep (with you getting in on the ground floor)! You are going to need the marketing tools I taught you today!

2) A political plan that reveals the party name, the platform, and the startling campaign strategy. (The campaign strategy will boggle your mind!) Until then, you need to go to the political state breakdown on the secret web site and get organized state by state.

This is so important that I am going to repeat myself: you are now part of the group that will change the world! Everything you learned today will be crucial for you to transform into a world-class marketer. You know by now that Neothink® is not hyperbole. It is the only movement with the engine capable of changing the world.

Once again, going public will start in two ways:

1) Spreading Neothink® by bringing outsiders into The Neothink® Society, our growing Neothink® family. This will be formatted in a way that Level-Four apprentices can begin to make good money doing this — a REAL ground-floor opportunity! A REAL Friday-Night Essence!

2) Spreading Neothink® by bringing people into our political party. This will be formatted in a way that Level-Four apprentices can begin to acquire honest power doing this — also a real ground-floor opportunity! Both approaches require an enormous marketing job to succeed! You now have the proprietary Neothink® marketing tools.

You are the fortunate forerunners. However, that is enough foreshadowing for now! Let us come back down to Earth, back to the foot traveler taking one step at a time. Everything you learn this month is going to build your horsepower next month for marketing both the Neothink® Party movement and the Neothink® Society movement. Those Neothink® movements could become your FNE. Both Neothink® movements involve historic value creation. You will be free to pursue numbers and make Ten-Second Miracles. Making a difference in this world will be exciting for all Neothink® apprentices, including those of you trapped in a job of labor.

Your homework is:

First, in a week, view this master-link lesson a second time.

Second, go back into the Second Heirloom and study Visions Three, Four, and Nine. I want you to really understand the Forces of Nature, the Forces of Neothink, and common denominators. As you read Visions Three and Four, you will read about supersociety stimulations that out-stimulate spiral-of-death stimulations, which will come into play in our next meeting together.

Those with a business to market…common denominators, Forces of Nature, and Forces of Neothink are the three pieces to the powerful marketing puzzle. I do suggest starting with the first two pieces only…until a certain point is reached where you can introduce secret-message marketing to the child of the past within.

In closing, I have said all along that this is a two-fold journey:

1) A journey for YOU to personally succeed.

2) A journey for our NEOTHINK® GOAL to succeed.

I have also said all along that those two paths can and will eventually join together. Remember, Neothink® Society members are the only individuals who can do this because our child of the past is alive and reaching. Only we see the C of U. Sometimes, when sustenance is met, self-enrichment can become very fulfilling by contributing to the Neothink® Goal. This is an exciting opportunity for all of us, including those stuck in stagnation traps...for making our deepest dreams come true, the dream of our Child of the Past.

Before entering our next historic meeting, view this entire master-link meeting a second time and read your assignments. Practice, practice, practice developing the three puzzle pieces revealed in today's Essence Meeting. And those who have not subscribed to the secret webs site should do so now to reside where the two great public movements will be released, organized, and orchestrated.

I will follow your efforts there at the secret web site. In fact, I am going there right now.

Level-Four Essence Meeting
Introduction

Hello and welcome to your Level-Four Essence Meeting. As you know, this is the meeting in which, for the first time in the history of The Neothink® Society, that we will be going public. This historical meeting will come at you in four parts: 1-The Intro, which we're going through now about going public and marketing, 2-Part One, a network marketing opportunity for you which is a natural Friday Night Essence for many of us here today, and 3-Part Two, the political movement, which is a natural Friday Night Essence for many of us here today and Part Three, forming the formal structure which is starting the C of U on earth.

Let's start off with talking about going public. Now, when I say going public, what we're actually going to do is bring people in, bring the public in, bring anyone in. Bring in as opposed to reach out. Bring in as opposed to spread out. By that I mean people must come in to our society to get the advantages. In fact, the concept of the Secret Society, the Neothink® Secret Society, changes to the Neothink® Society of Secrets or simply The Neothink® Society.

Now, you are beginning to engage in marketing. Recall, in the Level Three Meeting, we talked about Forces of Nature impulses, Forces of Neothink® residuals, and common denominator formats. We'll go into those Neothink® Marketing concepts throughout the three parts of this meeting here today. Now, from your homework in your Level Three Meeting you learned that the driving force behind both Forces of Nature and Forces of Neothink is stimulation. We also talked about common denominator formats. Recall how in Ford Motor Company the common denominator format was the assembly line and we talked about some other common denominator formats. In your case, it was finding the child of the past, searching within you. And it was that common denominator that we used to select you to join or "come into" The Neothink® Society.

Now, getting back to the Neothink® movement of going public…We will find that our common denominator format is going to take the form of Clubhouses and their meetings. For example, the Clubhouse will become a place of belonging, a place of life advantages. I suggest you will set up weekly meetings to bring potential new members in to what I am calling the Introduction Meeting. It is in these Introduction Meetings that you will sign your visitors up as new members to attend Clubhouse Meetings, which are meetings for members only. Some of those new members will subsequently join the political movement and the political meetings. As you'll see, these meetings, these Clubhouse congregations, will grow into the common denominator format for going public.

You will also learn today that you are in the process of turning into a super Neothink® marketer. Remember, the Forces of Nature in your reading and in your homework from our last meeting, you learned that those amount to spiral-of-death stimulations. The reason for that is we're no longer an animal of nature. On the other hand, Forces of Neothink® amount to super-society stimulations. We are now conscious man and should be living in a limitless super society.

Super-society stimulations out simulate spiral of death stimulations. You read in Visions Three and Four the irresistible attraction to Forces of Nature. But those are spiral of death stimulations because they come from nature and we leapt beyond nature 2000 to 3000 years ago. For example, to spread one's genes by mating randomly and recklessly is poisonous to a Neothink® romantic love relationship. We are no longer animals of nature.

When man's nature-created bicameral mind broke down 2000 to 3000 years ago, mankind leapt into a new man-made mind space known as human consciousness. Once we properly market and format super-society stimulations, they will out stimulate the under evolved, spiral-of-death stimulations of the anticivilization.

No one has ever explicitly formatted and marketed super-society stimulations because no one before Neothink® could understand and decipher such a thing without knowing about our next mentality, our next evolution into the mysticism-free God-Man. We are the first. You're going to ultimately format and market super-society stimulations which have never been done and therefore has huge potential.

Remember, the child of the past, the infant Zon, is inside everyone. It's the largest common denominator yet it's the toughest to tap. In your last meeting you learned the three-piece Neothink® marketing secret – the common denominator format, the Forces of Nature impulses, the Forces of Neothink® residuals. Now, I'm going to mentor you how to kick off what will ultimately become the greatest marketing dynamic for mankind delivering the greatest product for mankind…Neothink®.

First, let us talk about, "honor and glory at all costs" which is actually a powerful Force of Nature. Remember, in your last meeting we called the maximum and fastest prosperity, power, popularity, prestige for the least amount of energy spent "honor and glory at all costs". We first see this phenomenon in Ulysses from Homer's Iliad. There's no regard for honesty, no regard to earned prosperity, power, popularity, prestige. "Honor and glory at all costs" means taking, pillaging, and plundering by force for instant gratification. That Force of Nature, "honor and glory at all costs", drives the anticivilization. It drove ancient Ulysses and it drives many of our leaders today, especially our political leaders.

One way or another, most everyone is trapped in the spiral-of-death Forces of Nature, either seeking "honor and glory at any cost" or accepting and following those who are. A few climb to the top often through deception, force and fraud. Many more "succeed" off of the shoulders who those on top walk on.

That Homeric anticivilization lead by the plundering and pillaging Ulysses can be out stimulated by us, by those who understand the C of U and who can therefore skillfully offer super-society stimulations.

Indeed, Neothink® offers each person the opportunity to become his own Ulysses but minus the dishonesty. Now, think about that: Become your own Ulysses, become that meaningful, that eternally meaningful, important person. It's a large, *impulsive* common denominator but by adding in there the missing ingredient of honesty. Taking away the dishonesty beckons the underlying Forces of Neothink, that child of the past, the largest common denominator.

Everyone in his or her own way wants to be a Ulysses; a person leading a meaningful and important life and looked upon with respect and reverence. However, most good people don't have access to or desire for a dishonest destructive, quick path to the top.

Before I go on though, I must inject here that there are C of U leaders in this anticivilization who got there through honest wealth, power, and prestige by creating values for society. Now, everyone's deepest dream, most deep-rooted desire is to lead a meaningful and important life. They want to be meaningful; they want to do something important and valuable with their lives. If any person, any ordinary working man or woman, any retiree or housewife could live that meaningful and important life, become a Ulysses minus the dishonesty in his or her own way, that would out-stimulate whatever he or she experiences now. Stimulation guides our choices and now we can out-stimulate the anticivilization. Imagine this, having your shoulders walked on versus rising up yourself, never to be walked on again.

In short, my friends, out-stimulating the forces-of-nature stimulations of the anticivilization is the theme for the political movement, for the network marketing opportunity and for the Society of Secrets formal structure. That will be Parts One, Two and Three of today's meeting. In our C of U dynamic of value creation, everyone can contribute to society, be a self-leader, a God-Man and rise without stepping on others' shoulders. Instead, you will reach down and pull up your fellow man as I'm doing with you. You will reach down and pull up those you bring into your Clubhouse. Yes, now everyone can be a Ulysses minus the dishonesty.

The brand new Neothink® World paradigm of value creators allows the C of U phenomenon which is so much better than the way it has always been. More and more people will make the leap into the next mentality of self-leading value creation as they leave behind the current mentality of following mode value production.

If you can deliver *the* greatest message anyone wants to hear, you will succeed. The message: You can live the Ulysses life. A stimulating and exhilarating life-long journey filled with honor and glory, meaning and importance while always helping others. That message is filled with forces-of-nature impulses and laced with Forces of Neothink® residuals. That message, *the* message, is going to be your key to going public.

In the anticivilization of bicameral-like mentalities, the marketing message must come with forces-of-nature impulses and forces-of-Neothink® residuals which we learned about in our last meeting. You must also format those two huge common denominators. Now, let's explore how you will 1) push those forces-of-nature impulses, 2) plant those forces-of-Neothink® residuals and 3) format those huge common denominators.

In Parts One, Two and Three of this essence meeting, I'll dig into the marketing of the Forces of Nature and Forces of Neothink®. Right now though, I want to introduce you to how to format those common denominators. Using a little power thinking here, let's start with the end accomplishment, formatting those huge common denominators, that is, formatting people looking for forces-of-nature stimulations and people looking for forces-of-Neothink® stimulations.

So, how do we format those huge common denominators? Prior to this group of apprentices, The Neothink® Society was a loosely knit secret society that very rarely congregated. Even then, the congregation was very selectively chosen, limited to a couple of hundred hand-selected members only. You are the first Neothink® generation where we allow you to network and meet one another and to congregate. There's something huge about that, which you can't fully appreciate yet. For two generations, we've patiently laid the enormous ground work necessary prior to this day, the day when we would allow Neothink® members to congregate and bring in people from the general public without our very involved, very expensive, purposefully limiting, filtering process allowing only a select few, whose child of the past was still searching for the C of U.

But now you can bring anyone to the Introduction Meetings at your Clubhouse. The Neothink® Society is being allowed to grow, no longer growth-restricted as in its past. You can bring in anyone, family, friends and beyond. Before it was only limited to your children and spouse.

We'll stay close to our roots for now and still maintain an inside society status not a secret society status but still an inside society status. We're no longer a secret society but we are a society of secrets.

We'll have people, non-profiled people, come into our society of secrets. We'll let The Neothink® Society grow larger and larger causing the Business Alliance Dynamics you read about in the Miss Annabelle's Story. If the general public wants these secrets and competitive advantages — life advantages — they have to come in here to get it. Instead of saturating the public by putting our knowledge out there through selling it, we'll build mystery and momentum by exposing our secret knowledge only to those who come inside; by inviting people into The Neothink® Society. A point will come when to remain competitive to get the Neothink® advantages that others now possess, people will be motivated to come to us in large numbers to get in to The Neothink® Society and get our competitive advantages that will help them discover the life they were meant to live.

And now we're formatting this approach through the power of your meetings. The three initial meeting structures will be the Introduction Meetings which we'll cover Part One, the Clubhouse Meetings for the members once they join which we will cover in Part Three of this meeting and the political meetings. People who are motivated and inclined to change society we live in will be drawn to these political meetings.

So, we have Introduction Meetings; Clubhouse Meetings; Political Party Meetings. In all three meetings there is a general recognition or sense that things are not right with the world and that there could and should be something more in our personal lives. In these meetings, we seek to uncover the creative, wealthy, happy person we were meant to be in the safe, prosperous, free society in which we were supposed to live. This sense that The Neothink® Society will improve the world we live in and improve our personal lives establishes huge common denominators. Improving the world around you draws one into the political meetings. Improving the person inside you draws you into the Clubhouse meetings. In both cases, to become a member of The Neothink® Society to improve the person inside you or to improve the society around you, draws you to the Introduction Meetings.

Okay, we have learned that meetings are the powerful common denominator format for you to take Neothink® to the public. Let's move on now to Part One which will bring you to the Introduction meetings which for many of you will become your Friday-Night Essence.

Level-Four Essence Meeting
Part One

So many of you have written to ask me if you can tell your friends about Neothink®, that you want to spread Neothink®. After all, you spent your life searching for that something more the child of the past within you kept alive even in this anticivilization. So this will be a natural Friday-Night Essence for many of you; bringing people in and spreading Neothink®; introducing Neothink® to others and thus bringing to them that C of U dynamic that we have here in The Neothink® Society. And, as you bring people in, they will join the Clubhouse meetings which is where the C of U on planet earth begins.

Now, your first three Level Essence Meetings with me were crucial preparation for this. Introducing the general public to Neothink® will become for many of you your Friday-Night Essence and a place in history. And, you're going to *play* doing this. This will truly be the way you feel the sensation I talked about in the first meeting; *playing* at life. When you are creating values, you, as an adult, are *playing* and this will be the opportunity for so many of you to create values and to *play* at life.

You'll be able to use numbers to make Ten-Second Miracles doing this, bringing people in, changing the anticivilization to the C of U. You'll be able to apply the Neothink Marketing Secret, all three pieces, to become more and more effective, have more and more fun, achieve more and more success and make more and more money.

We'll get into the marketing approach as we go through Part One. Now, let me get into this opportunity for you. This is a Network Marketing Program with you at the ground floor. That is huge. I've had world marketing experts asking me to let them release this to their own teams to take Neothink® public. The country's top marketing experts wanted this

Neothink® Network Marketing Opportunity first and they've wanted this for twenty years. I've repeatedly said no and turned down a billion dollars to let my hand-picked apprentices, my loyal readers, have this first.

To take advantage of this tremendous opportunity that I saved just for my apprentices and loyal readers, you will assume a mentoring position to the flock of newbie's coming in. That puts enormous responsibility on you. I put enormous trust in you. This is *the* movement to change the world. This is so big — too big for many to grasp — but it is happening. This is not a sudden, fly-by-night fad. This has been meticulously, patiently evolving for generations. You are in the right place at the right time. You, as Jake was in the Miss Annabelle's Story, are thrust right in the middle of the Neothink® movement.

We searched years to find you. You are the chosen ones to bring the Neothink® Network Marketing Opportunity to the public, the political movement to the public and the Clubhouses to the public and you will help mentor all the newcomers.

So, let's look more closely at the Neothink® Network Marketing Opportunity. Recall we said the Introduction Meetings are formatted to introduce potential members to The Neothink® Society. Your Introduction Meetings will:

1) inspire the visitors to join the only path to a stimulated, exhilarated life which they were meant to live and

2) inspire the visitors to sell the only product that everyone eventually needs.

Think about that; marketing a product that everyone eventually needs. When you bring someone into The Neothink® Society, they come back and profusely thank you just as we all feel so thankful to be part of the Neothink®

family. And that knowledge gives you confidence. It's a confidence builder in your marketing effort.

Let's look closely at the contents of your Introduction Meeting: "selling" the value The Neothink® Society. The reason the Introduction Meeting is your format is teamwork. There's something powerful about having a team of people presenting values, presenting their own experiences, the values they've reaped from being a member of The Neothink® Society. You need a congregation of people to witness with your own eyes how Neothink® is a universal value. And I recommend that during the Introduction Meeting some designated speaker stands up and gives his or her own personal testimonial. Such a personal testimonial shows your visitors the exhilarating life that awaits them. You'll talk about things such as discovering your Friday-Night Essence, and reaping the rewards from Neothink® by having help from advanced Neothink® mentors. You will tell them how you discovered *playing* as an adult and Ten-Second Miracles. You will teach them how to market Neothink® and they will be surrounded by people who feel like family and who will be an enormous support in your new life journey. Here in The Neothink® Society they will learn secret knowledge, secrets that work and a way of life that leads to really good things. And, you will want to tell them about the Heirloom Packages and what they've meant to you and what they will get out of those.

Remember, we are requiring them to come in to The Neothink® Society. We are not putting our material out there for them to get their hands on. You are selling a new life. You're selling them the life that they were born to live but are missing out on. You are, in a non-religious sense, their savior, as I was yours. You're turning them onto a very stimulating, excitement-filled and love-filled journey to a new life. You're showing them how to become a Ulysses without the dishonesty. You are showing them a new way of thinking called Neothink®. Again, you will be there to help them with that and they will receive information through the Heirloom Packages and through the meetings with Mark Hamilton, with myself, as their mentor.

You'll talk about the love and the affinity that you've had with your family, your Neothink® family. Your sense of belonging here, you'll talk about the security, how we help each other and you'll talk about the life advantages that you gain in The Neothink® Society, about your friends for life, about the romantic possibilities, about the web site which brings them a national networking capacity with the chat room and discussion boards. Of course there is the Business Alliance that opens up a multitude of business opportunities for them.

You'll talk to them about the strength of the secrets in their Heirlooms that expand and escalate with the monthly Essence Meetings with Mark Hamilton combined with the live meetings at their local Clubhouses.

You can talk about becoming part of a rare watershed event in history that is changing the world and about what a feeling that brings to you, knowing you are part of that.

Of course, you can talk about the social gatherings and events as well as the specialized, exciting meetings that they may be interested in such as the new political party dynamic, the Neothink® music and bands, live arts, film projects, business opportunities in the U.S. and overseas.

Keep in mind, we are all one team in the sense that we are one unit working on the superpuzzle to bring Neothink® public. We're one unit but we're broken into essentially these different mini-companies all across the country. Therefore, Clubhouses need to communicate to each other through the secret web site. You need to share what is working, what's not working which will bring strength to the other Clubhouses. Remember, this is a superpuzzle, the same superpuzzle that we saw in the Miss

Annabelle's Story. And, as in Miss Annabelle, you must keep in mind the importance of what we are doing here and thus always want to help others who are part of that superpuzzle. We are changing the world and our secret web site will act as our communicator.

Now in the second part of your Introduction Meeting you will show your visitors the rare financial opportunity for those interested in making money. You'll explain that this is just beginning and, as I said earlier, is an opportunity that world-class marketers have been trying to get from me for twenty years. I repeatedly turned down those offers. I turned them down and, at the same time, turned down a lot of money. But I always kept in mind the superpuzzle and what really Neothink® is going to achieve; the goal is biological immortality. And, taking Neothink® public through you apprentices is part of that superpuzzle.

So, this is just the beginning, it's that head of steam that has been building pressure for generations. So you can communicate to your guests that they are getting in early on this.

Neothink® is the only product that could eventually reach everyone because it's bringing people the exhilarating and adventurous life they were meant to live. More and more people will need The Neothink® Society to stay competitive as we grow. It's those Business Alliance dynamics that are described in the Miss Annabelle's Story. When you understand all this you realize that the Neothink® Network Marketing Opportunity will go for a long, long time and penetrate civilization deeply. The money making potential here is huge for those getting in now. And, our format makes it easy. You just bring people to the Introduction Meetings and membership will basically sell itself. You will develop skill and technique that's going to serve you well on your marketing venture.

Remember, you can't escape the fact that we have the universal product that everyone needs and as The Neothink® Society grows the pressure on those who don't have these advantages is going to grow as well. This will give you confidence. Remember that those you bring in are going to come back to you and thank you over and over again for saving them from stagnation and boredom. And, many of them will also make a lot of money through the network marketing.

To summarize these Introduction Meetings; you'll have two parts, the **value** and the **opportunity**. The **value** you are demonstrating and offering your visitors is the Ulysses life minus the dishonesty...the life they were all meant to live. Only here can they become the person they were meant to be. They will discover and actualize their passion. For their monthly membership fee they will have access to the world's most highly-guarded secrets, visions and powers. They will become the person they were meant to be while taking their monthly course, their monthly Essence Meetings with me, Mark Hamilton for the first twelve months. They will enjoy the web site with the national discussion boards, chat rooms, chat sessions, help from others, questions, answers. They'll enjoy local meetings monthly at the Clubhouses, with people from whom they receive intellectual stimulation, friendships, business opportunities, and perhaps even romantic relationships. They're welcome to any meeting around the country at any Clubhouse and they will have access to specialized meetings and projects such as the political meetings, medical meetings, business meetings and opportunities.

The second part of the Introduction Meeting will consist of the **opportunity**. The Neothink® Network Marketing Opportunity has got to be one of the greatest network marketing opportunities of all time. Why do I say the greatest marketing opportunity? Because everyone wants and needs these highly-guarded secrets. Everyone wants and needs to become the person he or she was meant to be. Everyone wants or needs an environment of friends who will benefit and lift their lives because everyone wants and needs what The Neothink® Society has to offer.

The Neothink® Network Marketing Opportunity will go longer than anything out there. A lot of people will join The Neothink® Society for the **value** and a lot will join for the money-making **opportunity**. A lot will join for both the **value** and the **opportunity**.

All your life you have searched for the C of U without realizing that's what you were doing. You are all searchers. You did not resign to the anticivilization. You are looking for something more out of life. And therefore, that persistency that non-acceptance of the anticivilization, is going to make you the natural salesman for Neothink®, the natural messenger for the C of U. And, as you become comfortable with this role, it will expand within you and become your Friday- Night Essence. I don't see that there will be any stopping you.

Now selling will be new to a lot of you and takes some getting used to, however, what I would suggest is for you to get together with your apprentice teams or A-Teams and start forming the elements to the Introduction Meetings. Assign people or choose people who are going to stand up and give an account of their life, their experience, their search and what they found in Neothink®. Keep in mind all of the marketing elements we've discussed; the Forces of Nature and the Forces of Neothink. Forces of Nature are reflected in people looking for wealth, romance, health, and happiness. The Forces of Neothink are reflected in people looking for that meaningful and important life that the child of the past once sought. You can bring those together during your deliveries. Also, remember the analogy to Ulysses minus dishonesty; an action-filled, meaningful and important life…the life worth living, the life full of adventure, a journey. When one comes into The Neothink® Society he or she begins a journey, a life-long journey, of action, adventure, excitement, growth, romance. This Society has secret knowledge that will make you a wealthier person financially and personally. Your personal stories about those values are what will sell people on The Neothink® Society.

If you're not used to selling, I believe very soon you will be filled with motivation, a deep-rooted motivation as these Introduction Meetings become your Friday-Night Essence. It will go from, initially perhaps, some anxiety and maybe not feeling quite secure with your delivery to an exciting and exhilarating experience as you feel your value that you are bringing to the world; as you introduce people into the life they were meant to live.

Now, you see why I say it's very important for you to get the Neothink® Clubhouses going strong. We are going to talk about that in Part Three of this Level Four meeting. It behooves you marketers to get the Neothink® Clubhouses going strong in your areas for those are going to be perhaps the greatest reason for people to continue paying their membership fee monthly.

To be clear, the Clubhouse doesn't necessarily mean a specific place. The Clubhouse is the actual monthly meeting. It could be at a restaurant, it could be at somebody's home, it could be anywhere, it's the meeting itself. After your new members have been exposed to and absorb all the literature, then those fulfilling local meetings, the Clubhouses, will sustain their ongoing membership for life. We'll talk more about this, as I said, in Part Three of this meeting.

I want to make one more important point about these Introduction Meetings and that is your Introduction Meeting's designated speaker or speakers who stand up and give a personal account of his or her own life and journey with

Neothink®. This is where both the Forces of Nature and Forces of Neothink can play a powerful role. Here's how:

In the Introduction of this meeting, I told you that everyone down deep wants an important and meaningful life of lasting significance. The Forces of Nature bring us Ulysses. The Forces of Neothink bring us God-Man which is a Ulysses life minus dishonesty. You will not use the term God-Man in your speech. You will instead use the expression, "the person you were meant to be". In short, someone in your A-Team will give the personal account of his or her own life. How it transformed from a boring and stagnant life into an exhilarating adventure full of action, meaning, friends, money, love. That personal story will have an enormous impact and go a long way in convincing visitors to join because that personal story touches the child of the past within all of us. Deep down, everyone wants the exhilarating eternally important life, the romantic life of Ulysses minus the dishonesty. The important exhilarating romantic life you were meant to live.

Now during the second part, the money-making opportunity part of your Introduction Meeting, you'll express that unlike other network marketing products Neothink® is universal, everyone wants and needs Neothink® for the exhilarating, adventurous, meaningful and romantic life we were meant to live. All that can be found in The Neothink® Society.

As you bring people in, in essence, you become their personal mentor. You will help and answer their questions and before long you become a mentor to many as I am. Let me tell you from my heart, it is very rewarding.

Upon bringing people into this society of secrets, The Neothink® Society, you'll want to explain that they will receive our most highly-guarded inside secrets. You want to explain to them that they will come to their first local Clubhouse meeting on such and such a day and place that you establish. You want to tell these new members that they will have immediate access to the web site that will put them immediately in the middle of thousands of members for questions, guidance, chats, discussion boards and access to any Clubhouse meeting anywhere in your state, nation or the world. You'll want to let your new members know that they'll begin their one-year journey with their Senior Mentor, Mark Hamilton, that will change any ordinary person over the course of that year into the person he or she was meant to be, living the life he or she was meant to live.

Tell your new members they will have access to you and other local members for mentoring and let them know that they will discover a rewarding social network in their local Clubhouse. And let's see what happens when a new member gets into The Neothink® Society..

They will also have access to the political meetings or any other specialized meetings. Say there are meetings about business projects, medical meetings on medical longevity or live arts. They'll have access to all of those meetings, too.

I advise you to approach first your family and good friends. Get comfortable with the process, bring them in. Remember, they will thank you later for bringing them into this more exhilarating, exciting life. Then, as you get comfortable and feel good about doing this, then bring in the public. You can advertise in any way you wish to bring people to your Introduction Meetings but you can't use our copyrighted material. The only potential exception to that is if you present me with a specific package and plan and get my signature of approval.

So, get together with your apprentice teams and you should start preparing your Introduction Meetings. Get together and discuss how you're going to hold your Introduction Meetings. The Introduction Meetings, when developed and done well will sell the membership on their own and then all you need to do is go out and bring people in.

Start with your family and friends and then branch out to the general public. You may use any form of advertising as I had said before. You may post bulletins on telephone poles or around town. You can advertise on your television, radio stations, send flyers through the mail. Whatever you learn works to bring people in to your Introduction Meetings and well done Introduction Meetings will sell the memberships.

So, that is your starting point. You want to form your Clubhouses. You want to make a conscious effort to work together to make it the most exhilarating, exciting two-part meeting that the public, your visitors, have ever experienced. You want to sell the values. Sit down with your fellow apprentices, enumerate the values, be sure those are well expressed in your meetings. You want to determine who's going to talk, who's going to talk about themselves. You may want to split that responsibility around, rotate those speakers.

Down deep, you all share the same goal, the same Friday-Night Essence, that same search for that C of U. And, you can work together as teams, teams to bring people in, into the Clubhouse, which we'll talk about in Part Three. This is different, of course, from the way you came in to The Neothink® Society. You were selected through our highly-restrictive profiling methods and you were selected for the purpose of being who you are and where you are right now and being our chosen ones, so to speak to bring Neothink® public.

Remember, the secret web site is www.activeneothinkmember.com. This site is going to become more and more important to us as we bring Neothink® to the public. It's going to become our communicator. We are going to be able to help each other through the web site. We will be able to share with other Clubhouses across the country what is working, why it is working, what you're doing, how you are progressing. The web site is going to become valuable to us to learn from each other. Remember, bringing Neothink® public

101

is all new; it's cutting edge. You are in the first phase of this development which brings you the greatest profit potential in the end.

After two generations of keeping the Society secret and internal, I am very excited to see this next step unfold of taking Neothink® out there to others, to the public. And I must say here, my apprentices, I am excited for you. This could be truly your Friday-Night Essence. And, with some experience, this could be a way for you to make a lot of money. I really do believe in you, my apprentices.

Now that we have gone through the mechanism to take Neothink® to the public through this great marketing opportunity for you, let's move on to Part Two of the meeting where we're going to see how to bring Neothink® to the public through a political movement.

Level-Four Essence Meeting
Part Two

Let's move into our political party name, party platform and party campaign strategy.

The name — how do you choose a name? Well it's very, very tricky because you can get too specific or too broad. The time in history plays a role, too. I could spend today's entire lesson on this one subject on how to choose a name. Famous marketers have written about this since the beginning of marketing itself. Even billion dollar Fortune 500 companies get this wrong more times than they'll admit.

I want to say I appreciate the dozens of political party names submitted by you apprentices. As one apprentice suggested, I appreciated seeing your integrations. However, the party name we will go with is The Twelve Visions Party. There is so much reasoning behind the selection of that party name. Let me just say we understand that marketing can propel something to success. The key here is not just what is being said but also how it is being said. In both cases, this is where my skills come in. I'll provide you, sometime between now and the next meeting, with the fundamental, non-amendable portion to the party's Constitution and I'll provide the National Platform. You need this before registering the Twelve Visions Party with your Secretary of State.

I must ask you to exercise patience for beyond the enormous deep thinking that goes into this comes many long meetings among different lawyers to work through the legal and intellectual property issues. The Twelve Visions, of course, tie back to the Twelve Visions in the Heirloom Packages.

By the way, I'll take the Twelve Visions in the Heirlooms and rework them for the public move, for bookstores, once the political party gets traction.

Let's talk about the National Platform. The National Platform will reveal our plan to de-politicize America, but without ever using those words. When we understand that our success depends on not just what we say but how we say it, you realize we're talking about marketing, stimulation. We must do something unique to have our platform stimulate the masses. I'll provide you with that unique National Platform before the next meeting. As you'll see, I explain that the problem with political platforms is that one cannot reach ahead far enough to see the outcome. They all sound great but people need to see into the future to what kind of world those platforms create.

I go into the new concept of Neothink® and what that is. About bringing in knowledge like puzzle pieces and snapping those together into a puzzle and as that puzzle comes together and forms we can see what the puzzle picture is going to look like even before all the pieces are there, which is, in essence, seeing the future. That's what the Twelve Visions are. They are Twelve Neothink® Visions that are showing us the future.

The platform needs to be unconventional Neothink® visions and be stimulating. I want you to read Visions Ten, Eleven and the first portion of Vision Twelve in your Heirlooms. I'm editing those into our National Platform, a stimulation- based platform with all the planks snapping into those Neothink® Visions. Unconventional, yes but very effective.

Read Visions Ten, Eleven and the first portion of Twelve. You'll see how those Neothink visions will stimulate the masses. I'll give you a little insight into how effective this stimulating approach can be.

Back in 1992, I put feelers out for a Mark Hamilton for President Run. For that I wrote a book that was my manifesto called "A Future of Wealth Belongs to You". Back then I was beginning to grasp the stimulation based approach. I had a successful infomercial running on television that gave away my book for free. I had just started when Perot made his announcement on Larry King.

Well, the Perot campaign and my campaign had several parallels so I sent Perot my manifesto. A few days later I got a call from his Campaign Manager and she and I talked for awhile on the phone. She was very impressed with what she had read and there were particular expressions that caught her eye such as Career Politician and my expressions on how market businessmen will come in and replace the career politicians. She then asked me if I would mind if the Perot campaign used some expressions from my manifesto and I gave her my blessing. And, at that point, I stopped my exploratory committee for president and watched what happened with the Perot campaign.

Well, this added dimension to Perot's '92 campaign, for he implicitly emphasized moving competent business dynamics into the incompetent arena of politics. The people loved it. Perot's campaign became largely a stimulation- based campaign. As effective as those campaign gems I turned over the Perot campaign were, my advisors and I know much more now than we knew then.

Stimulation is the key. For example, our slogan is: The Twelve Visions Party is the Party That Will Make the People Rich – Make the Poor Rich". How? Through super-rapidly advancing new technology. Super rapidly advancing new technology always leads to cost dropping to fractions.

For example, consider the computers, the information revolution and the communication revolution. That's what the Twelve Visions Party is all about. The Twelve Visions Party represents a new political paradigm which set the conditions that allow technology to race forward unencumbered, with a purpose of making the ordinary person, even the poor person, live with a rich standard of living.

Everyone knows there is far too much bureaucratic red tape, regulations, bad law, and destructive litigation. The Twelve Visions Party dedicates itself to that problem. The more you learn about the Twelve Visions Party the more you discover how it truly is the Party that will bring the average citizen, even the poor citizen, remarkable wealth, health and safety, unlike any time before. It's what everyone wants except those in power for they're going to lose much of their power.

Understand that everyone wants the Neothink® World, even poor welfare dependents. They just may not know it yet.

So let's walk through what you need to get started in your state:

Well, you need a party name. We have that now, The Twelve Visions Party. You need a Constitution and Bylaws and you need a platform. You're waiting for me on the non-amendable, fundamental portion of the Constitution and you're waiting for me to get to you the Party Platform.

Now, you should be looking at some political party's constitution and bylaws. Look at those in your state and look at some around the country to get a feel for what you'll need to establish around my fundamental, non-amendable portion of the Constitution.

You need to establish when conventions are held. You need to have a method for electing members or assign members. You can start working on that, getting together to assign or select different temporary members. Get organized. In fact, in some states you can even begin, prior to getting registered with the Secretary of State, getting signatures. You will then take the completed constitution, the platform, the bylaws and your list of temporary members and you will then submit that to the Secretary of State and you should be then a registered party.

Then the next step is getting qualified to be on the ballot. You'll need to begin serious organizing, petitioning, getting people to run for office on the ballot. People who pledge to uphold the Party's Constitution or lose their Party status. Once you get to this point, then campaigning begins and your campaign will have a slogan that is shown and seen everywhere. And, you'll want to announce this to the media. Think about it, think about it. The Twelve Visions Party is the Make the Poor Rich Party. The media would not be able to resist that. It's a new political paradigm that makes the ordinary citizen, including the poor citizen wealthy, healthy and safe.

Now, the campaign dynamic is stimulation based. It's based on Forces of Nature AND Forces of Neothink®. What are the Forces of Nature in this campaign? Think about it. It's wealth without lifting a finger. You know the old Force of Nature to get the most out of the least energy spent. Well, we're telling people that we get the Twelve Visions Party in and technology will be unencumbered, will race forward like the computers did at the end of the last century and your buying power will multiply, a hundred, a thousand times. Wow, living like a millionaire without lifting a finger. That's a Force of Nature.

Tell people how this rapidly advancing new technology will lead to rapid health advancements, disease cures, rapidly falling prices in the health industry, in the medical industry and you will attract the elderly. In the end, you're going to live younger much longer.

These are all Forces of Nature. All of you have read the Heirlooms know the Twelve Visions and understand that the nature of this political party is reducing down to a protection-only government.

Now, realize this is how I explain our Party to you because I am educating you. But we will not talk to the public like this. I know from experience that we do not want to educate the public. We can leave that up to the Libertarians but they will never get anywhere. We must stimulate. We don't want to slip into educating. We want to stay clear of that. When you try to educate such as the Libertarians do, people's eyes glaze over. In a campaign you can't tell people how great business is and how bad government is. That's like trying to talk C of U to an anticivilization bicameral like person.

Instead you go to WHS — Wealth, Health and Safety. That's stimulation based. You don't even have to get into the complicated concepts of freedom or right versus wrong, or left versus right. Just get the citizens listening to wealth, health, safety...the Forces of Nature.

All right now, you know last month we talked about the Forces of Neothink® and I explained to you how that is the largest common denominator, the child of the past, inside everyone that has resigned to the anticivilization. How are we going to reach that child of the past in a campaign to the masses? We do that through expressing how, sort of like we have talked, ourselves. How you are going to discover a new person you didn't know could exist within you. That person is the person you were meant to be. When The Twelve Visions Party comes in and technology soars, your standard of living skyrockets, your health improves, your longevity improves, your safety improves, all of this without you lifting a finger by the way, without risking a thing. You express how you're going to go through a personal renaissance and you will meet that person you were meant to be and live that life you were meant to live. You will be waking up the child of the past in the masses.

You can also express how their job is a stagnant rut most people have to experience because of the division of labor today. You can express how the leaders of business for the most part suppress you — the great suppression — because of our politicized society and how all that will change when the regulations are lifted and technology is free to soar. We can start talking about these entrepreneurial jobs of the mind, the division of essence and playing at work as an adult.

But remember, as you express yourself, always keep at the forefront of your mind that we don't want to get too deep. We want to stay on the surface in almost a slogan realm.

Suppose the media begins to dig deeper during our campaign and you're asked how do you propose removing the red tape and regulations, bad law and destructive litigation and how will you free up super rapidly advancing new technology? Well, we'll give the basic answer that we will depoliticize America. And we will mention the Protection Only budget naturally and we will mention to secure Protection Only we will introduce the Party Constitution as an amendment to the U.S. Constitution. But then we will say, to get the details you need to study Mark Hamilton's Heirloom Packages, specifically the Twelve Visions. You can direct the media to the Miss Annabelle's Secrets. We have the details. They are in the Heirlooms.

Now we're going to market this. We're going to appeal to the Forces of Nature, wealth without lifting a finger, health without lifting a finger, safety without risking a thing and we're going to appeal to the Forces of Neothink®. Discovering the person you were meant to be in this Neothink® World, this new technology world, living the life you were meant to live. It's the key point here and I'm going to say it over and over again. You do not ever want to get into educating or trying to teach the C of U to the bicameral-like anticivilization whether that's the media or individuals or crowds.

You just need to perfect short, brief slogan-like statements about wealth, health and safety and about the life you were meant to live. That is how we will successfully run a stimulation-based campaign not an education-based campaign. Always refer the deeper details to Mark Hamilton's books. The key here is to avoid getting into educating. Just keep stimulating, not educating. Those who want deeper education can buy the books but the public does not want deeper education, they just want stimulation. I cannot say this enough, a successful campaign must be stimulation based, not education based.

Now let's say a Neothink® candidate is in a debate and the line of questioning forces him into some of the details about depoliticizing America, perhaps about the Protection Only Budget removing all elements of initiatory force including bad regulations, bad law and litigation. What does he or she do at this point? Always end with stimulation. We need to remove initiatory force, bad law, bad regulations, litigations to free technology and bring us rising standards of living, wealth, health, protection and safety to all our people including the poor. I want you to think, after today's meeting, think about this for a bit, how sweeping this approach is.

If someone were to just go in and read the literature, they could come out and say, oh, you're just for the rich guy, for the business owner. You just want to get the government off their back. But we're pulling in everybody. We're pulling in the welfare dependent with this type of stimulation-based campaign. We're pulling in the socialist left media, we're pulling in the Oprah Winfrey's, we're pulling in everybody with this campaign because its stimulation based. And that's exactly why this Twelve Visions Party is universal; everyone benefits and we can keep it on track by staying focused on the Forces of Nature, wealth without lifting a finger, health without lifting a finger, longevity, safety and Forces of Neothink®. Things will change and you will live a new life, a fulfilling life, a romantic life, a wealthy life.

Right now, state-by-state organizing needs to occur. You need to meet with your A-Teams to understand what needs to be done and then do it. I encourage people running for local office under the Twelve Visions Party all the way up to eventually getting the Twelve Visions Party on the Presidential Ballot. You need to set up A-Teams in your state geographically throughout your state. This has to be organized by you, my apprentices, for it is a grassroots movement.

Also, study other political party's Constitutions and Bylaws on the Internet. For you'll be forming that yourselves once you get my portion of your Constitution and once you get the National Platform from me. Be sure to wait for my portion of the Constitution and my National Platform before registering the Twelve Visions Party with your Secretary of State.

Also, I want to remind you that in some states you can start accumulating signatures even before registering the political party.

You do have a lot to do and I do believe in you.

Level-Four Essence Meeting
Part Three

Going public goes beyond the Neothink® Network Marketing Opportunity and the TVP political movement. It means establishing a formal structure by which The Neothink® Society can root and grow. This will begin the C of U on earth. Ultimately the C of U will grow as people leave the anticivilization and choose to enter the C of U, the Neothink® Society.

Consider that becoming organized is perhaps the most powerful force in the cosmos such as The Big Bang through immeasurable organization of all matter in the Universe. Let's look at this powerful force here on earth:

Consider the powered explosion when random occurrences become a tightly organized force. Consider wind, for instance, as random occurrences you merely have breezes. As a tightly organized force, you have a hurricane or tornado. That explosion of wind power can be compared to the explosion of Neothink® power, when you organize random Neothink® people into a tightly organized structure of Clubhouses.

In other words, before, you could easily go through your entire life and never meet another Neothink® person interested in you or in the things you feel are important.

In an organized Neothink® Society, however, you'll walk into a hurricane of people not only interested in you and what you feel is important but people like you actualizing those important challenges.

Once organized into the formal structure, you'll immediately feel their force swirling around you when you're there in the meetings. You could even find yourself swept up by a tornado of individuals interested in you and in your value creation. I know this will happen by organizing into these monthly meetings. In the organized Neothink® Society, organized into local Clubhouses with a national web site, there will exists a hurricane, a power explosion of value exchange. In the end, our Neothink® Society and the opportunities within will be unstoppable.

Before now, you were lone, random Neothink® people. Now you're becoming organized and will grow into a hurricane force. In the Clubhouses, you experience growing business alliance dynamics, growing acceptance and love, growing numbers of friends, lifelong friends. Perhaps even romance, and perhaps even a spouse, if you're single.

In the Clubhouses, you'll feel growing support from others, where Neothink® ideas and C of U ideas are the norm. Creation of values becomes natural here. You're inside an environment for winners. Your children will meet other Neothink® children. Things such as political movements, Neo-Tech Schools, they'll all originate here. Indeed, the organized Neothink® Society is the microcosm of the C of U on earth. Your quality of life rises.

If one is not interested in the Neothink® Network Marketing Opportunity or the TVP political movement, The Neothink® Clubhouses bring you a new society on earth of Neothink® people like you. A lot of people will join for this value alone.

Through the marketing Neothink® through the Clubhouses our Neothink® Society will grow into a small civilization. The advantages will add up and draw in more and more people to our little civilization. The Neothink® Clubhouses are the beginnings of the Civilization of the Universe on earth. In the end the C of U will grow and out-stimulate and out-compete the anticivilization.

To start these monthly meetings, your Clubhouses, the A-Teams need to come together and give shape and form to these meetings. You must give feedback to all. We'll set up a place on the secret web site dedicated to this sort of communication and feedback. From your feedback, we'll gradually evolve and formalize the structure.

Your Clubhouse, by the way, is your monthly meeting itself, not the "building" in which you have your meeting. And your Clubhouse will keep your local members in the society for a long time, perhaps for life.

Those moving on the Neothink® Network Marketing Opportunity revealed in Part One must take charge in starting the Clubhouses to secure their monthly income. The Introduction Meetings and the Clubhouses are pieces to the same puzzle. These local Clubhouse meetings will become a vital part of the monthly membership fee, for the Clubhouse is the place of congregation. People need to congregate, to socialize, talk, plan things. They can have specialized meetings such as the political movement, Paradise City, the business alliance, health and fitness, medical. From these meetings, members find a place they belong to. They find opportunity, they find new ideas and directions and adventures. They find fun, they find love, they find the life of Ulysses minus dishonesty. The superpuzzle for Biological Immortality eventually comes through creating this formal structure where ideas and opportunities and movements grow from.

This formal structure, the Clubhouses, is the foundation for the superpuzzle. The first piece to the puzzle has begun with the Twelve Visions Party. I'm impressing on you that the public movement is much more than the marketing opportunity itself. We are, for the first time ever, establishing the beginnings of an organized, formalized structure for Neothink® to grow and to bring in the general population. The outcome of this will be deeply moving on both a personal level and a societal level.

On the personal level, the friendships and the love will be fulfilling that "something more to life" you always searched for but never found. Yet there's something even deeper; the spontaneous generation of your creativity in this environment. Your Friday-Night Essence will come to life; your Ten-Second Miracles will come to life. This environment will lead to a hurricane of creativity and wealth.

On the societal level, the Neothink® Society will grow one per state, then two, then three, then several per state, which will start the pressures of the business alliance described in the Miss Annabelle's Story. The organized Neothink® Society will eventually cause a brain drain where sharp, intelligent people will begin leaving the anitcivilization and come into The Neothink® Society. They'll leave behind the anticivlization and come into our Clubhouses to get the Neothink® life advantages.

You all will become mentors and teachers. This is a big responsibility. You must never walk on others shoulders. Instead, you must reach down and pull others up with you. That's the nature of Neothink®. As we go public, we will not use the expression, Church of God-Man. We all know what that means having read the Heirlooms. When bringing in the public we'll instead use the expression, The Neothink® Society and our Neothink® Clubhouses.

And remember, we pull people in but give nothing out. That's the business alliance dynamic; if you want these incredible secrets and advantages you must come on in. We're not selling. We are inviting the public into our wealth of knowledge. Instead of burning out as we grow, that is, if we sell, instead we will pick up steam if we bring people in. Get in or get beat! That's marketing, starting at the ground floor. This could be huge. You see, people have to come in. They have to join because of the business alliance dynamics. They need to join; they need to come in for the advantages that are in our Neothink® Society, in our Clubhouses.

However, before anyone gets into a Clubhouse, he or she must be a subscribed member. Most will subscribe through the

Introduction Meetings. It is in the Introduction Meetings where you'll convince family, friends, acquaintances and strangers of something fantastic in life.

You'll bring in people through mediums you are most comfortable with. One fellow wants to knock on doors. That's where he is comfortable but maybe not for you. Others will want to post bulletins around town perhaps at universities or on the streets, on street light poles. Others will run radio ads and many times you can get free local PR. The same goes for television; sometimes you can get free television spots. At a certain point, people who are very successful at this will find that they want to buy advertisement because they're so successful at bringing people in and making a profit from having them become subscribed members. Some of you will learn how to use the newspapers to run newspaper ads or PR. Others will hand out flyers for the Introduction Meetings. Others will just simply approach people they meet.

You are merely making introductions. You're letting people know about The Neothink® Society of secret knowledge and, after generations, the Society will give them a peek into the Society's secrets to wealth and love. You're inviting them to the public unveiling.

Now, if you run PR or advertising, be sure there's a way for you to receive the credit for those coming to the Introduction Meetings because of your ad. Never use literature from my company, copyrighted literature or advertisements. Always use your own words. This will also get you into the integrating mode. With time, with what I've been teaching you, you will become very effective marketers.

I suggest your Clubhouses meet once a month. That's critical for your network marketing as a value motivator and it's crucial for you for emotional, intellectual, social and financial fulfillment. Your Clubhouse can meet over lunch or dinner or at any location. Have both a basic agenda and free time to talk, with additional time to socialize. Develop a format to incorporate a chance for members to talk, share, discuss the Heirlooms, help one another, socialize and time to embrace the business alliance. The Clubhouses will form now because of the public marketing movement.

Now, after all these years, Neothink® is formally going into the public and I'm going to enjoy the rewards, my apprentices, along with you. I'm here for you each month and even though I don't answer questions sent into me for sheer logistical time limitations except for some very rare exceptions, I still do and always will keep close track of you and your questions. You may have noticed that each meeting has been designed to answer your most pressing needs and desires. Look where it's taking you in just four meetings and I've come to know many of you through your actions and through The Neothink® Society's web site. So, keep posting and expressing yourselves on the secret web site. That's how I get to know you personally. I know many of you very personally by following your posts. I've developed genuine affection for so many of you. I celebrate your successes and I feel bad during your losses. I'm in a unique position to see your development from a wider perspective than you.

A father will do everything in his power to make things wonderful for his children. But his children will sometimes get sick and sometimes they'll make wrong decisions. The loving father will continue to do everything for his children through his guidance and knowledge. I pledge to do the same for you. Even if we don't see each other, I feel internal joy from your growth and I must tell you I feel a deep sadness when I lose one of you to the anticivlilization. I want you to know that I hope to bring each and every one of you into the Civilization of the Universe. That is my goal. Is it unrealistic? My answer: Never ask a loving father if it's unrealistic to expect to bring up all his children into a wonderful life. For, I know that in all of

117

you that innocent child of the past is reaching out, reaching out for this C of U life that is the goal of our journey.

Now I'm doing everything in my power to help. Therefore, your Level Five Meeting is going to consist of me answering your questions. I believe the timing for an essence meeting of this kind is right. You'll be leaping ahead this month more than ever before as you engage Level Four. You are going to run into challenges and that's what the Level Five Meeting will be all about, me helping you with your obstacles and challenges. So, I want your big questions. Remember how, in your first essence meeting, I was only able to answer ten or so of your questions. I want you to feel free to communicate with each other and perhaps collectively form your question or questions of highest importance. Be careful not to use this offer to block your own 100% responsibility. Go back and re-read that section on 100% responsibility in the Self-Leader System, The Vision Climax in your Heirlooms. Carefully choose your questions over the next month and post them on Meetings web site, Meeting Level Four. I will answer those questions in our Level Five Meeting.

In the meantime, you need to begin forming and organizing your Clubhouses to prepare for your three public movements.

1. Your Introduction Meetings to bring in and sign up members.

2. Your clubhouses to establish a formal structure through which a new civilization, the C of U, can take hold and grow on earth.

3. Your grassroots political movement to get candidates on the ballot in your states and to get stimulating campaigns going to the general public.

So get organized and get prepared. It's time to turn random breezes into a hurricane. And remember, during these organizational A-Team meetings you can determine the questions of high importance for me for our next essence meeting.

With that, I'll end today's historic meeting. I'm thinking big when I see our journey ahead...apprentices and mentor building a superpuzzle together. Let's see what you can do. I'm counting on you, my apprentices, to get organized in order to start implementing these three public movements. I also really appreciate you and your crucial role in changing the direction of mankind. You'll become an eternal part of future history books. And, remember as you take on these new challenges, you'll soon discover what I really mean by *playing* as an adult. For, you'll soon uncover that inherent Friday-Night Essence all of us in the original Secret Society share...the quest for the C of U on earth.

Level-Four Essence Meeting
Follow Up One
Introduction Meetings Supplemental Instructions

Hello apprentices. I want to stress a few very crucial points made in your Level Four Meeting that will help you set up your all-important Introduction Meetings.

I have seen some early questions posted on the Level Four Meetings web site and I will start with the notion of getting a script from me for your Introduction Meetings. You do NOT want a script from me for your Introduction Meetings. Here is why: You are not making a blind sale. You do NOT want to use the same selling techniques per se that you saw in your original Orientation Booklet from me. That was a blind sale and techniques were used accordingly. In your case, you are bringing people together with the apprentices, in the flesh so to speak, congregating in your Introduction Meetings. There they meet you and others, perhaps they already know you to some extent, they see and feel the love and respect and competence and happiness among you apprentices, they feel the child of the past all around them in the room. Remember in the Miss Annabelle Story when Jake and Jasmine attended a Church of God-Man? Remember how they felt?

Your presentation must come from YOU, from your personal experiences. You will get in trouble using a script from me. With a script from me, you will come across disingenuous. If you are not making big money now, then do NOT go there. Instead, go in the direction that YOU feel…say, the home you found in the Society, the love, the special people and lifelong friends. You were searching before for something…for something more, and now you have found it.

When you do make big money, then you can state it loud and clear in your Introduction Meetings. Then, you will be in the honest position to mentor your apprentices and help them do the same. You will come across with confidence and sincerity when you talk about making big money, and you will be able to answer questions with ease. You want to be YOU, and that will be your most powerful sale.

In the Level Four Meeting, when I pressed and pressed for you to use stimulation and NOT education, I was talking about the political movement. Your Introduction Meetings require stimulation, true, but there are different forms of stimulation. For example, while on the Disney Cruise with my kids, I listened to a speaker selling a lifetime cruise vacation club. I was a casual observer until he started talking about his daughter and how fast time passes and how his closest times with her were here on the ship. He told moving stories of their times together, including how she would sometimes subconsciously revert back and call him "Daddy" when they were on the cruise together. I admit, I got tears in my eyes and ended up in his office signing the contract. Yes, he touched my child of the past. He never mentioned money.

In this setting, your sales must come from your heart. I am not saying that you need to always use the child of the past approach...use money when you make a bundle through this network marketing opportunity. What I am saying is: speak from your heart. Speak with sincerity. During your presentation, you will be presenting Forces of Nature and Forces of Neothink®. It will be moving and believable. That real approach will get their attention. Remember Ulysses. Remember the exhilarating journey through life...that is what everyone wants, and that is what you have found in the Society.

Express your own passion. The Forces of Nature and the Forces of Neothink® will come through you expressing and emphasizing your own journey. The fact that you are on a journey and that your life has meaning and purpose will draw people in. They want that too; they want what you have. And the price is now affordable. The values are very tangible.

Let me reiterate: The direct mail piece you ordered your Neothink® Heirlooms from is a blind sale. It is cold coming through the mail versus the warm, breathing, physical contact of the Introduction Meetings. You must sell your own personal passion. THAT will make you big money...YOUR personal feelings for and commitment to the material and the people in The Neothink® Society.

As you apprentices begin to make good money, even big money, from this program...cheer out that fact in Part Two of your Introduction Meetings. View the Level Four Meeting again to understand Part One and Part Two of your Introduction Meetings. Yes, you will be using all the Forces of Nature and Forces of Neothink® in your exhilarating yet honest, heartfelt Introduction Meetings.

You have a few weeks of hard work in front of you before you can start. You need your A-Team in place. You need your Introduction Meeting in place. You need your first two or three Workshop Meetings in place. You need your Clubhouse Meetings up and going.

As the launch date approaches, I will provide you with rules of compliance, especially regarding advertising. In essence, there can be no claims made that are not possible and are not true. In a congregation such as the Introduction Meetings, as I wrote earlier, such a hyped approach will cause potential members to walk away, turned off. Instead, touch their hearts with YOUR life journey. I have read some heart-rending stories on the web site that would make powerful presentations in person. Do not look too closely at the NT approach that brought you in, for that was a different medium. You would be missing the most powerful aspects of your medium: the warm, human touch.

And do not forget, there is a Part Two to the Introduction Meetings that encourages the Neothink® Network Marketing Opportunity and its potential. The apprentice in your A-Team who is making the most money doing the Network Marketing would perhaps (but not always) deliver the most qualified and most powerful presentation, revealing his or her own success selling memberships. Here, in Part Two, you can inform potential members of the money they could make.

I do not want apprentices complaining about the time it takes to get this going. This move has been anticipated for decades. If it takes a few weeks to get it right, then so be it. You have as much work as I do to get this going. You need to get everything I listed above in order, and then report your ready-to-go status to me by posting on Level Four Meeting at the Level Meetings web site. I want a list of names in your A-Team and their roles in the Introduction Meetings, the Workshop Meetings, and the Clubhouse Meetings. Make that status report as brief and succinct as possible.

In closing, some of you have expressed a fear of marketing. In this benevolent environment, just be yourself, relay your experience, and explain the values YOU have received from the Society. You do not have to be a strong marketer per se, although you will become stronger and stronger with experience. For now, though, you just need to be yourself, for that is what potential members will respond to. Moreover, your sell becomes not only affordable, but appealing when the potential member sees all that he gets for that money, namely the highly-guarded secrets, the one-on-one workshops, a local mentor in you, entrance to the clubhouse, admittance to the national web site with discussion boards and chat rooms and more, the journey with national mentor Mark Hamilton, the social contacts including lifelong friends, and the wonderful network marketing opportunity. In this benevolent environment, just be yourself, relay your experience, and explain the values YOU have received from the Society. You do not have to be a strong marketer per se, although you will become stronger and stronger with experience. For now, though, you just need to be yourself, for that is what potential members will respond to.

My apprentices, we are on a great journey together. Tomorrow will bring us wealth, health, and happiness.

Level-Four Essence Meeting
Follow Up Two
Political Opportunity Supplemental Instructions

To be successful against political behemoths, we have to deliver the punch no one saw coming. Over the past twenty-five years, I have developed that phantom punch.

The Level-Four Meeting did not allow me the time to dig down into the complex psychology for you. Over the next few meetings, that psychology will increasingly surface.

The '92 Perot campaign came out of nowhere and almost decked both behemoths. But after Perot staggered the Republicans and Democrats, he could not follow through and put them away. He went the distance but lost a unanimous decision.

To begin to give you a taste of the psychology behind our political potential, let us first go back to a parallel event over two hundred years ago: Whereas the Revolutionary War began in April of 1775, the colonies still sought favorable peace terms. In January of 1776, Thomas Paine published his pamphlet Common Sense. Soon, all states called for independence. Six months later, the Declaration of Independence was ratified by the Second Continental Congress.

The sweeping psychological shift from seeking favorable peace terms to seeking independence rose from that very stimulating little 50-page booklet. No one really saw that coming. Thomas Paine and his Common Sense knocked out the behemoth, the Kingdom of Great Britain.

Paine's little book sold an equivalent of fifty million copies today. If you noticed, throughout The Twelve Visions, I state several times that once fifty million people see the Twelve Visions, then an unstoppable change begins toward the Neo-

Tech World. The stimulating style of Common Sense differed from the philosophical, educational style of Paine's Enlightenment contemporaries. The stimulating style of The Twelve Visions differs from the philosophical, educational style of the other nonfiction Neothink® works.

Are you beginning to see something here?

Over a decade and a half ago, I began to understand the differences between stimulation and education. Until that point, all my writings were educational.

With that growing understanding, I began a long journey to develop a phantom punch. Perot's original '92 campaign manager picked up on my stimulation-based approach when she read my political manifesto. She talked to me and got my permission to use elements of that stimulation from my political manifesto.

For the next fifteen years, I dug deeper and deeper into a stimulation-based delivery of Neothink®, found in only one of my several nonfiction books — in The Twelve Visions. Although most people cannot know it, I have created via that publication the perfect "body" for delivering the phantom punch.

Now, back to the Twelve Visions Party and the National Platform: it will look like nothing ever seen before. It will consist of an introduction that explains why political platforms all sound so good, but how the people do not see the society caused by those platforms until it is too late.

Then, in that introduction, I will introduce Neothink® and explain how Neothink® Visions legitimately show you the future, namely the society that will come about from our platform. Neothink® is a legitimate way to see into the future by seeing the missing pieces to a growing puzzle-picture. The National Platform will essentially consist of Neothink® Visions Ten, Eleven, and a small portion of Twelve. It will look like no other platform ever before, but that is the power in it. Combined with our stimulation-based campaign, this has the ingredients to knock over the unsuspecting behemoths.

Let me back up for a moment. Because of the wide-reaching marketing of Neothink® (in 193 countries, 14 languages), I have received mega-money offers to bring my books into the trade (i.e., into the bookstores). I have turned down every such multi-million-dollar offer because Neothink® has always been a secret society. I would not breach that secrecy no matter what the offer was. I would remain anonymous to the public. I would not relinquish my secrets and turnkey techniques outside our secret society. Money was not and has never been my authority. As you know, I am building a superpuzzle — the superpuzzle you read in the Miss Annabelle Story.

Although I have never let a Neothink® publication into the trade, I will eventually let a shorter version of The Twelve Visions go into the bookstores. The interplay between the political party and the stimulating book itself will add momentum and credibility to the political movement. I will also put portions of The Twelve Visions on the political party's national web site being developed now. Will we get fifty million eyes on the Twelve Visions? A successful campaign could conceivably cause that many eyes to see the Twelve Visions, if not the book itself, then portions of the book on the web site.

Now, changing subjects: In the Fifth Essence Meeting, I will spend some time talking about the different essences of Frank R. Wallace and Mark Hamilton. Although dealing with the same subject matter, Dr. Wallace was developing the fundamental belief system. I was developing the fundamental application system. We both needed each other. We had the perfect division of labor/division of essence. A comparison can be made to Christianity. Jesus was developing the belief system. Paul was developing the application system.

Dr. Wallace's essence: he had to integrate the fundamental ideas, no matter what they were about. He could not be concerned about people's reactions. He had to remain concerned about the fundamental reality of the idea itself.

My essence: I had to integrate the fundamental applications, no matter who the end users were. I had to be concerned about people's reactions. I had to remain concerned about the fundamental reality of effective application itself.

The dichotomy between Dr. Wallace's essence and my essence shows in the writings themselves. The Miss Annabelle Story, for instance, is a map to the C of U. Pax Neo-Tech is, too. However, many more people can read and actualize the life advantages found in the Miss Annabelle Story or in the Twelve Visions or The Self-Leader System because they all come from a fundamental Neothink® application system. Dr. Wallace's Pax Neo-Tech, on the other hand, is more challenging to read and apply directly into your life. You are more apt to intellectualize it than to apply it.

Because of the different essences, Dr. Wallace dug deeply into all areas of life in developing the Neo-Tech belief system of fully integrated honesty. His comprehensive belief system, for instance, deals with religion and God.

When running a political campaign, the Neo-Tech idea system for religion and God should not even enter the picture. For, the proper application of Neo-Tech in politics is Freedom of Religion. It is not up to a political party to dictate beliefs.

Therefore, the political movement must focus on Mark Hamilton's Twelve Visions, which deals with only the germane concepts and stimulants for political application. With today's Internet search engines, the political party must remain one step removed from Frank R. Wallace and his writings. As a matter of fact, he understood this and told me on several occasions that the political movement will be my essence and not his.

All will know that Dr. Wallace's original idea system planted the roots beneath this growing movement. Perhaps an analogy would be Ayn Rand's Objectivist philosophy planted the roots beneath the Libertarian Party. But, being one step removed, many religious conservatives still gravitate toward certain Libertarian ideas even though Ayn Rand was an atheist.

In the National Platform, I will refer to Neo-Tech, but in the context of super rapidly advancing new (Neo) Technology (Tech). Of course, you and I know that super rapidly advancing new technology is the result of fully integrated honesty in politics. But, we will let that deeper integration stay in Dr. Wallace's Neo-Tech writings.

Back to the topic of this supplement: The Twelve Visions Party. I see that apprentices in most of the states have acquired the requirements I had asked you to get. Still, I want the A-Teams in each state to call their Secretary of State and request a Minor Political Party Guide. That contains everything you need, from requirements on how to start the Twelve Visions Party in your state to requirements on getting candidates on the ballot.

Through some deep power-thinking, I can see that the A-Teams will more likely form and focus on the Neothink® Network Marketing Opportunity and The Neothink® Society. Therefore, I have decided that all A-Teams around the country must also incorporate the Political Movement, too. Whereas this might initially seem like baggage to some, it really ties into the common-denominator format. Remember what that is? Remember back to the Level Three Essence Meeting. YOUR common-denominator format is: your congregations, your meetings. Apprentices congregating – A-Teams. That common-denominator format will make this public movement powerful, just as the common-denominator format of the assembly-line made the early automobile movement powerful.

Now, this will not be difficult. Let me explain: The A-Teams will be designating certain people to do certain things...those things they are best at (keep in mind Friday-Night Essences). Some of those sitting in the A-Team will be best working the political movement (perhaps their FNE). But being a group, there are more of you to develop ideas and support for the political movement.

Of course, the problem here is: those working on the political movement do not make money whereas those working on the Neothink® Network Marketing Movement make good money. Well, I will solve that problem. Remember the highly qualified names I have to feed your down line? Those apprentices pursuing the political movement will get very healthy down-line feeds. Those down-line feeds will be worth a lot of money.

So, I want the Political Movement to integrate in now with the Neothink® Network Marketing/Clubhouse Movement. The greater pool of minds and bodies will launch the Twelve Visions Party. In the organizing stage of the A-Teams, the apprentices will decide who does what. I do not want a single A-Team without a political movement. It goes with the territory now. Going public is an essence (physical/mind) movement. That essence movement includes structuring the A-Teams, preparing the Introduction Meetings, preparing the Workshop Meetings, starting the Clubhouse Meetings, starting the Political Movement. You, my apprentices, have a lot to do. You are part of mankind's final psychological shift into the Neothink® World. You, my apprentices, stand to make a lot of money pursuing your FNE of spreading Neothink®.

It is a big plan. But it will move forward. I am looking for your big questions on the political movement. Get them to me soon, my apprentices, for I have to start preparing for your Fifth Essence Meeting.

One big step forward in our Level Four Meeting was combining the two public movements into one. The political movement will not get left behind. There will now be financial incentive in the lucrative down-line feed. And there will now be a full support system in the A-Teams.

Thank you for your growth, which I watch with pride.

Secret Teachings to My Exclusive Inner Circle

Level-Five Essence Meeting
Introduction

Welcome to the historic Level-Five Essence Meeting. We have a lot to cover today. Grab a pad of paper and a pencil because you'll want to take notes.

In Part One of this meeting I will answer your big questions.

In Part Two, I will reveal the formation of the Society of Secrets and we will get into the nitty-gritty of that process.

In Part Three of this meeting I reveal the formation of the Twelve Visions Party.

Level-Five Essence Meeting
Part One

In Part One of this historic Level-Five Essence Meeting I'm going to go through your big questions for me and give you answers. Also, I did something for this meeting that I don't do for the lower meeting levels. I saved those questions that I felt all of you could benefit by listening to my answer. So we'll start now with the first question:

Q: I have made several attempts to get a minor political guide in my state. I called my Secretary of State asking for the minor political guide. I have left my name but the person in the Secretary of State's office is having a problem getting a hold of that document. Apparently some states do not have this document. Or they do have it but the bureaucrats you're talking to don't know they have it, which has been the case in a couple of instances.

MH: So, just call your Secretary of State and tell them you need information on starting a political party.

Q: How do the A-Teams refer to themselves and their Clubhouses? Do they refer to themselves as the Society of Secrets Wisconsin Chapter or the Society of Secrets of Wisconsin or do they come up with some other name altogether?

MH: Basically, the first approach is best; the Society of Secrets of Wisconsin. In fact, that will break down even further perhaps to the city and perhaps even further eventually. Then at some point in time when this is proliferated around the country basically we'll just call them the Society of Secrets Clubhouses and that's it. We won't need, necessarily, a definition. But right now we do because this is all being launched.

So, the Society of Secrets of Wisconsin or in other states where there are several A-Teams, we will need to mention the city, as in Society of Secrets of the city name here.

Q: Good evening Mark. I need to know can we schedule our meetings in the topic chat room due to the high cost of gas, since we're a team of 5 that is a distance away from each other.

MH: Yes, of course, use that as a tool as a matter of fact. I plan to talk to the computer staff about setting up a schedule where people can sign in times and topics and people can see those scheduled topic chat sessions and look forward to joining. But as far as this question goes, using it for an A-Team meeting, yes, by all means, please make use of that.

Q: Mark, when we start going public how do you think the media will react to our party? I could see all the talk shows, radio and TV have a field day with this and drive a lot of new members to us.

MH: Yes, historically the media has ignored, avoided or is afraid of Neothink®. But I think we have a real coup here in the political movement especially with our slogan, "How to Make the Poor Rich". That is going to cause a lot of media attention to the political movement. We can really work that. How can the media ignore a plan to make the poor rich? They can't. I've already tested the waters with some media personnel and I think that they will go crazy over the Party that will make all the people rich including the poor.

So, the Society of Secrets itself may not get much media attention but The Twelve Visions Party political movement will. I will help you deal with the media. You'll learn a lot during this meeting and in the meetings to come on how to deal with the media.

I'm just to paraphrase the next question. Basically, the apprentice is asking about web sites in the Internet that use our terminology and names yet have no direct affiliation with us, our Clubhouses or the Neothink® Society.

You must understand our terms and names are all registered trademarks and all our literature is copyrighted. This is all intellectual property of mine or the Neothink® Society.

Now, as we go public, those using our words must come into compliance. That, in fact, is my next job. I need to sit down with my lawyers to review all of this and to develop a licensing agreement that will allow apprentices and others who are using our names to continue to use them as long as they're in compliance.

You must understand, when we go public, there is a whole new dynamic. The seniors of The Neothink® Society must maintain control over the use of those words. If I let some use these words and others I don't, I lose my trademark protection on those names so I have to, across the board, universally, have people sign licensing agreements. Now, that's the only way this can be done.

If I lose protection of those words, that will be a very bad situation. That would be a disaster because those words would get raped by greedy people looking to make a quick dollar and it would ruin those words.

It's very important that the seniors at The Neothink® Society maintain control and protection of those words.

So, I will be preparing the licensing agreement so everybody sanctioned can use those words. Those web sites out there will have to come into compliance.

Q: My question is, are you running for President?

MH: At this time, no. I need to see how this puzzle comes together and how quickly the dynamics fall into place. We have too much work to do first in building the Twelve Visions Party.

A lot of apprentices don't really understand the vast gorge we need to travel traverse first, from where we are today to the point of talking about running for President of the United States. I've been travelling that path since 1989. It's a long path that will require a lot more hard work. That's the point that we're at now. As presidential elections arise, we'll have to see as that time approaches what's happening here with building this party. We first need to build the party.

Q: Mark, hello Mark, I was wondering if I'm allowed to share the National Platform for the Twelve Visions Party with other non-Neothink® members that I trust? Can I send it to them by email or print out a copy and mail it to them?

MH: Yes, in fact, we're going to do something better than that as you'll learn in Part Three of this meeting. I'm going to print that Platform along with some other materials into a pamphlet and I'm going to send that pamphlet to the A-Teams by the hundreds initially for the political committee to use to start handing out. In that pamphlet the A-Teams can place their contact information, scheduled events and so on. Not only may you but we are going to start handing out that National Platform.

Q: I'm a Level Four member and I have something very important to talk to you about. I understand you are a very busy man so I will cut right to the essence of this message: I would like to begin by saying I can't thank you enough for what you have done and what you stand for. Recently, I've been experiencing some very powerful visions, emotions, thoughts and I felt compelled to share them with you.

The first that jumps out of my mind is that recently, I saw where you are directing us. I was able to see the world through your eyes and see where you are pointing your finger. I was able to see this group of Level Four members through your eyes and what you are building is far more detailed than the phrase C of U can illustrate.

I think of you as family and I must tell my family what is going on before my eyes. I see a great divide, a splitting of the Society taking place. Some have lost patience, they are saying things like, "things are not going quick enough," or "we are Level Fours and we should be a lot further along than we are". "Mark Hamilton could be doing a lot more than he is for us."

I do not mean to spread rumors or try to derail your efforts. I know that would be impossible. You have one of the strongest visions on the planet and I know there is nothing that can take that from you. It's just that I really care about my family and I was hoping that this will help you in any way it can.

I know that you face these kinds of obstacles but this kind of mysticism is stemming right out of our group. They are flooding each other's efforts with hidden cancer. I can hear it in their voices.

If there's one thing I've truly learned from Neothink is that we must confront mystical thinking, not back away at every confrontation, especially in ourselves.

But some of the members are building an army of followers. Instead of trying to free each other or more precisely, themselves, they infect each other and it's repelling the positive numbers away from the web site.

I also understand the frustration you must be going through. All of your efforts for the last 25 years have been placed on this group of apprentices and, to be perfectly honest with you, a lot of them are buckling. I don't want to point fingers, but I do want to make it known that I can see it as clearly as you do. I just wish there was something more I could do but I understand that each person will have to make a choice sooner or later.

To end this message, I would like to say that I love you Mark Hamilton with all my heart.

138

MH: Well, first, thank you. I really appreciate your reflections.

The concept of negativity will be dealt with later in this meeting, specifically at the end of Part Two of this meeting. But I will take a moment here to express to the apprentices that I understand and I know that the apprentices can't impossibly see the big picture that I see. It's just not possible yet and I hold no one to blame for that. It's just the nature of things. And, I actually do understand the apprentice's frustrations.

The effort to achieve the shift to the public after 25 years is huge and to the end it all falls on me. It all must come from my mind. For instance, I can't have a staff member do the things I'm doing like reworking the Heirloom Packages into twelve mini-heirlooms. That one task would take a professional writer 15 hours a day for several months just to accomplish. And I'm doing that. It all falls on my shoulders. No one else could possibly do that.

The operations of my entire company are now being moved to another facility. This is a huge change and again, much of this falls on my shoulders, the majority of this. Realize though that I am making this change to benefit you, the apprentices. This will open the way for us to what I see coming. I'm taking this very expensive preemptive step to move to another facility, a larger facility in order to handle what's coming down the road for you.

The computer operations, including the web site, the software being created, setting up the network marketing programming, this is all moving to a much larger facility and much of this falls on my shoulders, the majority of this does.

The reason why it all falls on my shoulders alone is a lot of these moves that are being made can't, like other businesses, just be made for business sake, for the business sake alone. There's so much more, decades more, of deep integrations that all link back to the product and how it's going to function to serve the goal. And that all falls on me. It must come out of my mind.

The legal work, the lawyers that set all this up, is enormously time consuming. I have marathon meetings with intellectual property lawyers. In fact, right after this Level Five Meeting, they want me to come and sit with them for 3 solid days to work through the licensing agreement and the other legal forms that are going to enable us to launch or marketing program. So, I'm doing all this for you, to benefit you. This all falls on my shoulders. This is the only way this can happen. The questions for Mark Hamilton take an enormous amount of time. Tracking your posts, tracking the web site takes an enormous amount of time. No one can do that for me, that all falls on me.

Certain comments I've heard in the past just shows a lack of understanding of all that I am handling, of the weight that I'm balancing on my shoulders. And again, of course, that's all falling on me but it's all to benefit you. That's the point I want apprentices to understand here.

Beyond all that, what I just mentioned, the deep power thinking, yes, the Neothinking, to make all this happen. Everything, every direction you see, everything I talk to you about today, the power thinking, the Neothinking to bring all this together and to make it work and make it successful, all falls on me. All that must come out of my mind.

This whole program could be in jeopardy if I rush this. So, there's just no way around that, it all falls on my shoulders.

Let me just put it this way; it is beyond human capacity what I am handling right now and it's only because of my many years of developing the business techniques that I'm able to handle this and able to do this.

Like I said, unlike other movements that are just strictly business based, this involves so much more. This involves an entire philosophy, it involves decades, actually generations beyond that of integrations that must all properly be worked so that this best serves the product, the integrations. That's the object here; it's not just to go out and make a lot of money per se it's to make this work. We have an end goal with all of this.

So for those who think I'm not doing enough, first of all, I want you to understand, I don't hold that against you. I understand, I completely understand. You just don't have my side of this picture. You don't have the bigger picture.

I hold no animosity whatsoever toward any of my apprentices. I'm balancing enormous weight on my shoulders to go live and I'm really pushing everyone out there. Realize it's not just me and me alone saying 'let's go live'. I have printers printing books and computer software companies building programs. I have companies taking over all the order processing that is going to take place when we have new members.

We're starting from scratch with new companies, working all around the country, Ohio, Chicago, Florida who are beyond my control. I can push these people but I can push them only so far.

The point is you have to decide as apprentices yourself if you're in this for the launch. That's a decision you have to make. I know that you are the right people for this. You are the chosen ones. Even with the negativity occurring, I hear this from many different apprentices. I expected this. I'm trying to lay down some perspective and we'll lay down more perspective at the end of Part Two of this meeting.

But you have to make the determination; are you in this for the launch? I do believe that those who are in this first launch have an incredible opportunity and I believe it is my opinion you are going to make a lot of money. I'm not promising, I've never done this before, but just from what I know after 25 years there's one heck of an opportunity here. And you just have to make the decision. I'm here until the launch. It might take 2 weeks and it might take 8 weeks. That's just the nature of what we're launching here. Anything that's real and anything that's big never comes easily and quickly. This is real and this is big so I want you to understand that.

Again, I'm not out to "bust" or get after any apprentices. I understand where you're coming from. I want you to have this perspective I'm laying out today. You must use some discipline now that you've gotten this perspective not to continue being negative and influencing others around you. That is very important for your own prosperity and for your our whole mission to succeed. If you drop out because you get too negative you will miss an enormous opportunity.

The bottom line is I'm working hard to make this a great success for you. Try to keep that in mind.

Q: The topic of security is forefront in many members' minds. As the group is trusting and open, we are posting our email addresses, phone numbers and home addresses on the web site.

Let me say that until now, all the apprentices were thoroughly profiled by The Neothink® Society and had a long relationship with Neothink®. Most have bought all three of the Heirlooms, read and digested them. They were all, up to now, have been the chosen ones to do what we are doing, take the Neothink® Society public. They are highly qualified people.

From the beginning I have not been one to really support putting your personal addresses out there for people to see and personal phone numbers but if it's okay with you, I'm not going to stop it either. So, each one has to use their own standards in dealing with this.

This particular apprentice asked if we could change the posting to not include the first and last names and actually that may not be a bad suggestion and where we would put your first and last name, you can put your first initial to your last name because you get too many first names that are the same and it's nice to know who you are communicating. This aids in building relationships with those on discussion boards. We could try that. In fact, I'm going to recommend that or actually direct the computer staff to do that. We can set that up.

This apprentice also pleads for people to use more discretion in the chat rooms. The security has been raised in the chat room. This apprentice advises people to communicate more securely and I'm all behind that, definitely.

There's a concern down the road about religious zealots getting phone numbers and first and last names and where people live. Well, I need to just take a moment here and say, security is one of the major reasons I have posted several times on the web site not to build lists, particularly lists beyond your local area. I have urged apprentices not to respond to people, other apprentices, who are trying to accumulate these lists.

Security is a big reason for that; you never know where these lists could end up. You just don't know. My company has been doing this for a long, long time and we have security where people cannot get to our names and addresses.

I know what I'm doing; we know what we're doing, and you're going to get what you need when you need it. Not necessarily when you want it but when you need it, to best serve the bigger picture.

So, I'm going to ask those apprentices who are trying to accumulate databases and accumulate names, please stop that activity.

Q: Are you afraid the government will try to shut us down or harm us in any way?

MH: No, I don't feel that way. Those few apprentices who have been with The Neothink® Society for a long time know that I'm not naïve to what the government can do including the use of force.

But I feel the government is probably relieved to see The Neothink® Society's going into the establishment, into the political system. As you know, it's almost impossible for a third party to get started no less to have any success. So they're not going to worry about us.

By the time that they do have something to worry about, we are protected by the first amendment.

So, I'll repeat, I'm not naïve to the ways or to the potential ways of the government and yet I do not feel any danger.

Q: I have four children and four grandchildren that I would like to become Neothink® Society members and join with me in the network marketing program. They live in Washington, Pennsylvania and California. Many people may also have this concern.

MH: Well, this is an issue concerning long distance references. The problem I see is the work that goes on at the Clubhouse level. In this electronic day and age someone could develop a sexy web site for example that directs thousands of prospects or leads to different Clubhouses around the country.

Whereas that would be great for the society, for me, for the growth of the Society, I want to be as fair as possible to all who are involved.

There's a lot of work that goes on creating and developing the Introduction Meetings, the Workshops Meetings, the Clubhouse Meetings, the mentoring at your local level. Having done a lot of thinking about this, I'm concluding that the fair thing to do is to split the commissions between those who refer and those who, the assigned or designated apprentice at the Clubhouse, who gets that particular incoming prospect.

This split makes sense when you consider the prospects are long distance leads, is the marketing side of the equation, and the development of the Workshop Meetings, the Introduction Meetings, the Clubhouse Meetings, the mentoring, the helping, is the product side. So, what we're doing is we're splitting 50/50 the marketing side with the product side. I feel that's fair to all. I talked to the computer house and they said that can be done. So, that's the plan.

Q: Mark, often you have said that the Level Four apprentices are the first Neothink® Society members to go public. Additionally, you have said that Neothink® has been evolving for several decades. From that some of us deduce that there are Neothink® members before us. Several of us were wondering if you would be willing to, with the individual's consent, share those names with us? Would a member in our geographic area be willing to guide us or work with us?

MH: I put deep thought into this and there are many, many Neothink® members before you, brought in through the Neo-Tech dynamic and we have nearly two million Neo-Tech members worldwide. Some of those are very well-known, some of those are very rich and some of them are very famous. But you, the chosen ones, over the past two years have been oriented differently. You've been oriented and chosen for this dynamic of going public. This is a unique journey that you're going through with me that the prior Neo-Tech members have not gone through. You have just been oriented differently.

In fact, I regularly receive requests from prior Neo-Tech members to come into your clubhouses or into your A-Teams and participate in your essence. And, I rejected those requests because they were oriented differently. I think you'll understand a little bit more as to why in Part Two of this meeting when I explain the dichotomy that is occurring now between our past, our Secret Society dynamic and our terminology and words that we use and the face to the public going forward and what your job is, what our job is here.

But let me say this: After the clubhouses are up and running, at that point I will allow prior Neo-Tech members to contact you, to join your Clubhouses, but not until then.

Q: Will there be guidance from you or your staff on establishing our political party locally?

MH: Yes, there will be guidance. In fact, that guidance is going to start very strongly in Part Three of today's Level Five Meeting.

By the way, this person again asked for the Minor Political Party Guide and they're having trouble getting that and again, I said some states don't have this or they do, they just don't know they have it. But simply tell the Secretary of State's office to send you information on how to form a political party and that should take care of that.

And although all the states have different requirements, when we start the A-Team Space on the computer in about a week, you're going to pick up a lot of natural guidance as well from your fellow A-Teams when you see what they've done and what they're doing.

I know that the A-Teams are having difficulty developing the political movement and I am going to step in quite strongly to get that done.

Q: The Indy A-Team has several questions for you so we thought we would condense them into one email. Your email this morning answered several of our questions, thank you. Here are the rest: Will there be an SOS web site to use for recruiting?

MH: The answer to that is yes.

If so, could each A-Team have an information section?

MH: Yes.

Q: Or will this be done through The Neothink® Society web site?

MH: No, a different arrangement will occur on The Neothink® Society web site in about a week and that's the A-Team Space. It's basically internally just for us to see each other's progress during this journey.

Q: Will the new Society of Secrets (SOS) members have immediate direct access to the forums?

MH: My personal concern is if new members are given access to the forums before they receive their first book some comments made by higher level members will chase them away before the true value is apparent.

One possible solution would be to have an SOS forum for each of the twelve levels each month as they receive their book, your essence meeting and our workshops, they would graduate to the next level in the Forum. This adds a little complexity to the management of the web site but I believe would reduce the fallout.

It also maintains a separation between the SOS, The Neothink® Society, and Neo-Tech until they have been through the entire twelve months and then granted access to the remainder of the Neo-Tech literature. This separation will basically be levels prior to introducing Frank R Wallace's works and those separating from those after receiving Frank R. Wallace's work which I'm going to get into in Part Two.

This dichotomy I started talking about on the supplements to Level Four is going to start kicking in here to where they won't be introduced to certain terminology, certain words, or to Frank R. Wallace and his works until they have gone through about six months of the Secret Society's monthly literature and workshop meetings with you.

By the way, I just want to add here that I have been very impressed with many of the A-Teams and take this opportunity to say this and I think you all will be impressed with each other next week when we get the A-Team Space up on the computer, web site, www.activeneothinkmember.com.

Q: Are the three Heirloom books available in Spanish?

MH: I've been asked this question by several other apprentices, so on and so forth. Yes, they are available in Spanish.

We're starting this now in America in English to simplify everything but once this gets up and running smoothly, we will open this up to 193 countries in all the major languages.

Q: How do you think the anticivilization will respond to our going public?

MH: Well, first of all, from my experience, they will all avoid us. However, at a certain point the slogan for the Twelve Visions Party, "Make All the People Rich Including the Poor" cannot be ignored. The media will respond and be drawn to us because of that slogan. As I've said before, who can resist a political party that's going to make all the people rich including the poor?

Now, as I said earlier, I do not feel any threat from authorities at this point. I feel no threat whatsoever and that's not being naïve. I've been around the block in the area of government and the use of force. The few older Neo-Tech members here know that I'm quite aware of what can happen, but I don't feel those problems now at all. In fact, I feel the face of Neothink® is going to be far less provoking, and confrontational than ever before. The government is basically relieved that we're going into the establishment now, into the political system.

Q: Concerning state and local elections, how do we decide who will run for specific elected offices?

MH: That is up to you, I'd say, but you will all have to sign — any Twelve Visions member who runs for office will have to sign a contract and we will get into that in Part Three.

Q: Concerning the FDA, when will it be time to make open challenges to the destructive activities of this organization?

MH: It's not necessary. Just concentrate on stimulation right now not education. We're talking about the political movement, don't educate. Don't go in and give philosophical integrations, just stimulate. Stick to the fact that we are the party that's going to make all the people rich. I'm going to help you along from meeting to meeting as to how to talk to the media in that regard. You'll get more of that in Part Three of this meeting.

The more recognition the Twelve Visions Party gets, the more people will look for the Twelve Visions. That's what this really is; a Lead Conversion Program. It's a one-two punch. People get curious about the Twelve Visions by what they hear you talk about in the news, in the media, in the newspapers and then they want to find out more about it. And then they get hold of the Twelve Visions. Fifty million Twelve Visions, that's our goal.

Q: Regarding Biological Immortality, can you share with us the latest developments in this area? How close are we to achieving this goal?

MH: Well, this is the end result of a superpuzzle. Specific advancements, per se, are not going to achieve biological immortality. It's too complex, it's too complicated, too much of a combined effort as demonstrated in the Miss Annabelle's Story.

We're part of the superpuzzle. What we're doing here is actually pieces, major pieces, including the political movement. Once we have the Neothink® Society open to the public, the freedom will exist for geniuses of society to soar.

The restrictions will be removed from people so they can enjoy life and play at life and feel their Friday-Night Essence. Once those two elements occur, the two *causes*, the *effect* will be this drive for biological immortality as we saw in Miss Annabelle's Story.

Q: As the SOS gains momentum and popularity, we will no doubt attract the attention of the media. Can you share with us specific ways of dealing with this attention so that our interactions will help, not hinder our efforts?

MH: Number one, the media will try to ignore us for a period of time but when the slogan gets out there in bigger and bigger numbers, we're the party to make all the people rich including the poor — there will come a point where the media can no longer ignore us.

Now I'm putting the National Platform into this pamphlet that can be handed out in large numbers and read. But one thing I want to stress here, start talking your beliefs, your political beliefs or ideas in front of the media. Even on The Neothink® Society web site we don't discuss the political points. Those are a big dud. Everyone's heard them, everyone's heard all the arguments and then you're just going to be positioning yourself either with the right or the left and immediately alienating a big chunk, 50% or more, of the population. Just stay away from issues, no matter how strongly you feel about them. You're going to learn why in Part Three.

When you're in front of the media, being interviewed, you continuously express how this is the only opportunity ever, in the history of mankind, to make all people wealthy, to make all people rich. You'll learn more in Part Three on how to talk like this to the media — stimulation, not education.

Q: Due to the political and social nature of what you want to achieve, I would like to know when we do face resistance, how will this affect our personal assets in the market and real estate? For, any time there is a change first there will be chaos. What can we do to protect ourselves? We're not in positions right now to know the legal issues of this event. Fear sets in and nothing gets done, hence many have left our A-Team. Fear only begets fear although there is only the three of us left.

MH: Okay, as I've said before, I don't see anything here to fear from the government. We are going into the establishment, into their system, which is rigged against us, stacked against us big time. They're not going to worry about us. In fact, they are going to be relieved that Neothink® is going into their establishment system. They're just not going to worry about us right now.

When and at what point they do worry about us, we're protected by the first amendment, number one. And number two, the swell will come so quickly, it will be that phantom punch that they didn't see coming. "This is an idea whose time has come" to paraphrase Victor Hugo.

Q: How are we to handle the legal issue of Clubhouses when we get to where we start collecting money to rent or build? Is there going to be a countrywide incorporation or are we locally going to have to research and decide what legal entity we will form?

MH: The A-Teams must take care of their meeting locations for now. In the long run, we will look at this again. But for now the answer is; you take care of your own location and your own meetings.

Q: I'm a commercial writer, producer, announcer at the national level. I'm considering producing a short video, 7 or 8 minutes for the Intro Meeting. My question is, do you already have plans to do this or can I offer my services to you? It is crucial that any representation of Neothink® be done at the highest level of professionalism.

MH: I have my crew to do this but what I do suggest is when you do produce that video, put it on the A-Team Space at The Neothink® Society web site so we all can see it. Who knows, perhaps you can step into that role of producing nationwide for the A-Teams.

Q: In a few words, my question is deceptively simple: How does it all work? How do Neothink® concepts of thoughts, ideas and visions, work when out of billions of people only a relatively few Neothink® people can behold the visions? What boggles my mind is that the illusions created by the neocheaters feel so real.

MH: The objective of this journey, these twelve levels you're going through, will answer that question. The journey you are traveling with me will answer your question. Indeed, that's what we are answering, how to do this. We're combining the philosophy, the ideas, the techniques, the actions, the application system, we're mixing this all together into a powerful take action event of taking Neothink® public. That is what we're doing here together and you are part of the way here at with Level Five. Remember, we're going through twelve levels.

In reading over the progress report from the Seattle A-Team, I saw a question to the Communications Director to herself and I'll answer it right here. It says, find out if we will need to be set up to take credit cards. I'm assuming the answer is no. And, she's right, the answer is no. You will have your new members fill out a form and then you will either fax, email, or mail that form to us with all that information.

Also, Seattle A-Team, you're doing fantastic. Reviewing your Introduction Meeting script, you're off to a good start. However, remove all the political references from your Introduction Meeting. We're going to really get into the political movement in Part Three. Do not discuss the political movement in your Introduction Meetings, workshop meetings and the Clubhouse meetings and I'll explain why later, in Part Three.

For the Introduction Meeting, have people stand up and give their own relaxed, enjoyable personal experiences with Neothink®.

Q: Mark, I think it needs to be stated that the Twelve Visions Party will be for all levels of politics. Some of my fellow apprentices think that obtaining the Presidency is the only objective. Depoliticization will need to happen at all levels. Also, some think that growing the party will be through the Neothink® Society only. It needs to be addressed that reaching out to all voters separate from the Society should be done.

MH: Of course, the political movement will be part of The Neothink® Society of Secrets but the movement doesn't have to be limited to our Society activities and members. The Twelve Visions Party needs to have its own membership and marketing activities. This is truer than anyone realizes now. I'll elaborate on this in Part Three of this meeting.

Q: I cannot be more excited about the financial incentives that you have given us to kick start the political movement. However, the lack of interest in the movement has been extremely disappointing until now. I realize that the political movement is a key puzzle piece to our mission. I believe most haven't been involved for the same reasons most of society ignores politics. The reason can't be explained any better than how you state it in the People's Party Manifesto.

MH: Which is interesting, the People's Party Manifesto. I wrote that 17 years ago. I'm wondering if he's referring to that actual publication. He makes very good points and it's very true. That's why I'm stepping in now and going to take a stronger lead in getting the political movement kicked off. We'll get into that in Part Three.

Oh and I need to make a note here for all of you. Nobody is to submit anything to the Secretary of State as far as the Constitution or Platform. That's going to have to properly come through me. I'm going to need to see everybody's before they send them in to the point that you and your local states will be signing a licensing agreement so we can continue to protect the intellectual property words that are being used in this whole endeavor in State Constitutions and State Platforms.

Q: It would be nice if we have an on-line recruiting tool where some prospects could go ahead and join on –line without having to attend Introduction Meetings.

MH: I know that you would want to use the meetings as a way to use a more personal approach but I believe that some prospects, at least in the beginning, will not be within reasonable range to actually attend the meeting and it would be a shame to miss a potential member just because of a distance problem.

And I whole heartedly agree with that. The problem is so much of the value of membership comes from the social interaction, hand to hand, face to face workshop meetings, the learning, the mentorship, the Clubhouse Meetings, the intellectual and social stimulation. The social interaction, the life advantages, the friendships, the friends. But I'm completely open to ideas on this.

One point I wanted to make. The Washington A-Team is doing a very good job of spreading A-Teams across the state. I'd really love to see the other A-Teams do the same. Instead of just having one A-Team in the state, try and organize several A-Teams to geographically cover the state.

And why that would be so beneficial to you to do, to set up, is it will enable me to send many more names in your direction and to cover the whole state. That would be a great win/win situation and that would quickly take care of this distance problem if we could get that started.

Q: Is it possible to have a national SOS meeting to meet you and other senior members and current apprentices face to face before going public? It would make all the difference in the world to me, perhaps to others as well.

MH: Well, the answer is no. I cannot do that. And that is not meant to be a rejection per se. It's just that I don't have the time now to handle this and all that I'm handling and have this particular meeting with my apprentices.

I also want you to tap your self-leadership strength. You've all been profiled, I know that exists and that you have that and you will be stronger because of it.

One thing that's going to help all of you a lot is going to be A-Team Space that's coming to the web site soon.

I know this is nerve-wracking to many of you but it's an obstacle that you will get over and once you do something a couple of times, you'll become an expert at it after maybe 3 or 4 times I'd say.

Q: I have to keep a positive attitude all the time but some of the members just seem to keep trying to bring everyone down. I hate to even admit this but on several occasions I caught myself wondering if some members might even be cancer seeds.

When I got done with each part of the meeting, naturally I was excited. I went to the general discussion board to share some of that excitement with others. A lot of the members were as excited as I was. Some of the others started in with all the criticisms right away. It wasn't long and the members who were excited did not seem to be any more.

I still remain excited every day. I set out to set the world on fire in every way that I can when I post with that enthusiasm. When I post with that enthusiasm I get ridiculed. When I try to help people overcome some of their issues, he gets ridiculed, I get ridiculed.

When the issue seems to be solved, then those same people move right to another issue, just one right after the other quarreling about things. I have stopped posting anything on the general discussion board altogether. I still read them, searching for the ones that do have value but the quarreling continues.

I read through it all every day, I realize they are thinking for themselves but it sure doesn't seem like they are heading in the right direction with their self-thinking. It seems like mysticism is still trying to rule over some members or still running through the veins of some members.

My questions are as follows: Are those people cancer seeds? If so, what can be done to fix this problem? Is there something, some benefit of all out of this quarreling that I am not seeing? Are you frustrated? Is this why you made some of the changes you made? Am I going to still receive some down-line fees? Is this all just part of the growing process? Will we all continue to grow and improve, especially with all of this going on now?

MH: Well, the answer is yes, we will continue to grow dramatically.

I'll address negativity toward the end of Part Two. Are they cancer seeds? I read through the entire web site and I know exactly what you are talking about and I've seen this myself. But one thing needs to be answered; before I address the issue of negativity in Part Two, let me just ask you, the apprentice who sent this letter, do you ever feel that any of these apprentices are out to destroy The Neothink® Society? Are they out to destroy us? And if you answer no then everything's okay, as you will see why in the negativity portion in Part Two.

Q: I'm writing to see if there can be a business alliance or global directory placed on the web site maybe under the Business Alliance; a meet-others forum, a place where members can post their business information for others to keep as much business as possible in the Neo-Tech family. This value would benefit both existing members and is another sale point at Intro Meetings. Imagine having a listing to go to where one could find honest business men and women in just about any field that you may need. Thank you for all your time and I love what you are doing. I love what we are set out to accomplish.

MH: Yes, this would be awesome. In fact, this is being developed now. It won't take the shape of the forum because of security reasons. Being a director, you can access but you will send us what you are looking for and we will actually have a team of people go out and find what you're looking for and present it to you.

Q: Are we letting the cat out of the bag, so to speak, in our National Platform? In other words, are we creating a road map for the value destroyers to follow and prepare for?

My second question is, do the average citizens in the anticivilization have enough knowledge at this point to fully grasp the integrations of the National Platform? I know for me, as I read it, it was very invigorating and extremely exciting but I am far more knowledgeable on this subject than the average person in the anticivilization. Are they prepared enough to understand and see the overall picture like we can? I also wonder about the perception of it. Will they be wondering who is this Mark Hamilton guy and why should I care what he envisions or thinks?

MH: First of all about letting the cat out of the bag; no, no one's going to know what we're doing here. It's not going to be a problem whatsoever. It's never been done before, this whole stimulation-based politics and we have decades of literature behind all this as people get into this more.

Now look here. I am holding in my hands the National Platforms for the Republican Party and the Democratic Party. Look at these. How many people have read these? Very few people have read those National Platforms.

But many people are going to read our National Platform. When I print this pamphlet and the title of the pamphlet is: "Make All the People Rich Including the Poor" people are going to read that. This is the power of the stimulation-based approach. It is the phantom punch they won't see coming.

Now people won't care who Mark Hamilton is but they will care about how they become rich? If I'm poor or an ordinary person, how do I become wealthy? That's what they're going to care about.

So, they will take an interest in Mark Hamilton in so far as he's the author of this pamphlet. And they'll take an interest in getting Mark Hamilton's Twelve Visions. And it's critical, a crucial puzzle piece to this puzzle, getting Twelve Visions Party members elected.

Q: Why do I keep getting offers from people who say they are Neothink® Society members but I know they are not?

MH: Many people abusing the names, mailing to our members without my permission, basically trying to sell their own thing that they're into.

Let me say this: The upcoming Neothink® Network Marketing Opportunity is going to be huge. I know it is. I can't promise you or guarantee you anything but I just know in my heart, this is going to be big. It is going to be the biggest opportunity you ever had, much bigger than any opportunity you are currently involved with.

Those of you who may be accumulating Society member names for the purpose of selling your own product, you just need to stop because you jeopardize your position, you jeopardize this once-in-a-lifetime opportunity that's coming your way. You must stop.

Not only do I not want apprentices to respond but I want those people turned into me. The lawyers have advised me that I have to kick these people out of the Society because they're just violating their privilege.

Q: What will you do with the money you receive after the first year?

MH: I want to start a new school system similar to what you read in the Miss Annabelle's Story…The School of Geniuses. The new school system, number one and number two, anti-aging research being done by certain specific scientists to start the Association for Curing Aging and Death.

But you remember, curing aging and death is still an effect. The cause is freeing the geniuses of society through the Twelve Visions Party and creating a desire allowing people to find the desire to live longer, to live forever by finding their Friday-Night Essences and living as value creators — not value producers but as value creators — in this exhilarating life when they want to live forever.

So you have the demand and then you have the ability to bring in the supply by removing all the politicization so that the scientist and businessmen or doctors are free to really soar. The geniuses of society to create the product that people want so badly.

Q: Can the lower levels join you in your Twelve Visions Party movement, the going public movement, the SOS? And, if so, how much information can I give them?

MH: I've decided the answer is yes, they can join. And you just give them everything they need. They're part of this journey, they're there, if they want to be part of this at this point and time, go ahead and bring them in.

They'll get what I give them when the time comes. But go ahead, bring them in, tell them whatever you want at this point. Let them help you in any way they can.

Next month post your questions at www.activeneothinkmember.com in the Level-Five Essence Meeting Comments section.

Level-Five Essence Meeting
Part Two A
The Formation of the Society of Secrets

Now we're going to talk about the Neothink® Network Marketing opportunity, the Introduction meetings, the Workshop Meetings, the Clubhouse Meetings and I also want to make a point here; there will be people who come into the Society who are not interested in the Neothink® Network Marketing Opportunity, they are not interested in the political movement and we need to understand that and make room in our Clubhouses for those people as well. There will be people who want to join just for the value of the product itself. In fact, that's going to become a large percentage of our members.

Let me say this: I have had a number of apprentices write to me and tell me they are having problems in their marriage because of the stress of Neothink® or the stress of becoming involved with the Society of Secrets. Starting next month in the Level Six Meeting, we will be getting into the whole area of relationships. We will talk about and work through relationships next month along with other personal issues and the value that Neothink® and the Society of Secrets can actually bring and add to those relationships.

Now back to what we are focused on today, the Society of Secrets formation: We will talk more about the dichotomy between Frank R. Wallace and Mark Hamilton. We will talk about the terminology, words to use, words not to use for the face of the Society of Secrets, to the public. We will get back to this in a moment.

We're going to pursue a different course here than most marketing programs that are focused mostly on the opportunity, the marketing dynamics. Our program is very different. Our program is product intensive and I'm going to walk through that today and focus on what your job is, what your part of the product is. Your product is your mentorship with the new members who join. It's your accessibility to these new members.

Your workshops are going to be critically important. Imagine the value of receiving the mini-heirloom package and then having a workshop meeting to make it all come to life and applicable to the new members.

That is your part of the Neothink® product; your Clubhouse is your product with those intellectually and socially stimulating meetings and congregations. Even your Introduction Meetings are your product and I call them your product because that's where the value begins. It begins in your Introduction Meetings.

Imagine, for example, people who own 3 of the Heirloom Packages coming to an Introduction Meeting, the excitement in the air as you reveal to them, you express to them, your journey through life in the Neothink® Society of Secrets and what this means you. The ability to change the world, this Ulysses-like journey but without the dishonesty.

So, you have to make your product awesome. The way to make it awesome is by increasing the value of your product. And, you must make your product addicting and the way to increase that is through making your product stimulating; stimulation is the key.

I want to point out that you do not mix politics with any type of marketing dynamic whatsoever. As you know, religion and politics are just things you just don't talk about.

Now, the fact that our political campaign is unprecedented and it is going to be stimulation based, we may find that it will work into our whole Neothink® Society of Secrets dynamic including the marketing.

For instance, if you're out there exposing the public to the Twelve Visions Party and the Platform, people will become interested and start coming in. When they come in you can actually introduce them to the Society of Secrets. In other words, they can become powerful leads for you to send to the Introduction Meetings at which time a certain percentage will convert to members. And I will get more into how to do that as we get into your portion of the meetings in Part Three.

Now, back to the dichotomy and this process of going public. Recall in the supplement to Level Four Meeting I made a clear separation between Dr. Wallace's materials and terminology and Mark Hamilton's materials and terminology. Frank R. Wallace and Mark Hamilton have two separate essences. Although dealing with the same subject matter, Dr. Wallace was developing the fundamental belief system. I am developing the fundamental application system. Both needed each other. We had the perfect division of labor, division of essence. Dr. Wallace's essence was to integrate the fundamental ideas, no matter what they were about. He could not be concerned about people's reactions. He had to remain concerned about the fundamental reality of the idea itself. My essence is to integrate the fundamental applications no matter who the end user's were. I had to be concerned about people's reactions. I had to remain concerned about the fundamental reality of effective application itself.

The dichotomy between Dr. Wallace's essence and my essence shows in the writing themselves. The Miss Annabelle's Story for instance, is a map to the C of U. Pax Neo-Tech is, too. However, many more people can read and actualize the life advantages found in the Miss Annabelle's Story or in the Twelve Visions or in the Self-Leader System because they come from a fundamental Neo-Tech application system, the Neothink® System.

Dr. Wallace's Pax Neo-Tech, on the other hand, is more challenging to read and to apply directly into your life. You are more apt to intellectualize it than to actualize it.

163

Because of the different essences, Dr. Wallace dug deeply into all areas of life in developing the Neo-Tech belief system of fully integrated honesty. His comprehensive belief system for instance deals with religion and God.

When running a political campaign the Neo-Tech idea system for religion and God should not even enter the picture. For the proper application of Neo-Tech in politics is freedom of religion. It is not up to a political party to dictate beliefs. Therefore, the political movement must focus on Mark Hamilton's Twelve Visions which deals with only the germane concepts and stimulants for political application.

With today's Internet search engines, the political party must remain one step removed from Frank R. Wallace and his writings. As a matter of fact, he understood this and we discussed this on several occasions. Dr. Wallace was the one who said the political movement will be my essence, Mark Hamilton's essence and not his.

All will know of Dr. Wallace's original idea system after being in the Society of Secrets for about 6 months. We will introduce them to all of Frank R. Wallace's works when they are ready for it. But the face, the face of the movement to the public must stay away from those polarizing, controversial and alienating concepts.

Now perhaps an analogy would be Ayn Rand's objectivist philosophy that planted the root between the Libertarian political party. But being one step removed, many religious conservatives gravitate toward certain Libertarian ideas even though Ayn Rand was an atheist.

So, for the face of the public, for the public movement, here are the words to use and the words not to use:

We will not use Neo-Tech. For example, if you key Neo-Tech into a web search engine, we see negative comments attached to Frank R. Wallace and the belief system. These comments will alienate many segments of the population.

We're going to move away from the word mysticism. We're going to move away from the word Zon. We'll move away from the person, Frank R. Wallace. We will not discuss religion in our Intro Meetings, in our Workshop Meetings and our Clubhouse Meetings.

Words that we will use; Society of Secrets and the acronym SOS, the Twelve Visions World instead of the Neo-Tech World, we will use Twelve Visions World. We will use Neothink®. We will use God-Man but sparingly. We will use the person Mark Hamilton for this face to the public.

Now, let's get into the Network Marketing.

I've been sent certain ads from certain apprentices and most of them are very well done. There are some who are promising the moon and are just unrealistic and those have to change. You can't promise people that they are going to make an astronomical amount of money if they attend. You just don't want to go there. You want to work the human touch which I talked about in Level Four Meeting and wrote about in the Supplement One to Level Four. (Study the Supplements again to the Level Four Meeting, that's very important.)

In fact, this particular person who continually emails me and others who have emailed me about making money – well, this is going to be enjoyable. She could use her charm and develop wonderful new friendships and relationships this way. It's a wonderful way to become rich.

Remember you must focus, it's so important now, and you can focus now that we're removing much of the stress and anxiety on the marketing side, you can and must focus on the value, on the product, on making the value greater and greater, making the stimulation great and greater. That makes it addicting, the value makes it something that is so rewarding to the new members.

Level-Five Essence Meeting
Part Two B

Okay, so how do you increase the value of your product, the Introduction Meetings, the Clubhouse Meetings, your Workshops Meetings? Remember, you're not there to hype the Society. You don't need to hype the Society. The life that is an exhilarating journey is what everyone wants and it's not hype. It is the value attainable right here in the Society of Secrets…A great journey, a Ulysses-like journey.

Okay, so let's look at the Workshops Meetings:

I'm going to go through the first six Workshop Meetings with you. That brings us up to the point where we go through much of Mark Hamilton's literature which is what is needed for the face to the public. Starting in the second half of their debut membership year, they will start getting into the Frank R. Wallace works in the seventh, eighth and ninth months. So I'm going to today, walk you through the first six Workshop Meetings.

The first Workshop Meeting is currently titled "The Neo-Tech System". Here I talk about the mini-day/power thinking team, about the division of essence, about the mini-companies as MINI Companies, about the essence tracking reports, the essence meetings, the integrating coordinating functions. Now, my experience from giving seminars on this particular product is, the way you can best help those who attend is simply walk through the exercises I use in the Neothink® literature.

For example, they'll come in to your Clubhouse meeting and you would work through the process of writing out their mini-days. You could walk around and notice a majority of them have subject matters listed as their mini-days. Of course, what you need to do then is go through the process that you see in my Neothink® literature of listing the **actions** that they performed and separating those into physical movements, not subjects but physical movements such as making the phone call, writing the letter, having the meetings. Those are physical movements of their mini-day schedule. Whenever I would do this in a seminar the eyes would pop open and smiles would appear on faces…it would be that eureka moment! And, all it takes is following the exercises in my Neothink® literature.

You'll have people attending your Clubhouse workshops who are interested in starting their own business. They'll be extremely excited about the whole process of breaking their business down into areas of purpose, money-making purpose and you can help walk them through that process, first by listing the basic responsibilities of their area of purpose and then going through, just like in my literature, how each responsibility exists due to or because of "X". That's how you find the areas in the business that can make money. With those, you have are areas of essence for starting the division of essence. Then we group the basic responsibilities under those areas of purpose, I call them, my areas of money-making purpose.

Now, getting back on track here, we separate those purposes or we list them under the money-making purposes throughout the business and you have a division of essence occurring for the business they are starting or existing business they are growing. This applies to all size businesses as shown in my Neothink® literature. I get great reactions when I walk through this process with entrepreneurs.

Now remember, the division of essence is the ultimate evolution of the division of labor. The division of labor was fantastic. It accelerated the Industrial Revolution. It brought about mass production starting with Henry Ford and the assembly line and really honing the division of labor down to the very specific movements of driving in the rivets or what have you along an assembly line there and that was a huge boost to human prosperity.

But the division of essence, which I've identified in my Neothink® literature is the next leap. It's the ultimate evolution of the division of labor. It's what we need in the 21st Century, in this world, where we bring our mind into our jobs. Society, the human race, cannot continue just driving in rivets. We need to now introduce the mind into the physical movement. We need to combine the mind and body and when you do that there is no limit.

As a division of labor, there's a limit to that fellow on the assembly line. But a person in a job of essence, a job with a money-making purpose, that person has no limit. Why? Because we bring the mentally-integrating responsibilities to that movement. Again, when I used to give seminars on my Neothink® products, the whole room would light up and fill with excitement, everyone leaning forward.

So, that's just the process of walking through my Neothink® literature in your Clubhouse Workshop meetings. You do not have to be an experienced business person to deliver this seminar. Believe me, I've experienced this through my life. Once you do something 3 or 4 times, you become an expert and it becomes a piece of cake. After 2 or 3 of these workshops, it's going to be very easy. At first it may be a little stressful. But remember, just stay tight with the actual exercises in my Neothink® literature and you'll do well. Pretty soon you'll be an expert at it.

Now the second workshop meeting will be the Twelve Visions. For example, we have Vision One which is discovering your Friday-Night Essence. That is a huge, rewarding Workshop. People loved when I conducted that seminar because it's so self-rewarding, a self-discovering. You are helping people make this self-discovery that's going to change their whole outlook on life. They can now play as an adult. They are discovering their passion in life. It's their deepest motivational root. Discovering one's deepest motivation root excites and reawakens the child of the past. Use all of those expressions in your workshop meetings. In many cases your new members attending the Clubhouse Workshops are going to find that building the Society of Secrets itself and the Twelve Visions Party is their passion in life, just as it is for many of you. And that's great.

Some of them won't find their Friday-Night Essence during your initial Workshop. Again, that's okay because you have alerted them to it. They know it exists out there. They see examples of others in your workshop meetings. That's very important. So, once they know it's there and it exists, they will be more apt to find it sometime within the following workshop or two. They will have a firm understanding that something more to life *does* exist and it is their route to *playing* as an adult and really enjoying life.

Now, as you go through the entire Twelve Visions, the Visions Climax, and the Self-Leader System, you want to show how those Twelve Visions apply in your everyday life. This requires your workshop to be fluid. You need to go with what the people are looking for or need at the time. If they want to work on the Vision Climax, work on it. If they want to work on the Friday-Night Essence, work on that.

Another possibility is to having more than one workshop for each part of my Neothink® literature. In fact, you can do that with any publication including Inside Secrets. You can conduct the first workshop on the mini-day/power thinking team, the self-capture secrets; the second can be on the company-capture secret for starting your own business. You will learn as you go along.

The third workshop meeting is going to be based on "The Three Insights". This is going to be 13 huge and controversial insights that will open up enormous and exciting discussions. In this workshop meeting you want to enlighten your attendees as to how those insights actually occur. These are world changing insights, profound insights into the nature of man and society, into the way things are and, more importantly, the way things need to be. And you must point out the integrated thinking that occurs in each and every one of those insights and how like puzzle pieces they come together, are snapped together with each insight. You are not only discussing the insights themselves but you're also showing your new apprentices the application of integrated thinking. Combine your workshop with my Level Two Essence Meeting, which deals with how everything snaps together to create a Ten-Second Miracle.

Continually nudge and guide your apprentices making them aware of the thinking process. Integrated thinking leads to these Neothink® puzzle pictures.

Your fourth workshop meeting will be when you introduce Miss Annabelle's Secrets. Miss Annabelle's Secrets or the Superpuzzle is a trilogy. The first book of the trilogy which is called "Conceiving the Superpuzzle". This will be a very exciting workshop especially because you are working with faction. And, this workshop will most likely be the first time that the subject of biological immortality arises. Sitting in a room full of apprentices with their mentors discussing biological immortality is extremely stimulating as you will discover.

Now you will be asked about the genre of Miss Annabelle's Story. It is non-fiction or is it fiction, what is it? Read the Forward to see that the story rose from factual experiences. Though the story itself moves into the realm of fiction, the line of logic is pure non-fiction. When I wrote the Miss Annabelle's Story, I could have gone into sub-stories and other plots that would have been extremely exciting and stimulating to read. But I refrained from that because everything in the Superpuzzle is a pure line of logic that is pure non-fiction.

The fifth workshop meeting which will be the second installment of Superpuzzle, "Putting Together the Pieces", when the children grow up and putting together the pieces to the puzzle, the puzzle picture that is biological immortality.

Time limits me from going through that and walking through that story again here with you. But let me say, this is going to be a very eye-opening, extremely exhilarating and stimulating workshop. For this is when your apprentices discover they are the twelve students. They are putting together the Superpuzzle along with you. Your apprentices will bombard you with questions. As that time approaches, I will give you some guidance on what you can and cannot divulge to your apprentices. But, believe me, this is going to be a thrilling revelation for them.

Another very interesting dynamic that will occur this fifth workshop meeting is the huge percentage of your apprentices suddenly wanting to join the political committee. They're going to see how the role, the critical puzzle piece, the political movement, plays and they are going to want to become part of that movement. This will feed dramatically the political committee.

Your sixth and final workshop meeting will be the third installment to Superpuzzle, titled "Beholding the Puzzle Picture". This workshop will be a very stimulating and fun experience because you're going to be exercising Neothink. You're going to be looking into the future, like psychics but not mystical.

By the time you read this Workshop you, my current Level Five apprentices, will be Neothinking. You will be seeing and predicting the future in ways you have no idea of now. This Workshop meeting will introduce Neothink because this is the segment of the faction work that looks into the future. It's going to get all your apprentices looking into the future. It's going to become your most rewarding workshop as your apprentices experience integrated thinking, some for the first time in their lives. When that happens, those apprentices are going to benefit you in ways that are going to shock you, just as you are benefitting me by launching this public movement. I could not do it without you. You're going to find similar benefits when your apprentices begin integrated thinking, Neothinking, from the Neothink® Network Marketing dynamic to the Twelve Visions Party dynamic to just the experience of succeeding with our grand Superpuzzle.

Now, the following six Workshop Meetings will get into Dr. Wallace's works. Now your apprentices will be well prepared and ready, they will not be alienated by Dr. Wallace's idea system. They'll be open to any beliefs that may rub against their former belief system. Do you see the process we are taking your apprentices through? And because of this process, we will develop some form of separation on the secret web site for those who are more advanced versus those who are just getting into the first six Workshop Meetings.

So, the workshop meetings we just covered, the first six Workshop Meetings, are the value, the product of what you are doing. The Society of Secrets and the Neothink® Network Marketing is a product-intensive period. You bring in your down-line into these workshop meetings. They are going to stay with you because they get such value from you and the Workshops. And, *they*, in turn, are going to be more motivated to bring in new members which all serve your down-line. Remember, the Neothink® Network Marketing Opportunity is product-driven.

This brings to mind an important Workshop you are going to want to add immediately. You will find it valuable to get your network marketers together and hold workshops for them and discuss what's working, what's not working, sharing your successes and motivating them. That's another whole set of workshop meetings that you can, once this gets rolling and kicked off, that you can have the complete liberty to hold. But keep it separate from the product Workshops.

A crucial part of your product, as we said, are your Clubhouse Meetings where you will have both intellectual discussion and stimulation. You'll have social interaction where you can cover a wide range of topics. I would suggest that you develop an agenda throughout the month of what will be covered during this Clubhouse Meeting to keep some order and time constraints on them.

Now you could also add an essence dynamic in that Clubhouse Meeting to track your progress in areas of Clubhouse functions to separate the two, as you will have members who are not interested in the Neothink® Network Marketing Opportunity or the political movement. They just want to come in and learn the life advantages and to be students of Neothink®

Now, I'm going to address once again the concerns expressed by some apprentices about negativity forming within A-Teams. It's not as serious as some of the apprentices, and rightfully so, fear or are concerned about. I'm not a psychologist and I've not studied in that field but just through live experiences I have learned that people tend to naturally talk about negatives. That's where gossiping comes from. I believe that it very well could stem back to our primitive minds. If you stop and think back to the bicameral times, man would act and would be forced into a decision during that period of leaping from the bicameral mind into the conscious mind under conditions of stress. Stress threatened survival. Think about that. For our survival we need to talk out the negatives first. Getting all the "negatives" out on the table explains why gossiping persisted and probably will continue in society at least until we're in the C of U.

So negativity is just a vestigial part of our survival mechanism where we tend to talk out our negative feelings up front.

Now, if you consider that you do not have the big picture that I possess, naturally you might feel stress, certain survival pressures that arise from not knowing what I do. But you must realize I've been doing this for nearly 3 decades. It's impossible for you to have the big picture that I have. So naturally there's going to be missing puzzle pieces, things you don't understand, don't see that cause you to jump to conclusions. Since the whole puzzle is not there, you naturally have negative thoughts that arise as a survival mechanism. And those negative thoughts are going to flow out and flow into discussion. I see such negativity as rather innocent.

The problem arises when such innocent negativity turns into envy. Envy is what we have to watch out for. Envy is the desire to *destroy* values. Now I have not picked up that any of the apprentices have a desire to destroy Neothink® or the movement. Some are frustrated because they don't see the full picture as a natural function of negativity as it flows out into discussions. And, I fully expected that. It's not the first time this has happened. But the one harmful emotional reaction you have to watch out for is envy.

And envy is tricky. The problem with envy is, because emotions are involved, we tend to too quickly jump to the conclusion that somebody is exercising envy. That can be very disastrous. We could ostracize or remove somebody who is a wonderful person and would be a wonderful valuable part of our movement. Therefore, we have to err on the side of giving the benefit of the doubt.

So the basic point I'm making here about negativity is that the primitive mind is naturally hard-wired to flow out negativity out of survival. That's innocent and will disappear once the momentum starts. Also, the fact that you cannot see the bigger picture yet causes frustration and is innocent. Once momentum gets going, that, too, will disappear. I know it's very disheartening to see some of this on the discussion boards but realize it's not envy.

Now, that's not to say you won't run into envy as you confront the public. You will run into envy and I will be there to help you through those situations. As of now I have not seen that.

Now this leads me to something very important that makes me proud. I see in your occasional arguments on the discussion boards how some of you work through such disagreements. The negativity is coming out in the forums for all apprentices to see. What happens is apprentices coming into the discussions express why it's not that way or giving further integrations and try to help those with negativity. I have seen most of those situations actually evolve to the proper Neothink®, if not C of U, conclusion. It's really very rewarding to see this.

As a result, there's just a long list of apprentices I would like to thank but it would just simply take too much time to do that now. I wanted to throw those thanks out because your contributions to such discussions have been such a great value.

And, I want you to know I will be following the chat sessions and I'll be tempted to join in but purposely won't and let you develop your self-leadership skills. This should give you as A-Teams enormous confidence in your working together as a group.

Well, I'm going to go ahead and end this part of the meeting by saying that going public is a huge job for all of us. If I didn't have the tools that I've created, the business tools such as the power thinking, the mini-day, Neothinking and the tracking reports and so on and so forth, I wouldn't be able to do this. It's simply beyond the human capacity but with my tools

176

I am able to accomplish this huge task. When we get into Part Three of this meeting you'll see the enormous amount of work involved in launching the whole political movement. Tell yourself, "I'm in this for the launch." Be patient and it will happen. It is going to happen.

Level-Five Essence Meeting
Part Three

In Part Three of today's meeting we're going to talk about the Twelve Visions Party and the political movement.

One problem I'm seeing with A-Teams is trying to blend the political movement into the Introduction Meetings and Clubhouse Meetings, which we don't want to do. The political movement is too polarizing, too alienating. We may find as we build this stimulation-based campaign that we might be able to blend that right into the Introduction Meetings. But right now we cannot do that. The political movement must be basically its own committee that is not promoted.

And there's a real bonanza that can occur for those apprentices handling the political movement. Let me go through that bonanza here: Through the process of you independently bringing the Twelve Visions Party concept to the public through stimulation not education. You will have people interested in the life they were meant to live. That is what the Twelve Visions Party leads to…we are the party to make all the people rich including the poor. We have a very solid platform and approach to doing that. The Twelve Visions Party will bring us a wealthy world, a healthy life, a safe life. That is the stimulation- based presentation of the Twelve Visions Party.

Now imagine you have a group of people you're talking to about the Twelve Visions Party and the life they were meant to live. And you go on to explain that these ideas evolved out of a Society of Secrets. And in the Society are the secrets to a wealthy, healthy and safe life. If you are interested in having that life now, the life you were meant to live, you don't have to wait for the long- range plan of the Twelve Visions Party. You can come to the Introduction Meeting and become a member of the Society of Secrets where we reveal to you the secrets of life. Bingo! You just established for yourself very high-qualified prospects to bring to your Introduction Meeting. This could be a huge bonanza. Never has a political movement been tied to a network marketing dynamic.

Those apprentices moving on the political movement really will have an eye-opening moment when you learn how to financially tie your political movement to the Neothink® Network Marketing Opportunity. That could be the motivation factor that really causes the political movement to blossom. And I'm going to help your cause here. I'm going to print the National Platform into a pamphlet and the pamphlet is going to be titled, "Make All the People Rich Including the Poor".

Speaking of the National Platform, let's contrast our platform with the National Platforms of the Republican Party and the Democratic Party:

The 2004 Replication Party National Platform is titled, "A Safer World and a More Hopeful America". And the 2004 Democratic National Platform is titled "Strong at Home, Respected in the World". Let me ask, how many people have read these? My guess is very few. The Replication National Platform contains over 33,000 words, just reading a lot of politics. The National Democratic Party Platform contains about 19,000 words, reading a lot of politics.

Now let's contrast a "Safer World and a More Hopeful America" and "Strong at Home, Respected in the World" with "Make All the People Rich Including the Poor" in a little, easy to read 5-1/2" x 8/1/2" pamphlet that's passed out by the hundreds, then by the thousands, then by the millions. Who's going to read that pamphlet? Just about everyone who receives it, because it's stimulating them about something they really want in life; how to become wealthy. And, of course, the pamphlet goes into the other great benefits of the Twelve Visions Platform of health and safety, and finding the life you were suppose to live.

So, I'm going to print and send these pamphlets to those apprentices who are managing the political movement. You will have a space to put your name, contact info and your schedule of meetings; this will be a great recruiting tool for you. You'll be able to hand those out by the hundreds and then by the thousands creating this great stimulation-based political movement, not educational-based, not like the Republican and Democratic National Platforms. People will read our pamphlet.

Remember Thomas Paine's "Common Sense". In January of 1776 that pamphlet was published and sold to the public and in the end equivalents, if you adjust for population figures, 50 million pamphlets sold of "Common Sense".

In 1775 the Revolutionary War began but the Colonists were just looking for better peace-time terms. It wasn't until "Common Sense" in January of 1776 that the Colonists really shift over and want their independence. "Common Sense" was the phantom punch.

The Twelve Visions is the phantom punch. Remember this is a stimulation-based campaign. You're going to get people very interested in this political movement and you can reveal to them that this evolved out of the Society of Secrets, the Neothink® Society. That there are secrets now available that can get them the life they were meant to live. Send them to an Introduction Meeting.

Now let's talk about the Constitution to the Twelve Visions Party:

When you get down to the irreducible fundamental of something, often a paradigm shift occurs. I'm going to draw an analogy here to Henry Ford. His great invention came from getting down to the irreducible fundamental of the division of labor. He reduced the division of labor down to that

180

fundamental of a single movement, the rivet man driving in rivets on the assembly line.

Well, that concept of not bringing the workers to the work but bringing the work to the workers, to the assembly line, of course, that changed everything. That caused a huge prosperity explosion. There's an analogy here to the Constitution of the Twelve Visions Party.

The Constitution of the Twelve Visions Party with the Prime Law gets down to the irreducible, fundamental of protection. And there, at the fundamental level, a paradigm shift will occur. I'll get into that shift as we go through this meeting.

The fundamental concept here is that we are not going to let the lawmakers manage the laws. Instead the Prime Law is going to manage the lawmakers which will change everything as you'll see. And the result of that change is going to be a huge prosperity explosion.

So let us now take a close look at the political party itself:

For a long time I dreaded starting this political movement because we're dealing with man. Man has faults, man has mysticisms, temptations, ego, drawn toward greed, drawn toward corruptions and dishonesty. Even the most Neothink® people have their bubbles of mysticism. They're entrapped in a society that's full of illusions and they just may not have enough insights or knowledge or integrated thinking to know what's right or wrong. They're just not able to integrate deeply enough. There's just too many things blocking those integrations in the society.

How could a political party ever work? I struggled with that for years. That was when I realized that a fundamental change had to occur. And that change was the fundamental decision making had to come away from the party members and into the Prime Law. We do not let the party members manage the party. We have the party manage the party members.

To do this, I've developed a contract that all party members who run for office will sign. That contract will hold them true to the Prime Law. Every decision they make will have to hold true to the Prime Law. With that contract, holding members to the Prime Law, the political party will work beautifully.

The biggest problem I see among the A-Team is establishing the political committees, I understand why that is such a problem and so I'm going to step in and take a very strong lead now in getting the political movement off the ground. As most of you understand by now, the one proper purpose of government is protection. Anything else takes away from our freedom and therefore will take away from our prosperity. Indeed, throughout history, the freer a country, the greater the prosperity.

For the first time, with the Prime Law, we are talking about a fully free country, a purely free country that's never existed on our planet. For the first time because of the correlation between freedom and prosperity, all people can become rich including the poor.

America originally rose so quickly and was so prosperous, much more than the other countries because it was brilliantly controlled by the rule of law, not by the rule of man as most other countries. Man is full of faults. He's driven by ego, pulled by temptations, attracted to corruption and dishonesty.

The Twelve Visions Party takes the rule of law to another level. It takes it one step further by going down to the biological fundamental of protection, no initiatory force. The Twelve Visions Party removes man from recklessly creating new laws that have nothing to do with protection and it removes man from recklessly interpreting the law.

To see how the Prime Law dictates man, dictates the lawmakers and not the other way around, let's look at a sample of a State Constitution that I'm working up for you right now:

I'm going to read through a sample State Constitution that I'm going to provide to you.

Let me just take a moment here to also mention as one astute apprentice identified, should not all the State Constitutions be the same, aside from the leg work, from how to form committees and hold conventions to select members who can run for office? That will vary from state to state but the actual philosophical fundamental part of your State Constitution will be the same for all 50 states. That is what I'm developing.

I just grabbed the state Massachusetts. Now just fill in your state as I read this

The visionaries of Massachusetts envision a profoundly free, wealthy, healthy and safe society protected by rule of law. We believe, however, the lawmakers should not dictate the laws. Instead the Prime law should dictate the lawmakers.

Now, I'm going to read the Prime Law to you:

The Prime Law
Preamble

The purpose of human life is to prosper and live happily. The function of government is to provide the conditions that let individuals fulfill that purpose.

The Constitution of the Twelve Visions Party guarantees those conditions by forbidding the use of initiatory force, fraud or coercion by any person or group against any individual, property or contract.

Article I

No person, group of persons or government shall initiate force, threat of force or fraud against any individual self, property or contracts.

Article II

Force is morally and legally justified only for protection from those who violate out Article I.

Article III

No exception shall exist for Articles I and II

Now on the web site, www.tvpnc.org I also posted a Constitutional Statement. You must go and rear that closely if you haven't already. The Constitutional Statement explains and identifies that government for the past century has been existing for two purposes, number one, to protect the people and number two, to promote the social good. It also explains why promoting social good is a bogus function of government. There should be one and only one proper purpose of government and that is to protect the people. And I will sum up that long Constitutional Statement by reading two paragraphs.

With that one Prime Law in place it essentially becomes our supreme law to which every law must answer. For the supreme law will filter out every law and regulation and violation, namely of so called, promoting the social good which requires initiatory force.

The Prime Law is the biological fundamental, the point of origin, the beginning of all law. Therefore, no further unhealthy law or misinterpretation of the U. S. Constitution could occur. No more violations could happen. Government could not tell us how to spend our money or force us to pay taxes. As long as we did not commit initiatory force we would be completely free. We would not need ego and power driven lawmakers stirring up legislation with lawyers and bureaucrats using those laws to drain us.

We would no longer need that parasitical ruling class that destroys our prosperity. Their deceptions could no longer pass through the individual rights amendments including their forced taxes.

Let me explain the individual rights amendments:

At some point we will submit this as an amendment to the U.S. Constitution and that's where that expression came from. I'll read the final paragraph in that long Constitutional Statement:

With the Prime Law in place via State Constitution and eventually the Individual Rights Amendment. Excuse me; let me start that paragraph over. With the Prime Law in place via State Constitutions and eventually the Individual Rights Amendment to the U. S. Constitution the prosperity explosion described in the National Platform would never end. Think about the potential wealth, happiness, love and health described in the National Platform. We would soon live the wealthy, healthy and safe life we were meant to live.

Now, going back to your State Constitution, I'll read the Prime Law and a small portion of the Constitutional Statement. Those will be in, with some adjustments, your State Constitution and that will be followed by this comment:

Lawmakers' dictating the laws has caused the steady erosion of our beloved freedom. Every elected visionary will sign a contract that every decision in an office will be true to the Prime Law.

I'm going to read you that contract. It's still in a very rough form. As I said when I realized the A-Teams were struggling with, this I stopped:

So I'm going to read a very rough draft of this contract. Note that it will be worked and edited and brought up to the point where we feel comfortable with it:

There's a premise that protection only will lead to the people's greatest prosperity as demonstrated in Twelve Visions. That is reality. I understand the thoughts of man cannot alter reality. Yet while dictating law that attempt to is continually made such as this law or that law will improve the people's prosperity. Whether innocently or guiltily all those government actions beyond protection, everyday, slowly kill our freedoms bit by bit and steadily age our country and lead to its eventual death.

The purpose of this contract is to establish the reality of protection which is the one purpose of government, and establish that reality as the unchanging Prime Law of no initiatory force that dictates man and his lawmakers.

I pledge to subordinate all my many preconceived thoughts, despite how strongly I feel, despite whether I believe with certainty or with reservation for with external and internal confusions and illusions that accompany a power-based government, I honestly acknowledge that always reaching the proper decision is merely impossible.

Serving my Party's objective to return to a protection only government in order to unleash an unprecedented prosperity explosion will make all the people rich including the poor.

I fully understand the mechanics come down to consistently, always, without exception, supporting the biologically irreducible fundamental act of protection, which is The Prime Law of no initiatory force as spelled out in the State Constitution of my Twelve Visions Party.

That Prime Law of protection must dictate the lawmakers, not the other way around. Therefore every decision I make even if it goes against the very grain of my mind, my skin, my heart and soul will be made purely based on serving the Prime Law.

I realize in the end that policy will bring forth our vision to make all the people wealthy including the poor. That policy will bring forth our vision of a profoundly free, wealthy, healthy and safe society.

If I knowingly go against the Prime Law for any decision, for any reason whatsoever or if I show a trend of unknowingly going against the Prime Law, the Twelve Visions Party will immediately and publically disown me and will no longer recognize me as a member.

As I said, that will be developed and edited into a contract that any Twelve Visions Party member running for office will need to sign.

Let us now move to your State Platform:

As you all know, we have a National Platform now on the web site, www.tvpnc.org. I'm going to develop for you your State Platform, at least the fundamental portion of it, and we'll get into that here. We're going to talk a little bit about the part I'm not involved with directly afterwards because we can run into a lot of problems there. So let's first get through this part, the portion I'm going to provide you. Of course, this is all in rough draft form but I'm going to read to you an approach that I'm developing for your State Platform. It will come in the beginning of your State Platform called the Preamble and we can call it the Preamble and Mission Statement:

The visionaries do have a great vision which is a soaring standard of living in which all the people become rich including the poor.

In this day and age of rapidly advancing technology, buying power soars as we have seen with the computers. Visionaries believe that all citizens can soon live with great buying power, great wealth, if the government returns to its one proper purpose of protection only and removes itself from its improper purpose of promoting the social good.

The dynamics of this return to a protection only government and resulting explosion of wealth for the people in this age of rapidly advancing technologies can be clearly seen in the National Platform of the Twelve Visions Party. There you will witness why we are the Party to make *all* the people wealthy including the poor.

The mechanics of becoming a protection only government bring us to our Constitution. There we state the visionaries of the place, your state (here I say Massachusetts) envision a profoundly free, wealthy, healthy and safe society protected by rule of law, The Prime Law.

The Prime Law of no initiatory force brings us back to a protection only government and sets free our great technological revolution to quickly bring unprecedented wealth, health and safety to all citizens.

Lawmakers, man, must not dictate the lawmakers. Men and women dictating law can lead to anything. Can lead a country anywhere, even to the point where it becomes law to kill others, as we have seen around the world throughout history. No, the Prime Law must dictate the lawmakers.

If we want to live in a wealthy, healthy, happy, peaceful, safe and truly free society then the Prime Law of Protection must first be adopted as the contract of members of the Twelve Visions Party today, must gradually become the Constitution of each of the 50 sates tomorrow, an amendment to the U. S Constitution eventually, the overarching constitution de facto of America in the Twelve Visions World. The overarching constitution of the world ultimately ending force, war and crime, country by country while unleashing soaring technology, standards of living, buying power and wealth among all people including the poor.

That is our vision and all members running for office under The Twelve Visions Party will sign the contract to serve the Prime Law for every decision in quest of our vision.

Man with all his faults of ego, greed, envy and innocent lack of knowledge and his vulnerabilities must not be left to dictate laws and interpret the Constitution. Man with all his vulnerabilities and faults dictating law is a recipe for destruction. Instead our country must adopt the Prime Law.

Now, that would make up basically the Preamble and Mission Statement of your State Platform. As you know in that State Platforms they enumerate a number of planks, positions on certain issues. Let me read this as introducing the planks:

The Prime Law, not men and women, not elected lawmakers will dictate all political decisions and actions and base them upon no initiatory force, from that all people, not just elected politicians can determine the consistent and universal unchanging action here, referring to the planks.

Who is in office becomes irrelevant. What Party holds power becomes irrelevant. The Prime Law and nothing more remains relevant. The consequences of these decisions and actions locked down to the Prime Law will be staggering as demonstrated in the National Platform.

The geniuses of society will finally be free to accelerate the technological revolution and drive our buying power higher than we have ever seen.

This millionaire phenomenon will come to all people including the poor as demonstrated in the Twelve Visions National Platform. The name of that National Platform by the way is "Make All the People Rich Including the Poor".

Other spectacular consequences are shown in the National Platform such as unprecedented health, happiness, love, peace, security and safety.

At our state levels every plank listed by the Republicans and every plank listed by the Democrats, all listed below, will either be moved eventually to the private sector, if it has nothing to do with the one proper purpose of government, protection. Or it will fall under the Prime Law and its protection.

I'm going to list the planks from the State Platform of the Republican Party and the Democratic Party, and then show or perhaps categorize them as to those that are on their way out according to the Prime Law. That's the Great Displacement Program moving to the private sector where they truly will be handled properly and those categorized under the Prime Law and that's the Prime Law of Protection, no initiatory force.

I will show when you move those planks out that the Democrats or Republicans are looking to impose on the people, it clears the way for the geniuses of society to soar and to do what they did when in the computer revolution; increase our buying power thousands of times over, up to a million times over. In other words, this Great Replacement dynamic brings about a society in which we will live like millionaires, all of us.

I want to make the point that when visionary Henry Ford discovered the worker should not manage the work, the work should manage the people, society went through this enormous prosperity explosion. The reason behind that is, of course, mass production, the assembly line, production line. His shift in production accelerated the Industrial Revolution. The Industrial Revolution came out of the division of labor. That's what started the Industrial Revolution. The division of labor was the impetus, the key puzzle piece behind the Industrial Revolution.

Now there is a connection here to what we are doing here. By taking the rule of law to the next level, not allowing the lawmakers to dictate the laws, the Prime Law of Protection dictates the lawmakers. We're going to have that explosion of prosperity which I believe all my apprentices understand. This will happen because it frees up the geniuses of society as we saw in the computer world who are going to drive the values toward infinity while costs drop towards zero as we've seen in communications, the Internet, and computer high-tech world. Those geniuses of society will do that across the board in all industries because they will be *free* to do so. The result of that is all of us living like millionaires.

The reason that explosion will happen is because by having the Prime Law dictate the lawmakers it frees up these geniuses of society to accelerate the technological revolution. So, what Henry Ford did to accelerate the Industrial Revolution, we're going to accelerate the Technological Revolution with the same results; skyrocketing standard of living. I call this the Millionaire Phenomenon; everyone's going to live like a millionaire.

And, this is not hype. This is actually going to happen. It is unprecedented. This economic model has never been seen. We've been held down in the darkness as I say in the National Platform. We now know with Neothink® we can see the future. The puzzle pieces have been brought together, the puzzle picture is there for all to see.

Okay, so I'm going to stress here that the Twelve Visions Party is the Party that will make all people rich including the poor. It literally is the Party to make all the people rich. That is our vision. It's not hype; it's truly a Neothink vision.

Now, one apprentice made an important point I want to address. His concern was how, in the Constitutional Statement, I used the first person two or three times.

First, I want to express how the posting on our Level Meetings Site is a personal interaction between you and me. I track that every day. I follow your posts, I follow your questions, I receive your questions, I spend a good amount of time each and every day looking closely at questions as that is my essence tracking report. So, because this is a personal communication between us in the Constitutional Statement I made the comment referring to the Constitution, "I said non-amendable". In other words, I used the pronoun "I". And I said "my protection only budget" in one place and I think there may have been another place I used the first person. Also I used, which this apprentice did not pick up, the second person as well a couple of times like, "as you all know", or "as you know". So I'm making a point here, that's a more personal communication. But when this goes into a formal document then the first person comes out. When I provide you with your State Constitutions for example, there will be no first person in there and there won't be, most likely there won't be a second person in there either. There will not be the use of "I" or "my" or "you" in those formal documents.

I wanted to just make this point because I don't want anyone to think that ego is playing any role in what I am doing or what we are doing. Everything is very calculated each step of the way. In fact, I don't want to get too far off on a tangent but you all know from the Miss Annabelle's Story why Daniel Ward was one of twelve who could have successfully run for President because with anybody else's ego or self-centered dynamic could eventually enter in. With the escalation of power, it could go to one's head. But with the twelve students in Miss Annabelle's Story, becoming President of the United States, taking control of the Oval Office was simply a puzzle piece to the grand puzzle of biological immortality. In fact, what was important to the twelve students was not becoming President of the United States. What was important to Daniel Ward was ultimately serving as a piece to the puzzle to achieve biological immortality. So therefore, he had no deeper motivation, no other motives, no risk of ego taking over. The same goes for me. My end goal is biological immortality and these are simply puzzle pieces to achieve that goal. Ego does not and will not and cannot enter my psyche on this process.

Now I want you to understand, a similar analogy occurs with Thomas Paine and "Common Sense. "Common Sense" was the key puzzle piece to launching the Revolution, the fight for independence. Twelve Visions is the key puzzle piece to achieve our Twelve Visions World. That is the key puzzle piece to bringing about a Twelve Visions President.

I am the author of Twelve Visions. Twelve Visions must be promoted through this process. I look at this as a two-step process; the campaigning, the public eye, your public movement which generates leads who are drawn to the Twelve Visions. The pamphlet I'm going to provide you is going to help dramatically with that goal. But we need 50 million people — eyes on Twelve Visions — so if we use the name "Mark Hamilton", we're doing that because he's the author of Twelve Visions. We need Mark Hamilton and Twelve Visions to be out there in the public now. We need that.

For 25 years and more I have kept all these movements very secret. I've turned down a lot of money to go public. But now is the time to go public. Twelve Visions is the key puzzle piece. Mark Hamilton and Twelve Visions need to be promoted to the public. This has nothing to do with ego.

If I had any problems with ego, I would have, decades ago, been involved in the public mode. So, I want to make that very clear, so you understand what we are doing. We are promoting Twelve Visions.

On your State Platform I do not want any apprentice to start putting in their own beliefs or thoughts, trying to form planks. That will lead to disaster. I have seen a small number of attempted National Platforms and they do not work. Just for starters, the moment you begin putting down a position, you create a polarizing dynamic which is a dud, a big giant dud.

People have seen all that before, the arguments here and there. That's not what we're about. We're about a phantom punch, a unique campaign strategy that has not been used. We're going to come in with a stimulation-based campaign. I'm going to help you through this now. I'm going to work with you to create your State Platform, your State Constitution. I do not want anybody trying to develop planks themselves or positions. That just won't work.

The Prime Law is what this is all about. The Prime Law, freeing up the geniuses of society, to create great wealth and prosperity. That's what this is about. That's what we're going to put out there. That's our face and that's how we're going to deal with the media. I'm going to show you how to deal with the media and give you the approach.

I want to recap some key points here:

The Society of Secrets is a product based Society, The Neothink® Society. I know we're on the political side now but I want you to always keep that in mind. The Society of Secrets is a product based dynamic. Down the road the political movement is going to tie in very tightly with the Society of Secrets.

Because we are a product-based movement, there are going to be a percentage of people coming in who do not want to be part of the Neothink® Network Marketing Opportunity or the political movement. They simply want to be in The Neothink® Society to learn. They are students who want to learn and eventually become mentors and that's absolutely okay, that's absolutely fine.

And, to that point, our essence meetings here starting next month are going to resume with me teaching you concepts that are valuable to you. For instance, some of you are having issues or problems with your spouse or significant other. There's concern about you getting involved in this movement I can give you the tools to greatly relieve a lot of these situations. Not only relieve them but actually change that dynamic into a great positive where your spouse or significant other is very involved with you. It could spark a whole new romantic relationship.

Also, let me clarify a point I made in last meetings Supplement: Your political movement is not to be part of The Society of Secrets or a part of the Introduction Meetings. It's not to be part of the Clubhouse or Workshop Meetings. That may be confusing to some because I said in the Supplement I would be combining these. What I meant by that is no Society of Secrets can exist without having a political arm or committee. This is all going to turn around and beautifully feed the Society of Secrets as you will see with time.

Well that about covers it. I will be in contact with you through the web site throughout the month leading up to our next essence meeting.

Secret Teachings to My Exclusive Inner Circle

Level-Six Essence Meeting
Introduction

Welcome to the Level-Six Essence Meeting. I have an extraordinarily exciting meeting for you today.

As you know, we launched some of The Society of Secrets (SOS) Clubhouses in a test market phase. And, that's basically what this meeting is going to concentrate on.

By the way, those of you who are not really participating now, the fence sitters, just watching from a distance, seeing how this goes, understand this is a very special time. These are very special meetings. This is a very special, intimate transition from a closed Secret Society to a public Society of Secrets, to the Neothink® Society. So you are witnessing something that is historic and you can enjoy it for that and that alone.

Now, I did say I would talk about relationships during this Level 6 Meeting and I will touch upon those and that topic. However, I am postponing the in depth treatment of relationships to a future meeting because the timing is so critical right now to launch the A-Teams that are out there now in the real world.

I will repeat myself throughout this long meeting at points and I do that purposefully, strategically. Those points that you hear come up 2, 3, 4, 5 times, realize I'm not doing that because I'm being forgetful. It's because I need to drill that into your mind. It must stand out. It's like putting something in bold or italics or caps so when you hear something for the fourth or fifth time please don't say "Mark, I've already heard that". Realize my repeating a point is critical for that point to stay in your subconscious. When you're up there in a pressure situation in front of 600 people and you're delivering an Introduction Meeting, that little voice in the back of your head that's helping you out and pulling you through that meeting is me repeating that point 6 times in this meeting, for example. So, realize there's strategy behind my repeating a point. Don't tune out when you hear something repeated several times.

So back to the fence-sitters:

I know there are fence-sitters who will join the A-Team when they're ready at different capacities. As you'll see there are four basic people I identify in here who will be joining and they can join in any one of those four capacities. They don't have to contribute; they can just be in your Clubhouse for the sheer enjoyment of being in The Neothink® Society and receiving its advantages. Or they can be aggressively building it, there's different categories; we'll get into that.

We're going to concentrate now on the launch of the Society of Secrets and the Clubhouses, and talking about the program, about the programs coming down the road; what to expect.

So let's begin with Part One of our Level-Six Essence Meeting.

Level-Six Essence Meeting
Part One

Today's meeting will be focused on the launch of the Society of Secrets (SOS) Clubhouses.

As you know, we've contacted a few of the A-Teams who we felt were ready and they felt were ready to partake in the test market of the launching of the Clubhouses. Just today I received from the printers the first Heirloom, "SOS Secrets". We will send this to the A-Teams who are involved in this test market so they can look at the changes that have been made and work those changes into the Workshop Meeting.

The way this particular test program is going to work is as follows:

People out there who we've selected will order from us that Heirloom Package. And the reason we call them Heirloom Packages is because these advantages, these life advantages, these secrets and these visions, these powers will be passed on from generation to generation.

They will purchase from us that first Heirloom Package. When they receive that book, these buyers will receive a letter from us explaining what the Clubhouse is and giving them the opportunity to experience the Clubhouse, experience the Workshop Meetings, experience the Clubhouse Meetings.

We will provide a phone number for them to call. When these new buyers of the first Heirloom package call that phone number we will then contact you and put you together so you can talk to them directly, give them information about your Workshop Meeting, time, place and date of your Clubhouse Meetings.

This is only one of many programs to bring you contacts, names. There are several programs that will feed leads to you. It's going to be a very powerful, unique program.

Let me run through this a little bit further so you get the big picture:

You are the chosen ones. You have been the initiators of the A-Teams. You have worked hard on developing the Introduction Meetings, the Workshop and Clubhouse Meetings. You've been dealing with or will be dealing with the issues of real estate, where to hold these meetings, how to expand as you grow your Clubhouse. Basically, you have taken responsibility for your Society of Secrets Clubhouse. As your reward and because of the unique relationship that we have, I'm going to feed you these highly-qualified names.

For example, for those buyers of the first Heirloom Package, I expect a very high percentage of conversion of them to membership in the Society of Secrets. It's early to throw out numbers but once you have your Workshop Meetings, Clubhouse Meetings, really up to where these people can be brought to, you will get 75 percent, perhaps even higher percent conversion. They will, in others words, join and convert and become members of your Society of Secrets Clubhouse.

That's an astounding number, 80 percent. What's perhaps even more astounding is the engine this will become as I feed these names to you. It will be a continuous feed, week, after week, after week. And there are several programs I will be testing and developing that will generate names for the A-Teamers.

Here's just an overview of that: I see two basic feeds. One is "the buyers coming in". For example, these people will have purchased the first Heirloom book. I will recover the money for that and that will be kept by me because of the acquisition costs and so on. But when they convert, when they attend your Society of Secrets Clubhouse, it is at that point the split occurs where they provide you with their credit card and you send that into me.

I will not cut that off after a year. I have restructured this, into an evolving program. I'm trying to basically give as much out there for the most incentive and reward as I can. So there will not be a cut off after a year. This will go on as long as the life of the program. And, the fact that these values are eternal values, I don't see this program ending. I see it going on eternally.

Now those are buyers coming in. There will be different buyer programs. This is simply the launch and I'm going to launch this conservatively. Everything until now has been done in a slow, methodical, conservative pace. And this launch will be no exception. But once we get it up and running and I feel comfortable and you feel comfortable then we simply can turn up the volume.

The other half of the feed of names that I'll be giving you will be what I call leads. These will be people who will be 10 times as likely to convert as the best prospects you will find in your general life around you. You know, you meet somebody at Starbucks or at work and they become interested. This lead I provide you with, because of our sorting mechanism, will be 10 times as likely to convert. (The buyers I send you are 100 times as likely to convert.) As I said, when you develop your program to where it should be you will convert 75 to 80 percent of the buyers and you will convert anywhere from 10 to 30 percent of the leads. That's yet to be determined and perhaps even higher.

This is a completely new venture for me. I'm basing this on some legacy data but this is an entirely new development for Neothink®. This whole going public concept and we will learn as we go along but minimally these, well let me put it this way, these are conservative figures I'm throwing out. But you will be given a large feed from me of leads and buyers.

Now what you've been working so hard on for the past several months is developing your Introduction Meetings, developing your Workshop Meetings and developing the basic Clubhouse Meeting format premise information. Those have been your real efforts these past several months.

Now let me show you why those efforts are going to payoff for you very quickly:

The buyers coming in are not going to go through the Introduction Meeting and I know those A-Teams who have been contacted by Steve Rapella, my General Manager and my right-hand man, have been told that the Introduction Meeting is not necessary and it's not for buyers coming in. These people are calling you to get to your Workshop to really learn and have help applying the mini-day/power -thinking team from their first book. They want help, they want your advice, they want to sit down and have you help them develop their mini-days. That's the self-capture portion, of course, and you have the company- capture, setting up the mini-companies, the tracking reports; they want help with that. And, of course, you have the world-capture and they will be looking for help with all of this. And, as we discussed before, this could be anywhere from one Workshop Meeting to two, up to three Workshop Meetings. But they're coming to you for that human interaction and help and human mentoring. That is your role now. You are teachers, you are mentors.

That value, when they come and they experience that value and they also experience the Clubhouse Meeting and the intellectual stimulation and the social stimulation of the Clubhouse Meeting, those values that you've worked hard developing are going to be what motivates these people to join and become a member month after month. So, they skip past the Introduction Meeting.

Now the leads that I begin to feed you *will* go through the Introduction Meeting. I can provide you with 10 times the number of leads the buyers I provide you. When I start providing you with leads, they go to your Introduction

Meetings. These people will not have bought anything yet. They will come to your Introduction Meeting wide-eyed, curious. They will have read literature from me and they will be excited to meet people instead of just reading through the mail the Orientation Booklet. They now get a chance to come and meet people and listen to people talk, to see how Neothink® will affect their lives. That's where the value of having developed your Introduction Meetings come into play.

So, now you have a little bit of an understanding why I've had you work so hard the past several months developing the Introduction Meetings, the Workshop Meetings and the Clubhouse meetings. They are going to become your tools, your mechanisms for building your membership, building your Clubhouse, building your Society of Secrets and making money.

Now, let's look how this beautiful, well-oiled machine is going to work:

As you bring in these people and convert them through your Workshop Meetings and your Clubhouse Meetings, you convert these buyers that I feed you and through your Introduction Meetings you convert the leads that I feed you. These people then become your marketing team.

Now your team is not going to receive a feed from me. Instead they're going to be the other leg to this program. They are going to become your Neothink® Network Marketing Team. They're going to be the ones bringing in their family, their friends, people they meet. They are going to develop ideas to bring people in for the Introduction Meetings which you by now are becoming experts at delivering.

I feed you the highest, by magnitudes, the highest-quality names; you convert these names through your Workshop Meetings, your Clubhouses Meetings, through your Introduction Meetings. These people then, not all of them, but

a good percentage of them become interested in the Neothink®
Network Marketing Opportunity and they recruit people,
convince people to come into your Introduction Meetings that
you're just running week, after week, after week. And those
people who become members get converted, etc. It becomes a
formula and there will come a certain point where you will
know, just as I can know from my legacy data in my business,
exactly what percentages you're going to convert. And you're
going to learn techniques and you're going to evolve and
you're going to watch yourself drive up those percentages as
you become more and more effective at really communicating
the true value of the Society of Secrets, the secrets within The
Neothink® Society.

Now, each month, the first year your members are going to
receive these enormous advantages, these consistent
advantages that they can get nowhere else. They can't get
these advantages, these secrets in bookstores or from other
people. It's just been a very, very secret small group of people
who have been exposed to these life advantages. Each month
these advantages and secrets are going to just flow to these
people. This is part of their membership, these life advantages
coming from my publishing company, just flow to them each
month.

That will be basically their one year journey. Whether or
not you find that advantageous to explain that or not, that will
be left up to you. You basically can present that each month
they're going to get enormous advantages. After a year they
are going to be so tied in socially, they're going to have such
friendships, such bonds, such values from what you developed
from these Clubhouse Meetings that they can get nowhere else,
they will never leave.

The first year is the real hook; it's the literature. After that
they're not going to want to leave. It's like any other society
where people discover life advantages from churches that

people belong to. I've identified in some writings the reason churches have survived in the modern era is because of the life advantages that people actually get. The same thing happens with certain clubs that people belong to, certain societies. They're there because they receive certain life advantages, whatever those may be, whether it's certain opportunities in business, certain friendships, a certain sense of belonging, a certain sense of security. That's all going to come into play here in the Society of Secrets.

For the first year these people are going to be essentially, really, without exaggeration, they are going to be blown away by the advantages that they receive. Then that combined with the Workshop Meetings, the Clubhouse Meetings, this is going to be just a new society, a new experience in life for these people. They're going to evolve. They're going to learn that this Neothink® Society is truly the society that they want to be part of.

Remember, it wasn't until your third meeting that I explained you are searchers and that is how I found you. So you will understand when these people come in that they are searching for the life they were meant to live. That's the child of the past and you know more than they do. Just like when I you brought in. I knew more than you do. You can deal with these people with that type of love, understanding, warmth and acceptance. You want to help them achieve and reach that life they were meant to live. You want to awaken the child of the past. This is your role.

I will ultimately have people come to you at different levels. There will be people who come to you who will; have received the first three Heirlooms directly from me. These are people who will need more literature prior to being introduced and interacting with people.

Once they come and they discover that you *are* The Neothink® Society where they belong, you will have the forms, they will sign up, they will become a member and they will then receive the fourth Heirloom, which is the first very emotionally moving book of the Miss Annabelle's Heirloom Trilogy.

So this is sort of the overview here of where we're going. Everything that you've done up till now has been critical for you to present and bring to these people, the feeds that I give you. These feeds that you receive directly from me will become very lucrative. These feeds will make us basically unstoppable in the long run.

Now I want to temper everyone's expectations. First of all, I'm going to start this off conservatively. Don't expect to make a lot of money instantly. But as you're A-Team develops and matures I will turn up the volume and feed you larger and larger amounts of names.

But during this program, the test market A-Teams that are launching this. At some point I want the test market A-Teams to tell your leads that, for a year, they're going to receive these enormous advantages. Remember, they're going to be very happy campers when they get this first book because they're going to see something they haven't seen in any book stores or any program. So they're going to be pretty happy about what they've received here already. You want to tell them that as they absorb these highly-guarded secrets and life advantages, you're going to help them. You are going to mentor them, to integrate these advantages into their lives. We're going to bring them together to meet others. They're going to gain advantages and friendships. You're going to offer this outlet for social activities, human interaction where lifelong, powerful friendships will develop. And after a year they're going to find that they will never leave this exclusive society. Everything is here, everything including the life you were meant to live, lifelong friends, soul mates. They will take a lifelong journey. They'll begin with a one-year journey after

206

which they will want to be a member for life in The Neothink® Society

Now the people that are coming in with this first product will have a basic orientation from me. They're going to be brought in having received one-third of the Inside Secrets from Mark Hamilton. So their perception is "I have one-third of Mark Hamilton's Inside Secrets. There must be more!"

Level-Six Essence Meeting
Part Two

Now, the next book they will receive the second month is going to be "Twelve Visions" which is the first book of your Second Heirloom Package. The third book that they would receive is book two of your Second Heirloom Package which is currently called "The Three Insights" that's going to be called, "God-Like Powers". The front cover of both those books, by the way, are going to be "SOS Visions" for their second book which is "Twelve Visions" and the third book will be "SOS Powers" which is "God-Like Powers".

So, they're coming in from that perspective that they've got one-third of Mark Hamilton's secrets which is one of three books of mine which reveal basically the non-fiction secrets. So they are going to be primed and anxious to continue on, to continue on to get the next two books.

When they come to your Clubhouse and experience the Workshop Meetings and the Clubhouse Meetings that's going to add just a whole additional dimension to the value. They are going to be quite excited to sign up to get the next third and then the next third. During this process, of course, you are going to express to them that this is another society, a parallel society to the society of the masses; a small, exclusive society that receives these secrets that no one else knows about. The only way you can find out these secrets is to become a member of the Society. This is the point where they realize, WOW, I will be able to get these advantages, these life advantages, not just for two more months but ongoing and they will make that transition.

Your most important and most critical Workshop Meeting is going to be the Workshop Meeting or Meetings that you have for the first book of your Heirloom Package. This is your conversion tool. This is when people say, "Where do I sign up?"

All right, let's move on to a very important value of the Society of Secrets, of The Neothink® Society; The Business Alliance:

As the human interaction in our Clubhouse grows and you meet and interact with people you may find you have particular needs or a business idea you want to get involved in. Someone might say, "I'm a lawyer, here call me, I can help you with that" or "I'm a realtor. If you're interested, sure I can help you" or "I'm a doctor, I can certainly see your children." That's the essence of the Business Alliance and it's very simple. People who are in The Neothink® Society are given first consideration. That will become a very powerful dynamic. We see that in certain religions, for instance, in the Jewish religion where they give first consideration to anyone who is Jewish which tremendously shifts the odds. If there is somebody else who's not Jewish who has a better, more advantageous arrangement then of course, the open market dynamics will bring them there. But giving first consideration is a very powerful concept. The Mormons use this practice, too. You also see this dynamic in clubs such as The Rotary Club or in other societies such as the Masons. This is an often-used practice and is a proper use of the Business Alliance.

Improper use however is using the members as a name bank to push other MLM programs. For example, to aggressively advertise your product through the Society that is not a Society-endorsed product or without The Neothink® Society's permission is not the proper use of the Business Alliance. In fact, that's abusing the Business Alliance and now that we're launching the movement to grow the Society, I cannot allow such abuse. This has been allowed to slide a little bit and I know this abuse is taking place. Now if there's a genuine value say like a technical communication dynamic that can be beneficial, sure it's fine to tell people about it. That's all fine and dandy but to aggressively push it is a cancer to our Society.

Why is this cancerous? Because you will have people joining the Society and then suddenly they're bombarded with people trying to sell them something, especially something that is not a Society-sanctioned or approved product or service. You will drive away a member who could be worth a lot of money to you.

So to enforce this I will cut off the feed to those who are turned into me as violating the Business Alliance and that is assertively calling, emailing, pitching or sending out letters and pitching to our members. That must end now. Of course, at any time I can change the rules but right now this is how I'm setting this up. So keep that in mind.

Now, I'd like to address the issue of growing your Clubhouse. Some of you are jumping ahead here. Like I said, you need to start this slowly. I want you to keep your expenses down but have a plan, have a fix on rapidly expanding your real estate capacity when I turn up the volume. But in the meantime I would recommend keeping your expenses as low as you can. And, I'm talking right now to the A-Team in Washington where there's been some talk about purchasing a building or perhaps leasing a building. Do research on this, yes. And have things lined up to move in that direction. But I'd like to see you have a supportive core membership first. Arrange to keep your expenses down by having Workshop Meetings at different homes. I'm not up there with you; I'm not in your situation so you will have to make those decisions. This is just some insight I'm passing on to you. This is a new venture for all of us, me included. I don't want to see you stress coming up with lease or mortgage money each month if there's any other way that you can work around that.

And I control volume here. If we need to keep the volume down just so you can build that supportive core then when that happens we can turn up the volume on leads and then you can have your building or your place where you're leasing your space.

Now, we will set up Tracking Reports to where all this runs like a well-oiled machine.

Level-Six Essence Meeting
Part Three

I will be setting up these Tracking Reports. The most important Tracking Report right now is your A-Team Neo-Space on our Active Neothink® website. Those whose A-Teams are launching the test market, for your own survival and profit, you must get into your A-Team Neo-Space and really update with everything that's going on and I'm going to tell you why.

Your most important connection is your connection directly with me. If you remember, in your first book of your Heirloom the integrating and coordinating functions of the CEO. Well, that is our relationship. As a matter of fact, one apprentice posted on the web site a Ten-Second Miracle. He suddenly realized that this was like the division of essence — mini-company and the CEO, that relationship, with tracking reports. And, he's absolutely right. My relationship with you is that of CEO. I handle the integrating and coordinating functions. These level meetings that you're having with me are our Essence Meetings. This is where I give you guidance. My most important essence tracking report is what you write in your A-Team Neo-Space. I'm going to actually have my computer staff isolate those A-Teams that were launched and they are going to be the first thing I look at now when I go to the web site. I'm going to go in on a daily basis, I'm going to look at your progress and how you are moving along. That's going to feed me with the integration that you need for success.

Starting tomorrow morning, I want everyone in your A-Team to get on the website so I can look and see your name. I want to know you by your first name. That's important. I want to see what you're doing; I want to see what each person in every A-Team is doing.

The way I see the value of your A-Team is that each person has different strengths and weaknesses. And it's completely up to you how you break down your division of labor and your division of essence within your own A-Team. Some people may excel at giving testimonials or life experiences and so those people may want to run those Introduction Meetings. Others just may be good at understanding the product and how to apply the techniques, so they would run the Workshops. Others may be good at making phone calls and talking to people, getting them to the Introduction meetings. Others may be good at other communicators, while others are basically the secretary, keeping things organized and keeping communication flowing. Others may be very good in real estate and handling the real estate issues.

You must determine what those strengths and weaknesses are. I believe you've been doing that and I need to get more integrated with each of you in your A-Team, specifically what roles you're playing. We want everybody to contribute to their greatest capacity into each A-Team. And, I am going to assume that each person is an equal value to your A-Team. Maybe somebody doesn't work as hard as somebody else but perhaps they have another overwhelming value. Maybe such a person can afford the leasing or contributes the real estate while others are doing enormous work with their time and effort. Those are mutual value exchanges and that's completely allowed and acceptable.

Additionally, an A-Team should have the ability to vote somebody out. And, any A-Team member can, for any reason, leave an A-Team. Doesn't mean he has to be voted out. Let's say someone's spending 18 hours a day devoting him or herself to the business of the A-Team and the others aren't that interested. That person can elect to leave and start his own A-Team.

I get into these issues now because we're launching and it's time to sober up and buckle down as we say in business. We need to see reality for what it is and get down to the nuts and bolts of how this is all going to work. It is important to have the nuts and bolts nailed down as we move into the next important phase where you become mentors.

This year of our mentoring has been very special between you and me. I've put a lot of effort into this. I've been tracking you more closely that you probably know. This has been created out of nothing, this new program. After decades of being rooted in a secret society, we are turning it inside out so to speak. But this mentoring that I've been doing with you, this is going to now pass on to you. You will now become mentors to your members. You will be there with them in your Clubhouse providing the personal touch. You will be a phone call away; you will be a Clubhouse Meeting away. You will be a Workshop Meeting away. You will be down the street; you will be a drive away. You will be there for your members and you will be their mentors. You will experience what I'm experiencing with you; the great rewards and fulfillment of bringing Neothink® to others and mentoring them to be that person they really were meant to be. There is tremendous happiness for you when you bring happiness to others. This rewarding experience is passing from me to you.

To this end of making you the mentors for your members, I am backing off from certain communications as you begin to develop. I'm going to remove "Ask Mark Hamilton a Question" from the web site because those questions need to be answered by you. It's part of the process of you becoming mentors and teachers. That responsibility is coming to you. It's an extremely rewarding experience and you will feel the great responsibility when you are involved in lifting people's lives and futures.

Soon I will stop reading emails. Only emails I will read are those that I request. I will continue for a while to answer your big questions each month and bring those out in the remaining Essence Meetings. But aside from that I'm not reading emails any longer.

I will open up another concept to you. I have no issue with ambitious A-Teams members starting A-Teams around their entire state or beyond. I've seen that in Washington, for example, where you have your core, super A-Team with satellite A-Teams around the state. Now I'm not asking you to go out and do that right now but I'm saying that option is open. Now you can't just stake claim to this A-Team over here, in this part of my state. You actually have to spend effort and time there in that A-Team and work with the people and develop them to the point where they are providing great values, the human interaction, great Workshop Meetings, great Clubhouse meetings, great Introduction Meetings.

I am bringing this up now because we have certain A-Teamers who have endless amounts of energy and organizational skills. This is an open opportunity for them to go ahead and begin to set up A-Teams around their state. It's going to be tough, hard work but that option is available. And you can have A-Teams doing that as a group. You don't have to have one person splintering off doing it. If this entire A-Team, Seattle A-Team, for example, wants to start an entire A-Team in another part of the state, they can be given credit for having developed that particular A-Team. So these options are open to you and we will just see, as we go along, how that develops.

All righty let's move on here. Just remember, any A-Team needs a core. You need a core of people to handle the Intro Meetings, the Workshop Meetings, and the Clubhouse Meetings. You're going to need at least a dozen Workshop meetings. You need people coordinating social activities.

Remember, this is all part of the appeal of the Clubhouse product. The people you convert, who become members and remain members, particularly after the first year, need that social interaction. You need a core of people to run these Intro Meetings, to run the Workshop Meetings, to handle the operational details, to handle the real estate issues, to handle the coordination of all your meetings, to handle the social activities, the secretary, and the communicator. There are a lot of things that need to be done in any one A-Team to make it a great value. So you need a certain number of people. There will be an optimal number of people that we will discover, an optimal number of people you will discover. We don't know what that is, but right now, in a sense, the more the better.

Remember, this is a product-based marketing opportunity. The whole move to take Neothink® public thing is driven by the product and the value of the ideas and what that can lead to. So we need manpower in there for the Intro Meetings, Workshop Meetings and Clubhouse Meetings and for setting up this great, well-oiled machine.

Now I'm going to throw a term out here, a term that we had backed away from but I don't want you using this term outside our essence meetings. This is just between you and me. Originally I called this the Church of God-Man and in your Level One meeting I talked about this as the Church of God-Man. In your Third Heirloom Package, the faction piece in the Miss Annabelle Story talks about the Church of god-Man and in my mind and in your mind you can look at it that way. This is like a church but we cannot use the expression, the terminology, a church because it's too polarizing, too alienating. It just shuts off people right from the get-go. But between you and me you can look at it that way. You know how in neighborhoods across the country you have many different churches. Well, we will be setting up, ultimately, many different Clubhouses and that's what we're calling it.

We're calling it Society of Secrets Clubhouses because that's inviting and enticing. It's not alienating and polarizing.

But in your mind think of churches, how you see them on different corners and neighborhoods all over the place. That's essentially what we are doing. This really is a Church of God-Man program. You are the ones building your church. We are not going to discuss it and call it a church outside of these secret meetings that are between you and me. We're going to call it your Clubhouse, your Society of Secrets but it really is and your thinking tools it's the Church of God-Man. And you know that for such an endeavor, starting a church, you need manpower and that's why you need a substantial A-Team.

And, like a church, people keep coming back over and over for the life advantages they receive. That is your responsibility to, every week, every month; provide these great life advantages through the Workshop Meetings, the Clubhouse, through the social activities, through the intellectual and social stimulation.

Level-Six Essence Meeting
Part Four

This is a superpuzzle and we are all pieces in the superpuzzle. You all know that by now. Each of you is a crucial piece to the grand superpuzzle so anything you can do to help the other pieces evolve is part of a wonderful win/win situation for everybody. That is why I have done everything I can to remove my profits from this, to get this out to you because in the end this is how this is going to work. Do not fear other A-Teams in competition.

For one thing, A-Teams are in totally different geographical areas. If a person in Wilmington, Delaware discovers a particular technique for recruiting that is working and puts that up on his Neo-Space A-Team, he is not going to be hurt one bit if a Team in Fort Lauderdale, Florida, for example, uses that technique. In fact, in the long run, he's going to be helped as this takes on that synergy that I have had hoped would have taken on by now. So, we need to get that information, that tracking, your notes, your meeting notes on those A-Team Neo-Spaces now.

Okay, I'm now going to give you an "Ace up the Sleeve" for your Introduction Meetings. It's both a Force of Nature and a Forces of Neothink. That's what makes this "Ace up the Sleeve" so powerful to your Introductory Meetings. It's a powerful sorting mechanism for mating for women selecting a mate, for men selecting a mate. This is a powerful sorting mechanism for those who become creative and become successful in life. It's a very powerful Forces of Neothink, becoming creative, the value creator. It's an anticivilization concept of being perceived as smart. "He's smart" and bingo, the women look at him differently, his peers look at him differently. "He's smart". His boss suddenly looks at him differently. "Smart" is a powerful, powerful Force of Nature and Forces of Neothink®.

As you go through the first Heirloom package and you learn and then teach in your Workshops, keep this in mind, how "smart" one becomes when you really know how to apply this stuff. "Mark Hamilton, a very rich man, is just an average Joe, but look how smart he became because of these techniques." In reality, it's not really smart, which is an anticivilization expression but it's really this ability to integrate. That's what it really is. But if you say he's an integrator, people aren't really going to understand. That requires integrations to understand. But if you just stick with the term "smart", people who really grasp this and understand this are going to out-compete the people who went to Harvard Business School. I'm living proof.

During your Workshop Meeting people will become very excited as you show them the power of Neothink® techniques…how they've never seen these ideas in any self-help course, in any bookstore. These are very different, unique ideas that work and they're going to see how they work in your Workshop Meetings. And you are going to plant the idea, the Force of Nature and Forces of Neothink® in their head by saying, "With these Neothink® techniques you will become smarter than those people with PhD's and MBA's. You're going to run circles around them."

The concept of "smart" is powerful. Work that through your first Workshop Meeting. Using such an anticivilization expression like "smart", a person would be a fool not to sign up. It's like that old commercial, "When E. F. Hutton talks, people listen." That's what this is. The word smart is a code word for success in business and relationships. It's a code word so use it.

Level-Six Essence Meeting
Part Five

I want to get back to the terms we use amongst ourselves versus terms to be used in your Clubhouse Meetings: We will not use the expression C of U, or the Civilization of the Universe in our Clubhouses. It's just too grand. It's beyond a complex concept. It's a puzzle in and of itself; it's a puzzle picture that you grasp simply because you're a Level Six apprentice. But the ordinary person will shut down before you get even one-quarter of the way through articulating that puzzle picture to them. So, instead of using that grand superpuzzle, Civilization of the Universe, we will talk about us as a Super Society and about the Twelve Visions World. For instance, we are coming into the Super Society as a result of Neo-Technology racing ahead so rapidly. You can tell your members that they are going to discover this out in the second month, in the second Heirloom. We are racing ahead so rapidly that it creates a Super Society where everyone becomes wealthy including the poor, which is the Twelve Visions World.

So, instead of using the word C of U, we'll use words like the Super Society and like the Twelve Visions World.

Now back to what you are building and how we will work together:

The Neothink® Clubhouses, our network of Clubhouses around the country is a product-based value that is facilitated by the Neothink® Network Marketing Opportunity. Keep in mind that we're building these churches. Remember, we're not calling them churches to the public; we're calling them Clubhouses in all neighborhoods around the country, offering these life advantages. That's how and why our Clubhouses will proliferate around the country and then around the world.

Now, I have seen in some of the A-Teams something that is preventing your success. Some A-Teams are using the Forces of Nature too much. You need to understand the value of how to use the Forces of Nature and be careful not to overdo them. You are the human touch, human interaction part of our Neothink® product. The Forces of Nature are more important in a cold sale, a cold contact which is what I have to deal with in reaching people through the mail. It sometimes will hit people the wrong way and create negative responses. But when you have the warm, human touch as you do in your marketing, you can concentrate more on the Forces of Neothink® in helping them become that person they were meant to be.

Again, let me throw out that concept I threw out earlier that Ace up the Sleeve concept of "smart". That concept works both the Forces of Nature and the Forces of Neothink®. If the recruit is single, smart tugs the Forces of Nature that leads to finding a mate or attracting the opposite sex. But if they're happily married, "smart" is going to tug on that Forces of Neothink®. "Maybe I can become that person I always dreamed of" thinks this person. And that's a deep-rooted force because right now they're saying "I'm an average Joe stuck in a routine rut. What more can I do? My hands are tied." You know, with the division of labor business structure in the anticivilization, the mind, the whole essence of man, has been cut out of 99 percent of jobs. People are trapped. So when they hear "smart", if I can become smarter, that touches the child of the past.

Now, as promised, I'm going to answer some of your important questions. There's no particular order to these:

Q: Should there be a hierarchical structure that governs the actions of local A-Teams? Or is it possible that a hierarchal structure could denigrate the amount of control and influence that Mark Hamilton personally has in the movement and allow mysticism to enter the process? If there is to be a hierarchal structure due to the need for the Twelve Visions Party to remain separate from the SOS will it be permissible for an official in the Twelve Visions Party, state level party, to act in an official capacity within the Society of Secrets state chapters.

MH: I want to thank you for this excellent question. This is so important to help remove ambiguity and bring clarity to the A-Teams. I recommend within the A-Teams having a contract that will create the control needed now. I think there's a beauty in working together as self-leaders with a certain controlling element. It's almost like your own little constitution. It's like in Thomas Paine's' "Common Sense", you're a microcosm, a little society, a small C of U out there. You are great self-leaders and searchers working together and you have this contract in case certain innocent or guilty conflicts arise. You all agree to it, sign it and off you go.

Natural hierarchies will occur and I want this to be clear. And this brings us back to an area where some readers of the Neothink® materials get confused. There would be leaders in a super society. They would be business leaders. They're legitimate leaders that are encouraging and helping others become self-leaders because they benefit everyone. Legitimate leaders, not leaders who subordinate you and specialize your job. There will naturally be legitimate leaders helping others become self-leaders.

There will be natural hierarchy occurring within you're A-Teams and that should be allowed. For example, you'll have certain people who are just excellent speakers. Let them take leadership roles in the Introduction Meetings. There will be others that are excellent teachers. Let them take leadership roles in helping others learn in the Workshops. There'll be excellent business people. Let them handle and take leadership roles in handling certain business dynamics. It's a win/win for everybody. Such hierarchies help you learn from each other just as you're learning from me. I'm in a leadership, a mentorship, a teacher-like role with you.

Forbidden Revelation

What about the control and influence of Mark Hamilton? Let me give you an example of where and how my control and influence is so important:

I sent an email to the Ohio Twelve Visions Party a couple of weeks ago expressing how the real force and power internally in the Twelve Visions Party is going to come from the removal of man from everything; the removal of man from dictating the law, from interpreting the law. We have these great educated federal judges and Supreme Court Justices who are highly regarded, revered, and educated in the law. But they're now turning proactive, violating their role in interpreting the law. It's just all going down the tubes. And, the reason why is we've allowed man to interpret the law. We've allowed man to dictate the law. We realize and understand the removal of man from the decision making process by having that Prime Law in place.

That is the reason it's so important for me to have control of the Twelve Visions Party. What is happening with Supreme Court Judges is going to happen here. It will happen, innocently at first, but it will grow like a cancer for the nature of man will enter the picture. When I say man, of course, I'm speaking men and women alike. Man will enter the picture and will, for whatever reason, start injecting his own ideas, the way things should be, his own egos, desires. It's unavoidable, it's human nature. We are all creatures of the anticivilization and that will simply destroy everything that we're trying to do here. I know exactly what to do and how to do it.

Yes, I'm a man but the reason Mark Hamilton right now is the legitimate influencing factor is my whole interest is beyond anything, any political piece, beyond everything. Very few people alive today outside of myself really understand my position. That's not to put anyone down or to question anyone's devotion to the goal.

The Prime Law removes Mark Hamilton, removes everything, removes all man from the dictating and interpreting process of law. We will get into that next meeting when we launch the TVP. So, yes, we're a society and man must proceed but we must remove man from the interpreting and dictating of the law and the Prime Law will do that.

Now, the next question is more of a statement from an apprentice that I want you to pay close attention to.

Q: Although our format is MLM let's consider it to be multi-level mentoring of an entirely new paradigm in the advancement of human consciousness. It will require commitment of time and energy before initiating to absorb the material and quite frankly, we don't want anyone who is not committed to advancing this new paradigm to be able to influence anyone into the Society of Secrets. We are selling a new way of life and a new way of thinking. We are offering the opportunity for an individual to achieve optimum health, romantic love, superior intelligence, carefree security, stimulating career and abundant wealth.

MH: What a wonderful email and perfect reflection of what we are formatting here. And this statement brings out his understanding of Forces of Nature and the Forces of Neothink®.

Q: I'm glad to know that you will be touching on the subject of relationships in the Level Six meeting. My husband and I are not on the same page. I want to share with him my inner feelings and I did that at the beginning of our marriage but he is a distrusting person. He has used things I had told him against me. The subject of relationships is so important yet it's not taught anywhere so we have to learn by trial and error and this cost is too much time and pain.

MH: Very good point. Now because of the importance of this launch, I put topics on hold this month to keep focus on the launch but I did mention I would bring up relationships so let me take a moment here just to say something and I might, a little bit later on, say one other thing about relationships. I received a few emails and I saw quite a few posts on the discussion boards that my apprentices have a great outlet here in the Clubhouses to meet friends and their spouses are giving them a hard time about it or think they're joining a cult. Their relationships have suffered or been destroyed and in some cases the apprentices have come to me saying, "Unfortunately I'm thinking I have to leave my spouse." I said to these apprentices, try and see this from your spouse's eyes. Realize much of the aggravation with them toward Neothink® stems from insecurity. Basically, they're afraid of losing you to another love of some kind and that's why they resort to calling us a cult. It's irrationality from a jealous person, saying certain things, upsetting you, becoming upset displaying immature behavior. But always look deeper at situations. When you look deeper, a lot of times that's just because they're insecure and you must also look, always look deeply at anything you value.

Realize, too, that when you first married your spouse there was something very deep there that was coming from your right brain. There are many things that your right brain knows that your left brain does not know and those things are still there. So, your left brain may see reasons or problems when in fact the right brain still knows you are still very much in love. There could be something very deep and powerful worth salvaging and sometimes your actions must be the opposite of what your feelings are telling you or what your left brain, what your thoughts are telling you.

Instead of shutting out your irrational, immature spouse who is name-calling and saying things that are just not true, try doing just the opposite. Show love, give them a sense of security and tell them certain things like you're still deeply in love with them. You may be quite surprised to find the relationship is closer than it's ever been because now there's security and in more than one instance the spouse is now part of the Society of Secrets and they're closer and more in love than ever.

So keep that in mind. Sometimes we overlook that.

Again, the tendency is to draw away from a spouse who is distrustful and fighting your sudden and growing involvement in the SOS. Sometimes you don't want to draw away; sometimes it's just the opposite. You want to try to get close, try to feed them with security.

Q: Hello Mr. Hamilton. I was 27 years old in 1988 when I was fortunate enough to receive my first marketing package from you back in those days offering the Neo-Tech Discovery. For that life-altering experience, I am eternally grateful to you and your family.

I went on to purchase almost every product you offered me including the Grand Event, the Neo-Tech Protection Kit, the Consultation Packages, the Guns and Fists Newsletter, the Neo-Tech Guide Book, Cosmic Business Control, the Neo-Tech World, The Story and just recently the Neothink® Heirlooms. In addition, a friend purchased for me, a near mint conditions, used copy of Psychuous Sex back in the early 1990's

I've never been so completely satisfied with any purchase in my entire life. Unfortunately, I still harbor many personal mysticisms that have limited me. I've done relatively well though considering I was a box-boy when I first purchased the Neo-Tech Discovery. At the time, I was going nowhere, I was a loser. I now maintain a 100K career with AT&T Mobility and President and CEO of a retail store created by my wife and I and I have two beautiful half Japanese children, run several times a week for my health and love my life.

Neothink® and your family have been the source for these successes. My Neothink® emotions and integrations run deep within me. I failed however by only tapping into 1 percent or less of this extraordinary power. But now is a new day. Finally the opportunity has arrived to market and sell the only product that I can't find any inconsistencies with. A product I'm 100 percent proud of.

Already my mind races ahead with ideas as I re-energize, re-integrate more and more Neothink® concepts, re-reading the Heirloom Packages, re-listening to the SOS meetings, the Grand Event and Consultation Packages.

For many years I've hoped for the opportunity to market and the most spectacular product I've even purchased in my 45 years of life. My Friday-Night Essence couldn't be more obvious. What could surpass this opportunity? What could be more important than this? That's why I'm writing you today. I share the desire to collapse mysticism before it's too late for everyone. I'm emotionally integrated with the collapse of mysticism especially when I consider my children's future.

I recently attended the Washington State A-Team meeting. Washington State is shaping up nicely, although some members are a little bit confused about Neothink® concepts but they are very nice, sincere people. I tell you, I'm re-energized now just as much as I was in 1988. There's nothing I understand better, support more or wish to succeed than the world-wide collapse of mysticism. I'm here Mark, ready to seize this opportunity.

I'm editing my story and experience with Neothink® for our Introductory Clubhouse Meetings and I'm eager for it to get underway. By participating in the meetings, Workshops and Clubhouse, I'm reborn, so-to-speak after meeting other Neothink® members for the first time in my 20 years.

I'm looking forward to building the Neothink® Network Marketing Opportunity. My long-term experience with The

Neothink® Society has prepared me well. I have many skill sets such as CEO of a small corporation, presenting to large groups, sales, direct mail marketing experience, data base knowledge that I can leverage.

I'm power thinking and putting in place world capture for the Neothink® Network Marketing Opportunity including India and Japan. Leveraging my wife's knowledge of Neothink® and her knowledge of Japanese culture the opportunities to build the Neothink® Network Marketing Opportunity in Japan couldn't be stronger.

I've come up with a Ten-Second Miracle for reaching potential customers in India via Virtual Assistance. Indian citizens available over the Internet that will work, inexpensively as an assistant, so on and so forth. For marketing in the U.S., I will use the professional tools learned as a Neothink® practitioner since 1998.

My unique 20-year story will draw and fill my down-line one by one. Of course, I'm considering mass marketing approaches as well. My plan includes both horizontal and vertical growth of the Neothink® Network Marketing Opportunity by leveraging resources, integrating the values and the numbers, so on and so forth. Ready to start, looking forward to mysticism collapse and creating the C of U.

I look forward to the day when you attend a Washington State Meeting and shake your hand.

MH: That's great. Here we are two decades later and we're ready to actualize everything that was idealized, everything that you've read in our Neothink® literature. We're ready to set off the tipping point.

I will only read one sentence because it gets into too much detail about a particular negative situation. The first sentence reads, "Mark, we are in a negative way with one of the members on our A-Team." Now let me read an email that I got from this person five days later. By the way, that was the first sentence of their long, that person's long email.

Now I'm going to read in this email that came in 5 days later the very last sentence of a long email.

"I just want to let you know we have resolved this problem and we have all decided to help him along as long as it does not take away from the group as a whole."

MH: Hear that! They're going to help him as long as it does not take away from the group as a whole and that can be the basis of your contract that I brought out earlier, the contract I think each A-Team should establish for themselves, their Constitution. I'm just so happy to read something like that. In this little civilization we've set up you'll be surprised how well you will work through differences as I have in this business, worked through with some very important, very high-level Neothink® advisors, Neothink® practitioners, advanced Neothink® people where we've had very strong disagreements. We worked through them and in the end we evolve into something much stronger.

I have another email here that I will not read because it's much too personal. The essence of it has to do with self-love and one's lack of it.

Now let me say that certain religions, certain and perhaps most religions really work against self-love. That's important for subjugating the people and removing self-esteem and self-love. To people who have been heavily involved in religion, often times they have a lack of self-love and a lack of self-esteem. Not everybody, not in all cases.

Let me also say that self-love is not always so apparent but it does not mean it's not there. Now again, this is something earlier I mentioned about relationships, there's that right brain influences. Your right brain is just an amazing, amazing thing and in the day-to-day stresses and strains there are certain

229

habits we get into and certain things that just sort of obscure the artistic beauty in our relationships with everyone; with our children, our parents, our siblings or our spouses, and, particularly with ourselves. Just because you don't see the self-love, or it's not obvious to you, doesn't mean it's not there. Sometimes it's just a matter of tapping that and by the person's letter I feel very strong self-esteem, self-love. It just needs to be tapped and touched and reached, that's all. It's the child of the past, you are tapping these yearnings and longings and sense of something missing, a sense of lacking. With what we are doing, those yearnings will be fulfilled. Things will change.

That's it for this Level Six Meeting. You have the tools to move forward. You have a good overview of what we're doing, the asset, the well-oiled machine, how it's going to work. We have one of the best programs ever developed, not to mention the best material, the best product, in the history of mankind.

I'm very proud and excited about having people like you, my apprentices, on this team. You are my soul mates. We can really bring about the C of U on Earth. We are going to accomplish the tipping point to actualize everything you read about for the past 20 years.

Next month, I look forward to launching the amazing Twelve Visions Party and showing you how we're going to tie it into the Neothink® Network Marketing Program and have something very valuable and very powerful that could sweep the nation. The inner-workings of the Twelve Visions Party focuses on removing man from the equation with all of his corruptions and mysticisms. That's going to be the key, internal workings.

Now, externally the face to the world is stimulation; making the people wealthy, all the people wealthy including the poor. This is not just some slogan. We have the only political party in history that when you actually delve into it from an economic formula and scrutinize it, you see that is true.

The TVP is the only program that can make the poor rich, in the history of mankind. And what's so mind boggling about this is those that hate us have to love us because we're saying the same thing. They're going to study this and see that this formula for making the poor rich is real. And you will start loving those people who are poor because you see that you are offering them a second chance at a fulfilling life. You are offering them something beautiful and wonderful to bring back their child of the past.

So you will find you will develop this emotional love for people. You won't be able to help it after awhile. But your love will be real and your program to help them is real. It won't be this toll booth compassion, using an expression out of Neo-Tech, that is expressed by the Clintons or Bush or the whole political establishment supporting the state or religion...that toll booth compassion just leads to subjugating people and suppressing society.

Your face to the world is this powerful, unprecedented approach to make all people wealthy, healthy and safe, including the poor and underprivileged. The TVP is the only thing out there that could ever bring this about.

You've read the National Platform, which as you recall, I am turning into stimulating pamphlets that you're going to receive. In there you see the Twelve Visions Party is not hype or rhetoric or a gimmick. You're going to feel this with every ounce of your body. The TVP is what can sweep the nation, my friends. Next month we launch the Twelve Visions Party.

Secret Teachings to My Exclusive Inner Circle

Level-Seven Essence Meeting
Introduction

Welcome to historic Level-Seven Essence Meeting.

Today's meeting is going to transcend everything you have learned to date about Neothink® and about our actualization of what we idealized in the 20th Century, what we plan to actualize now in the 21st Century.

This meeting will be mind-opening. It will be a historic moment as you see how we will now trump the anticivilization, we will trump the twin pillars of the anticivilization; those being religion particularly organized religion and politics.

Today the final puzzle pieces will come into place for you. You'll see exactly how we will actualize the C of U here on Earth.

In Part One of this meeting I will discuss creative cycle in business and what that means to you and your A-Team.

In Part Two I of this meeting I will discuss trumping religion and in Part Three I will discuss trumping politics. And, finally, in Part Four, I answer your big questions.

It's going to be an exciting meeting that will to give you insights you have not seen before, and it's going to reach me at a more personal level where we've been before.

Level-Seven Essence Meeting
Part One

Hello and welcome to Part One of the Level-Seven Essence Meeting.

First I want to talk a bit about something called the Creative Cycle.

Business, to grow and advance the great boundaries, business goes through creative cycles. Let's think back to Henry Ford when he started his creative cycle on developing what eventually became the assembly line.

Well he started in his shop by attaching the carriage to horses that would pull the carriage along, stop at a station while the men did their part. Then the horses would move on to the next station, stop while the men would do their part, so on and so forth. Later, Henry Ford developed pulleys to make things more effective and then again later, Henry Ford developed methods using gravity to start what became the assembly line up high and work its way down with the use of gravity, stopping at the stations along the way to let the men do their work.

The movement to bring Neothink® public is a business and as such we are in a creative cycle. When a puzzle piece does not fit or is not right then we must continue to work to find the puzzle piece that does fit and is right to move this puzzle picture forward. That's what we must do.

When you understand the creative cycle in business, you understand that we must always look for the signs that direct us to make changes and improvements. This is what ultimately creates a solid business model that will not die out because of its own bloated weight. When you understand the creative cycle that is natural in starting and growing a business, the opposite happens; you get creative and power think, we do integrated thinking, we Neothink® and continually increase and enhance our value and therefore increase and enhance our profit.

Now some words of wisdom about profits. From day one my whole concern has always been the goal, the value. I never concerned myself with the money. People who know me know this. They'll see me turn down a lot of money, much more money than I would make on my own path. I've turned down big money over the decades because I had the single goal in mind to achieve, a goal that requires a relentless focus on what the superpuzzle is and how to create the pieces. I perfected and increased the value, the pieces, starting with idealizing this small group of writers, Frank R. Wallace, myself, Eric Savage and a very small handful of others who we've worked with like Tracy Alexander, who has a piece in the First Heirloom.

We idealized the Twelve Visions World in the 20th Century. Now that we're in the 21st Century and some of you old timers remember my piece, "Will America Go Neo-Tech" subtitled "Get Rich After 2001". In other words, back in the 80's in the mid-80's, I envisioned this Twelve Visions World in the 21st Century. Now here we are in the 21st Century and we are actualizing what we idealized.

What I learned is, don't overly focus on the money. I remember over 20 years ago conducting essence meetings with my executive team. In these meetings I taught my team the danger and the harm of what I called money madness. Let's avoid money madness now. Let's really focus on the superpuzzle because in the end my friends, focusing on this superpuzzle is going to make you, I'm not going to say wealthy here, but I'm going to say it's going to make you more money than if you were overly focused on how to make money right now. First build your business.

The old timers know what I'm talking about when I refer to the 99% principle of marketing. Most marketers will say, "How can I sell to that 1%? How do I intrigue that 1% to buy from me and all their focus is on that 1%." My focus at The Neothink® Society has always been, yes, to sell the 1% but also to leave the other 99% with a residual, to have them walk away with a value that's in their mind because somewhere down the road they will come back. As a matter of fact, going back to the greatest marketing campaign in history to Christianity, where they talked about the residual that was left in those who they encountered. The 99% Principle is a Neothink® marketing concept that has guided us from day one because the focus here is on the goal, is on the value.

So we keep pushing and pushing and pushing on the value…and the money came. I want you to do the same. Push, push and push the value. You now have your business and we have the Neothink® System, the business model with the ultimate division of essence here in The Neothink® Society. Concentrate on the value. Stay focused on the value because the value is real. As I said, the money will eventually come and the potential here is huge because this is a movement that is unprecedented. We will reach a tipping point and we will change the world. And you are at the very beginning of this public movement.

I've studied creativity cycles throughout history and every creativity cycle was met with chaos, then control, then chaos and then control. I went through this myself developing the Neothink System and I developed that when I was out of the country, the speed at which the company evolved was breathtaking. But I met resistance and cancer seeds because people like a bicameral setting where they are led and become comfortable in set routines. That doesn't happen in a creativity cycle. There will be change. You must be ready for it.

The creative cycle is a change that will in the end improve the business but will create momentary chaos. From the chaos, you regain control. Why is there chaos? I'm going to use a metaphor to illustrate what I mean. When you sit down to put together a puzzle, you start out with chaos, pieces are scattered all over the floor and you begin to put them together. The same occurs with your Neothink® puzzle. At first it's chaotic, this piece won't work here and that piece won't work there. But eventually as you begin to snap together pieces, a wonderful wave of control begins to move in.

Let me give you another example:

Throughout the years, back in the tough embattled days of the 80's and 90's we had a lot of fights with authorities and some heavy-duty authorities. Frank R. Wallace actually spent time in a prison because of his unwavering principles and for resisting the very dishonest. From those battles, from that chaos, Frank R. Wallace created a series of literary masterpieces; the Guns-and-Fists Newsletters, The Protection Kit that caused a great debate in the Senate that resulted in congressional hearings. We created a major change in this country that led to a freer structure in this country were it not for those battles, that chaos, that we went through. Someday the inside story will be told. There's chaos, and then there's control, and there's chaos and control.

Another example: One apprentice pointed out cancer seeds while another extolled his love for promoting the supreme value in the universe, consciousness. It was a beautiful debate in which two honest apprentices, coming from two different perspectives, sorted out something very important. It was a wonderful debate that came to an honest, valuable conclusion; that we must be aware of those who are dishonestly outright attacking versus those who are frustrated and just simply need more attention and mentorship. I thank both apprentices for that.

I even saw some web posts accusing Mark Hamilton of poor planning and even dishonesty. Again, that comes from not understanding the concept of the creative cycles in business. And, I'll just tell you right now, history will show a completely different perspective than those misguided feelings. History is going to see a program and a plan, one of genius. And I include all of you when I say genius, not just me. This is a plan, a puzzle of genius that is going to change the world. It's unprecedented and there's nothing else out there like it. As good as the Libertarians might be or Ron Paul, there's nothing out there, as you will see when we get into the political section, that can really effectively change the world.

Before his death, Frank R. Wallace talked about how it really comes down to what we are doing in creating this Neothink® puzzle. He said that achieving the superpuzzle comes down to two pieces of literature; Pax Neo-Tech and what was titled then The First Immortals which later evolved into The Miss Annabelle's Story and the SOS Superpuzzle. Those two pieces came to us not out of the anticivilization but out of the C of U...from a non-fiction standpoint, Pax Neo-Tech, from a faction standpoint The First Immortals or The Miss Annabelle's Story, SOS Superpuzzle. And actualizing what we idealized, actualizing with your help is pure genius. It's Neothink® and that is how history will view this and I want each of you to feel confidence and to feel proud of your role in this rare movement.

So, today there are about 300 of you who are going to handle this initial launch nation-wide. Those numbers will expand as we rapidly expand this program. But as it stands now, I'm going to be marching into the anticivilization to actualize the Twelve Vision World with my "300". My "300" are the strong ones who realize that money's not first but the value is first, the goal is first.

I'm a wealthy man today but many of you don't know that I was once just absolutely dirt poor. But this goal was something that just took me over. All my focus and energy on that goal and its potential became everything to me. I immersed myself in it and as a result I'm a wealthy man today but not because wealth was my goal or my objective. I've turned down mega money over the course of my history, mega sellers, best sellers and opportunities and mergers. I turned them all down because I won't be side-tracked or distracted from this goal. The money will take care of itself. I've always told people in the long Neothink® will be, you will be, much bigger and much more wealthy, by just stubbornly focusing and staying on the goal and providing the value.

My deep inner drive is what you read in the Miss Annabelle's Story. That's my blue print, my superpuzzle. The Trilogy, the SOS Superpuzzle is what we are going to actualize here on planet Earth. This is a once in the history opportunity. There will never be another opportunity like this, ever. You have a chance and you have a choice to be part of this history.

In Part Two of this meeting, I'm going to present you with a bit of a surprise. I'm going to show you how we will trump organized religion.

Level-Seven Essence Meeting
Part Two A

In Part Two A of this Level-Seven Essence Meeting I will discuss how we will trump religion. In your second Heirloom Package, the Second Insight says God-Man is God. Of course, all of you read this and I'm going to walk through some portions of this with you right now. Here's how we are going to trump organized religion:

The Second Insight, God-Man is God, starts off talking about how the conception of God came about to begin with. You have bicameral man living like all animals, in the here and now. And because man was bicameral the epic poems passed down through the ages were written like a newspaper reporting the news. The two most well-known of these epics are Gilgamesh which was written before 2000 B.C. (completely bicameral times) and the Homeric epic The Iliad. In these epics, there was no past, there's no future and there's now introspection.

But the books of the Bible were different. They introduced the past, the future and the inner self to humanity. Those books were written over an 1100 year span from about 1000 B.C. to about 100 A.D. And in that span of time, we see the transition from bicameral man into fully conscious man, which we see with Jesus and the New Testament.

The books, the Hebrew Bible, the Old Testament, were written about the 10th Century B.C. through about the 6th Century B.C. during completely bicameral times. However, they were very different from other writings during that time. There's thousands of other writings at the time and different epics at the time, stories of warriors and kings. But only ones that survived for four thousand years were stories starting with Abraham in 1850 B.C., almost 4000 years ago. The only surviving stories are those found in the Bible. Why is that?

Well, as you know, in the Second Insight, I demonstrate that when you understand human consciousness versus the bicameral mentality, you come to the breathtaking realization that all the stories that became Holy Scripture were of bicameral man having breakthroughs, moments or glimpses of human consciousness. We can see that transition, the different stages, through the stories of the Bible; bicameral man breaking through into human consciousness. In Insight Two I reveal how the Bible, prior to the stories in the Bible, particularly starting back in the Old Testament, man was meaningless. He was just a pawn to the Gods and his world meant nothing. The world of Gods was real but the world of man meant nothing, it wasn't real. He was just there for the fancy and whims of the immature Gods. (Similarly today with our government structure, we are pawns and here for fancy and whims of our government leaders.) The Bible, in the Old Testament, was the first literature ever that brought importance to man, "the chosen ones." Suddenly, man's world became real through the Bible.

Thomas Cahill writes in his wonderful book, "The Gift of the Jews", how the Bible brought about, for the first time, a sense of importance, a major shift in the mentality. Cahill didn't understand the difference between bicameral and consciousness, but that's what he's getting at. His book is a wonderful read by the way, "The Gift of the Jews", Thomas Cahill.

But we see in his wonderful book the power of this new breakthrough in mentality, starting with man being the chosen one; man's importance in this world. And we see the true nature of the Bible. History becomes suddenly important; where we came from and when that became important to man. Then man where is headed becomes important; man's the future becomes important to him.

And then we have the stunning breakthrough in literature with Ten Commandments. Now, for the first time, man was being presented with a choice. Remember, bicameral man never had choices. The choices were all in the world of the Gods, hallucinated Gods as man "heard" the higher Gods. Man was an automaton who would just follow the Gods and the whims and the voices, the directions of the oracles and the Pharos, those in the upper hierarchy. He would follow his Ka under stressful situations. That was the "voice" he heard in his head. There was never, ever, prior to the Ten Commandments, a situation where you literally had a choice. Choice was associated with consequence which suddenly gave man a sense of control. Control over what? Control over his future. A stunning breakthrough in the human mentality is demonstrated in the Bible, and only in the Bible and no other literature of its time.

Let's quickly walk through some of the stories in the Bible:

We have Abraham, who left his comfortable surroundings in Haran and went into the desert and had his confrontation with God. Now this is an amazing breakthrough in mentality. Up until now, man was a polytheist believing in many different Gods. Abraham not only reduced down to monotheism, but actually had such a strong sense of individuality that he had a conversation with this God. This is a major step. You need a strong sense of yourself, an individuality, to make the leap into human consciousness. So we have in the story of Abraham the first leanings toward the conscious mentality.

Another point about Abraham: Abraham was this lowly desert nomad when he went on his journey. Yet he deceived the most powerful man, who was considered a God-King, the Pharaoh. Yet Abraham deceived him. He deceived him; it would be certain death if the Pharaoh knew that Sarah was Abraham's wife. So Abraham deceived the Pharaoh by telling him that Sarah was his sister. Bicameral man cannot deceive, cannot create deception, that's a conscious act. So, here you have Abraham, showing two very strong breakthroughs toward conscious mentality. That story is in the Bible.

Each and every one of the stories in the Bible shows a breakthrough to the conscious structure of our mind, the mental structure of consciousness. For instance, "Why were the Hebrews the dusty ones? Hebrew means "the dusty ones from the desert." Why were they the chosen ones? In the Second Insight I explain that for the breakthrough into human consciousness from bicameral man, two ingredients are needed. One was the metaphor that uses something to describe something else. The other ingredient was the event which allowed the mental structure for man to, for the first time, step back into an inner mind space and view subjectively the world around him and his place in it. It gave man that other dimension, the ability to form thoughts, introspect and to think subjectively.

But what sent man into developing this metaphor? What created that new way of thinking? Essentially, what allowed man to become a decision maker, one with God, to become a God-Man at that ancient time? Well, he couldn't do it from comfortable surroundings, in the luxurious and well-provided environment such as the thriving civilization of Sumer, Egypt and Babylon. The Jews, however, faced tough survival pressures. Every story in the Bible is about tough survival pressures from Abraham leaving the comforts and going out into the desert leaving the comforts of Haran, to Moses and the Exodus, taking the Jewish slaves out of Egypt into the Sinai Desert living in those harsh conditions at the foot of Mount Sinai for 40 years...or when the Jews were deported to Babylon as slaves during the exile in the 6th Century B.C. The struggle for survival, for physical survival is the second ingredient needed that forced the mental structure of bicameral man to such an extent that his way of thinking changed from the bicameral mentality into the conscious mentality.

Metaphors and the pressure of survival are those two ingredients that created the new mental structure known as human consciousness. And it was the Jews who broke through. The gift of the Jews was the breakthrough into human consciousness having those two ingredients throughout their history.

Then, we have the spectacular story about King David where we see the breakthrough into human consciousness. The use of word "I" meaning "I, my inner self" occurred in the Psalms of the Hebrew Bible. And David is known to have sung some of the Psalms using the word "I" meaning that inner mind space. We would not see that in any other literature for another 400 years.

Then there are the prophets in the Bible who warned of major coming catastrophes for the Jews. When you understand how bicameral oracles and prophets worked, you understand why they were quite accurate. Using the right brain, data collection, the almost computer-like processing of that data, under stress, a prophecy was created that were often quite accurate. The prophets predicted the exile of the Jew, and they were absolutely right. The Jews ended up right back to where they started 700 years before. The elite Jews, the very prosperous Jews, were back as captive slaves. Those severe survival pressures forced them to look back and reflect upon what the prophets had warned. They began to look back at themselves and the choices they had made, the consequences they were now paying for such choices. It was those survival pressures that caused that inward look at themselves, the journey within, the spiritual journey within, which again reflects the mental structure of consciousness. The writings of the Bible were unlike anything ever before. There's no counterpart in any literature of this time...the journey of the spirit.

Then we move forward, issues like justice and judging, and trying to understand things such as why must the good man suffer? These forms of justice, these thoughts are conscious thoughts. Bicameral man cannot think in those terms. You see in the Old Testament an attempt being made at answering why the good man must suffer. It's not really answered until the New Testament of Jesus. That is reflecting a conscious man dealing with issues of justice, judgment, suffering, why, honesty. These are fully conscious integrations that came about in the New Testament with Jesus.

Jesus, as you know, confounded his followers and his leaders because Jesus was a true self-leader. Much of what Jesus taught and said was left with puzzled looks and confusion. But Jesus was putting together a puzzle, a superpuzzle that others didn't see including Paul. Paul was a very innocent, good man who misinterpreted Jesus.

Jesus' integrations as to why the good man must suffer is something that both Dr. Wallace and I observed and understood as being on the edge of yet another leap of mentality, into Neothink®. Jesus was on the edge of bringing consciousness to the bicameral peasants. He was on the edge of the first leap of human mentality, now on the edge of the second and final leap of human mentality, from mysticism plagued consciousness into mysticism free consciousness which is from consciousness into Neothink®.

Dr. Wallace and I completely understood why the good man must suffer. In other words, we observed over the years that the more man is invested, the more materially successful man is, the more he will recoil from this coming leap. They're set in their comfort zones; things are working for them in the anticivilization so why change?

On the other hand, the less invested, those materially suffering the more naturally they can accept, grasp, and desire the new mentality, especially the more survival pressures they're under.

Do you see so many of the apprentices, "the down trodden", the financially suffering are beginning to see why you are the chosen ones? I needed for you to have this other ingredient, this survival pressure. Those of you who are not so materially ensconced in a comfort zone in the anticivilization, who are willing and able and feel the pressures to make this leap; the downtrodden, those who Jesus loved and supported and wanted to see change for and knew needed the change. But those educated elite who were suppressing, similar to today, the educated elite, the leaders, the political leaders, the judicial leaders, the establishment leaders who suppress the downtrodden, suppress society, are doing so because they don't want to change. They're going to fight Neothink®; I dealt with an authority this past month, a potential threat to our movement, no threat to you and to the movement itself, to Neothink®. They are trying to wipe Neothink® from planet Earth. But they aren't going to do what they did during the 80's and 90's. However, today's another ballgame.

So the downtrodden, the suffering, those with survival pressures, those are the chosen ones. You are the chosen ones. And with your digestion of the three Heirlooms combined with everything that's going on in your life, with certain survival pressures, intermingling with those who are not suffering and with those who have been with Neothink® for a long, long time, who will help guide things along when needed. I see certain old timers I call them, come along and help guide others with their deeper insights. This is a chosen balance to keep this superpuzzle growing.

So Jesus answered that question with a full conscious mind. He was bringing this kingdom of God, this fully conscious

Man-God, this God-Man, to his beloved bicameral peasants around the countryside, who were suppressed and taken advantage of by the conscious, educated elite. That was the light of Jesus.

So from Abraham, to Moses, to David, to the Prophets, to Jesus, the Canon of the Bible brought together the accounts of man's fascinating leap from the bicameral kingdoms ruled by the imagined Gods, into only Kingdom of God ruled by one's own consciousness. In the proper context, the Bible was a working document. It was the light of day for making the leap.

Now, with the aid of Plato, the church turned from a journey into human consciousness to a journey into mysticism. And for 1600 years the Bible has been viewed from the illusionary context of man serving his supernatural being in order to gain this organized religion, to gain this political structure over the suppressed, the downtrodden. Much like the Pharisees did with the Torah, the church now controls its people in the name of God.

Through Plato's definitive philosophy combined with St. Augustine's prolific literary genius, they created a mutant bicameral mental structure and irrevocably tied that to the Judeo-Christian religion, specifically to Jesus Christ and the Bible; a completely inverted, upside down interpretation.

Jesus Christ was the very man who was leading the bicameral peasants out of that bicameral mentality and into human consciousness. Suddenly, the Bible takes away all of man's importance and puts it back out there in this context of the organized religion, with the ordained priests and the leaders of the church basically taking control again, just as the educated elite monopolized literature during the Dark Ages to gain control of man, just as he was coming upon a great power, as he was becoming the God-Man of that ancient time through his evolution into consciousness.

The Plato, St. Augustine combination separated Jesus' God-Man into God and Man or God over man, right back to the bicameral perception in value structure. The church now uses the great power of the Bible out of context as a self- serving political tool to rule over man in the name of the Almighty God above man. All meaning in value now lay with God and the church. Man is once again the pawn, the powerless. The Bible, once the most valuable document ever written, is turned into the most destructive document ever written. Instead of freeing the bicameral peasants, the church enslaved them for 1000 years. Jesus, who gave his life for his love of the struggling peasants, would have been eternally heartbroken upon learning this. And at that time, his enemy won the war of two worlds.

Now my writings and Dr. Wallace's writings give us a cosmology that Jesus would have strived toward had he not been murdered just 3 years after his ministry began. Neo-Tech/Neothink® writings complete our final evolution into God-Man which is the message that Jesus himself wanted you to know. And Insight Two does justice to Jesus and humanity which has been robbed for 2000 years.

Note that during his years as a peasant, Jesus witnessed the dishonesty and hatred toward human life, especially toward the working class as displayed by those educated elite, specifically, the conscious Pharisees, the scribes and Hebrew leaders. Perhaps without actually explicitly understanding this Jesus at least implicitly understood that the elite's consciousness was flawed with dishonesty. In Insight Two I show how Jesus actually through his ministry of pure love was trying to promote Neo-Tech back in those days. Jesus was trying to bring honesty, the missing ingredient, into human consciousness. It attempted to enter through Aristotle, through the educated elite, but was lost. Why? Because it was easier for the educated elite, with their ability and advantages over the masses through this consciousness, to dishonestly suppress, subvert and live off the bicameral peasants. Jesus picked up on this dishonesty and, through a ministry of pure love requiring the act of honesty, was introducing that missing ingredient to conscious man. To come into the Kingdom of God, man needed to be honest. One needed to be good at heart. Very interesting; Jesus was bringing honesty and bringing the early beginnings of Neo-Tech to civilization.

The dogmatists would claim, of course, that they're the ones who serve, preserve and protect the morals. The Pharisees were the dogmatists and they decried that Jesus was the one attacking the principles and morals of the Hebrew Bible. But Jesus understood with the change in mentality from bicameral to consciousness that no, he was actually the one who was protecting the morals and principles. But context had changed with that major leap from the bicameral to the conscious structure. He lambasted the Hebrew elders for their teachings, which created great havoc and the authorities chased Jesus and eventually, of course, was crucified.

But Jesus basically knew that as man evolved beyond his external world mentality, he must evolve beyond the external world laws of the Torah and the dogmatists. And the religious dogmatists demanded the same literal application of the Torah. They were merely creating a power structure from which they could dishonestly place themselves as the authority and live in a comfortable world under those harsh conditions and suppress the bicameral peasant. That's what Jesus was so heroically out to change. He was changing external authority that ruled others into the internal authority of self-leadership, the kingdom within. There are many lessons throughout the Bible of Jesus' battles with the Hebrew elders.

Dogmatists have destroyed great idea systems all throughout history. They destroyed Jesus and his idea system. They destroyed the beautiful, benevolent working document that the Bible truly is, in proper context. They destroyed Aristotle during the Dark Ages and they are now destroying Ayn Rand. The dogmatists are basically Neocheaters who are setting themselves up as authorities to become the rulers and suppress the followers.

How did Christianity, originally one of the many competing sects within Judaism, take hold and become the largest religion on Earth? Consider Jesus' teaching becoming combined with the Hebrew Bible to form the Canon of the Christian Bible. As obvious as that seems today, at the time of Christ, the odds would be highly against Christianity even surviving the period, no less joining together with the Hebrew Bible that the Hebrew elders, the authorities so despised. It just didn't make any sense.

Yet Jesus' teaching, even throughout all the accusations of his ministry and his teachings being blasphemous, even to being ostracized from the Synagogues, were destined to become part of the Canon and Christianity was spread over the world.

Why is that? Why Jesus' teachings were destined to permanently join with the Hebrew Bible is based on evolution, evolution of consciousness. We must understand that the Bible was not originally a religious document per se. It was certainly not in the context, the destructive, mystical context that it is today. The Old Testament was the recordings of evolution, of man's human evolvement into human consciousness. And Jesus' teaching represented that leap into the new mentality. Therefore his teachings were destined to become part of that historic document. The scribe of history would not and could not have it any other way.

So now, by understanding the historic context of this working document called the Bible, you can begin to see something fascinating and ironic. And that is how Neo-Tech itself, of all things, will become part of the Bible.

Now to put it all into context, Neothink® is the final evolution of human consciousness; the mysticism-free, human consciousness. The Neothink® mind is the final evolution and thus also belongs as part of this working document the evolution of human consciousness. Now this may seem enormously ironic and awkward. Incidentally, the driving force of all those Internet flames against Neo-Tech is a small group of religious fanatics who are attacking what we are doing out of fear. They go so far as to make it appear as though others are doing the attacking, but it's really them inflaming others. That group is the fanatically religious, close minded right dogmatists. These people who are responsible for the flames on Neo-Tech are equivalent, in a sense, to the Hebrew elders and the Pharisees and the Scribes who would attack and flame and inflame the people against Jesus. Jesus joining the Hebrew Bible, his ministry, it was incredibly ironic and awkward in its time, just as Neo-Tech is going to be here.

Are you getting a sense of something bigger than life occurring here, something historic and for the millennia? Are you sensing this? Are you picking this up? This is going to occur over the next year. So when you really understand the context of the Bible and its obligation to the Scribe of history, we'll see Neo-Tech has to become part of the Bible. There's no other choice.

Now it's true that Frank R. Wallace, in his writings, specifically attacks the Catholic Church and it was true, that Jesus attacked the Hebrew elders, the Pharisees and the Scribes. And it is true, that the religious right attacks Neo-Tech and it is true, that the religious authorities, in their time, attacked Jesus. Frank R. Wallace had to confront every issue directly, and therefore he completely confronted and attacked the Catholic Church. That particular attack on the Catholic Church and organized religion would shut too many people off in the early stages of bringing them into The Neothink®

Society. My writings don't do that. My works are coming from a different angle of actualizing and creating the application system. So, for example, in my works, the Twelve Visions, it doesn't matter what religion you are or not, that has nothing to do with politics and replacing the ruling class or removing the ruling class.

Jesus' teachings were the very last literature the Hebrew authority's 2000-years ago would have ever imagined would join with the Book of Moses. And Neo-Tech teachings are the very last literature the Christian authorities today would ever imagine, or allow, to join with the Holy Bible. But in both cases they're destined to join together.

Now I am currently working on a publication that brings together the Christian Bible with Neo-Tech. This might be one of those rare cases that I may release this directly into the main stream public such as in a trade publication, in a bookstore.

This product, the new Bible, will be so much more stimulating and rewarding. Think about this. Imagine love, pure love, not for a mystical Supreme Being or higher authority but rather pure love for the supreme value in the universe, conscious beings. The supreme value, this pure love for oneself and his fellow man, is occurring now in our Clubhouses and on our web site. It is a microcosm of the C of U.

Now you see by comparison the rhetoric love professed by organized religion is hypocritical and self-defeating. You eventually break through with anger as you realize that you selfishly sacrificed yourself for nothing. Instead now we leap beyond that hypocritical, self-destructive selflessness and love is directed toward something that is real and valuable and you can feel it. It is a mutual value exchange with others. It becomes so real, so exhilarating, and so euphoric. This product I am working on could be stunning and it could go like a wave across the country.

The unreal rhetoric, this unreal love, this false love, this fools love I talk about in the first insight, the conflicts and the contradiction and hypocrisy, all that fades in the face of what the SOS Bible will present to the world.

So we have this SOS Holy Bible that will come out, and let me tell you what that's going to do. It's going to kick off the Church of God-Man. Out of our growing and flourishing Society of Secrets, we will have two stunning events coming. We will have the Twelve Visions Party and we will have the Church of God-Man, driven forward by this SOS Bible. The stimulation and exhilaration of something so real, exciting and harmonious with conscious life will trump organized religion just as The Twelve Visions Party will trump politics and government.

When we launch the Church of God-Man, imagine the power that will be coming out of your SOS Clubhouses with both the political movement and the Church of God-Man. That is enormous power that you will be sitting on, my friends. The Church of God-Man is going to focus on the supreme value, which is your life. You get a sense of this in the Miss Annabelle's Story, the SOS Superpuzzle. We're going to work on your life in the Church of God-Man, on discovering and releasing the secret in your heart.

Now in addition to the stimulations in our Clubhouse Congregations, our mega-Churches, these life advantages, getting connected, the Church of God-Man will deal heavily in the realm of immortality. Remember in the Miss Annabelle's Story how Jeremiah worked on shifting perspectives. For example, he didn't concentrate on immortality per se, that's too alien. He concentrated on more cosmetic things, like anti-aging. He brought in the huge anti-aging crowd by going that route, and then they would evolve, and eventually they began to realize that they wanted immortality as things progressed, as they become successful by Neothinking, bringing together pieces of the Superpuzzle.   Here is how we will approach immortality in our Clubhouse Congregations:

Level-Seven Essence Meeting
Part Two B

I'm going to develop that same approach introducing immortality. And you know when you're young, mortality is nowhere in sight. Then when you finally get up into your mid-life and over your forty, you begin realizing your life is running through your hands like water. You begin to realize and feel this more and more often with great sadness. Then when you grow old, you play out your end game with great lament, some in disbelief. And, I have seen some who simply accept it. My three major non-fiction titles SOS Secrets, SOS Visions and SOS Powers and my faction trilogy, the SOS Superpuzzzle show why most human beings accept death. The secret is in their heart and they don't know it. That secret, yet of course, is the child of the past, the Zon within. Deep within mankind's deepest desires, deepest secrets, is his unknown self, yet to be discovered.

The secret in our hearts is to live happy and live healthy. To live means not dying. That is the secret in our hearts. But immortality is just too big to really comprehend. Remember in the Miss Annabelle Story, the challenges to basically create the demand for immortality. It's an enormous challenge. However, I'm going to develop an approach that will coincide with the release of this publication, and it will be a program that we will use in the Church of God-Man. The concept is creating a shift in perspective brought to the large anti-aging market. I'm going to develop the understanding about the growth cycles in our lives; how it would be to grow and develop and enjoy those cycles twice as long…just keep it going twice as long. Starting in childhood and having twice as long to develop, to gain our education, and learn, too in order to establish success and happiness in life. Your young adult years are sort of like your apprentice years, that growth cycle.

What if we could have twice as long in our apprentice years to develop our skills, and talents, our integrated thinking in order to build success puzzles.

Then, what if in our adult years, our accomplishment/achievement years, we had twice as long accomplishing and achieving. Imagine what one could do with twice that time!

And then of course, think of our mature adult years, where we develop, and we have wisdom and ability to be a teacher, which is so extraordinarily rewarding, and a mentor, that growth, the growth period. What if we could double that growth period? And, then of course, in old age where we learn how to take a philanthropic look at life, to help others, and leave our legacy that will benefit mankind. What if we could develop that? Everyone really wants to experience all five of those growth cycles. So what I am saying is what if we can experience all five? Then what if we double the length of each of those? You would say yes, indeed, I would love to double it. It gets rid of the bigger, overwhelming question about living forever. As a parent you would also say "Oh yes, I would love that. I would love seeing my child be best prepared for major success in life. I'd love to see him double his education time and his learning curve and his apprenticeship. I'd love to see that. I'd love to double my time with my child, and the enjoyment that we have together." Time with your children goes by so fast. You blink and they're in high school, then they have their driver's license, and then you don't see them much anymore, they're gone.

Now, I developed this basic working model for our Church of God-Man program. As time goes on something's going to fill your member's soul. Here's what's going to happen: As they understand these five growth cycles and if we could double each one, this ultimately means slowing down aging. Slowing down the whole process so we have twice as long in

these different growth phases of our lives. It's a Neothink®
breakthrough, a Ten-Second Miracle, when you realize I don't
have to remain isolated to my one growth cycle. Indeed, I can
actually, at any age, experience all five together synergistically.
That is what I personally, Mark Hamilton, experience in my
life. That brings about the immortals stimulation and
exhilaration that makes you not want to die.

Through my program and the Church of God-Man, we will
create this process that your members will go through.
Suddenly, at one point in their life, they're going to realize the
synergy, and this is where the great stimulation, the ultimate
stimulation, the immortals exhilaration comes from. That you
will never will cease when you start having all five growth
cycles occurring within yourself, all synergistically together.

For instance, currently, my growth in education, which is
basically associated with childhood, is a phenomenal growth
cycle right now! On the other hand, I am in a philanthropic
growth cycle where I'm helping others. I'm also in my mature
adult cycle as a mentor to you. I am in my accomplishment,
achievement growth cycle big time, as I build the superpuzzle.
I'm integrating all of these growth cycles together
synergistically, and the exhilaration, stimulation is
phenomenal. This is a process that we'll bring the people in
the Church of God-Man. They will have that eureka moment
where suddenly they will feel it. They want immortality and
that's the course of the Church of God-Man; understanding the
supreme value of the universe.

In that First Insight, I talk about pure love, universal love,
as opposed to fools love. Our Society, with such stimulation
love will lead us to universal love, not tthe love of the mystical
organized religion that leads to anger, disappointment, sense of
failure, of cowardice, of meekness, of subjugation. Love is
based on mutual value exchange, which say between a man and
a woman is conditional. But when you begin to emotionally

awaken to the idea that conscious beings are the supreme value in the universe, then you begin to awaken to universal love. In the anticivilization where you have dishonest, evil people, you have to have conditional love with judgments and conditions.

But in the C of U and on our microcosms forming in the Clubhouse Congregations, we are headed for universal love. That's where the Church of God-Man will take us, along with the Twelve Visions Party and the Twelve Visions World. All this comes out of your SOS Clubhouse Congregations. There is no dishonesty in the Twelve Visions World, in the C of U on Earth.

We will experience universal love because we will love our fellow man. We will love everybody because we are all contributing such great values to civilization, to society, to you and your family. That is mutual value exchange.

The coming mind-blowing SOS products that will trump the anticivilization are the SOS Bible, subtitled Universal Love which could generate millions of interested people in your Clubhouse Congregations and the other product subtitled Universal Wealth will trump politics. Imagine universal wealth. There's no hypocrisy talk or political rhetoric filled with contradictions here in The Twelve Visions World. When we say we are going to make the poor rich, our numbers will prove that we can. Unlike the illusions and political rhetoric from the liberal left with their universal health fairy tale or the false morality of the conservative right there, the Twelve Visions Party is real. We actually have evidence throughout history of putting together pieces of puzzles to show indeed this is going to work. We *will* have universal wealth. Not political rhetoric of making the poor rich, giving the poor tax breaks or giving the poor welfare, of giving the poor universal health. We're talking the real wealth because we are the real deal.

This leads me to Part Three, trumping politics.

Forbidden Revelation

259

Level-Seven Essence Meeting
Part Three

Recall from our Level-Four Essence Meeting, I talked to you about the political meeting having to be stimulation-based. That's very true and it has to be. When we come up with the technical documents such as the State Constitutions, the State and National Platform of course, they will always be tied back to the stimulating aspect of this "Make All the People Rich Including the Poor".

And, as I said, this is not political rhetoric. We are poised in time and with technology to have this prosperity explosion.

Never before has there been such an opportunity for us. For the first time in our human history, we can all be rich including the poor. We have arrived at a unique moment in time and technology in which that millionaire phenomenon can happen. The Twelve Visions Party is highly aware of this rare opportunity, and is here to actualize it. The premise of the Twelve Visions Party is simple: man is imperfect. Again, the premise of the Twelve Visions Party is simple: man is imperfect. Man is flawed; man is vulnerable to incorrect opinions, selfish agendas, destructive temptations, misguided behaviors, dishonest corruption, even manipulative evil.

By removing all imperfections, by removing man, a perfect power reactor explosion of prosperity, love and wealth will overwhelm society sooner than later. The problem in the political and legal systems ever known to man are, they are all directed and interpreted by man. The American political system for instance, whether liberal left or conservative right, in both cases, is directed and interpreted by man, by flaw-filled imperfection.

Civilization will take an unprecedented leap forward by removing imperfection, by removing man and his endless opinion and agendas from dictating and interpreting and enforcing law. The method to remove man is The Prime Law. The consequence is shown throughout this book. There's millionaire-like prosperity for all the people including the poor.

Once we recognize and remove the inherent problem of man as a flaw-filled being, easily influenced by power and money, then ordinary people will become wealthy, even the poor, as we will see in this book.

Positions of ruling class power must be taken out of the hands of man. The freedom and prosperity of any country will steadily decay with man both dictating and interpreting the law. On the other hand, the freedom and prosperity of countries throughout history soar as man is removed from the political controls.

Our own country soared as we removed the rule of man, a monarch. To complete the evolution into universal prosperity, the powers of the legislature, judicial and executive branches, must be taken from the opinions and agendas of faulty man, and put into a fundamental Prime Law.

If you take 100 well educated men and women and asked them thoughts on important current events, they will bombard you with the many different opinions and agendas as exemplified by the U. S. Senate. Moreover, once in positions of political power, surrounded by the trappings of power and wealth, their answers will be directed for their own benefits, for their own political clout.

Man is an easily influenced, easily corrupted creature. Therefore, the laws that govern man, that is, protect man, must be free of man. The only way to be free of man is to reduce law, reduce protection to the fundamental nature of protection. Once at that fundamental nature of something, there's no going deeper.

All the opinions, agendas, illusions, dishonesties and corruption, all man's faults, no longer matter. The fundamental nature stands unchanged, unscathed, unconditional, uncorrupted, plain for all to ever see and know which is the nature of the Prime Law.

Indeed, the fundamental biological nature of protection is, the Prime Law that supersedes all law. The Prime Law removes man, including all the smart law school graduates, from the decision making process of law. Law leaps to another level altogether, for the first time, completely free of man.

The Prime Law controls the creation of new laws, not man with his endless opinions and agendas and faults. The fundamental nature of protection of the Prime Law controls the interpretation of laws, not man with his endless egos, selfish desires, and many flaws. The Prime Law controls the enforcement of laws, not man with his intoxicating power, rampart dishonesties, and capacity for evil.

When the Prime Law removes man from creating, interpreting and enforcing law, something amazing happens. The heavy and corrupt ruling class of man comes off society. Society and technology soar. The great technological revolution takes off and causes our buying power to multiply a thousand fold, making everyone rich, including the poor.

We already saw the forerunner with the uninhibited computer information revolution. Let us now introduce a new political party, with the sole objective, to remove man from creating, interpreting and enforcing law, in order to make all people wealthy, including the poor.

Instead of man governing our country, the fundamental nature of protection, the Prime Law will govern. The name of that new political party that removes man from governing and removes the ruling class, is the Twelve Visions Party.

Let us now see how the Twelve Visions Party will do that. Let us go through Visionaries State Constitutions and State Platforms.

Now I'm going to get into the technical document:

First, the Constitution of the Twelve Visions Party of your state, say Massachusetts would begin as follows:

Preamble and Purpose: The visionaries of Massachusetts envision a profoundly free, wealthy, healthy and safe society protected by rule of law. We believe however, that man, even the most educated man or woman is by nature, a flaw-filled creature. Any idea or thought put before man generates endless opinions, arguments and agendas.

Moreover, man is predisposed to egos, temptations and irresistible power. Man, by nature, tends to quench his own appetite first. In other words, he puts his own clout before society. At the expense of society, politicians migrate toward political clout and re-election power. In recognition of man's inherent shortcomings, the visionaries of Massachusetts aspire to lift the rule of law to a whole new level not yet seen on Earth.

Historically, the more successful a political system is at removing man from making, interpreting and enforcing law, the freer the nation and the wealthier and healthier the people. Without going through a history lesson here, America advanced that evolution more than any other country with its brilliant Constitution, its separation of powers and watchdog branches of government.

The Twelve Visions Constitution goes to the next evolution of removing flaw-filled man from making, interpreting and enforcing law. That next evolution will lift society into unprecedented freedom, and its people, into never before seen wealth, health and safety.

To accomplish that next evolution in politics and law, we proudly introduce the Prime Law. The Prime Law completes the millennia-long evolution of removing man from creating, interpreting and enforcing law and will lead us to the wealthiest, healthiest and safest nation to ever exist on Earth.

For the first time, law will be completely out of the faulty incentives of man. The lawmakers, judges and regulators will no longer dictate and control law. Instead the Prime Law will dictate and control the lawmakers, judges and regulators.

And the Prime Law comes next and you all familiar with the Prime Law.

Now, The Preamble: The purpose of human life is to prosper and live happily. The function of government is to provide the conditions that let individuals fulfill that purpose. The Constitution of the Twelve Visions Party, guarantees those conditions by forbidding the use of initiatory force, fraud, or coercion, by any person or group, against any individual, property or contract.

Article I – No person, group of persons or government shall initiate force, threat of force or fraud against any individuals self, property or contract.

Article II – Force is morally and legally justified only for protection from those who violate Article I.

Article III – No exception shall exist for Articles I and II.

Politicians, lawyers, judges and bureaucrats, flaw-filled creatures controlling our laws have caused the steady erosion of our beloved freedom and prosperity.

The Prime Law Amendment demonstrates how the Prime Law permanently removes flaw-filled man from subjectively creating, interpreting and enforcing agenda law and ego justice.

No longer will flaw-filled politicians, lawyers, judges and bureaucrats control our laws, as instead, the Prime Law will control our flaw-filled politicians, lawyers, judges and bureaucrats. Perfection will control imperfection.

The Prime Law Amendment to the U.S. Constitution statement shows why the Prime Law was the one missing ingredient our forefathers needed to forever preserve the beautiful country they created.

Every Twelve Visions Party candidate, every elected, appointed or hired visionary will sign a Twelve Visions Party contract, that is TVP Contract. That TVP Contract binds every Visionary's decision in any local, state or federal office or position in all branches of government. The TVP Contract binds every visionary, yes, flaw-filled man to the Prime Law (read the Twelve Visions Party Contract at www.tvpnc.org).

The results of removing flaw-filled man from controlling government and its law creation, law interpretation, law enforcement will be unprecedented prosperity. That is not a hypothesis. Prosperity explosions have occurred among civilizations throughout history. By removing flaw-filled man from the controls of government including agenda law, that's agenda law ego justice and political policy law enforcement. In fact, our country is one example of such an evolutionary leap from a man-controlling monarchy, to the nearly flawless U.S. Constitution controlled republic.

A great prosperity explosion followed over two centuries later, the Twelve Visions Party gives us an opportunity at the next and final evolutionary leap that completes the evolution away from flaw-filled, man-controlled government. The Prime Law was the ingredient our forefathers missed. That missing ingredient guarantees freedom forever, and its resulting rising standards of living. That missing ingredient makes the U. S. Constitution flawless and fully removes flaw-filled man. A great prosperity explosion will follow once again.

The Twelve Visions Party merely completes the final evolution of providing protection, and only protection , the purpose of government, without flaw-filled man as a result shown throughout the TVP National Platform in Part Two of this booklet. Removing flaw-filled man from the controls of government means the average American will live like millionaires without lifting a finger. Everyone will become rich, including the poor.

The Twelve Visions Party recognizes this opportunity and offers the method to the new experience of universal wealth for the first time ever on our planet. The next evolution of freedom will bring all Americans a wealthy, healthy and safe life. And that is the end of your State Constitution, the Preamble and Purpose section.

All 50 states will have what I just read once it's perfected and the integrations are all complete. You will submit that with the technical aspects to your Secretary of State.

All right, the Twelve Visions movement: When you get down to the irreducible, fundamental of something, often a paradigm shift occurs of magnificent proportions. I will give you one of many examples:

When Henry Ford got down to the fundamental nature of production, down to the physical movements of production, the assembly line emerged, and caused a worldwide paradigm shift of mass production. Do not let the workers manage the work, instead let the work manage the workers. That changed everything, a prosperity explosion followed.

The Prime Law gets down to the irreducible, fundamental nature of law, down to the physical protection of the individual and his property. A paradigm shift will occur of magnificent proportions.

Do not let the flaw-filled politicians, judges, and bureaucrats manage the law, instead let the Prime Law manage the politicians, judges, bureaucrats and that will change everything. A prosperity explosion will follow; a great, unhindered, technological revolution, in which buying power will rapidly multiply.

Now let us take a close look at the political party itself:

For a long time I dreaded the idea of launching a political party. I knew that all people, including loyal visionaries, were flaw-filled man with all his short comings, vulnerabilities and temptations. How could the Twelve Visions Party survive the faults of its members and officials? The answer, I continued to conclude, was it will not survive the faults of man.

How then, could my new political party idea ever work? That was when I realized I needed to take the fundamental decision-making process away from the Party members, yes, away from the visionaries, away from the visionaries themselves. In other words, do not let the visionaries, that is, opinionated, flaw-filled man, manage the law. Instead let the unchanging, flawless, Prime Law manage the Visionaries.

Yes, and with that, with that fundamental of law, the Prime Law, I could do this. I could finally start the political party. The Twelve Visions could now work and truly bring the millionaire phenomenon to the people. To control this all Party members who run for office must sign the TVP Contract that every decision is made according to the Prime Law.

Now the political party will work beautifully. The Twelve Visions Party can now actualize the unprecedented opportunity to make all people rich, including the poor. Indeed, we are in an unprecedented moment in time and technology, T & T, to ignite a never before seen prosperity explosion.

Here's the Twelve Visions Party TVP Contract:

The Premise: A protection only government will lead to the people's greatest prosperity as demonstrated in Twelve Visions. That is reality. I understand the many opinions of man cannot alter reality. Yet while dictating, interpreting and enforcing law, the attempt to alter reality is continually made.

This law or that law will improve the people's prosperity whether innocent or guilty, all those government actions beyond protection, every day, slowly kill our freedoms bit by bit, steadily age our country and lead to its eventual death.

The purpose of the contract is to establish the reality of protection, which is the one proper purpose of government.

We established the reality of protection through the unchanging Prime Law of no initiatory force which controls the lawmakers, lawyers, judges and bureaucrats and their endless opinions, biases, agendas, motivations, egos, desires, delusions and illusions.

No longer will those flaw-filled creatures control law and politics.

Contract:

I, (then write your name), pledge to subordinate all my many preconceived thoughts, despite how strongly I feel, despite whether I believe with certainty or with reservation, for with external and internal confusions and illusions that accompany a power based government, I honestly acknowledge that, always reaching the proper decision, is merely impossible.

In serving my Party's objective to return to a protection only government in order to unleash an unprecedented prosperity explosion that will make all the people rich including the poor. I fully understand the mechanics come down to consistently, always, without exception, supporting the biologically irreducible, fundamental act of protection, the Prime Law of no initiatory force, as spelled out in the State Constitution of my Twelve Visions Party.

That Prime Law of protection must dictate the lawmakers, not the other way around.

Therefore, every decision I make, even if it goes against the very grain of my mind, skin, heart and soul, will be purely made, based on serving the Prime Law.

I realize, in the end, that policy will bring forth our vision to make all the people wealthy, healthy and safe including the poor as articulated in the Twelve Visions Party National Platform.

Again, that policy will bring forth our vision of a profoundly free, wealthy, healthy and safe society as articulated in Twelve Visions.

If I unknowingly go against the Prime Law or any decision, for any reason whatsoever, or if I show a trend of unknowingly going against the Prime Law which is self-evident, the Twelve Visions Party will, immediately and publically, disown me and will no longer recognize me as a member.

Lawmakers, man, must not control law. Men and women controlling law can lead to anything. Can take a country anywhere, even to the point where it becomes law to kill others, as we have seen around the world throughout history.

Man with all his faults of ego, greed, envy and innocent lack of knowledge, and his vulnerabilities, must not control laws, and interpret laws, and interpret the Constitution. Man with all his vulnerabilities and faults controlling law has always been a recipe for destruction.

No, the Prime Law of protection must control the lawmakers. If we want to live in a wealthy, healthy, happy, peaceful, safe and truly free society, then the Prime Law of protection must first be adopted as the contract of members of the Twelve Visions Party.

The Prime Law of protection must first be adopted as the contract of members of the Twelve Visions Party today, must gradually become the Constitution of each of the states tomorrow and an Amendment to the U. S. Constitution eventually, the overarching Constitution De Facto of America in the Twelve Visions World. The overarching Constitution of the world, ultimately ending force, war, and crime, country by country, while unleashing soaring technology, standards of living, buying power and wealth and health among all people, including the poor.

That is our vision, and all members running for office will sign the contract to abide by the Prime Law for every decision and quest of our vision.

And we have a Sign Here place by members of the Twelve Visions Party.

Now I talked about a Twelve Visions Amendment to the U. S Constitution and that will become a real possibility. Here is the introduction to that section:

The Prime Law Amendment

The one proper purpose of government is protection; anything else takes away our freedom, and therefore our prosperity. That fact is demonstrated in Twelve Visions. Indeed, the freer our country, the more prosperous, as shown throughout history.

For the first time, with the Prime Law, we are talking about a protection only government, and therefore a fully free country. There has never been a fully free country. For the first time, we have reached the time and technology to experience a universal prosperity explosion. If set free, we can ignite that explosion. All people can become rich including the poor. (Go to www.tvpnc.org to view the Twelve Visions Party National Platform).

America originally rose quickly, and was so much freer and more prosperous than other countries, because it was a country brilliantly controlled by the rule of law, not subjected to the rule of man, as so many other countries. Indeed, man is full of faults, driven by ego, pulled into temptations, attracted to corruption and dishonesty. Man is imperfect, including all visionaries.

The Twelve Visions Party takes the rule of law one step further, by going down to the biological fundamental of protection, no initiatory force. The Twelve Visions Party removes man recklessly creating new laws that have nothing to do with protection, and it removes man recklessly interpreting the law. For any law or interpretation beyond protection against initiatory force, requires force.

The Prime Law insures a pure protection only government. A pure protection only government will ignite the universal prosperity explosion. The Prime Law has the potential to become an Amendment to the Constitution of the United States.

Let us take a close look at that possibility:

With that one Prime Law in place, it essentially becomes our supreme law, to which every law must answer. For the supreme law will filter out every law and regulation and violation, namely, those who serve the bogus purpose of so called "promoting the social good", agenda law, which requires initiatory force.

The Prime Law is the biological, fundamental, the point of origin, the beginning of all law. Therefore, no further unhealthy law or misinterpretation of the U. S Constitution can occur. No more agenda law or ego justice, no more violations could happen. Government could not tell us how to spend our money, or force us to pay taxes, as long as we did not commit initiatory force, we would be completely free.

We would not need ego and power driven lawmakers stirring up legislation with lawyers and bureaucrats using those laws to drain us. We would no longer need that parasitical ruling class of man that destroyed our prosperity. Their deceptions could no longer pass through the Prime Law Amendment, including the forced taxes.

Here's another important paragraph from the long Constitutional Amendment statement. This is the final paragraph:

With the Prime Law in place, via State Constitutions, and eventually the Prime Law Amendment to the U. S. Constitution, the prosperity explosion described in the National Platform would never end. Think about the potential wealth, happiness, love and health described in the National Platform. We would soon live the wealthy, healthy and safe lives we were meant to live.

The political pamphlet that I will have for you by Meeting Level Nine will include your State Platform. And I will be providing you with the Preamble and Purpose and the Conclusion. You will fill in the planks as I recommended to you. You'll simply state the popular issues in your state. You'll probably take planks from both the Republicans and Democrats and line them right on up there in your State Platform, showing which ones would fall under the Prime Law and which ones would not. Some would have to be spinoffs of private businesses and institutions that would take those over. Or they simply just go by the wayside.

Here is the working draft of a State, the philosophical portion of the Preamble and Purpose and Conclusion for your State Platform:

The visionaries have a great vision, which is a soaring standard of living, a country in which all the people become rich, including the poor. In this day and age of rapidly advancing technologies, when buying power can soar, as we have seen with the computers, visionaries believe that all citizens can soon live with great buying power, great wealth, if the government returns to its one proper purpose of protection only, and removes itself from its improper purpose of promoting a social good.

The dynamics of this return to a protection only government and resulting explosion of wealth for the people in this age of rapidly advancing technologies, can be clearly seen in the National Platform of the Twelve Visions Party (Go to www.tvpnc.org).

At our web site, www.tvpnc.org you will witness why we are the party to make all the people wealthy and healthy, including the poor. The mechanics of becoming a protection only government bring us to our Constitution.

There we state that the visionaries of, say Massachusetts, envision a profoundly free, wealthy, healthy and safe society, protected by rule of law, the Prime Law. The Prime Law of no initiatory force brings us back to a protection only government, and sets free our great technological revolution, to quickly bring unprecedented wealth, health and safety to all citizens.

The Prime Law, not men and women, not elected lawmakers, will dictate all political decisions and actions and base them upon no initiatory force from that fundamental, all people, not just the elected politicians, can determine the consistent and universal unchanging planks stated here.

As I said, you'll go in and grab the popular planks in your state and you may even just run down the list of Republican and Democratic planks, and list them right there in your State Platform. The process will be quite easy. You determine which plank falls under the Prime Law and which does not. And anybody, any citizen, can determine that, not just the politicians.

So now who is in office becomes irrelevant. That's interesting, isn't it? Who's in office actually becomes irrelevant. Personal agendas and endless opinions become irrelevant, party affiliation becomes irrelevant. That's amazing when you think about it. What party holds power becomes irrelevant. The Prime Law and nothing more remains relevant.

The consequences of these decisions and actions locked down to the Prime Law will be staggering as demonstrated in the National Platform. The geniuses of society will finally be free to accelerate the technological revolution and drive our buying power higher than we have ever seen. This millionaire phenomenon will come to all people including the poor, as demonstrated in the National Platform with additional spectacular consequences such as unprecedented health, happiness, love, peace, security and safety.

At our state level, popular planks listed by the Republicans and popular planks listed by the Democrats will either be moved eventually to the private sector if it has nothing to do with the one proper purpose of government, protection, or it will fall under the Prime Law and it is protection.

Okay, you need to go in now and show the planks, show how they line up. I can help you with this when you create your State Platform. When you complete it, email me a copy. Let me look at it so I can give you feedback before you submit it to the Secretary of State.

Then you'll have a conclusion to your State Platform:

When a 20th Century visionary discovered that workers should not manage the work, but rather the work should manage the workers. Of course, we're talking about Henry Ford here. Society experienced an enormous prosperity explosion. Mass production accelerated the Industrial Revolution and everyone's buying power skyrocketed.

When a 21st Century visionary discovered that the lawmakers should not control the laws, rather the Prime Law should control the lawmakers; society stands to experience an enormous prosperity explosion. The unburdened geniuses of society and their unbridled super rapidly advancing new technologies will accelerate the technological revolution and everyone's buying power will skyrocket. See the National

Platform for the Twelve Visions Party to get a clear understanding of this millionaire phenomenon for ordinary people at www.tvpnc.org.

Indeed, the Twelve Visions Party is the Party to make the people rich, including the poor. That is our vision. We have reached a rare moment in time and technology that could literally make all people wealthy including the poor. The Twelve Visions Party recognizes and reaches for the switch to ignite the prosperity explosion.

That concludes your State Constitution. And that wraps up Part One of the political pamphlet that I'll have for you by Meeting Nine and will have for your A-Teams to distribute.

Over the next few months, I will be locking down and perfecting the legalities of this, including the licensing contract that I will have each of you sign for the political movement. This is necessary in order to use my trade names and to create a necessary control over the political movement.

So you're seeing now two really powerful trumps over the anticivilization, the twin pillars; trumping religion as we discussed and trumping politics. And the Twelve Visions Party is the only real way to trump politics. Even Neo-Tech itself could not trump politics because, as Frank R. Wallace said, everybody has their bubbles of mysticism. He struggled with that in Pax Neo-Tech to get to the point where mysticism can completely leave our psyches. He still had a ways to go with that, but that was *his* struggle and *his* battle. And we had a beautiful division of essence going there. As he worked on that, I was working aggressively and moving forward with what we're involved in here today.

With his tragedy, his accident, I've had to step in and do a lot of work in his area which in itself is not the best division of essence. But nobody else can do this. So, it was necessary. Someday I'm going to write about that great tragedy.

But today we have the twin pillars that trump the anticivilization in a very exciting way, with a real movement that's no longer rhetoric. In politics we have a plan, a real solid plan, backed by evidence that can make the poor rich and create real universal health and true universal wealth. We have that. And we have the SOS Bible that will trump religion. With the twin pillars and with universal love we talked about, we will reach that tipping point.

We are part of this long term process to change planet Earth; to change human kind from a self-destruct, dishonest civilization, to an honest, super civilization with all its wonderful gifts — it's breathtaking.

Next meeting, in Level Eight, I'm going to talk about the science and medical area and how we're going to move into it in the near future. Also we will move into the Arts and start a program to expose the SOS Clubhouse Congregation to the potential in the arts.

Now, on to your questions:

Level-Seven Essence Meeting
Part Four A

Our first question is from an A-Team coordinator who is part of the launch:

Q: We are concerned about the liability of our members resulting from our mentoring and teaching activities. We can form an entity and attempt to limit liability, but we cannot stop lawsuits and the resulting legal fees against both the company and the individuals.

MH: Well, when you get your Starter Kit from us there is a contract that indemnifies you in there that you and your team will sign. And, of course, you can set up a limited liability company which will give you protection. You know, it's not a risk free or perfect world, but you'll be as protected as you can be.

A side note on that: We have an incredible track record of standing up to just about any authority, on any playing field ourselves, without high-powered lawyers. I'll sometimes involve lawyers, but in the end, it's my integrations that would stop authorities cold in their tracks. We have quite an arsenal built up to stop those overly-ambitious lawyers looking to get something for nothing.

Q: We are concerned about logistics and our ability to handle more than one location. We can handle 12 books in one location but how do we handle several geographical locations which will be required in the very near future?

MH: You're setting up a business entity and you're on a creativity curve with Ten-Second Miracles and I think that will all work out. You're getting into a more manageable structure here with the Inner Circle, not just everybody filing into those workshop meetings. This business model that I'm laying out here now is much smaller. And conceivably, down the road, a one-man apprentice could start an A-Team through this business model. That lone apprentice, that single-person A-Team can hire people to work for him or her which enables you more flexibility.

Q: Our understanding is that the masses are looking for three things; first, money, second romance and finally health. What are we offering? What is the incentive for the masses to join, and continue in this program, and then join with us to start new A-Teams and finally to join the political party, to move the entire program to biological immortality?

MH: Let me take the Socratic approach to these questions and ask you, why are the mega churches around the country such a smash success? Is it money? Is it romance? Is it health? What are they offering? I want you to ponder this because you're going to discover what you need to do in your clubhouse congregations.

What is the incentive for the masses to join and continue in there, that is, the mega churches program? I can tell it has nothing to do with worship. It is the life advantages. That's what makes the mega churches grow. It's the life advantages combined with the stimulation and the exhilaration of fun. It removes the boredom of one's life to attend these highly spirited mega church congregations.

So we are bringing life advantages then getting connected, even meeting potential business opportunities. We offer a security blanket, in a sense; having friendships, a brotherhood or sisterhood and friends, a support system. We create an environment for someone's having a hard time making connections for a business opportunity or having a difficult time meeting someone of the opposite sex. These are all life advantages that people get by going to any church.

It is from the success of mega churches that we've learned the art, the secret of stimulation, socializing and entertainment. That's the opposite of our boring lives. These mega churches now are out-stimulating the traditional churches that are more locked down to just the sermon and ceremony.

So the masses are going to get life advantages, they're going to get stimulation, they're going to get fun and excitement and get connected, all from your Clubhouse Congregations. They're going to get what people get at mega churches. From the literature, the masses will receive what people get out of the Bible; the actual lessons and secrets of life.

Then, of course, to answer your question further, your members are going to receive your Workshops, the personal mentoring, the enhanced secret web site.

Q: How is SOS considered exclusive if anyone can join? In my fraternity we voted for new members, I don't propose that, but I'm concerned how to explain this.

MH: I think the answer is very simple. I'll start off by saying the leads that I sent you in the past were all screened. They always will be screened. Now, you're running a business and you're allowed to go out and advertise. You're allowed to run radio spots and television spots, anything that you find that is profitable for you.

How are we an exclusive society? Although we're opening up the Society to the masses you are bringing people to the concepts, our advantages and life-altering secrets. People have to become members in order to see, read, experience these advantages. Because of our exclusive advantages, people will say, "You know, I've got to get myself into that Society of Secrets. Look what people are learning, look what I'm missing out on". Remember in Miss Annabelle's Story how eventually people had to come into the Church of God-Man in order to remain competitive any longer?

So, people have to have us. I think it's simply an ingenious concept to bring people into the Society. Anyone can basically come in, true, but they still have to come inside The Neothink® Society and reap the benefits.

So, what does that do? Curiosity, the need for our secret life-advantages in order to survive, forces people to you and your Clubhouse Congregations. That's your business.

Level-Seven Essence Meeting
Part Four B

Okay, next question is about relationships:

In an earlier meeting I mentioned something briefly about relationships and received quite a few responses. This particular response is a glowing testimonial to Neo-Tech. This couple's marriage was on its way out. Part of the problem was jealousies that created a lot of drama in the relationship. Such drama and jealousies would eventually destroy any relationship. Then as they read Neo-Tech and understood mysticism, their marriage was saved. It's a beautiful marriage now, they're happy and in love.

And I just want to add from Neo-Tech you recall that can't control or help your feelings. You can only control your actions, how you act or don't act on those feelings. So once you understand this you will allow yourself to just have a feeling of jealousy. Nature hard-wired jealousy into man. The reason, of course, is that the superior man is the man who would stay and raise his children.

In the Insights, I talk about love. Love as a reflection increases with evolution. The more evolved the animal from the insect, to the dog, to the human being, the greater the love is. So, the man who would stay with a single family and had a sense of duty, was the superior man. Mother Nature did not want man raising the offspring of an inferior man. So, the way Mother Nature dealt with that was to instill jealousy in man, to be more suspicious and keep a watchful eye on his female, on his spouse.

By saying that, I hope that might help this fellow in his relationship. Do not deny your feelings nor suppress them. That will lead to problems later on. To feel them, recognize them, but then take the conscious approach, not the animal, bicameral, approach; that is to override the feelings with conscious thoughts. And apparently, that's exactly what he's done. Congratulations, that's an example of Neo-Tech working in personal relationships.

Q: Why are you insisting Neo-Space and A-Team be dependant to one another? I am not interested in putting my personal data on Neo-Space.

MH: You're setting up a business and the information I ask you to post on the national web site is actually my tracking report. It's not a matter of wanting or not wanting. It's simply a matter of you gaining the advantage of having your CEO track you, to integrate and coordinate the big picture which is going to help accelerate you. This information I ask for is going to greatly benefit you. If you're concerned about putting up your personal information, I'm sure your A-Team can post in such a way so you're not giving out personal stats. But I need to see your notes, your progress, your meetings that you're holding, your plans, your videos, if you take videos. I need to track you. That is to your advantage, for my integrating and coordinating function, so I can come back to you through our essence meetings to give you guidance.

Q: I would like to video tape our meetings. Do you see any issue or concerns with making video recordings of our meetings?

MH: Well, one concern is filming people without their permission. You can't do that. But you can have people sign a release form. And I've held large seminars in the past with several hundred people and I had no problem with them signing releases. In fact, a lot of them will be involved in such a video-taping. For those who don't, simply sit them in a place in the room where they will not be video-taped.

The other concern I must consider is our secrets, our copyrighted literature and materials getting in the hands of someone who blasts it all over the Internet. That's a very real concern. Yet there can be a tremendous value in videotaping your workshops where good workshop meetings are uploaded to our national web site which enhances our overall value tremendously. So I do see great value in such recordings but they have to be done right and uploaded only to the subscription secret web site.

Q: I really miss my religious roots. Would it be okay for me to go back to church?

MH: That is very interesting. The very thing that's drawing him back, the very things we're going to use to trump organized religions are the things that he's missing in life, the life connections, the life advantages, the brotherhood, a sense of place and belonging, this security blanket. You know, a person becomes unemployed there are contacts and introductions you can make at church. If I get divorced, you have the support network around you. This person misses that. And you know what he misses most? Playing the piano and singing with his brothers and sisters at his former church.

He's not going there to worship. He doesn't even believe in the mystical preaching. But he wants to go back and is going so far as asking me if that's possible.

That's what you all, my apprentices are providing to the public in your Clubhouse Congregations. You are creating what this apprentice is longing for. So, with that in mind, my answer to him is, sure. I'm not here to dictate your actions. We're just here to open your eyes and to help you see past the illusions to what is. And this particular apprentice sees through illusions to what is. But for social reasons he wants to go back. So I have no objections. I'm certainly not going to tell him no. But you all need to recognize how we're going to benefit mankind. This apprentice is going to be so stimulated by what we're doing that he's not going to need his church any longer. We're going to outcompete what he longs for.

Digest everything I'm telling you here. See how the timing of this question perfectly fits into what I'm talking about; the power and stimulation of your SOS Clubhouse Congregations. You don't need to necessarily teach Neothink®. I've done that job, Frank R. Wallace did that job, Eric Savage did that job.

By the way, in MLM's, I was told the average life of an MLMer is only two to three months. The average attendee of a church is many years and, in some cases, entire lives. That's what we're setting up, many, many years and entire lives.

Q: I know that Ron Paul is not Neothink®, but is he not a good jumping off point? Is his stance on the issues and his promises closer to what we are promoting? And, if he were elected to office, would it not be easier for us, afterwards, to win a campaign on the Twelve Visions Party after Ron Paul is in office? Or am I misinformed to his intentions, and is he just a big neocheater like everybody else?

MH: First of all, I do think Ron Paul is sincere. He's been at this a long time. He's basically a Libertarian running on the Republican ticket. He's not the most charismatic person to look at or to listen to, but he's very principled and very solid. But I've been down this road too many times to ever believe that any outside dynamic will help us in any way. We're simply off the radar screen. We have to do this ourselves. So I move ahead on my superpuzzle and my course without any consideration whatsoever what happens or doesn't happen with the elections.

I am very excited about our next Essence Meeting, our Level Eight Meeting. The excitement is beginning to grow. Feel the power that is coming your way. The Twelve Visions Party will result in a tipping point especially coming out of your Clubhouse Congregations. Imagine the insane curiosity in people; where are all these amazing ideas coming from? This curiosity is going to drive people to you. Your Clubhouse

Congregations are going to become the world's biggest celebrities.

Next month, we're going to introduce a couple of other major sources of power that will be coming to your SOS Clubhouse Congregations. One source of power is going to be in the medical and scientific field; the anti-aging market. The other is in the Arts.

I look forward to seeing you in the next Level Eight Meeting.

Secret Teachings to My Exclusive Inner Circle

Level-Eight Essence Meeting
Introduction

Hello and welcome to the historic Level Eight Meeting where the theme is the Big Picture.

I'm going to express a vision to you. My greatest Neothink® vision has never been written down before now. Last month, in the Level Seven Meeting, I never did ask you to send your questions into me and I did that for a reason. I want you to just hear my greatest Neothink vision, the Big Picture. I just want you to have that, to hold that in your head, and not to have the meeting drag out with anything but the Big Picture in your head. I want you to be able to hold the Big Picture in your head without any other competing thoughts or integrations.

Next month, I'm going to get back to launching the Twelve Visions Party. By next month, I will have the political pamphlet down to the irreducible, fundamental integrations that can hold for all time. I've been working hard on that pamphlet for months. It will be ready for our Level Nine Meeting where we will hit the Twelve Visions Party and the political movement hard.

I know the political area is not an area that most people, including you, my apprentices, would normally be interested in. But that's why we need to hit it hard. All SOS Clubhouse Congregations are going to be required to have, as part of their Inner Circle, the Twelve Visions Party movement. So, we're going to hit it hard and launch the Twelve Visions Party movement from that Level Nine Meeting.

This meeting you will see the Big Picture, the great Neothink® vision. Then in our next meeting we will be focusing on the first of several world- changing movements that you will see today in the Big Picture.

Level-Eight Essence Meeting
Part One

We spoke of man, flaw-filled man, and how, in order to make the political movement work, we needed to develop the Prime Law. And, it's the Prime Law that enables us to start the Twelve Visions Party. Now, if you remember, the reason for that is man, human beings, in this anticivilization by nature, are not perfect. Even the most innocent, even the Visionaries, will be taken in by illusions or not have all the facts or knowledge and cannot make the right decisions, the perfect decisions all the time. We also have a world in which temptation can be overwhelming particularly when people get in positions of power. So, in order to start and have a successful political movement, we needed to develop the Prime Law.

Similarly, with SOS Clubhouse Congregations, we're dealing with many people, many human beings who, by nature, are not perfect. Again, they're flaw-filled beings. Therefore, in order to make the Neothink® movement of Clubhouse Congregations successfully spreading around the country, we need to anchor them as we have anchored the political movement with the Prime Law. To this end, we have our great body of Neothink® literature in all Heirloom Packages. This great body of literature will be called The Prime Literature.

I want to draw a comparison between The Prime Literature and the stories in the Bible. The stories in the Bible survived and still exist today, 2000 years later, whereas the hundreds if not thousands of stories at the time — of kings, prophets, and liberators — did not survive. Why did the stories in the Bible survive? In Insight Two in your Second Heirloom Package I identified that the stories in the Bible were of bicameral man breaking into consciousness. That is what distinguished those stories from all others at that time and enabled them to survive.

Similarly, we have the literature that's been created here in The Neothnk® Society particularly by Frank R. Wallace and Mark Hamilton. Only Frank R. Wallace and I understand what it takes to create this type of literature. You'll see other writings that appear similar. You'll see on the Internet writings that use our expressions, our integrations. They are well-meaning people and some good writers but they aren't at the prime literature level. Only those around Frank R. Wallace and me realize what it takes to develop this Prime Literature.

To give you an example, my Twelve Visions took me 25 years of steady, daily work; hours and hours and hours on end with days that lasted up to 16 hours and beyond, day after day, seven days a week went into creating that material. Such literature requires a particular skill and ability that isn't in any other writing on our planet. Frank R. Wallace and Mark Hamilton's work get down to the fundamental, to the irreducible, fundamental integrations.

You can draw an analogy to art. You have the original creators who paint a masterpiece. Then you have a very good artist who can recreate that masterpiece. It will look very similar, very close to the original masterpiece but there's something intrinsic, a deeper, unmatchable, lasting value, in the original masterpiece not present in the copy. That intrinsic value just doesn't exist in the copy. And, it's the masterpiece that will live on for hundreds of thousands of years.

The Prime Literature that you read and that those who become members of your Clubhouse Congregations will receive is the prime literature from The Neothink® Society, from Frank R. Wallace and Mark Hamilton. And, there will be a publication or two from Eric Savage. There is no literature like this on the planet. Only we know what it takes to get down to a level of integration that is unassailable, that can withstand any attack, argument, and challenge and cannot be corrupted. Such literature will exist a hundred, a thousand

289

years from now. And, of course, one of the features of getting down to this irreducible, fundamental integration is at that level, we were able to discover and break through into the next evolution of our mentality.

Let me just backup to the literature that survived and became part of the Bible. That literature, the stand-out feature that I identified in Insight Two is that the bicameral man had flashes or momentary breakthroughs into consciousness culminating in the fully conscious teachings of Jesus.

The Prime Literature has broken through from our mysticism-plagued consciousness into mysticism-free Neothink®. And again, it's the breakthrough into the next mentality that has occurred as a result of us being able to get down to that fundamental integration that cannot be reduced further.

Frank R. Wallace began writing Pax Neo-Tech, a very small publication, on September 11, 2001 and he worked on that every day, from morning to late at night, seven days a week, until the day he died.

The Miss Annabelle's Story took me 9 years to develop and that was fast. However, the reason it only took 9 years was I'd spent 25 years developing the basic integrations for that piece of work.

The original Neo-Tech Discovery took Frank R. Wallace 15 years to complete. And understand, when I say 15 years or 25 years or 9 years, these aren't a normal writer's days. These are marathon days and weeks without a break, one after another, week after week, month after month, year after year.

I trust now with this integration you have a greater understanding and confidence in understanding the value members who join your local Clubhouse Congregations will receive month after month. There's no other literature on the planet, in history, of this nature, of this value.

So, I want to bring this back around full circle now; the SOS Clubhouse Congregations are full of people with flaws, who have bubbles of mysticisms. I want all of my apprentices to understand that what makes your Clubhouses a success is The Prime Literature. That is the anchor just as the Prime Law is the anchor for the Twelve Visions Party. The Prime Literature is the anchor for your SOS Clubhouse Congregations. People are paying to come to your Clubhouses for this Prime Literature.

Now the Clubhouse socials, the congregations are wonderful, added social value. Human beings are social animals. You are adding that value.

With that said, let's move on to the Big Picture:

When you received my first letter to you through the mail, I said you had hidden talents waiting to come out. When you received my first meeting on the Internet, I said you would be a different person, the person you were meant to be, at the end of your 12-step journey with me. Early on, I talked about living a life of romantic adventure, the life of Ulysses minus the dishonesty. The life you were meant to live is such an exciting adventure.

I talked about becoming a value creator, about playing at life. I talked about making Ten-Second Miracles using numbers as your tool. I talked about common denominators, puzzle building thinking, Neothink® marketing, Forces of Nature, Forces of Neothink®.

I told you that you can become powerful marketers, bringing the Twelve Visions World to the public. I told you that you can become value creators, living your Friday-Night Essences, playing at life by bringing the C of U to the public. I told you that would awaken the child of the past in the souls of good people everywhere. And, I told you that you will create the world you fell in love with while reading the Miss Annabelle's Story.

At the time, all of that may have seemed like exciting rhetoric. But now, it's all going to come true. The launch has begun. Folks have begun joining Clubhouse Congregations and this is only the beginning. We're moving now to the second wave of new A-Teams. The number of A-Teams is growing and the number of Neothink® Society members is growing. We're setting this up to have a strong steady growth over the coming months. What can stop us now? Nothing. The C of U on Earth now is simply a matter of time.

So, let's start grasping this Big Picture. All right, the Clubhouse Congregations are going to grow in numbers and locations. Realize that the local A-Teams that have launched may start marketing in your geographical areas. You've already developed your Introduction Meetings to handle this growth. You have my permission to begin your marketing efforts. Moreover, I'm going to start sending you large numbers of very strong leads for you to mine. These leads that I send you are going to be for you to bring to your Introduction Meetings along with those people who you market in your geographical areas.

The word of mouth will begin to take hold, your own marketing will begin to take hold and the leads I send you are going to begin flooding your Introduction Meetings, out of which you'll convert into Neothink® Society active members. As your Clubhouse Congregations grow, these people will also have access to the Neothink® Society active member web site. These people are simply going to want to get more out of the Neothink® Society. They're going to want to get more out of life, and this is where your Workshops come into play. All the serious movements, as you'll see today, are going to rise out of the tier-two Workshops. Focus groups are going to develop. Tier two is the Inner Circle of the Neothink® Society.

Now, I want you to think about that expression for a moment, the Neothink® Society's *Inner-Circle* members. The Inner Circle is where the power will arise. For example, last meeting we discussed we are going to trump the two pillars of the anticivilization. One is the Twelve Visions Party trumping politics and the other is the SOS Bible with its Church of God-Man trumping religion. Recall I said both of those movements will rise out of your Clubhouse Congregations. Politics and religion are going to rise out of your Inner Circle, the more serious members.

Can you begin to sense the power of the Clubhouse Congregations now…the power as a result of bringing these two world-changing movements to the public? The local chapters are going to be doing this in your Clubhouse Congregations.

Remember in an early meeting I said that the most powerful force in the cosmos is the force of becoming organized. All the way from organizing matter to the point where it reverts into a big bang, this ordering or organization leads to the greatest explosion, the greatest force in the universe. And it's that act of becoming organized that takes something that's powerless and makes it very powerful. I used the example of random breezes. When they become organized you have the force of a hurricane. Well, that's exactly what the local Clubhouse Congregations are going to become. They're going to become Neothink®'s hurricane that blows away the anticivilization. And who is hosting all of that honest power? You are. You are sitting on top of all that honest power.

Now, let us look more deeply at the Inner Circle of our Neothink® Society. You all read the Miss Annabelle's Story. Now there is a real place, an organized force, to actualize everything you read in the Miss Annabelle's Story. The Neothink® Clubhouse Congregations will be successful at actualizing everything in Miss Annabelle's Story for three reasons: Number one is because of the Prime Literature and the brain-sweating work that went into creating that incredible, irreducible material. Number two is because of the format, the business structure we set up here with 40 years developing such a business model; the effort and the challenges of taking the unlikely Prime Literature in your three Heirloom Packages and marketing that to the world. We're not marketing automobiles or bread or commodities; we're marketing Neothink® to the world. And to have taken that from the realm of philosophy and writers into the battle-ground arena of business and succeed is a breathtaking feat that only history will shed the proper recognition upon. It is an epic story that will one day be told. We do have a Neothink® writer working and developing that story.

But our network of Clubhouse Congregations is not a structure that's just been developed during the course of our time together. This has been a gut- wrenching battle since 1968, with all the incredible learning curves it took, the battles fought, including time spent in prison. All of that is part of the value that now exists here for you and for the network of Clubhouse Congregations spreading around the country and eventually around the world. And when I say eventually, that's not very far out. It's just a matter of nailing down the format in the United States and then replicating that out to 193 countries around the world where Neothink® has penetrated. We have people all over the globe chomping at the bit to do this with us.

Now I said there are three reasons we will succeed. I've given you two. I've given you The Prime Literature and business format, the structure we have set up here. For those who read my very original Business Control, you will realize those are two of the three components for success. We have the product, we have the marketing and now the third component is personnel and that is you. You are in my big vision, part of the Big Picture vision that I never wrote down.

But you, my apprentices, particularly my pioneering apprentices, you are the third reason we will succeed. You may not fully realize it yet, but you are some of the most integrated and smartest people alive today. Why? Well, you absorbed The Prime Literature, the three original big Heirloom Packages. I believe that amounted to over 3,000 pages of the most integrated material ever written. You absorbed and understand that literature better than anyone else.

Moreover, this has been a long journey for you, too. I think it's been about three years in total when you first received your first Heirloom until now. You have demonstrated to me that you are the kind of person who has the perseverance and persistency, the strong talents and characteristics of people who will succeed.

Now remember, originally, when I first contacted you I said you had hidden skills and talent that will surface. They are surfacing now. What will further enable your hidden talents and skills to surface is the format we've set up. Such a business dynamic will create a learning curve for you. You will, week after week, with such perseverant and persistent integrating minds, learn, adapt, grow and therefore succeed.

Right now, retention is your main focus, but marketing is going to increasingly become your focus as well. Persevering is the key. It was my key and my strong point. It is my strong point and it is your key as well. And these talents and characteristics, these traits that you have, your hidden talents, are going to increasingly surface as we move forward here.

Now, I want to go back to the Big Picture. The Twelve Visions Party will rise out of the Clubhouse Congregations, out of the Inner Circle. The Church of God-Man will rise out the Inner Circle. The Inner Circle is where the power really grows because the more serious, more driven, more successful members will be in your Inner Circle. And, from within the Inner Circle of your Clubhouse Congregations will eventually arise Project Life. With that organized force, that hurricane, as I call it, of your local SOS Clubhouse Congregations around the world, with more people joining your local chapters, there will come a point where I will actualize the Association for Curing Aging and Death for the local Clubhouses. It is this format with the talent flowing into the local chapters week after week that will enable me to actualize and start the Association for Curing Aging and Death which is going to lead to Project Life.

In your Second Heirloom Package, there's an open letter to the very successful people around the world. It says the successful people possess three special qualities; they love life, they know how to succeed, and they have extensive resources. I start the letter off by talking about Michael Milken and how he made more progress, more rapidly than any other effort in history. And he's a man who loves life, he knows how to succeed, and he has extensive resources. I pose the question in that open letter; what if we had Michael Milken and Bill Gates and people like that just coming together on this dream-team to make this effort to cure aging and death? It would be like the Manhattan Project.

But I go to explain in that letter why that doesn't happen, why it's not happening today. However, with our business structure that we have now, with the growing talent and power, the cure is going to happen in the local Clubhouse Congregations. There will come a point where these talented people will find us and will come into the Inner Circle to create that dream-team, a Manhattan Project, the Project Life dynamic. It will happen. And guess who's hosting and sitting on this honest power? You are.

I want to make a little side note here. The Free Masons, the Elks, all the secret societies and clubs all pride themselves on doing social good. As we are talking about the Association for Curing Aging and Death arising from the Clubhouse

Congregations, The Neothink® Society is going outdo any and all secret societies, all societies, all clubs and groups in doing social good. We're going to outdo everyone in the realm of doing social good!

Now everything you read about in the Miss Annabelle's Story will rise out of the Clubhouse Congregations. Remember the wide scope accounting lawyers? Remember Bruce who protected business and innocent people from political policy and those regulatory bureaucrats who damaged and destroyed their lives? That's going to rise out of the Inner Circle as the talented and powerful people come inside The Neothink® Society. And it just keeps growing and growing. It's going to happen. The talent pool is going to become so great with serious- minded people who understand the Big Picture that I'm delivering to you today. They want to actualize Project Life. And it's going to start happening right there in your local SOS Clubhouses.

There's going to come a time when the education movement is going to begin. Of course, you remember the Miss Annabelle's School of Secrets in the Miss Annabelle's Story. It will be given a different name but we will begin with one school at first, and then it will spread across the country and the world. And it's going to start where? That school will arise from the Inner Circle of your SOS Clubhouse Congregations.

In science, the Overlay Charts and the God-Man theorists are going to look at all the available data differently now. Now, they will understand from having read The Prime Literature that consciousness is the unifying component of the Universe that Einstein missed. Consciousness will very quickly take over mass and energy to control the cosmos. They will take all the available data and start looking at it differently. And from that data the Overlay Charts that Frank R. Wallace planned to uncover will arise. It's going arise out of the Inner Circle of your Clubhouse Congregations. .

In the news media, remember the Patterson Press in the Miss Annabelle's Story? That is a news service based on values. A value-based news service, for example, might look at the world of celebrities and drive a wedge between their meaningless talk of politics and world events, an area of life which they have no integration with and the one area of value they do extol; their sense of youth and health, keeping their bodies fit and healthy into their later years.

The format we have here to funnel large numbers of people into your Clubhouse Congregations, week after week, is the key to your success. And those numbers are going to grow with more and more people joining the Neothink® Society with greater talent and power.

In the early days, Frank R. Wallace made the comment that what separates Neo-Tech and why it will succeed over other philosophical and idea systems is that we are disseminating Neo-Tech through business. We've reached that point now where we will hit a tipping point, a point of no return, by setting up a real Neothink® System. I developed the Neothink® System with the identification of the division of essence. This is what we have developed and that several apprentices have identified in the local Clubhouses Congregations. We set up a Neothink® business system that is going to be very effective.

The honest power that will build in the clubhouses is going to create these world-changing movements, these paradigm shifts. I talked about the paradigm shift in politics with the Twelve Visions Party and in religion with the Church of God-Man. Now /that's going to become very powerful and appealing, as you'll see. We're going to have a world-changing paradigm shift in education with the School of Geniuses laid out in the Miss Annabelle's Story. The School of Geniuses will be similar to the mentors in the Guilds during the

Renaissance man or the tutors of the great Greek philosophers, where a child's thinking breaks through boundaries to see common denominators and linking them together into Neothink® puzzles. This is where one breaks through surface logic of what "appears to be" to reveal "what is". The School of Geniuses is going to cause a major paradigm shift and where is it going to come from? It's going to actualize in the Inner Circle of the Clubhouse Congregations.

There's going to be a major paradigm shift in science and the way we look at the cosmos. There's going to be a major paradigm shift in law. There's going to be a major paradigm shift in art where the power shifts from the art brokers and elites in the art world back to the consumer and to the artist. The artist will gain the power in art as was demonstrated again, in the Miss Annabelle's Story in grass roots charts, in the music field. This will rise out of the Inner Circle of your Clubhouse Congregations.

These are world-changing paradigm shifts with honest power on a world- changing level in not just one but in every imaginable area of life. Those powers will rise out of your Inner Circle with you sitting right on top.

Remember in the first letter that I sent you I talked about the newly emerging illuminati? Do you remember that? Well, my apprentices, that is you. You are the newly emerging illuminati.

A few years ago I was listening to a talk given by Objectivist Leonard Peikoff and someone in the audience asked him a question. She asked Mr. Peikoff when he thought an objectivist world will come about. And he immediately threw his hands up in defeat and said, "Oh, long after I'm gone." And, I remember my emotional reaction; my soul immediately recoiled. I want you to know that I plan to have this evolution to the Twelve Visions World to occur during my lifetime. How will that occur and why am I so certain? Again, there are three reasons: First, the product itself, the Prime Literature that took decades to get down to the irreducible fundamentals. It took decades to idealize the Civilization of the Universe. I use the expression Civilization of the Universe with you but we use the Twelve Visions World throughout the SOS Clubhouse Congregations.

The second reason is the business structure that the Objectivists don't have. We have the business format that has taken 40 years to develop. For someone to enter the Direct Mail business and succeed is a huge endeavor. But to take the Neo-Tech/Neothink® literature into Direct Mail and succeed is the most unlikely thing to occur yet we've done it and we are very successfully. And all of that power is poised and ready to dovetail with the Neothink® movement and your Clubhouse Congregations.

And the third reason we will succeed within our lifetime is personnel who I specially selected. You are now so very integrated, so very persistent, and so very motivated.

All of you have that deep-root of motivation, that Friday-Night Essence I talk about in The Prime Literature. My "300" who are with me now in the pioneering stages of the Neothink® movement have found their Friday-Night Essence. Your child of the past has joined you in this effort. Now, you sit atop this world-changing, honest power. You are to become the new illuminati. And metaphorically speaking, you will control the world by removing dishonesty and bringing about fully integrated honesty. We are bringing about the Twelve Visions World.

When you get very effective at delivering your Workshops I want you to video tape each of those meetings. Of course, you'll have to have your audience sign waivers to do that and if they don't want to be video-taped they can still be in the meeting outside of video camera range. Then we upload all your Workshop meetings to our web site. This will be an incredible resource for hands-on learning. It will be priceless.

Level-Eight Essence Meeting
Part Two

Now I want to tell you about my vision I never wrote down:

I had this Neothink® vision in my mind during my final two years of developing the Miss Annabelle's Story. But I knew I had to first complete the Miss Annabelle's Story before moving forward with this vision, before trying to actualize this vision.

You see, Miss Annabelle's Story is one of two publications in existence that comes purely from the Civilization of the Universe. The other publication is Frank R. Wallace's Pax Neo-Tech. I started writing the Miss Annabelle's Story on Thanksgiving Day in 1997. I finished writing the Miss Annabelle's Story in 2006, nearly nine years after I started.

The reason the Miss Annabelle's Story is so emotionally moving is because it's the only right-brain-driven literature from the Civilization of the Universe. Think about what that means. I wrote that story, that faction as I call it, from the emotional perspective of "the person you were meant to be". That long-lost child of the past in you was reading along with you when you read the Miss Annabelle's Story. And at times, the child of the past within you would reach for that world that it didn't have but should have had.

I received hundreds, if not thousands of emails expressing to me that while reading Miss Annabelle's Story their child of the past would breakdown and start crying. I've gotten emails from men who said they have never cried in their adult life, but would cry, cried several times throughout that story. Even as I wrote that, it would break me down to tears. That is because Miss Annabelle's Story is the only publication coming at from the C of U. That's why it hits you with such power without warning. I understood that emotional power as I wrote the story.

I also received hundreds perhaps thousands of emails and letters from readers who never wanted Miss Annabelle's Story to end. Frank R. Wallace felt the same way, too. He said he felt sad when it was over. And I know exactly why that is. Remember, for nine years I had to keep my head in that world, in Miss Annabelle's world, in order to create that literature. And when it was over, when I could not leave this anticivilization to spend hours on end in the Twelve Visions World in my mind, I felt as if something precious has died.

But, I replaced that sadness fairly quickly with the powerful determination to actualize that vision, my greatest vision ever that had been in my head in the two final years of writing the Miss Annabelle's Story. That vision of the Twelve Visions World is the Big Picture that I am revealing to you today.

I channeled that sadness into a determination and motivation to actualize that Twelve Visions World. I just swung in to actualizing that world when I completed the Miss Annabelle's Story.

And actualizing my greatest vision brings me to you, my apprentices. You are a major part of my greatest vision; this great vision of setting up a business-like structure around the country and then around the world with my chosen ones, who were completely integrated with The Prime Literature and who persevere because of their deep-rooted motivation to bring the Twelve Visions World to the planet. That was my vision.

The Miss Annabelle's Story permanently captures what was once only a fleeting mirage of an oasis in this anticivilization. And, of course, we all know now that that oasis is the Twelve Visions World. The Miss Annabelle's Story had to be completed first before I could move on to actualizing my greatest vision, the greatest Neothink® vision. For, The Miss Annabelle's Story grabs hold of that oasis and lays it all down on paper for us, like a blueprint of our future Twelve Visions World. I needed to complete that blueprint first in order to accomplish the most important Neothink® vision to date. And together we will make that fleeting mirage of the oasis of the Twelve Visions World a lasting reality.

The blueprint is done and it is The Miss Annabelle's Story. The construction phase has begun with the launching of the A-Teams, and now the growing of the local SOS Clubhouse Congregations. Now, together with our business format, we will build that C of U, that Twelve Visions World. That Big-Picture vision that includes you is my greatest Neothink® vision to date and that's what we are going to actualize. It encompasses and incorporates all my other visions, everything to date, including all the Prime Literature. It all culminated in your SOS Clubhouse Congregations. Using the anchor of the Prime Literature, interacting through this Neothink® business format, you are on a vertical learning curve, becoming more and more successful at delivering greater and greater value to serious-minded people.

This meeting today is so important. I chose to give you the Big Picture in a general format instead of in the specific format so that you can hold the whole Big Picture in your head. And holding that Big Picture in your head is important for our Level Nine Meeting where we are going to throw the focus on one of several of the major world-changing paradigm shifts. The first major movement that's going to come out of your local Clubhouse Congregations is the Twelve Visions Party. We're going to throw the microscope on that movement in the next meeting Level Nine. We're going to power our way through that meeting detail by detail in order to launch and really start that world-changing paradigm shift.

The vision has begun. The vision is happening. And it's important for you now to have the Big Picture in your head and to be able to carry it in your head as we move through the paradigm shifts. You realize the power, the honest power that you are sitting on. You realize what my greatest Neothink vision is and how it involves you. You understand our relationship, the business relationship. You understand now the nature of The Prime Literature. You understand the nature of the 40 years in developing the business to where it is today and you understand your role. We're not talking about little local church-like chapters. We're talking about something much bigger. We're talking about really and truly changing the world, about major world-changing paradigm shifts. This is Neothink® in action, my friends.

In Meeting Level Nine, you're going to see what the future of politics is. You're going to see how it's going to change, how it has to change. It's going to change history for your children and grandchildren. We are going to change all the major paradigms of our world.

Level-Nine Essence Meeting
Introduction

Hello, and welcome to the Level-Nine Essence Meeting. In our last meeting I revealed the Big Picture vision and the major movements that will eventually arise from your Inner-Circle members of the SOS Clubhouse Congregations. The first of those major movements is the political movement, the Twelve Visions Party. Today, I will reveal to you the political pamphlet. I've worked nine months to develop this pamphlet and it's nearly complete. Today you will take a close look at this political pamphlet for the first time. The title of the political pamphlet is "Make All the People Rich Including the Poor". And it is subtitled "The Secret Society Brings You the Forbidden System".

Level-Nine Essence Meeting
Part One

Now, that title certainly does not sound political but it's very stimulating. In earlier meetings, I talked to you about the role of stimulation in this political movement and the campaign process. I explained the difference between educating people about political ideas versus stimulating people. Our process will be to stimulate people. In Meeting Level Three we talked about the Forces of Nature, the Forces of Neothink® and common denominators that culminate in huge Neothink® puzzles. We call this the Neothink® Marketing Secret. This political pamphlet is perhaps the best job I have done at applying the Neothink® Marketing Secret.

Stimulation is a major part of our formula for success. With that in mind, I want you to read the Orientation to this political pamphlet on page 397. Do this now.

You can see in the Orientation that it is very stimulating. There's a lot of motivation to read through the entire pamphlet now. One doesn't feel that it's political because people really aren't that interested in political ideas. They get worked up during campaign season when they see the candidates in debates. But voting is more a civic duty than it is something that people are motivated to follow. Apathy is huge in this country. This is the problem with third parties like the Libertarians. They really don't have a chance from my years of understanding how the mind works, as well as marketing and motivation. I know how to get these otherwise unlikely ideas of Neothink® into the hands of the people. And, that is through my ability to touch the child of the past within people, while also stimulating their Forces of Nature which is a powerful drawing card in all people. And I have perfected drawing upon the Forces of Neothink®, the child of the past which is your largest common denominator that down deep everybody wants. Understanding the Forces of Nature and the Forces of Neothink® and how to achieve those through common denominators is what I have incorporated into this pamphlet.

Again, I'd like you to go back and study the Level-Three Essence Meeting on page 49 because that will help you in understanding what's going on now in the political movement starting with this political pamphlet which will lead to, down the road, the political campaign.

Now what grounds this pamphlet is The Prime Literature as we discussed in Meeting Level Eight. It's The Prime Law that does the fundamental work while stimulation does the marketing work. An example of that is the expression "make the people rich including the poor." Imagine that expression out there in the public arena. Who would have thought that the welfare recipients would read this from cover to cover and be very excited about it? But they will be!

The key to making the political movement happen is Forces of Nature stimulation, not education but stimulation. Underneath that is The Prime Law, but on the surface we are stimulating, using the Forces of Nature and the Forces of Neothink® to touch that child of the past inside the reader, including the faulting third generation welfare recipient. Even if a person doesn't immediately respond to this political movement, I will have touched that child of the past and thus leave a remnant in that person. And somewhere down the road, they will come back to the Twelve Visions Party. Why? Because the child of the past sat up and took notice. So the more pamphlets we get out there, the more people will be left with that remnant. You will understand of this Neothink® Marketing Secret effect as you read through the pamphlet. The Forces of Nature will stimulate people to drive through the material while the Forces of Neothink® won't let it leave their memory. Every person who reads this pamphlet may not act or talk about it immediately but it leaves a remnant and they will come back to us.

Other examples the Forces of Nature in this pamphlet are expressions like "become rich, including the poor" and "become healthy, happy and creative" and "live longer". These are huge common denominators among many groups of the population. Again, I urge you to study Level-Three Essence Meeting on page 49 in concert with reading through this political pamphlet found in its entirety beginning on page 395.

The real power in this pamphlet is that I'm not just presenting the political ideas. Every Twelve Visions World principle is in this pamphlet. People will perceive not just the idea but the result of that idea, the consequence of that idea.

For example, the beginning chapters of this pamphlet express how The Prime Law is going to bring about this great wealth and health. It will also bring about real universal health, not political rhetoric. I have in this pamphlet a working approach to getting real universal wealth for everyone and real universal health for everyone, not an Obama approach. This is a real, unprecedented approach.

People will be emotionally connecting these heavy duty political ideas because of the stimulation. "Wow, I could live like a millionaire" or "I could live longer and get affordable medical care." They will perceive that could be healthy and live disease-free, live longer and live like a millionaire. That's the secret behind this pamphlet; stimulation, the Forces of Nature, and the coded Forces of Neothink® that I have worked into this pamphlet. This political pamphlet is essentially our National Platform.

Now, let me ask you a question. Have you, personally, ever read the National Platform for the Republican Party? Or the National Platform for the Democratic Party? Or any of the third, Libertarian or any of the third parties? Do you consider yourself politically inclined? Have you ever sat down at a coffee shop with others and talked about the political National Platforms? Have you actually gone through those platforms with your brother, your friend, your parents, your children? Unless you're politically active, generally, the answer is no. And you probably never will. And that, my friends, is the majority of the experience out there. Maybe a few thousand people read the Republication National Platform and maybe a few thousand have read the Democratic National Platform.

But now imagine this: I have a goal to sell this political pamphlet. And I have a very powerful approach that I've been working on for nine months. Whenever I develop a new product, I always develop the marketing approach. For, when I work on the marketing brochure or advertisement, what I'm really doing is working on that ninety-nine percent principle; that is, 99% of people who do not buy will be left with a remnant, a value, a residual which helps me elevate the value of the product itself.

If I'm successful at selling the political pamphlet for, say, $9.95 or $10, it would indicate to me two very important things. First, it would mean that by selling this and recovering my costs to print and distribute the pamphlet, I could distribute hundreds of thousands of them annually. Remember, this is our National Platform in disguise being distributed, perhaps to hundreds of thousands annually. Second, if somebody pays $10.00 for this pamphlet, my statistics have shown that they will read it from cover to cover. I doubt that the few thousand who may have picked up the National Platform for the Republican Party or the National Platform for the Democratic Party read it cover to cover.

So let's do the math here: If I'm successful in a few years about 2 million people would have read our National Platform from cover to cover. And they'll be fully integrated and very motivated because of the Forces of Nature, the Forces of

Neothink® stimulating the child of the past. We'll have 2 million ambitious Americans wanting what is expressed in this pamphlet to happen. Now that may not sound like a lot of people. But when you figure the winning percentage of eighty to a hundred-million votes needed to win a presidential election, it's huge. It's like when Lenin, during the Bolshevik Revolution, knew that if seven people understood his principles, he would win. He knew the revolution was won. With seven people…we have 2 million people. We will reach the tipping point.

Now, I want you to read through the Introduction and Chapters One and Two of this political pamphlet on pages 405 to 416. Do this now.

Let's talk about Chapter 1. Although you are reading through some heavy-duty concepts of law and politics, all along there is motivation to keep reading. You feel excited that maybe there's something real here, like the idea of universal wealth. It's not that same old political rhetoric. You know you're in for something different. You see how I am working in the Forces of Nature and I'm putting in some coded Forces of Neothink® as well.

So, you're rolling through this intriguing Chapter 1. Then you move into Chapter 2. I want you to know that Chapter 2 will actually be your Twelve Visions Party State Constitution. Of course, you have your Bylaws and other leg work throughout the State Constitutions. But the philosophical integrations that comprise all 50 State Constitutions is going to be Chapter 2.

Now realize that there are actually two approaches to achieving the Twelve Visions World through our political movement:

One way is the Prime Law and that will occur through the Prime Law Amendment which is Chapter 5. The Prime Law and the Prime Law Amendment must come through the legislative branch, that is, through Congress. Of course, the Great Replacement Program must occur before the Prime Law would be proposed as an amendment to the U. S. Constitution. So that's a ways down the road.

The second way to achieve the Twelve Visions World is through the executive branch and the Protection-Only Budget. And, of course, the Protection-Only Budget mandates that funds and spending is for protection only which is the only valid and proper purpose of government: Protection from force and the threat of force or fraud.

So, the President could submit a budget that cuts say a trillion dollars and reduces spending to where our money should be spent; on protection. Now, of course, the Congress would come back and would return a basically normal budget. Then we would go through a two-year process that would provoke the Great Replacement Program. At that point, you would basically have a sweep across the country of Twelve Vision Party candidates coming into office. Now, of course, you would only have one-third of the Senate replaced but the pressure would be so overwhelming at that, in time, by the third year, the President would see his Protection-Only Budget pass pretty much in its entirety.

Also, as you'll see in Chapter 4, the Twelve Visions Party Contract that every candidate, every member, every appointed Twelve Visions Party member will sign. This contract will bind all of their decision making to the Prime Law. It won't leave decision making up to them, up to man. The contract will make that clear through The Prime Law and that will carry a mighty effect as we start seeing Twelve Vision Party candidates moving into office.

At this point in time, The Prime Law must be presented by the Twelve Visions Party and it must be presented in the State Constitutions, the TVP State Constitution. Again, the Chapter

2 is going to be the philosophical portion in all 50 State Constitutions for the Twelve Visions Party.

Moving on to Chapter 3; Chapter 3 will also be reformatted and become your State Platform. Previously I discussed that I'll provide you with this philosophical portion of the State Platform. Then each state would more or less look at the Republican and Democratic planks. You would, with the use of The Prime Law, determine which ones were valid and which ones weren't. Which planks were valid but not as a government function but as a function of the private sector. Now I've done that for you. I put the planks into your State Platform and not only did I put in the planks, but I put in the consequences of those planks. That's the secret behind all this, not just showing the political idea but showing the consequence, the powerful result of our platform. That's the power behind the National Platform, the State Platform, the Constitution, the pamphlet itself, our entire campaign.

Then we'll make clear the awesome tool of the Prime Law. We will make clear that the layman, the citizen himself, can use the Prime Law to look at any plank by any political party and immediately see which ones are bogus and which ones are valid. That's the beauty of the Prime Law; it's so simple that the layman can determine what's right and wrong, what the government should be doing and what it should not be doing. He won't be fooled by illusions any longer. He has The Prime Law that is black and white.

What I would like you to do now is read Chapter 3 which begins on page 417. This will become your State Platforms. Go ahead now and read Chapter 3 on page 417 now.

Having read Chapter 3, I'm going to provide you with the whole political package with your State Platform, the philosophical portion of your State Constitution and your National Platform and I'll also include the political pamphlet for you to study and understand thoroughly as well.

Let's move on to Chapter 4. There you will read about the movement and the TVP Contract which is crucially important. Also in Chapter 4, realize that I struggled for years with the idea of starting a political party. My concern was that it would run out of control. I know how all people, including all of you, including myself and the most integrated Neothink® person, integrated with the Twelve Visions World and all its concepts still has vulnerabilities, illusions, bubbles of mysticisms, bicameral longings that prevent one from through to "what is". That is just the way man is in the anticivilization. So, even with the best of visionaries, the party would eventually disintegrate.

But with The Prime Law we remove all of man's decisions including the visionaries, all decisions about creating, interpreting and executing the law, by removing all man. If the decision is always made by the Prime Law through the TVP Contract, then every decision a Twelve Visions Party candidate, politician, judge, every decision made by a Twelve Visions Party member is, no matter what one's personal feelings, agendas, thoughts, beliefs may be won't matter. With every decision made through The Prime Law, then I had no more concerns or fears about starting this political party.

So go ahead now and read Chapter 4 on page 423. In Chapter 4 you will read the contract that all TVP members will sign. Read now Chapter 4 on page 423 now.

You see in Chapter 4 if ever a Twelve Visions Party member intentionally votes or makes a decision that is obviously against The Prime Law or has a trend of unknowingly doing so, they will be publically disowned from the Twelve Visions Party.

Now, let's move on to Chapter 5 where we get into some heavy-duty, hard- hitting political ideas. But the ideas are always presented with the results, the consequences of those ideas. And the reason we can do this while no one else can is every other political party or candidate is merely rhetoric. In the end, they're going for their own political or personal agendas. They're building their career and power around promoting their own political ambitions. They may try to touch on some Forces of Nature but everybody knows down deep what it really is. The American people understand that one particular party is getting their re-election through promising the entitlements and the other political party is trying to push their personal religious and moral beliefs onto the public. The people down deep understand this.

We have no rhetoric and no promise of change. And everything here is real, demonstrated with examples. We have powerful proof behind what we say. That's going to cause us to become unstoppable once the momentum begins.

Now, in Chapter 5, we talk about the Prime Law Amendment to the U. S. Constitution. It's the one integration that the Founding Fathers missed. Had they made this final integration, the Prime Law, their beautiful U. S government idea would have never decayed the way it has over the past 200 plus years. The founding Fathers' original concept would still be alive and we would be in a Twelve Visions World right now. We'd be in that super society, and everyone would be wealthy and happy and creative, living and playing each day. Everyone would be living the creation-driven life they were meant to be living. They'd be healthy and living longer, hot on the trail of biological immortality. However, this one, simple, obvious integration was missed.

One of the first papers I ever wrote when I was a very young man was called, "The Obvious Theory". As I was getting into business and understanding the way the world operated, I realized some of the most profound and powerful breakthroughs often times happened to be the most obvious. And, I called that "The Obvious Theory." And much of my success, early on, was attributed to "obvious theory". I understood and looked for the obvious. Throughout history in business and science often times the most obvious things are what huge profound breakthroughs come from, breakthroughs that take us to the next level. With that said, you see then that The Prime Law is so obvious. Yet, the brilliant Founding Fathers missed this final integration. Had they pulled that final integration the world would be the way I described in The Miss Annabelle's Story".

Once The Prime Law is an Amendment to the U.S. Constitution, it, in essence, becomes the Supreme Law because every law, every regulation must pass through The Prime Law, as it filters out the bad laws and regulations that are all based on initiatory force. The Prime Law is the beginning of all laws. No new laws, at that point, can be created that violate The Prime Law. With The Prime Law, we will have a shift from a government based on power to a government based on service. That's a huge paradigm shift. Now you will not necessarily understand how profound a paradigm shift this will bring from reading Chapter 5 and that is intentional. However, in our Meeting Level Ten I'm going to reveal something that no one has ever read before which shows this paradigm shift away from a government based on power. As nearly perfect as the U. S. Constitution is, The Prime Law makes that final paradigm shift from a power- based to a service-based government.

Now I want you read Chapter 5 on page 429 as though you were a layman being handed this pamphlet perhaps having paid $10.00 for it. Read Chapter 5 from that perspective and see how it leaves you feeling. It leaves you feeling different than you've ever felt before toward politics and government. It generates an excitement, an enthusiasm inside for something different, for something you can sink your teeth into. Things really can be different!

So go now to page 429 and read Chapter 5.

An Amendment to the U.S. Constitution must start in Congress. And for that to happen, we must first experience the Great Replacement Program in which we replace Republicans and Democrats with the Twelve Visions Party members who have signed the Twelve Visions Party Contract. Now I don't know if that will happen before there's a Twelve Visions Party President or after a Twelve Visions Party President, as is the case in your Miss Annabelle's Story. Recall first Daniel Ward is elected President. Then two years later during the mid-term elections, we had the Great Replacement Program..

Now, if The Prime Law becomes an amendment to the Constitution following the election of a Twelve Visions Party President, our amendment must now move from the legislative branch to the executive branch. Then we would switch from The Prime Law to the Protection-Only Budget. Chapter 6 on page 437 describes such a switch and shows the full political system changes from a power basis to a service basis government. Read Chapter 6 on page 437. Do this now.

In Chapter 6, I tackled some very big concepts, the major changes that will occur, especially with the marketing approach behind both this stimulating political pamphlet and the future stimulating political campaign. People will be left with that remnant and they will be filled with stimulation…a very potent combination. The tipping point can be reached and when it is reached, everything changes.

The freedom paradigm begins when traction builds behind this political movement because things out there will start happening even before The Prime Law Amendment or the Protection-Only Budget. For one, companies and businesses will begin to sense that risk to invest money into research and development is lowering. The risk of losing such an investment is shrinking from the effects the Twelve Visions Party in the minds of ordinary Americans. Once this trend begins it will rapidly accelerate to a stampede. As the momentum builds a freedom paradigm will arise on its own. And this freedom paradigm will unleash more and more of the potential geniuses of society who have been suppressed, caught in that regulatory web, afraid or just simply cannot can't move up. They will break free, raising that lid on society while bringing everyone up with them.

So as the Twelve Visions Party and this political pamphlet begins having influence out there, businesses will start investing more money in research and development, which will lead to certain breakthroughs and advancement and more job creation. Geniuses of society will feel more able to develop their creativity, to take risks and move forward.

Chapter 7 gets into this whole effect of the geniuses of society when unhindered and loved. Today the geniuses of society are vilified in every movie you see and in every newspaper article you read. They're the villains. The most valuable people in society, the job creators, are the villains while the malevolent politicians and political and bureaucratic leaders are loved and revered.

When this political pamphlet gets into the hearts and minds of hundreds of thousands, it's going to start changing the psyche of the average American, the ordinary American. He'll start looking differently at the geniuses of society, at the business leaders, the entrepreneurs who take risks and live with risk every day to provide jobs and value to ordinary Americans.

In the super society, the geniuses of society are not going to just offer you jobs of labor with very restricted incomes. No, they're going to tap your Friday-Night Essence. They're going to establish jobs of essence. They're going to create jobs that you can fulfill with your Friday-Night Essence and limitless creativity. When the geniuses are loved and revered and those who try to hold them back are scorned, it will create momentum.

Read Chapter 7 on page 465. In Chapter 7, you will read the story about great geniuses of society. I often use the analogy of the computer revolution to explain what will happen in the Twelve Visions World with unhindered growth. But some have argued that the computer revolution was an anomaly. So let's not use high technology as an analogy. Let's go back a hundred years to the down and dirty railroad industry. So it is in Chapter 7 that I reveal the story of James J. Hill to demonstrate how everything I say in this political pamphlet has almost come true over a hundred years ago in an industry that had nothing to do with computers or high technology or communication whatsoever.

So go now and read Chapter 7 on page 465. Read about the geniuses of society and the Great Prosperity Explosion that's coming our way. Do this now.

People would tend to dismiss what you just read there in Chapter 7 as false utopian thinking, or showy political rhetoric but here's the thing:

The Soviet Empire collapsed. Why? People say we out-spent Russia. But the real reason is this evolution of free advancements from the communication revolution. The invention of the television, photo copiers and fax machines enabled more and more Soviet people to see proof what the freedom in the Western world could bring them. That's really what brought down the Soviet Empire. Once people see proof with their own eyes, it's like the Victor Hugo quote, "An invasion of armies can be resisted, but not an idea whose time has come".

Now with that in mind, we have the computer revolution as our proof. So now communism in China; its breaking down internally and business is beginning to thrive all because of the Internet and the satellite TV. That's what's breaking down communism.

The computer revolution is what's going to break down our political structure as we know it because the computer revolution was proof of unhindered geniuses of society being able to move forward without that regulatory web. The computer revolution happened so quickly and advanced so rapidly that the government didn't know how to get a grip on it. And so we saw buying power multiply a thousand fold and, in some cases, a million fold.

So we have proof that is going to stay with people. They're going to see the correlation between the computer revolution and the great technological revolution that will drive up our buying power in every single industry once we remove that regulatory web. And we have the actual system to do that. This is the Forbidden System because the leaders know this to be true. And, in fact, next meeting, I'm going to show you how this goes all the way back to Socrates. All the leaders from Socrates forward understood what's in this political pamphlet. It's the Forbidden System because it's been forbidden, withheld from the masses.

We're just going to blow the lid off this Forbidden Secret with stimulation. We understand the Forces of Neothink®. We know how to pull those together through the common denominators and we know how to code in the Forces of Neothink®. This pamphlet is going to do now what Common Sense did back in 1776. It's going to change the way everybody sees politics and how the world really works. It goes back to removing our bicameral mysticism. We don't have to necessarily say that here as that is too sophisticated a concept for the masses. People will see, through the Forces of Nature, how they can become millionaires without lifting a finger. Literally, they just sit back while their buying power goes through the roof.

I didn't lift a finger but I can buy a million times the buying power now than I could ten or fifteen years ago. My children enjoy outrageous computer technology; they play on it every day. Buying power from unhindered geniuses of society just blew away the regulatory web and off they go. And you don't do anything to receive the fortunes they bring you.

Now, I've seen post on our active member's web site from apprentices who have experienced this sense of urgency to launch the Twelve Visions Party. I appreciate the urgency. It's admirable as it shows me you understand The Prime Literature and the approaching catastrophic era in all areas of life. We see the economy deteriorating and we are facing some very serious medical catastrophes such as the avian flu and other unsuspected viruses and bacteria. So you understand the approaching catastrophic era and it is coming right at us. But remember, I'm in the driver's seat of this movement. The driver always has more of a comfort zone than the passenger because he has his hands on the wheel. Believe me, I would love to have this material come out much faster but that's not how Prime Literature works. But it's done now.

Chapter 8 next on page 489 reveals the medical world catastrophes we are facing as part of a wider catastrophic era. The one answer to saving us from the catastrophic era, and it is what I call the Great Rescue. This pamphlet is establishing the Twelve Visions Party, The Prime Law, The Protection-Only Budget all to free the geniuses of society. It will drive the geniuses, the doctors and scientists back into medical research. It will drive businesses to invest research dollars in medicine like never before.

Interesting point: You know anti-aging used to be considered quackery when my father, Dr. Frank R. Wallace first began exploring the whole concept of biological immortality. We were called cranks and crackpots back then. However today, every major medical project, one way or another, is linked to anti-aging. Of course, we were ahead of our time as is the case with people using Neothink®. In fact, because major medical projects today are linked to anti-aging is an indication of the Forces of Neothink® beginning to emerge in society at large. And, I see that emergence of Neothink® in society at large in the wide-spread damnation of politics and politicians. So, I'm beginning to see some signs of the Forces of Neothink® emerging. This is going to be a powerful drawing card when the great technological revolution begins as a result of the Protection-Only Budget and eventually The Prime Law Amendment, and generally the influence the Twelve Visions Party starts taking hold out there. Businesses will put more money into research and development and potential geniuses of society will start taking more risks.

When the great technological revolution begins, people will begin loving life, experiencing the life they were meant to live, experiencing creativity, experiencing their Friday-Night Essence and playing at life as they did when they were children. When people experience such happiness and exhilaration after breaking free from their stagnation ruts, the cry for health and longevity is going to be enormous. That's when the sleeping giant awakes and the geniuses of society turn their focus to medicine and research, Project Life will roar to life with vigor greater than the moon project or the Manhattan Project.

Project Life is going to take over with such velocity, it will be unlike anything the world has ever seen. And you got a taste of that in the Miss Annabelle's Story and the race for life.

Chapter 8 reveals what's going to happen when the Twelve Visions Party moves in and arrests the advantage now that the viruses, microbes have on our modern technology. Read Chapter 8 on page 489 now.

Reading Chapter 8, you saw how I coded the Forces of Neothink® and longevity in there to reach through to the child of the past. Chapter 9 really reaches in and grabs hold of that child of the past to leave a remnant with the reader they will not be able to forget. Everyone who reads this political pamphlet will not be able to forget. For in Chapter 9 I bring out the Forces of Nature and the Forces of Neothink®. Both are touched upon in Chapter 9.

For example, the propagation of species is a very powerful Force of Nature. That's why both political parties, the Democrats and Republicans, touch upon education during a campaign season. The propagation of our species, the well-being of our children is a powerful common denominator.

But Chapter 9 also cleverly touches the reader's child of the past within. Remember in Level-Three Essence Meeting I revealed to you how I tap into the child of the past in my readers. All the way from the initial marketing booklet that anyone ever received from me I tap the child of the past. I tap the child of the past in Chapter 9 more than anywhere else in this pamphlet as it is the last chapter. I am doing this intentionally to leave the child of the past with coded messages. Anyone who reads this pamphlet will not be able to forget the Twelve Vision Party for the child of the past within still longs to live the life he or she was meant to live. That longing, that sense of something missing in life as we get older is still inside all of us. I touch and thus re-awaken the child of the past more so in Chapter 9 than anywhere else in the political pamphlet, which is, as I said, our National Platform in disguise.

This remnant that I'm leaving with the child of the past in every reader will build the strength of our TVP in a geometric fashion and will drive us to that tipping point much quicker. Every reader will eventually be pulled back to the Twelve Visions Party. Combine that with the power of our distribution plans, the Neothink® Marketing Secret, marketing this pamphlet and getting it out to hundreds of thousands of people per year. Do the math and realize we have something very powerful in our hands that will grow with great momentum as each year passes. The Neothink® Marketing Secret will prevail.

Go now to page 501 and read Chapter 9.

In Chapter 9 you see the effect the geniuses of society are going to have throughout all industries and what that's going to do for you, for your family, for our country, for our future. You can see that we are held down in the darkness, held back from achieving that super society, that Twelve Visions World. The political pamphlet, however, is giving people a look forward into that Twelve Visions World. (One thing I express in the National Platform at www.tvpnc.org that is not in the political pamphlet is the full application of Neothink and why Neothink is the only legitimate way to actually see forward into the future.)

All right, now here's what's going to happen next. From this pamphlet, I'll now break out the State Constitution, essentially Chapter 2 of the political pamphlet, and the State Platform which is essentially Chapter 3 of the political pamphlet, and the TVP Contract which is Chapter 4 of the political pamphlet, and the National Platform which is essentially the entire political pamphlet, but it will be formatted differently.

I'll develop the license agreement for you that enables you to move ahead with my trademarked names. Then I'm going to put together a political package similar to how those A-Teams that have launched received a package from us at the beginning. Once you sign the licensing agreement, you will next submit to your Secretary of State the TVP State Constitution, the State Platform, the National Platform as provided in this package. You will then officially start our Twelve Visions Party in your state then nationwide. I will also send you several copies of the political pamphlet. I want you to study and know that pamphlet thoroughly for your own discourse and potential political campaigns.

Now, let's talk about launching the political movement. Remember, this is a tier-two dynamic. In your local SOS Clubhouse Congregations there will be a very strong percentage of people who want to see things change as they deeply integrate The Prime Literature. They will be motivated to do something about creating change. Those people are your Inner Circle. And it's in the Inner Circle where the Twelve Visions Party political movement happens along with the other movements that I talked to you about last meeting when I revealed to you the Big Picture. The Twelve Visions Party, the political movement, is the first major movement that will rise out of your local SOS Clubhouse Congregations.

Now you can approach the masses directly. You can create a movement on your own. You could put up posters or give talks or visit universities, run ads in newspapers about a new political movement. You can start a Twelve Visions Party movement separate from your SOS chapter. And this can become a very powerful recruiting tool to bring the public into your Introduction Meetings, into your Clubhouse Congregations. The masses that you approach with the political movement will see the millionaire phenomenon, the money that can come their way along with health, creativity, happiness and love through the Twelve Visions World. Then express to those individuals that although the Twelve Visions Party will deliver these values down the road, you can reap all the benefits of the Twelve Visions World today in the Neothink® Society. It is in the Neothink Society where you learn these advantages, these secrets, and how to apply them in your life today. This whole movement arose from The Neothink® Society. Now, you just brought in a new member to your SOS Clubhouse Congregation. The political movement will be a powerful recruiting tool.

Recall again in our last meeting when I revealed the Big Picture and the major movements, specifically the political movement that we are initiating now. I also revealed that the other twin pillar of the anticivilization, religion would be trumped by the Church of God-Man and the SOS Bible and will follow the initiation of the political movement. We also have the Association for Curing Aging and Death and the SOS Schools of Geniuses. We also have the SOS News media and SOS lawyers. Remember the wide-scope accounting lawyers in the Miss Annabelle's Story?

There'll be the SOS artists who take back the power from the elite and there'll be the God-Man theorists who break open the whole way of looking at the cosmos.

The Big Picture is coming together today with the political movement, the first of these major movements.

Next meeting I'm going to disclose the never-before-revealed blueprint for how the government will make the shift from a power basis to a service-basis government. There's never been a government based on a service anywhere ever. Because of the stimulation in the Forces of Nature and Neothink® the common denominators and The Prime Literature all coming together, a service- based government is going to seem very natural and very appealing.

Now, you finally have the thinking tools to be able to perceive the Neothink® picture that I'll reveal to you next meeting. And with this Neothink® picture in your head as you discuss politics with your gathering of people, you'll leave your audience in awe. The Neothink® picture that I will reveal to you next meeting is going to serve you very well at this time. I appreciate you, my apprentices, with all of my heart. I really do. You are a key puzzle piece in making this happen and bringing this to the public.

We're launching the political movement. I am getting together a package that will include your legal papers, reformatted State Constitutions, your State and National

Platforms and the political pamphlets. I look forward to getting this political movement officially started.

It's just a joy to communicate with you in these essence meetings. I look forward to our next meeting. Until then, read through the entire political pamphlet, the Forbidden System on pages 395 to 509.

Level-Ten Essence Meeting
Introduction

Welcome to the Level-Ten Essence Meeting.

What happens after your twelfth meeting with me? Well, that's when you graduate from apprentice to mentor. Now, you need to prepare. You need to start preparing now for certain issues that you will have to deal with when you become mentors. And today, I'm going reveal one of those issues that you've all witnessed; people's misconceptions about money, making money, becoming wealthy.

Level-Ten Essence Meeting
Part One

You see, in the anticivilization money is scarce and it's hard to accumulate wealth. In the Twelve Visions World, that will all change. You've read The Prime Literature so you understand how this will happen. You understand the Twelve Visions Party and the political movement and what that will bring to society; universal wealth, universal health, and peace to society. Money in the Twelve Visions World is abundant and easy, but as I said, in the anticivilization that's not the case.

Now, all the elements for making money even in this anticivilization are in The Prime Literature. However, few of you are making really good money and, of course, that's because making money in the anticivilization is very hard. That's because in this anticivilization the political structure, the business structure, the educational structure, the emotional and psychological structures are all geared for suppression and stagnation.

The sales literature that you originally received from me referred to certain people who evolved, who made the journey that you are now taking with me.; people who evolved into the Twelve Visions World, into the C of U dynamics here on Earth. Those people entered into the Twelve Visions World even while living in the anticivilization. Therefore, money to those people comes easy and it is abundant.

Now you've seen certain apprentices become disillusioned because they expected to have a monetary windfall when they walked into The Neothink® Society. Unfortunately, that's a mystical concept. In the anticivilization, such abundance is not going to happen the way these disillusioned apprentices hoped. Some were expecting such a windfall based on the letter I sent them. However, as I said, that letter I sent was a reflection of those who had gone through the journey and had entered the C of U dynamics and became value creators driving on their Friday-Night Essence. When you create values that did not exist before and live a creation-driven life, you will then enter into an abundance of wealth.

The human mind is meant for creation. The conscious mind is the only thing in existence that can create. Our purpose in life is to become value creators. If we don't then we fall into a life of stagnation. The goal of our journey together is to bring out your hidden traits, your hidden talents and skills. You are the searchers who I found and the child of the past within you wants to create, wants to become a value creator, who wants to live the life you were meant to live.

Now, as you graduate to mentors, it will fall on you to deal with this specific misunderstanding about achieving wealth. The reason it will fall upon you is those who come into The Neothink® Society through your local SOS Clubhouse Congregations are coming in with 1/12th of The Prime Literature. So, you're even more likely to run into such misconceptions about money. So I want you to prepare for that now.

Remember everything in this anticivilization, every structure of society is geared toward suppression. It's an anticivilization where a ruling class ruling, a parasitical elite lives off of your backs. When everything is geared toward suppression and stagnation, it is very difficult to make money, particularly to accumulate an abundance of wealth.

As your apprentices take their journey, receiving The Prime Literature each and every month, coming to the Clubhouse Meetings and the Workshop Meetings, they're going to discover "what is" just as you are now discovering. You are my first wave of apprentices, my "300". I need to be sure that you evolve to each new level before we move on to the next level. Remember when you received my Heirloom packages? I specifically spaced out the introduction of the next Heirloom, your next level. Most businesses would have you purchasing those three heirlooms back to back. It took most of you about two years to receive all three heirlooms. That's a long time and I did that very deliberately. Now, because of your integration with The Prime Literature, you understand why the

The Twelve Visions World of abundance, wealth, prosperity, health and peace will come through the political movement. There will be exceptions. If you remember from The Prime Literature, people will break through as those people had in the sales literature that I refer to. But for most people, entering the life they were meant to live is going to happen because of this much larger movement we are handling together.

I want to share with you an insight I had. At one point early on, I considered making wealth the focal point of entering The Neothink® Society. In the past I held seminars and worked one-on-one with people with the very specific objective to bring about wealth in their lives. And I was very successful at that. But, as you know, I have worked for all of my adult life with this Big Picture in my mind. This journey of mine has always been to achieve that Big Picture. For 26 years, I idealized my Prime Literature. Now we are actualizing that Big Picture. Focusing on generating wealth would not have brought about the Big Picture. The Big Picture was laid out as a blueprint in the Miss Annabelle's Story. There is no such thing in the anticivilization as easy or abundant wealth. What I did with you is I shifted the focus from money-making techniques per se to the Big Picture, to becoming the person you were meant to be and evolving into a value creator. Living the life you were meant to live is our Big-Picture journey that incorporates your Friday-Night Essence and Ten-Second Miracles.

Once you are racing ahead on your own vector of value creation, driven by your Friday-Night Essence where you love what you are doing, you will eventually break into a wealth-generating position. I've seen it over and over again in people who have read The Prime Literature and became an active Neothink® member. They are generating wealth through their Friday-Night Essence and value creation. They make Ten-Second Miracles through using integrated thinking and then Neothink® puzzle building. They become value creators. Once you are on that vector of value creation, on your Friday-Night Essence, making great wealth is possible.

So, that wealth-making dynamic exists but is very rare and difficult in the anticivilization. But you are moving in the right direction. It's a long-term journey and we're on this journey together. We're beginning to see now apprentices breaking into value creation. We're beginning to see that happening since this past meeting, since the Meeting Level Nine. And this is about when I expected to see these breakthroughs to happen. Now it's going to happen at a more rapid pace. Once a person makes the evolutionary leap into value creation, from a value producer to value creator, that person moves on a unique vector that bypasses all competition.

For example, look at the Neothink® Society. What competition does the Neothink® Society have? There is no competition. The driving force is the goal and the ultimate survival pressure of us dying, of us losing the battle to death, is our driving force. It's not competition.

Another example is the Twelve Visions Party. When we enter the extremely competitive fields — the political arena — with this political, you will see there is *no* competition. The whole political movement is an example of value creation moving on a vector, a unique vector of value creation with no competition. We're starting to see the breaks in the ceiling of suppression and we're starting to see apprentices break through as well.

Remember that when I first contacted you I said that you are the chosen ones and I literally meant that. I believe someday you will add values back into society. Recall that? We're beginning to see that now. We're beginning to see Level Ten apprentices creating value for the Society.

Also recall from our earlier level meetings, you as a group are actualizing the Superpuzzle as I presented in The Miss Annabelle's Story. My expectation of you now is different than in the past. You have a very great responsibility and many of you know this. I want to relate two recent emails from an apprentice who truly understands this great responsibility. I did not ask this apprentice for his input. It just showed up in my Inbox:

"Thank you for your continued kind words and effective support. Having the opportunity to use my Friday-Night Essence of business building and mentoring to spread your painstaking and well written words to the masses is an honor and privilege for me. The words of Frank R. Wallace and yourself have enriched me beyond dollar value.

"To realize I am truly a value creator is a gift I treasure. Thank you for the opportunity to search and find this and other valuable assets."

And a couple of days later, in my Inbox, addressed to Mark Hamilton, I found another email from this same apprentice:

"Thank you for your ongoing, continued support to offer me the opportunity to actively partake in the global face-of-the-world launch. It is a wonder to watch the vision unfold and be personally involved.

"The opportunity to continue to advance my integrated thinking, along with ongoing power thinking, is establishing a new and exciting world for me. Participating in the weekly national conference call, plus the preparation to conduct an effective meeting, as well as integrating with all of the current and upcoming A-Teams has forced me, happily, to step up my leader program and put into daily practice the seven power techniques. The results are amazing. I am feeling pretty amazing with the increase of my happiness by creating more and more value.

"Also, I am putting to use more and more of the tools offered in the heirloom books. My activity is giving me more cause to continue to stretch and use the effective methods you have offered to us.

"Note: Big dollars, big money should not always be measured exclusively in monetary value."

As you begin to bring in more and more people to your SOS Clubhouses, realize people read only one-twelfth of the Prime Literature. You, my Level Ten apprentices, soon-to-be-mentors must deal with their wide-eyed desire for instant gratification, for fast wealth and windfall money. You must be prepared, you must power think now how to answer these people, how to help them see the wider picture that our apprentice here just expressed.

To this end I want you to power think and I want this to be a joint effort. I want you to discuss among yourselves and post your good ideas and breakthroughs on our discussion board. You are preparing yourself to become mentors so I want you to prepare yourself to deal with apprentices who need a little guidance when they come in, a little push in the right direction. I am replicating my vision and passion to you, and then in turn, you are to replicate that vision, that Big Picture and passion to those who you bring in. This is how the movement spreads from myself and my very close associates, my "300", then to 3,000, 30,000 and 300,000 and so on until we reach that tipping point.

In the National A-Team Meetings, I've seen my apprentices comparing what we're doing now, bringing about the Twelve

Visions World, to the Founding Fathers bringing about our new nation. That is a very good analogy and I've enjoyed seeing that. It is a very good parallel to what we are doing now. As a matter of fact, the Founding Fathers were probably the closest Neothink® men than anyone who has ever lived; men like Thomas Jefferson, James Madison, George Washington, Benjamin Franklin, Thomas Paine.

Now, let's take that analogy further. I want you to imagine for a moment the focus of those Founding Fathers. I want you to imagine what it must have been like, sitting around having their discussions. Imagine their focus, driving on their Big Picture; for the first time taking the rule of man out of the hands of man into the rule of law and understanding the prosperity explosion similar to the prosperity explosion I envision. Those men back then had a very similar vision. Imagine their focus. It would be equivalent to my focus and drive. When those Founding Fathers gathered to share that vision just as I am sharing my vision with you, my Level Ten apprentices, let's call their meetings the Society of Secrets. Those men got together and they had their secret meetings and planned their strategies, shared their philosophies and how they were going to disseminate their vision, and how they were going to convince the man and achieve the tipping point. They were the Society of Secrets.

Now I want you to imagine during the Founding Fathers' meetings what their focus must have been like, their energy and intensity. Think about what they knew was at stake and what would happen if they didn't succeed. They knew what was at stake in their minds and they shared that with each other, they shared an emotional connection. And the Founding Fathers focused on their success on a united level, eventually on a national level. They exerted historic and heroic effort into their Society of Secrets, tirelessly, voluntarily, without pause, without pay, without fixating on money.

We need that same passion today in our Society of Secrets in order to succeed. And this is what I am looking for. My Level Ten apprentices, you have reached the point in time where you are among the Founding Fathers of the Twelve Visions World. You can become the Thomas Jefferson, the James Madison, the George Washington, the Thomas Paine of our time. You, my Level Ten apprentices, have their passion, their vision and focus, their drive to succeed. This is what it's going to take. You, my "300" with me are the Founding Fathers of the Twelve Visions World.

We have spent over a year together now as my selected few. I have been planning this Society of Secrets movement with my chosen ones, with my selected searchers for many years. This has been an utter and complete dedication of mine, developing this movement to where it becomes self-perpetuating, to where we reach a tipping point.

But from an opportunity cost standpoint, I am behind my normal course of value creation. Still I will not waiver in my commitment to you. I have always operated from the largest perspective and in the end, those who operate from that larger perspective, from an integrated thinkers' perspective, will achieve levels of wealth they never dreamed of. But I work with a long-term picture at the expense of near-term financial gains. I've always operated that way from my days of poverty until now. I view my energy, time and monetary loss as voluntary time that I put into developing you. In the long term, my investment is bringing me returns far beyond any other near-term gain. I am replicating my vision and my passion to you and from there, from replicating Mark Hamilton out there to my "300", you in turn, will replicate this vision and passion to the masses. And they will be able to replicate and soon. For a near-term loss, the long term will be achieved through this approach. This is a clear example of Neothink® at work.

Prior to physically starting this approach, I worked for 9 years developing and getting just right the Prime Literature, the Miss Annabelle's Story knowing all along this would be our blueprint, our guideline, our road map. When I selected you I stated right from the beginning with the hopes of value coming back into the Society of Secrets. Now that is happening. We've got our people and we'll be able to kick off the Twelve Visions Party.

We are now approaching our final 3 meetings, starting with today's meeting. This is the final leg of your journey with me. This is when apprentices start putting value back into the Society at the national level. So, I'm going to use an unusual analogy here. But because you are Level Ten apprentices and have read most of the Prime Literature in your original three Heirloom Packages, I believe you will grasp this analogy:

You are all very familiar with the concept of "Zon and The Long Wave, We the Creators of Heavens and Earths" written by Frank R. Wallace. That particular publication explains how, in the course of the universe, we are on either side of the long wave, either side of the explosion cycle or the implosion cycle where all conscious life would perish. As consciousness progresses and conquers —takes control over — nature, consciousness would not allow itself to perish at either end of the grand cycle. And Dr. Wallace, in other publications, explains how consciousness would prevent that universe collapse from occurring through black holes putting more energy back into the universe or creating gravity units or creating black holes to basically allow the universe to oscillate at the most optimal dynamic for conscious life.

And in my writings, I explain how a Zon which is Frank R. Wallace's expression for very advanced God-Man, who has long since developed biological immortality, evolving with knowledge progressing at nearly the speed of light for billions of years, could potentially have created our universe. What is the real objective of Zon then? The purpose of Zon, the most developed conscious being is value creation. Creating value is how our brain experiences happiness in life. The human mind needs to become a creator, needs to move into value creation.

Now as the advanced God-Man advances, more and more time passes, becomes an immortal and lives for thousands of years and tens of thousands of years. Well, what is the ultimate value creation? We understand that consciousness is a supreme value of the universe but the ultimate value creation is to create realms of existence where conscious life will evolve.

So if Zon created our universe I explain in my literature that the greatest joy Zon could experience is putting back value into the universe through conscious life.

Now I draw that analogy to a Zon creating the universe to Mark Hamilton creating the Society of Secrets which brings the Civilization of the Universe to Earth. And what would be my greatest joy? My greatest joy would be to see you evolve into value creators and ultimately put value back into the Society of Secrets, the C of U on Earth. The greatest value reflection a Zon could receive comes when life evolves, conscious life evolves in his new realm of created existence. Then that conscious life becomes value creators and eventually puts value back into Zon's house, into his universe or his galaxy.

Thus my greatest joy, my greatest value reflection on our way to the goal comes to me when I see you become value creators putting value creation back into the universe, into our house, into the Society of Secrets as we're beginning to see now.

My goal is not money. My goal is the same as Theodore Winter's goal in the Miss Annabelle Story. Theodore, being the world's greatest businessman, came to a point where the business and profits did not matter. Theodore wanted to achieve the Superpuzzle, biological immortality. The goal here is the same goal as in the Miss Annabelle's Story. And the Miss Annabelle's Story demonstrates what I know must occur, we all must all work toward making the Superpuzzle happen. We must all contribute what we can. Remember the twelve students when they realized what their Superpuzzle was at the reunion in the final chapter in Book 1 they realized what they needed to do to achieve their goal. They realize what the puzzle pieces were and what role they were going to play toward that Superpuzzle.

So that is the most important thing you could do for me and for the goal is to become one with the goal. You have been successfully replicated. You have successfully absorbed my vision and my passion. You are becoming geniuses of society. And I have proof of that. A real genius of society in the future is not a function of intelligence. It's a function of integration and evolving into Neothink®, where you can build puzzles that break through beyond what anyone has ever seen...to new knowledge that no one else can see. Right now, you can see beyond the anticivilization to the Civilization of the Universe, because you absorbed The Prime Literature. You see beyond what even the smartest people see. Further proof is when I see your interactions on the discussion boards. I see your growth and development where you may not.

Like siblings. When they live together, siblings don't see each other's growth, they don't grasp it. They see each other every day, every morning, every night. But when relatives come and visit, they're blown away by the physical growth they see in these siblings. This is what I see in you; growth that you don't see.

Here's yet another example and is a reflection of what I'm talking about. This past month a very high paid, high powered Intellectual Property lawyer out of Washington, D.C. needed to see our secret web site to deal with some trademark protection issue for us. Now mind you, this is a multi-millionaire, powerful, renowned lawyer. And he's a complete and total outsider coming to our Society. He was absolutely blown away by what he saw. He was blown away by the level of integrations being made and the discussions happening in the discussion boards and in the meetings. In fact, this high-powered lawyer was in awe of what we are doing and what you are doing. This was an honest lawyer coming in and looking to help me get the proper intellectual property protection as we go more and more public. And his response was almost one of intimidation. That's power coming from you now, my Level Ten apprentices.

So understand, you may not see your growth today but I and particularly outsiders see that growth, accomplishments, and level of integrated thinking. Make no mistake, you are now becoming value creators and forming vectors, unique vectors of value creation that you are moving on. You are building value, permanent values for the Society of Secrets that will always be there. Don't forget, the greatest thing we can do for the Zon that created the existence field that we live in and enjoy is to ultimately put value back into that existence field.

Remember in the Miss Annabelle's Story when the characters went from God-Man to Zon's and that was when they launched Trinity to go and rescue Beorapparaus, another planetary system. They were value creators, extending beyond their realm of existence and reaching out to help another conscious mind in another realm of existence, putting value back into the house of Zon and that's when they evolved from God-Man to Zons. I see you making a similar analogous evolution now as you now are putting value back into the Society of Secrets at the national level.

Now as you all know, I'm developing a new look to our secret web site and it's called the "Face of the World". Here we will be able to accommodate the values that the high-level apprentices are now bringing back into the Society of Secrets. An immediate example of this is the launched A-Teams who formed local SOS Clubhouse Congregations and will have real estate on this new "Face of the World". Now something that you can do immediately to put value back into the Society of Secrets at the national level is to create your virtual Introduction Meeting. Make it virtual, make it for the computer and upload that to the national web site because that's going to become your drawing card. It's going to become a beautiful expression of what the Society of Secrets, The Neothink® Society means to you and the value it brings to you.

Also, for several months now you've been working on your Workshop Meetings. Let's capture the value of those meetings by creating virtual Workshop Meetings. Videotape your best Workshop Meetings and upload them to the "Face of the World" web site to create the world's greatest show for someone who just happens to be cruising the Net. Now, someone you meet can be invited to check out this "Face of the World" web site. It's going to be a powerful drawing card. Additionally, imagine how those virtual meetings will benefit all the local SOS Chapters. Now any Clubhouse around the country can have a Workshop Meeting on the web site. You can have a big screen computer that you sit around to view the meeting. It would be a very effective way to hold the Workshop Meetings. If there's a particular workshop that's better than yours, you can use that virtual workshop. Or you can use that virtual Workshop to improve your Workshop Meeting. That is the synergy of us working together.

In the very original advertising literature you received from me I described the parallel society of the fortunate few. That's what we are building here, the parallel society of the fortunate few. There's the society of the masses, then there's this small society of the fortunate few. As we bring in more and more people and that tipping points are reached, we are eventually going to overtake the society of the masses. We will simply have the Twelve Visions World.

When people walk into your Clubhouse they are going to be walking into the life that everyone down deep really wants; that romantic, Ulysses-like journey minus the dishonesty. We are experiencing very hard economic times and they very likely could get worse. I want you to understand something about the value you are bringing to people:

A famous author and marketer, Ted Nicholas, said to me, "Mark, can you get together all the products that you have, all of them?" I said, "Well geez, you know, what are you planning to do with them"? Ted told me that he could sell my literature for some outrageous sum of money. I said, "You're out of your mind. You want to ask people to put out how much money?" And then he stopped me right there and said, "You need to think about what you're giving these people with your Prime Literature. You're giving them an entirely new life. You're giving them life, Mark. You're giving the life that they couldn't get otherwise and the value is priceless."

The reason I bring up this is so you to understand what you are offering people coming into your Clubhouse. You should not be embarrassed or sheepish about what is being charged. You're offering them life, a life they could get no other way. Life advantages that surpass anything they've ever come across ever or ever will. Without this Prime Literature people will die unfulfilled, without experiencing the exhilarating life they were meant to live. Hold that in your thinking because that is going to give you the confidence and passion to build your Clubhouse Congregations. It's going to raise the level of value you're offering. By you really understanding and feeling and expressing that value people are going to get more out of the experience. People, particularly as the economy gets worse, really need us, need the advantages found only in The Neothink® Society.

You need to get your Introduction Meetings recorded and uploaded to the Face of the World web site. You need to begin recruiting. Give your testimonials, projecting beyond that to what this means for your future, the priceless nature of The Prime Literature, the Workshop Meetings and the coming Twelve Visions World. These are values and advantages you will never experience without anywhere else.

As you begin contributing now your time, energy and value creation back into the Society of Secrets on both the local and national level, you become one with our goal, the goal that I have felt and tasted for most of my life. You become one with that.

When we move into the C of U which, here on earth, is the Twelve Visions World, properties of civilization are going to change. You saw that throughout the Miss Annabelle's Story. So keep that in mind as I go through this integration:

Last month we began the Twelve Visions political movement. And two meetings ago, I revealed the Big Picture and all the major movements that will eventually come out of the SOS from politics and the Twelve Visions Party, education and the Hamilton's School of Geniuses to religion and the Church of God-Man. The Business Alliance, too, will emerge soon after we launch the "Face of the World" web site. And the Business Alliance will serve its true purpose as articulated in the Miss Annabelle's Story. Other major movements in science with God-Man theorists and with wide-scope accounting lawyers, and the media with Patterson Press dynamics of the Miss Annabelle's Story will all rise out of your local SOS Clubhouse Congregations. All these, including the Association for Curing Aging and Death, will rise out of The Neothink® Society.

Why will all those movements rise out of The Neothink® Society? The answer is elegantly simple but earth shattering. To see that elegantly simple answer, we must look at our blueprint, the Miss Annabelle's Story. Let me ask you, what essentially was the climax of the Miss Annabelle's Story? Of course, it was achieving the definitive cure for death of mankind, achieving biological immortality. Now, driving that story to its climax was the joining of forces of human-kind to achieve that goal. That coming together, that joining forces toward the Superpuzzles of good comes from a heliocentric view of mankind, a Neothink® view of mankind as a living, breathing entity.

Remember the operation in the Miss Annabelle's Story to save Martin? Martin was a paraplegic, who had a very short time to live. Dr. Sally Salbert was the doctor who led the first attempt at saving Martin. There came a point when the whole world was viewing this operation. Televisions across the world were fixed on this 20-some hour operation to transfer Martin's head onto a cloned, young, healthy body. And then suddenly we come to a point when the operation seemed complete and no one was breathing. Everyone was holding their breath waiting for Martin to take *his* breath. And, as you remember, of course, that breath never came.

That scene is a metaphor for what will become when the properties of our society, of our civilization, change as we enter into the Twelve Visions World or the C of U on Earth. The whole of mankind becomes the supreme value and as takes over. Mankind as a whole, mankind and the individuals who makeup mankind is the supreme value of the universe. Separations based on power, based on ruling over others, man subjugating man, man fighting and destroying man is tantamount to an individual hurting and destroying himself. For, mankind then is seen as one supreme value where actions are based on benefitting the whole because each individual within the supreme value is a value creator "glued together" creating values for each other. Everybody is a value creator so everybody is invaluable to each other. Mankind becomes this unit that puts pieces into an interlocked Superpuzzle.

Once you emotionally achieve this view of mankind, love can overwhelm you. When you reach this emotional relationship with mankind, the existing anticivilization and what occurs here can really tear you up inside.

But now imagine the Superpuzzles that will help all of mankind. Imagine eradicating anything that can hurt mankind. Imagine removing crime through the Twelve Visions Party and its Protection-Only government. Imagine eradicating disease after disease through the Association for Curing Aging and Death. These are Superpuzzles in the Twelve Visions World. Imagine removing stagnation from everyone's life through the Division of Essence jobs.

Imagine removing guilt, fear, subjugation, and emotional suppression, removing organized religion through the Church of God-Man and the SOS Bible. You're beginning to get a sense of the love I write about in the Prime Literature. Love grows and deepens as one evolves as species, from the insect to the mammal to the primate to conscious human beings. Love rises to whole new levels as we evolve from the conscious human being to the mysticism-free Neothink® man to the God-Man. Indeed, this is why people got so emotional when they read the Miss Annabelle's Story. I want you to think about this next emotional level of love and this perspective of *mankind as one*, everybody benefitting and contributing to Superpuzzles.

Understand this is not egalitarianism nor collectivism, communism or socialism. Throughout history political and philosophical systems have hijacked the whole concept of love and loving mankind. They hijacked this with fools love. Understand that love has been hijacked and been presented and brought through in these horribly tyrannical political systems like communism, so-called love for one's fellow man. Love for one's fellow man in the Twelve Visions World will be a genuine love based not on this selfless sacrifice, but on mutual value exchange. The love I feel for the doctor who eliminated the disease that would have killed my child is the sort of love that you will feel for your fellow man because everybody will be contributing such great values to your life.

In the Twelve Visions World we will have universal love, we will have universal wealth, universal health and universal peace. And that explains why these major movements will rise out of the SOS. Other secret societies that exist today and have existed throughout history often times work for the betterment of mankind. They are sensing the relationship with mankind as one entity and to their credit, worked toward the genuine good of mankind. They're sensing what Neo-Tech idealized in the 20th Century and what the Society of Secrets is actualizing here in the 21st Century as the Twelve Visions World.

The 20th Century Neo-Tech idealizes as the Civilization of the Universe. Now in the 21st Century the Society of Secrets, The Neothink® Society is actualizing this as the Twelve Visions World. Hence, the Society of Secrets, The Neothink® Society is the most important development on earth today.

My apprentices, you are on the final leg now of our journey. You're an upper-level apprentice soon to become mentors. I want all you high-level apprentices to grasp the concept of mankind as the supreme value and hold on to concept. This is the opposite of communism and socialism in which the ruling class subjugates the people. Properties are changing as we move into the C of U. This is not collectivism but mutual value exchange. This is individualism. And, this is not unconditional love either for unconditional love is actually impossible in an anticivilization. The anticivilization is full of dishonesties and evil and the desire for power to rule over and subjugate others through force. So, unconditional love is impossible in an anticivilization.

As the Twelve Visions World is actualized, all the properties of civilizations begin to change. You're going to feel an amazing source of love come into your local SOS Clubhouse Congregations. It's going to be an amazing transformation for you and for those SOS members. Understand that's one of the amazing values that you are going to bring these people who will become your apprentices.

The Twelve Visions World is a world of universal wealth, universal love and peace. So I am having an emblem designed to reflect those values. That emblem will be printed on the back of that political pamphlet and is the symbol of peace, wealth and health with the words wealth, health and peace inscribed.

As you live and breathe as one entity, one value creation, each one of us is a piece of the Superpuzzle bettering mankind as seen in this Miss Annabelle's Story. Void of irrationality and dishonesty, living this exhilarating life, we can move into the structure of government never seen on this planet. Today I'm going to reveal to you the structure of government that's never been seen or even conceived on planet earth. The uniqueness of this government structure is removing the need for power. Once you evolve to this level — of living and breathing the Superpuzzle — there is no need for any separation of power whatsoever. Our government was by far the best government ever created in the history of our planet; a republic and controlled by our Constitution of the United States. That brilliant, ingenious document, however, was not fully conceived. It is missing The Prime Law. And good as our government is, it is still a government based on separations of power, checks and balances of power, all backed and based on force. Never has there been a government conceived in a complete and integrated fashion based on service. I want you now to read the structure of government as it should be:

What follows is the evolving, free-will government structure that will maximize its one and only purpose of protecting the individual against initiatory force and providing justice. I created this document of the new government structure three years ago. I built much of the background development in my second publication Neo-Tech Business Control, (Volume Six, Government Capture) twenty years ago. But I have held this document back, until now. You, my Level-Ten Apprentices, are the first to see this piece. You must integrate this Neothink® Puzzle now that we will actualize the Twelve Visions Party.

How Government Could Evolve Into A Value-Creating Business

The United States Constitution's three main principles of inherent rights, government by the people, and separation of powers provided the basis for the freest and most prosperous nation in history. Just imagine two centuries ago the new ideas of a nation created to ensure a person's right to life, liberty and the pursuit of happiness as written in the Declaration of Independence, a nation governed by the people, a nation with watchdog checks and balances on political and bureaucratic powers.

The delegates of the Constitutional Convention in 1787 also gave careful consideration to the division of power between the federal government and state governments. The U.S. Constitution, which emerged from the Constitutional Convention in 1787, is called the supreme law because the state constitutions and both federal and state laws cannot violate the U.S. Constitution.

The U.S. Constitution does a nearly perfect job setting down the principles and system of government. Things went wrong because of continual misinterpretation of the Constitution over generations, which led to repeated violations of the Constitution. What was missing was an overarching constitution, so to speak, the prime law of no initiatory force. What was missing now exists in the Prime Law of the Twelve Visions Party.

Had the Prime Law existed since the beginning, our country would have entered the wealthy/healthy/safe Twelve-Visions World generations ago.

If the Prime Law eventually becomes an Amendment to the U.S. Constitution — the Prime-Law Amendment — we could again have confidence in the U.S. Constitution and the state constitutions, for they brilliantly set down the system of government and separation of powers, starting with the three main powers of 1) making laws, 2) executing laws, and 3) interpreting laws.

There would be, however, a fundamental change with the Prime-Law Amendment: The concept of a government based on power — separation of powers, division of powers, checks and balances of powers — would change from a government based on power to a government based on service. That fundamental change from a power basis to a service basis would evolve a businesslike system — a businesslike protection service — as detailed in Twelve Visions.

The businesslike, service-based government would be both centralized and, at the same time, decentralized to handle the sprawling government. At first, that seems like a contradiction, but let me point you to the SOS System (in Book One, abbreviated in Visions Five and Six of Book Two), with its powerful decentralization through the division of essence of mini-companies within the company, and its powerful centralization through Essence Tracking Reports and Essence Meetings.

The evolution from a power basis to a service basis will gradually happen with the success of the Twelve Visions Party. I will lay out a very simplified, an oversimplified explanation of the highlights of the new businesslike government structure we would be aggressively working toward. The following potential scenario did not come to me as a Neothink® Vision; instead I put power-thinking to work here to develop the general idea:

With the nearly flawless job done in the original U.S. Constitution document setting down the law, we will not touch its main principles. We will repeal some of the Amendments. And we will work toward evolving the daily functioning of our government into the most successful business system ever devised — the SOS System (Inside Secrets, Mark Hamilton).

Let us look closely at this transition from a power-grabbing political basis of government to a value-creating business basis. In the briefest of highlights, here is a quick synopsis of the ideas:

The SOS System's division of essence is the ultimate division of labor because each job of labor also includes the mind — the ability to think and make the job more and more valuable.

The division of labor works by dividing a company into its physical movements, which become its jobs of labor such as the man driving in rivets on the assembly line. The division of essence, on the other hand, divides its business into its physical movements too, but movements that include the thinking mind in order to create and elevate values. Each value-creating movement or job becomes a crucial part of the value-creating business's essence. Each job in the business becomes alive and valuable in its division-of-essence structure.

The three branches of government as set down in the U.S. Constitution are 1) the Legislative Branch, creating laws for citizen protection, 2) the Executive Branch, executing laws for citizen protection, 3) the Judicial Branch, interpreting laws for citizen protection. Instead of three branches of government, we can now identify them as the three main physical movements of protection — the essence of government — that include the thinking mind in order to make the movements more and more of a value. This begins the government's ultimate division of labor, known as the division of essence. The purpose of government, the essence of government, remember, is protection.

So, the three main physical/mental movements of government protection are 1) creating the laws for protection, 2) executing the laws for protection, 3) interpreting the laws for protection. But, how does the government break down further?

Inside those large main movements of protection are smaller mini-movements of protection. They too are complete physical/mental movements for protection, just smaller value-creating subsets or mini-movements of the overarching main movements of protection. For example, under the main movement of executing laws for protection, comes four mini-movements: 1) executing foreign affairs, 2) executing money matters, 3) executing the military, 4) executing justice. Each is a physical/mental movement with a clear purpose of protection, the essence of government. Notice, those mini-movements are four of the thirteen Departments of the President's Cabinet — Department of State, Department of Treasury, Department of Defense, Department of Justice. In a protection-only government, the other Departments are not needed. Interestingly, those four Cabinet Departments were the original four the father of our country, Neo-Tech man George Washington, established in setting up our government.

The physical/mental mind-with-body mini-movements of protection are self-driven chunks of essence from the overall value-creating essence of the government, which is protection.

Collectively, the mini-movements of protection make up the government's division of essence. The massive government continues to divide into its physical/mental movements of protection or chunks of essence, down to smaller and smaller chunks of mind-with-body, value-creating movements of protection. For instance, the federal prison system is a complete chunk of essence, a full physical/mental value-creating movement of protection that falls under the larger movement of Justice, which falls under the overarching main movement of executing the laws. The police force, the armed services...those are chunks of essence, physical/mental value-creating movements of protection that fall under larger physical/mental movements of protection.

Those chunks of essence — mind-with-body movements where value creation toward the business's essence can occur — exist throughout all value-creating businesslike structures. Of course, the government's essence is protection. Chunks of essence — mind-with-body movements where value creation toward protection can occur — would exist all throughout our new Twelve-Visions Government. Those new mind-with-body value-creating movements of protection will cover all functions of the new government, bringing out the best protection service.

Vision Six in Twelve Visions demonstrated how the division of essence allows decentralization, while at the same time having strong centralization, which is exactly what a service-based U.S. Government will need. For example, in the division-of-essence structure, the fifty states would most effectively become their own chunks of essence with their own division of essence. In other words, they would function autonomously under their own constitutions. They could compete, and people would vote with their feet. However, the Prime-Law Amendment would filter out every state and federal bad law in the country, including existing amendments in the

U.S. Constitution. Therefore, all citizens everywhere would be protected by the Prime Law of Protection: no initiatory force.

Moreover, without getting into too much detail, once you understand how the division of essence works (study the SOS System) you will understand the mutually beneficial internal Essence Tracking Reports that will rise up from the states to the federal main Movement Heads. And you will understand the Essence Meetings that will bring centralized control over the decentralized U.S. Protection Service. The service of protection and justice, from the local level to the federal level, will snap together into one unbreakable Neothink® puzzle-picture through the Essence Tracking Reports. That Neothink® service — that intense value-creating thinking put in at every level of government — will deliver the greatest value creation to the American people. Peace unlike ever before will blanket America.

Let me pause here to make a point: The separation of powers and division of powers will no longer be necessary, for a ruling power will no longer exist. Whereas, as the saying goes, power corrupts; absolute power corrupts absolutely...our new government will be merely a service — a pay-as-you-use service. Instead of forced tax collection, citizens will voluntarily pay for superior protection. People will pay for peace.

There will be absolutely no ruling power, no reason to separate or divide power. All divisions will come by way of the division of essence to maximize the values being created — the protection of our citizens.

With that in mind, I see two possible scenarios here for the Twelve-Visions Government that would be determined based upon which one would deliver the best service when the time approaches:

Scenario One: Do not link the federal and the states' Essence Tracking Reports and Essence Meetings. The federal responsibilities stop with federal law, courts, prisons, national defense; the states' responsibilities cover state law, courts, prisons, police.

Scenario Two: Vertically link the federal and states' Essence Tracking Reports and Essence Meetings. The federal and states' responsibilities link vertically under one essence of protection. This is possible only because we are shifting from a power basis to a service basis.

The better approach is yet to be determined. Since the Twelve-Visions Government will eventually become the first government NOT based upon power, rather upon service, either approach will be valid. The determination will be made upon one factor: which approach provides the customer with the best service, the best value, the best protection!

Imagine…a value-creating businesslike government, structured upon the greatest value-creating breakthrough of all time — the division of essence. The division of essence is the next evolution of the almighty division of labor (Inside Secrets, Mark Hamilton). Indeed, that next evolution opens the door to break down not just labor, but value creation into jobs for the ordinary working person. Imagine, value creation broken into the workers' jobs by the ultimate division of labor that includes not just labor, but the mind as well, the superior division of essence. That division of essence in business has proven to bring forth the most creative, breakthrough-values, often by ordinary workers! And that is exactly what we want from our government: the most creative, breakthrough-protection.

We want no weapon to be able to penetrate our country; we want no criminal or terrorist to be able to violate our citizens. The division of essence ignites every man and woman's creative mind and will bring us what we want for our country.

I created the division of essence (presented in my book Inside Secrets) for maximum value creation. Indeed, the division of essence is a powerful value-creating force that will thrive in the Twelve-Visions World. The division-of-essence structure of business will bring us the creation of the most amazing consumer values in all areas of life including medicine. And now, we will bring that division of essence to the structure of protection. We will enjoy the best protection ever witnessed on our planet, even during a world of escalating terrorism.

The new division-of-essence structure of protection will adopt tools such as Essence Tracking Reports and Essence Meetings (abbreviated in Vision Six). I will not go into the details here, but you can understand those terms as well as Movement Heads, mind/body mini-movements of protection, their mini-movement heads — those at the state and federal levels — by understanding the concepts in my book Inside Secrets. That book explains all those terms and the value-creating power of the division of essence.

Neothink® Control

The Movement Heads will receive the daily, weekly, and monthly Essence Tracking Reports from their mini-movements under them. Those tracking reports are the Movement Heads' puzzle pieces. The Movement Heads will snap those tracking reports together like puzzle pieces into the big Neothink® puzzle-picture. Then monthly, they'll hold their famous Essence Meetings with their mini-movement heads. The three main Movement Heads will be the persons with the big picture of their respective movements, and they will guide each mini-movement head to best serve the big picture.

The three main Movement Heads have enormous responsibility. They are the best at the movement they serve; they rise to the top through superior performance. They give invaluable guidance to their mini-movement heads at the

356

federal level and to their fifty mini-movement heads at the state level (if the vertically-linked paradigm takes hold). Again, the Movement Heads receive their Essence Tracking Reports, snap together the big picture for their specific movements, and hold monthly Essence Meetings with their mini-movement heads in order to guide them through the big picture toward creating the best values — the best protection.

That big picture comes together from everyone's essence work revealed on their Essence Tracking Reports, from everyone's creative efforts to best serve their chunks of essence of protection.

The three main Movement Heads will be selected by a board of directors. (I will explain the board of directors in a moment.) The board will select the three main Movement Heads, as in any successful business, based on performance. The board will select the three persons best suited to snap together the big picture and guide the mini-movement heads.

Similarly, the mini-movement heads of protection will earn their powerful positions through performance. Remember, we are steadily replacing a political government based on power with a businesslike government based on service — a comprehensive protection service.

Because of rapidly declining terrorism and crime in the future Twelve-Visions World, the cost of the government — your protection service — would continue to drop year after year. Someday, when the entire world population has evolved into the Twelve-Visions World, the government — your protection service — might no longer be necessary. Government as we know it might become extinct.

Until then, the board of directors will select and assist the Movement Heads in their huge responsibilities. The board of directors will consist of nine persons with the most outstanding careers at serving the essence of government: three with the most outstanding careers in the legislative-protection movement, three with the most outstanding careers in the executive-protection movement, three with the most outstanding careers in the judicial-protection movement.

Those nine board members will advise the Movement Heads as they oversee and coordinate the three main movements of government. Remember, there will be many mini-movement heads and three Movement Heads. Each Movement Head will receive Essence Tracking Reports from his or her mini-movement heads. The Movement Heads will snap together the national puzzle-picture for their specific movements and guide their mini-movement heads across the country. They will meet monthly for their all-important Essence Meetings when the Movement Heads give their mini-movement heads big-picture guidance and expectations. In turn, the three Movement Heads will submit their own national Essence Tracking Reports to the board — the nation's Leading Head, so to speak. From those tracking reports, the Leading Head, the board, will snap together the final big puzzle-picture and, in turn, give the Movement Heads the final big-picture direction and ultimate expectations.

The board of directors will be responsible for replacing board members when the time comes. The board will replace any Movement Head if performance permanently slips. However, although the board will select the Movement Heads and advise and assist them, the hands-on Movement Heads will be in charge. With advice, big-picture direction, ultimate expectations, and possibly great pressure from the board, the Movement Heads will make the day-to-day decisions. Through strict protocols, the Movement Heads can eventually be replaced. But, except for very specific circumstances, they will make the final operating decisions until that day comes.

Since the Prime-Law Amendment guarantees no forced tax collection can ever exist — no IRS as we once knew it, no

Criminal Investigation Division — the people will have the legal option to withdraw from government protection and justice…withdraw from government protection against force being used against them, their property, or their contracts, and withdraw from the justice system that coincides with protection. With that legal option to withdraw from government protection, the government will have to competitively provide a genuine value that people want to pay for. Therefore, the government employees will have to work hard to offer a valuable service — ever-growing protection and peace.

For example, our police force today is not really a service of protection — of crime prevention. Today's police force simply follows up after the crime. We have crime follow up, not crime prevention. Thus, we really have no protection whatsoever, no elimination of initiatory force. Our police — through no fault of theirs — get involved only after the force occurred.

In tomorrow's Twelve-Visions World, we will have superior protection. The protection will be so good, in fact, we will want to pay for it. We will want to pay for peace. Movement Heads will oversee value-creating mini-movement heads who run the police force, the armed services, the judicial and prison systems, the legal work that will include filtering out bad law, revising law, creating civil and contract law, determining legitimate liability laws and punishment for violating laws. As a division-of-essence, value-creating protection service for the people, we the people will gladly offer our voluntary payment for a country of blissful peace, harmony, and prosperity.

As any value-producing institution, the board will keep their Movement Heads as long as they are the most competitive for bringing value — protection — to the people. Without forced tax collection, the government's value will be easily measured by the number of subscribers.

The Movement Heads of government will be the gate keepers of our protection as laid down in the Prime Law. And every subscribed American will "own stock" in protection — in his or her protection. So, American individuals will be "stockholders" in their own protection. If the people were unhappy about the board's performance or any Movement Head's performance, they could call for a general vote of "stockholders" — subscribed Americans. Also, the board will have the prerogative to call a general "stockholder" vote in the rare scenario the board prefers the "stockholders" to decide whether or not to remove a Movement Head. The specific choice for replacement, however, will always fall upon the board.

Why will the board of directors eventually be responsible for selecting the Movement Heads? As in any value-producing institution, the board members are closer to the company and its details than the stockholders. The board members know best who is most qualified to provide the maximum value to consumers and who will deliver the greatest performance to the stockholders. Therefore, the board will select the Movement Heads. Proven value-creating performance — not corrupt election campaigns with tricky propaganda — will select our Executive Movement Head, our Commander in Chief, for example. The massive election campaigns today are often designed to deceive a naive public into voting for a particular candidate — into voting for a deception. Those deceptions will be gone. Moreover, re-election fever will be gone along with its symptomatic, attention-getting lawmaking and spending programs that destroy our economy.

In tomorrow's Twelve-Visions World, anytime the people — the paying subscribers — grow discontent, they may call for a general vote to remove a board member or Movement Head. In such a rare scenario, the people tomorrow will not be caught up in propaganda and deceptions as they are during campaign season today. The people will know they are not happy about something specific and will use their power as "stockholders" in peace to effect a change. ...Each individual will be equal under the Prime Law of Protection. Thus, each individual will receive one vote.

The board will call such a "stockholder" vote if it feels the people need or want it. Remember, the people can always withdraw without being criminals, if ever the need arose. If enough withdrew, a competitive service would rise to meet the demand. But that technicality would only exist in theory, for without a force-backed government, only rational decisions and the best actions for the people can continually occur. The gifts of life — the wealth, love, happiness and health described in the National Platform of the TVP — will shower upon the people.

What you read is Prime Literature. This document is an integration that you have to understand in order to envision the new Twelve Visions Party government structure based on service not power.

Remember, you're the chosen ones to help me actualize what has been idealized. This is not a mystery. I laid it all out in the Miss Annabelle's Story. You are becoming the geniuses of society. You are, in a sense, the students now growing up, becoming the adults to put together the pieces to our Superpuzzle.

Now I understand some apprentices innocently want to study the advertising letters that Mark Hamilton sent to you and apply those marketing techniques in your Introduction Meetings. But the answer is no. That would really backfire because these are two completely different arenas. My advertising literature is reaching people cold, while your advertising approach is reaching people warm. I use the term "warm" to reflect that your market is a person you are meeting face to face. Your strongest approach to that market is simply to express the benefits you reaped from membership and from The Prime Literature. Do not say a lot about making money unless that is actually what you were able to achieve. Just emotionally express from within you what Neothink® and membership to the SOS Clubhouse Congregations has meant to you and the value you received. Express how your life is different now and how you see your future forever being different because of this invaluable, priceless journey you joined. This is how you are going to bring people in who will stay with you. If you just got up and started approaching them like my original letters to you, it would not work at all. At most, you'll get someone in for one meeting and then they'd leave. You have to approach the live public completely differently.

At some point soon, I advise reading the Miss Annabelle's Story again so you can internalize that blueprint to achieving the Twelve Visions World.

You are becoming the geniuses of society and I really mean that. I am not giving you an empty compliment meant to stroke your ego. I have spent many hours with scholars discussing different subjects. I have interacted with scholars from around the world, people with a lot more education than most of you. But they still don't see things that you see. You can out-integrate those very smart people. And, remember this is the value that you will be bringing to your apprentices. We are building the parallel society of the fortunate few. This is what people are getting into. This is what they're joining. They will start thinking differently.

As Level Ten apprentices becoming mentors, you need to contribute both at your local level and at the national level. I need you to be thinking of what value you can put toward the "Face of the World".

That basically concludes here our Level Ten meeting. Next month we're going to move on to another major movement and then the final month we're going to move onto the climax, the culmination of our journey here together. I want to let you know that you're growth is something to behold. It's wonderful and actually quite mind blowing.

Level-Eleven Essence Meeting is next. Soon follows your graduation from apprenticeship into mentorship. That is a tremendous accomplishment that has changed you forever into an integrated thinker, a value thinker, a value creator in the burgeoning Neothink® Society.

Secret Teachings to My Exclusive Inner Circle

Level-Eleven Essence Meeting
Part One

Our Neothink® Society has laid the groundwork to steadily improve the world. Now, with your role as mentors, let's look at how our Society works. And this is how you can express yourself to others:

The Society brings in newcomers and the newcomers learn inside secrets, inner circle secrets that help them achieve success in their personal lives. And the more experienced members, in this case, you, the Level Eleven apprentices, help the newcomers. Help them learn, help them evolve, help them develop; help them with the inner-circle secrets to success. And as members go through the journey with me, and interact with you on the discussion boards and come into the Clubhouses, they will evolve, improve and learn how to apply themselves. They too will contribute on a national level. They will become experienced members and, in turn, will help newcomers.

Now as members evolve and become experienced such as yourselves, you enter a realm, the very rare realm, of being able to do something that actually improves the world around you. Not too many people have that opportunity in their lives.

If you get down to the psychology of man beyond humans being animals, into being man who made the leap from the bicameral mentality to consciousness, you begin to understand what makes us happy. You realize that your ability to create and bring values to others is really the meaning of life because that ultimately brings you happiness.

The very process of going through these levels in our Society brings the more experienced, higher-level apprentices toward mentoring the newcomers. And that is what brings happiness. Working with new members is where your focus and energy will really pay off. That's the beauty behind developing the Clubhouses.

There are apprentices rising up around the country into this rare realm of helping others which is tremendously rewarding. Those who are doing this now understand and feel the euphoria and the true meaning of life.

By design, the Society works both left-brain practical turnkey techniques when you come in and, as you evolve, you move into an emotional right-brain satisfaction, this sense of happiness that comes from helping others. It's a very integrated process.

I'm bringing this up to you now because you are near mentors at this point. You're entering a new realm. You will be graduating from apprentices to mentors sometime after the Level Twelve meeting.

Today's meeting is designed to express to you the real meaning of The Neothink® Society. In science and philosophy, people can express what something is, but to really know and understand what it "really is" requires a deeper look.

For instance in science, take the concept of gravity. People think they know what gravity is but really gravity is a big mystery. Really understanding gravity is analogous to understanding the Neothink® Society.

Here is a paragraph I'm working on that will give you a sense of what the Society really is: (It's not in practice yet but it's going to help you to begin to understand really what we're doing.)

"Finally it's here. The Neothink® Society (www.activeneothinkmember.com) is a growing society unlike anything ever seen. Some amazing people are here, some amazing secrets are here. You can meet lifelong friends here at activeneothinkmember.com. Or you can go in the flesh to the many local Chapters and Clubhouses across America. You can physically meet and socialize with real people, with those you see on line. All ages, all religions, all income levels, all people, men and women of all ages, everyone benefits here at activeneothinkmember.com. Breathtaking secrets, amazing people, on line or at Clubhouses. You must first own the literature to get in. And you can get that literature only, if you have been especially selected by our members and have personally received our invitation.

You can feel from this something different is going on in the Neothink® Society. I am making our Society of Secrets more open to bringing in new members."

I want to take a moment to explain the uniqueness of our Neothink® Society web site at www.activeneothinkmember.com:

Anyone who comes to that site quickly senses a complete "other" Society. People are going to realize behind that landing page exists the Society of the Fortunate Few. Our Society of Secrets, the Neothink® Society is a black hole sitting inside the society of the masses. And that black hole is drawing people in slowly at first, one at a time. But we're going to pick up momentum just as would a black hole and eventually that black hole will destroy the anticivilization.

There is truly an entire society that we are building at www.activeneothinkmembers.com, a real society, an alternative. This new alternative society carries itself beyond the virtual world into the real world, into the physical flesh and blood via the Clubhouses. There is something powerfully unique about that, about being able to physically interact in the real world with those you see on-line. Contrast that, for example, to Facebook where you can have two hundred, five hundred, a thousand friends. After a while those friendships becomes meaningless. But friendships never become meaningless at www.activeneothinkmember.com. Members that you see in the virtual world don't become meaningless because you can meet those people. You can go to their Clubhouse. If you meet a particular person with whom you develop a rapport, you can visit them at their Clubhouse and meet that person in the flesh. There's something very powerful behind that.

I want to reveal to you a future PR piece that I am developing:

"This story may be an historic first. Writer Mark Hamilton published his own emotionally moving Trilogy Superpuzzle about a world free from abuse, crime, poverty, illiteracy, disease. A world that even defeats aging. Sounds like utopian science fiction. Not this time.

"Mark Hamilton is serious about someday seeing his epic novel about the future become historic non-fiction; if not in his lifetime, at least in his children's lifetimes. And he is having success.

"Amazingly, approaching two million people have read his self-published books which include his fact-based fictional Trilogy Superpuzzle and his non-fiction Trilogy Secrets, Visions, Powers.

"But his books are just the beginning of a burgeoning mass movement that includes local Chapters and Clubhouses springing up across the country. There are over sixty official local Chapters and more than a hundred more Chapters now are moving toward official status.

"National Meetings are held several times a week simulcast from Mr. Hamilton's web site www.activeneothinkmember.com.

"Mr. Hamilton plans to start, with the help of his national infrastructure of local Chapters, Clubhouses and thousands of members, a new political party named, The Twelve Visions Party, TVP, based on his twelve visions of the future, captured in his book by the same by the name. The title to his Party's

National Platform is, "How to Make All the People Rich, Including the Poor."

"His dedicated members are ready to file the new Party with their respective Secretaries of State when they get the word from Mr. Hamilton. The TVP brings to life the political movement right off the pages of Superpuzzle.

"Mr. Hamilton has begun a virtual School of Geniuses. Eventually, Mr. Hamilton wants to establish his own school system patterned off the Miss Annabelle's Schools of Geniuses, also in the pages of Superpuzzle.

"When you talk to the rapidly growing members anywhere in the country, you realize they too, take the puzzle picture created in Superpuzzle very seriously.

"In a recent National Meeting simulcast from Mr. Hamilton's web site, the meeting's host said to several hundred members in that meeting quote, "I want for myself and for my children what Mark Hamilton idealized in Superpuzzle and he is giving our Society the chance to actualize that world." We all know that if we, that is, his members, do our part it is possible to actualize his Twelve Visions World.

"His web site, www.activeneothinkmember.com is a private site for members only. However, take a look at the home page for yourself. There you can see a complete, entirely new Society is forming; a Society of the Fortunate Few.

"What is Mr. Hamilton writing about now? "Not enough," he says, "making Superpuzzle real is a major undertaking. It requires almost all of my time and focus."

"Did he plan this? "For over twenty five years," he says, "I knew I had to idealize this world first before I could hand pick my apprentices who would actualize it with me. After a quarter century idealizing the Twelve Visions World, standing on the shoulders of a giant learned about in the Society, I am now, along with my amazing apprentices, the new geniuses of society, together we're actualizing the Twelve Visions World."

"Mr. Hamilton's Twelve Visions World is a world in which everyone is happy, even exhilarated, in love, healthy, slim, wealthy, and eventually, no longer aging.

"Once one reads Superpuzzle, he or she realizes how reachable the Twelve Visions World really is," he says, "that's when and why many readers decide to join a local Chapter where the Twelve Visions World has begun on a small scale."

"Can this really impact the world? Mr. Hamilton says, "You see just how doable this beautiful Twelve Visions World is when you, yourself, read Superpuzzle. I'm now building the foundation to support the growth, once I release this to a much broader base. In the next few months I'll open this up to my readers in over two hundred countries."

Now I included that future PR piece because I want to begin to fill your thinking and your direction with the real meaning of what the Society is all about. I want you to really know and understand what we are doing here. As you become mentors I need you to grasp the Big Picture.

We have the Twelve Visions Party, we have the Schools of Geniuses, we have the Business Alliance, we have the Prime Literature and all those techniques and we have the Heirloom Review Meetings. Of course, we have Workshop Meetings in the Clubhouses Congregations. These are all pieces to our Superpuzzle. The mentoring at all levels in the Clubhouses, on conference phone calls, through emails and webinars on the discussion boards are all pieces to the puzzle.

Now, let's take a look at the final piece to this puzzle:

Our omnipresent focus is of course, that final puzzle piece of biological immortality. And the key piece to achieving that goal is the Association for Curing Aging and Death. Now this is my Big Picture: Everything I write, everything I do, this entire Society is moving toward that ultimate end. And I cannot outwardly express this puzzle piece. Like Daniel in The Miss Annabelle's Story, he, too, could not outwardly express that same puzzle piece. Even though Daniel ran for and became President of the United States, being the President was not his goal. It was biological immortality. He recognized that to be the number one fundamental piece to the Superpuzzle. Daniel was not really interested in being President other than the fact that, as President, he had the ability to snap that large puzzle piece into the Superpuzzle. But his end goal was beyond that. And his end goal of biological immortality qualified him as the ideal person to snap down that puzzle piece of becoming President. Daniel knew that becoming President was one more piece toward completing a much larger puzzle. And this fact also qualifies me for the position. Although I, emotionally, do not want to be President, when the time comes, I know I can fulfill that role for the particular puzzle piece.

However, I know that my time and focus can be more efficient and effective integrating and coordinating the entire Superpuzzle rather than fulfilling that puzzle piece. However, I would step into that if there were no one else qualified to do so. The way to become qualified and become integrated enough to step into that role and run for President would be to really understand the Forbidden System. One would have to dig in and understand what that Forbidden System and the Prime Law are really saying at the deepest level. I would have to be satisfied that they really understood the Forbidden System and particularly the Prime Law for someone to take on the position of running for President.

Many times I've wanted to run for President with the ultimate goal of achieving biological immortality. I even came up with some actual medical procedures and studies and PR campaigns, even a series of TV shows about actual medical processes and procedures. But I knew all along that those would be a bust because psychologically, people are not ready for the concept of biological immortality.

Now as I talk about in Superpuzzle, people can accept the concept of anti-aging or slowing down the aging process. Such a concept is within people's comfort zones. And that's as far as we can go right now. You can't come right out and say, "Look we want to end aging, we want to end, cure death". For the most part, that would not succeed today. People are not ready to hear about biological immortality. And this is why:

Achieving biological immortality is a cause-and-effect process. We first need value producers to become value creators. And, we need to depoliticize America and eventually the world. Recall from the Prime Literature, remaining a value producer eventually leads to stagnation, boredom. Eventually the meaning of life and happiness drains away. That's because the human mind was meant to create. It's not meant to just produce the same routine, process the same task and the same mental functions day after day. It's meant to create and break into vectors of creation in order to bring new values to society. That's what brings humans happiness. But as value producers, humans will stagnate and run out of happiness. A value producer cannot emotionally relate to immortality. And most people, by and large, are value producers, not value creators. Therefore, most people's lives are filled with stagnation and so cannot emotionally grasp or relate to immortality.

Part of the problem is the suppression of white-collar hoax, the ruling class and the political elite who lock people into lives of stagnation. The process of depoliticization will remove the ruling class and create almost a spontaneous generation a new business structure with the division of essence versus a division of labor; essence being the ability to create in your job, paving the way to value creation. Depoliticization will elevate everyone's job by bringing the human factor, the creative mind, into your job. The division of essence will eventually take over all business structures around the world.

But the process of going from value producers to value creators and depoliticizing our country will lead to the cure. That's all explained in Superpuzzle. Then you have the creative people on one hand and the happiness and euphoria in the masses which will create the demand for longer life. Not a tacit acceptance of death but a loud and passionate demand for life, for immortality. And without the ruling class suppressing progress, you would have the freedom to meet the demand, the demand for life…the supply.

So we can only achieve biological immortality when you understand this cause-and-effect dynamic. The cause is you depoliticize and you turn value producers into value creators through the division of essence which creates the demand. The effect, the cure is the supply. And out of that will rise the cure for death. That cause and effect will come through a synthesis of the Prime Literature, the SOS Clubhouses, the Mark Hamilton's Schools of Geniuses, the journey with Mark Hamilton and the Twelve Visions Party. Those will all synthesized and ultimately bring about the cure.

Do you see how SOS Chapters with their Clubhouse Congregations and your process of mentoring and helping new members rise up to these levels where they begin to taste the euphoria, the exhilaration of life is all part of the process. You have become, in a sense, the members of the Church of God-Man (or your Clubhouse Congregations as we refer to them to the masses). In the Superpuzzle, it was the members of the Church of God-Man who understood and were privy to the concept of curing aging and death. That is you, my apprentices. You are those people and the local SOS Clubhouse Congregations that are spreading all across the country is the Church of God-Man that you read about in Superpuzzle.

Realize I'm talking to you in a way I could never talk to any new member. You are entering a new realm. You must now look forward to the goal as part of that forward focus. You must also help the newcomers at the lower levels achieve certain levels of success and learn our inside secrets, help them with the mini-day/power-thinking team, help them discover their Friday-Night Essence and help them with their Ten-Second Miracles. Help them break down their jobs into an area of purpose they can capture, an essence of the company they work for. Help them break their small business down into a division of essence. Help the newcomers while at the same time look forward, as I do, at the Big Picture. Each and every day I ask, where are we headed? We're heading to curing aging and death.

And as I mentioned several times, newcomers coming in are very focused on the Forces of Nature. For example, one of the most pressing Forces of Nature on newcomers is making a lot of money...fast. You need to help them evolve beyond strictly concentrating on the Forces of Nature and start evolving into the Forces of Neothink®.

And you need to deal with complaints about their active membership fees. They must realize that what they're paying for is the most important life-changing secrets found nowhere else on the planet; secrets that will literally save their lives. These secrets, our life-advantages are priceless. And those fees for these life-lifting values are going toward making this undertaking possible and keeping these values flowing and growing. So I just want to put that in your thinking too, because you will run into such complaints from time to time.

Again, from the Big Picture perspective, we're bringing people into our world; we're not putting those advantages out into their world. That's an important concept. They're coming inside the Neothink® Society to learn these inner-circle secrets with our inner-circle dynamics. Like a black hole, we are pulling people in. And just like a black hole, light comes in and it stays in. Eventually, the society of the masses, the anticivilization is going to vanish eventually.

And as such, we will be pulling in all types. I want you to be prepared for this. All types of people who you must deal with. You're going to be dealing with the very wide-eyed newcomers; you're going to be dealing with the curious, cynical, paranoid and trusting. So you are going to have to develop skills to deal with these different types of newcomers. And you must be able to receive all of these people and help each and every one of them to begin their journey. You need to help them make it through and come out on the other side in the C of U.

Let me make this point: You own our Active Neothink® Member web site. That secret web site is yours. And by that I mean the discussion boards and forums are yours now. You're my Level Eleven apprentices. You are the controllers of those discussions and posts. You are the controllers of your burgeoning Clubhouses. The virtual Workshop Meetings is your baby. This is your home. This is your tool to do your part in growing the C of U.

Now I really need you to own the process of bringing people in. Start thinking differently about how you will bring in people such as family, friends, co-workers, people you meet, acquaintances, extended family. A lot of you are afraid to do this and I know why. You have come in through the three large Heirlooms. The three large Heirlooms immediately exposed you to some very hard-to-grasp and shocking concepts such as Neo-Tech. The concept of Neo-Tech is really inner circle; it's for the inner-circle of this Society. People don't really deal with Neo-Tech and mysticism, fully integrated honesty until the seventh month and that will be the process in your Clubhouses. By then, they're going to be very well oriented, prepared to tackle such concepts. The difference now is people

who you bring in will initially be exposed to just the Neothink®
life-lifting techniques. Step back and see it from an outsider's
perspective. There is nothing controversial. The Prime
Literature has been reconditioned, restructured to relieve that
emotional anxiety of bringing people in because the
controversial concepts come much later and are reserved for
your inner circle members.

So those of you who are still fighting the feelings of the
past, of being ostracized from your family and from friends
because of those controversial concepts, take comfort. Things
are different now. So I want you to feel more comfortable with
approaching people and bringing them in, bringing them in
through the process I've developed; through the restructured
Prime Literature. We are bringing the C of U to earth without
using the word or the expression Neo-Tech. They will learn all
of Neo-Tech through this process but it will come to them
when they are ready for it.

The process: To bring people in, we stimulate them and
begin to integrate them with the Twelve Visions World and the
C of U. By doing so, these newcomers begin to disintegrate
with the anticivilization, including the ruling class and the
political structure, the white collar hoax, their stagnate, routine
rut jobs as they learn our Neothink® concepts that have been
hidden from the world since the beginning of consciousness.

The people who come to your Clubhouse are not nearly as
integrated as you were. As mentors, to understand this and
work with these people to help them evolve, you will play a
very key role in their transition. You have the full Prime-
Literature integrations whereas they don't. So they will be
counting on you for help just as I count on you for help. This
is part of your role of becoming mentors.

You are the front runners in this shift from the irrational
anticivilization to the rational Civilization of the Universe, the
Twelve Visions World here on Earth. You're the ones, the front

runners, who are blazing the paths that others need to journey to get there, to get to the C of U.

Now and exciting new addition to our Society is the Hamilton's School of Geniuses patterned after Miss Annabelle's School of Geniuses. Several apprentices have emailed me letting me know how much they want to participate in a Miss Annabelle-type school. Recall in the Miss Annabelle's School, the most important lessons were the general lectures. I compare those general lecture lessons to the teachings at the Guilds during the Renaissance from which great minds arose. Going back to the Greeks, they had tutors who's pupils would come and live with them. The mentors would impart not only academics but these boundary-breaking lessons in life that caused the mind to work differently. It caused the mind to break outside that stagnate following mode and move into the integrating, self-leadership mode.

I'm giving you the opportunity, my apprentices, to participate in the School of Geniuses. To start, go ahead now and video yourself and upload your educational general lectures to our web site. When people click on Hamilton's School of Geniuses they will see a list of these general lectures provided by you, my high-end apprentices. We will start those lectures at a virtual level right now, on the computer and eventually we will move into the brick-and-mortar phase and actually start a flagship school. From there we will branch out into an entire educational system, replicated across the country.

Returning to the "Face of the World", we are presenting an entirely new Society, fully integrated into which people can jump from one society to another. When you explain a great concept or a great integration to someone, it's isolated unto itself. Someone can, perhaps, adopt that or develop that belief, but they couldn't go much further. It's just a single concept. But when have an entire society, complete, with schools and a new government structure and new business structure, new romantic structure, a new socializing outlet, this could trump the society we have now. It's more stimulating with more potential and excitement and can literally out-compete the society of the masses. So one could just jump ship; jump into a complete society versus just adopting a single belief.

Now a real stroke of genius in The Neothink® Society is the interaction between a virtual world and the real world. You take something so successful such as a Facebook for example, and you know there's only so far you can go in cyberspace, in the virtual world. But at www.activeneothinkmember.com you have this incredible, international society based on our Prime Literature that's been developed at the deepest levels for decades with people congregating both in the virtual world on our web site and in the real world at the Clubhouse Congregations.

Our powerful Neothink® dynamics are working in the virtual world and in the real world. As you participate in the Twelve Visions Party, the process to change and depoliticize the country, you can participate in socializing, meeting friends or a potential romantic-love partner. There's something just so powerful in this dual-world dynamic between the virtual and real worlds. And the Prime Literature makes all of this possible. That's the common denominator that pulls it all together.

Remember, I spent an enormous amount of time and energy along with my staff to select certain people I wanted to bring into the Neothink® Society with the ultimate goal of having them become my apprentices and eventually mentors just as you are. I spent time and energy in meetings and money to find such people. I send out my invitations to those who qualify and pass my sorting mechanism. I send out the letters that you first received. Now a certain percentage respond but a lot of people think that the Society is just not real. But our "Face of the World" site and this exclusive society with people doing these spectacular things is very real. This is not just some made up gimmick, fly-by- night company trying to separate you from your money. Look at www.activeneothinkmember.com as you what is really happening out there. That's the power in the "Face of the World" web site. There is a synergy that will occur and it's beautiful and powerful.

Those of you who have made it to this level are winners in life. Now I'm not saying you haven't had bad breaks and you may not be wealthy, but based on my criteria, you are winners. And not only that, you truly are the emerging geniuses of society and that will become historically known as you will see as time passes. You are the ones, you are the early originals in this transition that will be a watershed, the turning point of civilization.

Now successful people, productive people, know not to blame others for their woes in life. And you know how awful it is to witness someone who is sinking in life. They dwell on blaming others for their problems or for what they could have been. It's easy to blame others, to dismiss one's own responsibility. In fact, blaming others is how the criminal mind actually forms.

If someone has this obsession or over indulgence in blaming others, that will graduate to, expecting others to owe one a living and that is the definition of the criminal mind.

Now, you understand that there is valid blame on the anticivilization, particularly on the ruling class. That valid blame is forever there and the more successful you become as you rise up from Level One to Level Twelve you will realize the extent that the ruling class is responsible for people being held down, all the way down to poverty. I feel particularly bad for the elderly whose retirement funds or pensions, through inflation, have been depleted due to this reckless and irresponsible management, management by the government over all the years for short term gains.

Now with the Neothink® Society and our many movements you can do something about it. You can change this. You literally can change this. It's in your hands and you have the power. Instead of just blaming others and you can act and thus change the world. But to achieve this change we need hundreds, thousands, tens of thousands, hundreds of thousands and eventually millions of mentors. That will occur through this process of pulling in good people. This process is going to grow and gain strength as we make this world better and we break apart and disintegrate, disintegrate the anticivilization.

And a great tool for bringing in good people is The Twelve Visions Party and the political pamphlet. When you start your Twelve Visions Party you actually benefit doubly by not only building the members of the party, but members of the Society of Secrets, your Clubhouse Congregations. People reading the Forbidden System, the political pamphlet will see how powerful and potent we are. Then you say that we've got this same power here in the Neothink® Society in other areas of life, money and wealth and romance and romantic love and friendships. That is going to be a powerful drawing card to build membership.

Starting a political party that eventually has thousands of people and then hundreds of thousands is difficult to control. It could easily drift away as many parties have and will. Someone all of sudden is saying things that are completely opposed to the Prime Law, for instance. Someone doesn't have the depth of integration. So my big question was how do control this movement so it doesn't drift away.

The Twelve Visions Party contract is an important tool to prevent the drift I am concerned about. But I still need to keep this idea system sound. How do prevent what happened to Jesus with his teachings or to Aristotle with the scholastics and his teachings? How? I came up with the ingenious idea of using intellectual property rights. The Twelve Visions Party has become a registered trademark. So now I can license that name, The Twelve Visions Party, and at any time, I can end or revoke that license. No one in the political arena has ever created such a licensing. I have some of the top intellectual property lawyers in the country developing these contracts and there are many variables.

Once the licensing agreements are complete you can move forward and start registering with Secretary's of State. I will provide you with the political packet with your State Constitution, your State Platform and the National Platform, the TVP Contract, and of course the political pamphlets.

As we wrap up this Meeting Level Eleven, I want you to realize how much you've grown in the period of a year. You are very advanced now and very integrated and knowledgeable. When you speak, you carry a lot of responsibility whether it's on the discussion boards, in the forums, or at a Clubhouse Meeting. I want you to realize that what you say now carries a lot of weight particularly to the lower level members. You can and will have a very profound effect on people now. With great power comes great responsibility. And so, you must be clear about certain Big-Picture concepts:

I want you to have Neothink® in mind and what it really is; this other way of thinking, of building the puzzle pieces to create a puzzle picture that breaks through boundaries to values you could never see. You can surpass geniuses and the most intelligent people through Neothinking.

I want you to go back to Inside Secrets and understand the division of essence and how businesses, by and large, function through the division of labor today. What does the division of essence really mean? The beauty of the division of essence brings the real nature of man, his mind and creativity, to all jobs. An entire business can be comprised of jobs with essence. The division of essence rids us of routine-rut jobs where you produce values instead of create values. With the division of essence, you are creating values and building wealth as you drive on your own vector of creation.

I want you to have a good knowledge of the Twelve Visions and what those Visions are and the future they will provide.

I want you to understand what the Twelve Vision Party is and I want you to study the Forbidden System on page 395.

I want you to understand the new biblical paradigm and the SOS Bible found in your second large Heirloom, Insight Two.

I want you to have a good understanding what integrated thinking is versus specialized thinking, an understanding of the self-leader mode versus the following mode.

I want you to understand the Hamilton's School of Geniuses, the blueprint for which is found in the Superpuzzle.

I want you to have a sense of the economic and political paradigm shifts that are going to cause the Great Technological Revolution which alone is going to result in prices plummeting as they do whenever there's advancing new technologies. And, in turn, that is going raise the standard of livings for everyone, including the poor. I want you to understand that dynamic and how that all works. You can find that in Twelve Visions.

I want you to understand the Neothink® Marketing Secret found in Meeting Level Three on page 49 where I reveal the Forces of Nature. I want you to understand the Forces of Neothink® and how they out-stimulate the spiral of death stimulations that arise from the Forces of Nature. You will find that in the Twelve Visions, Vision Three.

I want you to understand the common denominators at work that pull together the Forces of Neothink® and the Forces of Nature and create the Neothink® Marketing Secret.

I want you to understand how adults play through value creation. I want you to have a good understanding of Friday-

Night Essence and how one discovers their Friday-Night Essence to become the person you were meant to be.

I want you to understand about Ten-Second Miracles, the spontaneous insights and how they occur. I revealed the Ten-Second Miracles in Meeting Level Two on page 25. Using numbers to create the puzzle picture that suddenly snaps into place, pours from your right brain into your left brain and you see the missing puzzle piece. Once that happens, you see the full puzzle picture and that is a Ten-Second Miracle.

I'm going to stop now with that. I've given you a lot to think about.

Finally, I would strongly recommend you re-read this Meeting Level Eleven multiple times. This meeting is your tool that ushers you into mentorship, this historic role you play in transitioning from the anticivilization into the Civilization of the Universe.

I look around the country and see such strong leaders rising up and stepping in and integrating and coordinating our movement, developing our Society of Secrets, The Neothink® Society that will replace the society of the masses.

.

Secret Teachings to My Exclusive Inner Circle

Level-Twelve Essence Meeting

As our children begin leaving the house, the manifestation of our mortality begins closing in on us. With our kids gone, the reality that we have no shot at our long lost dreams hits us hard. Our dreams are long gone. We look back and feel how fast our lives flew by. We look ahead and know our bodies are steadily breaking down.

As far as Mother Nature is concerned, we have fulfilled our purpose in life. We raised our offspring. We propagated the species and now Mother Nature begins breaking us down to remove us and allow evolution and natural selection of the younger generations to propagate and improve the species. And we oblige.

Without a lot of deep down reason to keep living and enjoying life, with our dreams buried under hopeless resignation, with our enthusiasm and energy fading, with our health sinking, we oblige.

We not only accept this, the gradual end game, but we have no choice. We all face this 25 year fall.

You stand in your quiet home after your youngest leaves and right then, when you feel the beginning of your end game, you feel that nostalgia rumbling through your body and dimming your soul. Somewhere deep inside a new light turns on.

For a brief moment in time you can go to the light, but if you don't, it will fade as quickly as it came. That light is human consciousness which is a power beyond nature. Human consciousness put you in charge of life. It's the power of God within the man.

With the children gone, free of distractions, that light shows itself to you one last time. If you ignore it, it will fade and be gone forever. If you go to the light, you have a fresh, clean shot at a new, very full life.

There's actually no limit as to how far you can go. When you pursue human consciousness to its fullest God-like power, consciousness, fully free of restrictions, you can experience Neothink®. Neothink® brings you the power of a God-Man or woman. The possibilities are truly limitless, ranging from great wealth to not aging.

Realistically, in this civilization where progress and business, science and medicine is held back by subversive regulations, great wealth is not readily available when starting later in life. Non-aging immortality is obviously not available now. So for you, there is not a realistic possibility, after the children leave, of coming upon great wealth and non-aging immortality.

However, those who are starting younger in life have more time to overcome those obstacles, for our movement to have an effect and ultimately lead to the Society in which wealth and non-aging immortality is eventually possible.

What I've done by founding the Society of Secrets, the Neothink® Society is bringing people together who pursue the inner light of consciousness. And they are pursuing the inner light of consciousness in order to transcend nature and its end game.

We learn the best techniques in the Neothink® Society to help us in our value creation efforts. We also actively subvert the subverters. In the Neothink® Society, I've built one roof for us all to come under. We are the people pursuing our power of consciousness. Here we open a door to our power and we close the door on those taking away our power. Here no one gives in to the end game designed by nature. No one accepts it, no one obliges.

The beauty in the tangible SOS structure and the growing SOS family is that those pursuing the light of consciousness can now pursue their Friday-Night Essence, what they love doing most. Granted, they may not be able to make a living through their Friday-Night Essence but they can experience the emotional sensation of actively pursuing their Friday-Night Essence. Pursuing your Friday-Night Essence immediately moves the psychological end game.

Now that leaves the physical end game. First, the physical end game becomes less and less acceptable to those who discover their Friday-Night Essence. Even those who do not discover their Friday-Night Essence but who are pursuing their light of consciousness, are searching increasingly and don't accept the physical end game.

In the Society of Secrets, the Neothink® Society, we understand the psychological and physical end games and our mission is to remove both. We have our SOS Clubhouse Congregations around the country working closely with the National Chapter. This is the depth of the value that SOS reaches, the force to undo the psychological and physical end games.

Let's look a little more at those end games:

Whereas the physical end game may be a long 25 to 30 year decline, the psychological end game actually begins much earlier in life. Actually it begins not only in early adulthood but, as I explain in my writing, it begins in school. It begins early on, even in first grade, when children first start going to school. That reasoning is in Twelve Visions and, I believe, particularly in God-Like Powers.

Now by understanding that psychological end game begins quite early on in life we realize that people are missing out on the life they should be living. They begin dying at an early age, psychological dying.

Now in the SOS with the Prime Literature, the SOS provides the powerful secrets for dealing with this gradual loss of life and happiness. The process of the SOS is to develop mentors who can help others coming into the SOS. They help members apply the secrets of the Prime Literature. The personal touch helps put into practice the deeply developed Prime Literature. The results is a better life financially and emotionally and the psychological end game which automatically begins early in life but hits us when our children leave the house. That psychological end game here in the SOS actually goes away.

So I want to tell my new mentors, I want to tell you, my Level Twelve apprentices, to recognize the great value that you offer members. You offer the opportunity to fully live life, to not slowly shut down. We don't have biological immortality yet, but most people begin slowly dying as adults. The full experience of the life they do not have largely shuts down in this world and you, along with the Prime Literature, can help members open the lid to the vast and wonderful experience of life. Now that's your great value.

The Prime Literature holds all the secrets and techniques. In this suppressed civilization, you can't readily make members rich. We all know that now. But that's not to say many have become rich using these techniques. And you as mentors will have the pleasure of helping some who will go on, particularly the younger adults, to become wealthy. Your role as teacher and mentor, believe me, is very rewarding. But those who become wealthy are the exceptions for now.

Your biggest reward as mentors will come from distinctly seeing the change in your members. You'll see in their faces the major change from succumbing under a steady loss of life to overcoming the negative forces, to rise up emotionally.

Remember Saul in the Miss Annabelle's Story? He was the fellow who just about committed suicide and then he discovered TGIF and his Friday-Night Essence and then went on to live an exhilarating, exciting life as one of the scientists.

He was involved in the Trinity, the ship that was going to rescue life on another planet.

Now I've said before that a person's deep-rooted motivational drive will lead that person to success. I have also said that today's education, regulation, litigation will steadily take away good people's deep, motivational drives. Therefore, they begin to stagnate and start the long decline fairly early in life.

By removing member's end game, by helping them discover their Friday-Night Essences, to become the persons they were meant to be, well, their deepest motivational drives returns, often for the first time in decades. Whereas it may be too late to overcome the obstacles to financial wealth, still opening that path to one's Friday-Night Essence brings back purpose, emotion and enthusiasm. Remember Saul in the Miss Annabelle's Story.

As we grow in numbers and strength, we'll become a major force. I'm talking about paradigm shifts occurring in politics, in education, in religion and business for a free, for the first time, a truly free and rich Twelve Visions World. Our twelve step journey has been a journey toward actualizing the Twelve Visions World.

Some of you have mistakenly thought our journey together was idealizing the Twelve Visions World. That's not what our journey was about. The journey was about actualizing that world and that means bringing you to this point of leaping off into mentors. This was part of the actualization of the Twelve Visions World.

With the A-Teams and Clubhouses across the country and our Active Neothink® Members web site, you as mentors the tools. With the Prime Literature, you have the tools.

Objectivist Professor Leonard Peikoff said that people don't really understand a subject until they teach it. Moving into this role as teachers, as mentors, gives you a great opportunity to really know beyond what you've ever known before about the techniques and the true deeper meaning of the Prime Literature. I guarantee you will reap great benefits as you experience being mentors.

Ok, now let me make something clear: The SOS with our Clubhouse Congregations is now a growing movement. The Twelve Visions Party is its political arm. Before the SOS, the Prime Literature reached a few chosen individuals and they were asked to keep the literature to themselves, which they did, so it did not go beyond them. That occurred throughout 5 different decades, starting in the late 1960's and going through the mid 2000's. During those many decades the Prime Literature was perfected, idealizing the Twelve Visions World and the C of U.

Now I founded the Society of Secrets and the Twelve Visions Party in 2007 as the turning point from idealizing the Twelve Visions World to actualizing it. My new mentors, you, are now a powerful part of actualizing a Twelve Visions World. So what should be your focus as mentors? The purpose of the SOS and the Twelve Visions Party is to eliminate the end game. First, we end the psychological end game and then we end the physical end game. The psychological end game begins in our childhood with our education and the physical end game begins in your mid-thirties.

As mentors, you need to be highly aware of the process to remove these end games described in Vision 4 of my Twelve Visions. That process is to end the psychological and physical death through a cause and effect process.

As mentors, this is your opportunity to be a force in the immortal movement that will forever rid the world of mysticism and tyranny. Your responsibilities lie in helping the members to integrate and apply the Prime Literature along with creating and encouraging a social environment. By finding ways to do this, you'll play an important role in removing member's psychological end game, replacing resignation with purpose, enthusiasm and motivation.

Twenty-one years ago, I realized that the goal of removing the psychological and physical end games ultimately required more than a person's integration with the Prime Literature itself. It also required the person's mental disintegration from the world he or she knows. For example, a person could click with and even really integrate well, the Prime Literature but they are still ensconced in the anticivilization; they couldn't leave it behind. That's all they had ever known. So intellectually they integrated with the Prime Literature and the C of U, the Twelve Visions World, but they could not disintegrate and leave behind the anticivilization, the society where they grew up.

People could not leave behind all they ever knew until now, until the SOS. By building the SOS with its physical SOS Clubhouse Congregations across the country, along with all that is developing on line, we're building an entire Society. We're building an entire Society that a person can simply step into. That person can just then leave behind that world from whence they came. One can allow the anticivilization to disintegrate mentally, disintegrate and dissipate as one moves into the Twelve Visions World.

The Neothink® Society is the manifestation of that insight I had 21 years ago. And I knew exercising great discipline and great patience while I nailed down the Prime Literature had to happen first. Not until then could we move forward and start the Society of Secrets, the public mode with the political arm, the Twelve Visions Party.

As mentors, you now become the gatekeepers of the SOS. You'll also be the innovators on how to add to the newly developing Neothink® Society. The Prime Literature locks down all integrations, down to the fundamentals. That 40 year job is now done. Your job is not to build the integrations. Your job is to build the disintegrations, the disintegration of the anticivilization. And, by bringing the world the great value, this new Neothink® Society that members can step into and leave behind the anticivilization, that meaningless "other" Society from whence they came. By bringing this great disintegrating value to the world, you enable the new members to reverse their psychological end game. Ending the psychological end game is the greatest value that you could bring another human being today.

Tomorrow, ending the physical end game will become the greatest value you can bring a human being. The physical end game is a process, a cause and effect formula to achieve our ultimate goal of biological immortality. The first cause is reversing the psychological end game by replacing stagnation with exhilaration. This cause occurs through building the Society of Secrets and mentoring the secrets, the techniques in the Prime Literature, making the transition from a value producer to a value creator, discovering Friday-Night Essence, living with purpose; a creation-driven life with exhilaration and enthusiasm. The other cause of this cause and effect is removing the suppressing ruling class that holds back progress and prosperity through our political arm, the Twelve Visions Party. That's an irreplaceable part of the cause and effect process. So now you understand that, even if you or few people care about politics, the Twelve Visions Party is different. This is not a political movement per se for it goes much, much deeper than that. It is the crucial cause in the cause and effect formula to achieving our Superpuzzle. And as we build a comprehensive society with education, religion, politics, business, science and the arts, people can leave behind that other society. So building the Neothink® Society is one of the causes of the cause and effect formula.

Your first responsibility is to create the Neothink® Society which includes the physical congregations, The Clubhouses which adds the social to the Society. Man is a social animal and he not only needs friends but mankind depends on others for his survival and living needs. So creating the social environment in your Clubhouse is absolutely critical. I want you to build that other world with me.

The Clubhouse coordinators' efforts forming a structure and detailed tracking reports to expand our Clubhouse network with continual congregations, meetings, Workshops, social gatherings has been a huge contribution to the Neothink® Society, to this alternative world we are building together.

And congratulations to those mentors who have taken the time on the discussion boards and in the forums to help those who need insights integrating the Prime Literature. The online community and the bonds that are forming throughout our Society particularly in your weekly meetings and conference calls all contribute to the growing Neothink® Society.

The more we grow the Neothink® Society together, this new Society of Secrets, the more people will disintegrate from the anticivilization, the dishonest, suppressive world, the only world they have ever known.

Through the SOS, new members can leave behind that world of steady loss and through the prime literature they can integrate with our Twelve Visions World of steady fulfillment. And you, our mentors, will help reverse the psychological end game that quietly burdens people's lives. And the new enthusiasm and motivation that members have here in the Neothink® Society will bring them a new lease on life. And, that new lease on life, really living life they were meant to live, will bring about the growing demand for ending the physical end game. Make no mistake, you as my mentors, play a major, historic role in the Superpuzzle as described in the Miss Annabelle's Story.

393

Achieving the Superpuzzle is possible because of the 40 years spent developing the Prime Literature, nailing it down. It is possible because of the past year and a half of getting the SOS Chapters, the Clubhouse Congregations spread around the country and getting the "Face of the World" web site built. And now it is possible because of you, my new mentors.

We are ready to roll! And I'll be right there steering this juggernaut from the widest perspective. I'll be the prime mentor steering the course.

As one of the two main creators of the Prime Literature and one of the three originators of this movement, I see this movement from the most wide-scope integration. I'm going to work closely now, hand and hand with you, my mentors as your prime mentor, giving you forward essence movement, holding essence meetings with you and giving you insights and encouragement and direction.

Forbidden Revelation

The Secret Society Brings You
The Forbidden System

Make All
the
People Rich
Including
The Poor!

Mark Hamilton

Secret Teachings to My Exclusive Inner Circle

Idealized in the 20th Century
Actualized in the 21st Century

To: My Level-Nine Apprentices
From: Mark Hamilton

Note: As you read through the Orientation below, realize that it is addressing new members who will have gone through the same selection process that you went through. I described that selection process to you in our Level-Three Essence Meeting. Read the following orientation from the perspective of having received this booklet from us, but not yet having been invited into our secret meetings.

The Forbidden System
Orientation

It was not easy to find you. We spent time, money, and held meetings to locate you. At some point, we will tell you what we were looking for and why we chose you. But for now, this booklet is meant only for you. There is something confidential I must tell you.

Those above you do not want you to have this forbidden information. In fact, this information has remained unwritten for a very long time. A world-renowned scientist tried to get this information to the public in 1990 and was instead sent to prison. Today, an exclusive association, a secret society, is releasing this forbidden knowledge to a select few people. You are one of those hand-picked persons. You see, your profile matched the character traits we are looking for to receive this secret information never before seen by the public. You truly are special. In fact, your character traits match those who are members of our exclusive association of some of the world's most important people. When you are part of our inner circle, we will reveal those character traits we saw in you. After you read through The Forbidden System (reserved for only you), you will then be ready for an invitation to our inner circle. Indeed, we are truly impressed with your character traits, and we want you eventually here with us.

But for now, that must remain a mystery as we focus on why we sent this forbidden knowledge to you: For 3000 years the information enclosed has been forbidden to the public — forbidden from the peasants of the past to ordinary Americans today. Our secret society, for the first time, has printed the Forbidden System that will bring ordinary people extraordinary wealth and love beyond what even the most selfish leaders hoard for themselves. As your profile indicates, the possibilities *for you* are endless. Realize, you are among the *very first* ordinary persons in 3000 years to lay eyes upon the Forbidden System, and you stand to benefit enormously. You are among the rare, early chosen ones to gain this forbidden knowledge. You display the character traits the men and women in our exclusive association seek out . We had to spend a lot of money looking for you. You do not know it yet, but we believe you will someday be part of this association of the successful few...a parallel society of the fortunate few. But that will happen after you read through your reserved copy of the Forbidden System – reserved for your eyes only.

Back to your Forbidden System: Since the beginning of civilization, there has always been a lucrative bank of knowledge that the leaders forbade the scholars to let out. If that forbidden knowledge ever did get out, then the highly-guarded hidden secrets to wealth would get to mere ordinary people. The leaders of society would lose their rank. So, this highly-guarded bank of knowledge always remained in the hands of the fortunate few, a safe-box for the leaders only.

They protected it with swift severity. In 1990, a world-renowned scientist tried to get it out but was sent to prison by the authorities. This Secret Society also consists of renegade writers who are protected by the First Amendment, willing to get the forbidden knowledge out to those with special character traits like you.

You are being exposed to an exclusive association, a secret society consisting of powerful and wealthy renegades who dare to release the millennia-old forbidden knowledge. The 3000-yearold forbidden knowledge contains the millennia-old hidden secrets to wealth, love, power, creativity, happiness, health and longevity. Only your wealthy and powerful leaders knew and exploited these secrets throughout history.

I must admit, we studied your profile. We spent labor and direct costs looking for you. The Secret Society has since determined that you have the character to be among the chosen few to see the Forbidden System of "unwritten" knowledge. The "unwritten" 110-page booklet in your hands reveals the forbidden turnkey system that will, for the first time, now allow ordinary people — allow *you* — to experience wealth. You have never seen this turnkey system before, and you will never see it…except through this "unwritten" booklet reserved in your name, only for you.

Never before has there been such an opportunity for ordinary people: For the first time in our human history, *they* can be rich, including the poor!

As you are one of the *chosen few* among the masses to be selected to receive this forbidden knowledge, you hold a civic duty to spread the news to others around you – those you care about – not so fortunate as to have received this priceless booklet. Indeed, the Forbidden System emerges from the shadows after 3000 years, and *you* are one of the selected few chosen to receive this booklet containing the complete Forbidden System. Here are four consequences of the Forbidden System as it unfolds before your eyes:

• **The Forbidden System — forbidden by all authorities — will allow ordinary people to live like millionaires without lifting a finger.**

• **The Forbidden System — forbidden since 1000 BC — will cure disease after disease and eventually cure aging itself.**

• **The Forbidden System — forbidden from ordinary people — will lift us from boring stagnation-fallen lives to exhilarating creation-driven lives.**

• **The Forbidden System — forbidden from love and marriages — will ignite or reignite romantic love.**

The entire Forbidden System is revealed in this 110-page booklet entitled *Make All the People Rich, Including the Poor!* You get the complete system in one *thorough* reading! Remember, we sought you out and ultimately want you in the Secret Society. So read this priceless information cover to cover. The authorities never allowed this highly-guarded information into the hands of the public.

Read the Forbidden System while you can. Your life will go through an amazing metamorphosis. The Forbidden System will show you how ordinary people can live like millionaires — even the poor! It will show you how ordinary people can live much healthier and much longer — even the elderly! It will show ordinary people how to break free from their depressing stagnation traps to soar with creativity into the exhilarating lives they were meant to live — even the hopelessly suppressed laborers and the dejected unemployed! The Forbidden System will bring romantic love to singles and bring back romantic love to couples. It is all in this complete Forbidden System — forbidden by the authorities for 3000 years. The Secret Society discloses the Forbidden System to a hand-picked few within the potentially very small window of time we have — you being one of those select chosen few.

Your Secret Society invitation will come after you have read the Forbidden System. That's right, we will give you two weeks to read this forbidden knowledge. Then, you will be ready to join us. We will send you an invitation to our exclusive association of powerful and successful men and women. You then decide. I will just say, for the record, we found you, and we like what we see. We want you with us eventually. You deserve the wonderful life of wealth, romantic love, and prestige…the life you were meant to live and can have in our exclusive association of the fortunate few. To qualify for our invitation in two weeks, you must read the following forbidden information from cover to cover.

Secret Teachings to My Exclusive Inner Circle

The Forbidden System

Secret Teachings to My Exclusive Inner Circle

The Forbidden System
Introduction

The premise is simple: man is imperfect. Man is flawed. Man is vulnerable to incorrect opinions, selfish agendas, destructive temptations, misguided behaviors, dishonest corruption, even manipulative evil.

By removing all imperfections — by removing man from making the political and legal decisions — a perfect "power-reactor explosion" of wealth, health, and peace will overwhelm society…sooner than later.

The problem in all political and legal systems ever known to man is: they are ultimately controlled by flaw-filled man. The American political system, for instance, whether liberal left or conservative right, in both cases is controlled by man — by flaw-filled man.

Civilization will take an unprecedented leap forward by removing imperfection, by removing man and his endless opinions and agendas from creating, interpreting, and executing law.

The method to remove man is the Prime Law. The rapid consequence, as shown throughout Part Two, is millionaire-like prosperity for all the people, *including the poor*.

Secret Teachings to My Exclusive Inner Circle

Forbidden Chapter One
Removing Rule of Man
for
Universal Wealth
Including the Poor!

"The Prime Law locks down the fundamental of law and government. The Prime Law removes man and his endless opinions and agendas and illusions. I can clearly see how ordinary people like me will become very wealthy."

— *A Neothink® Society Member*

Once we recognize and remove from politics and law the inherent problem of man — flaw-filled creatures easily influenced by power and money — then we will quickly rise into a wealthy world...even the poor will rise, as we will see in Part Two.

Ruling-class power must be taken out of the hands of man. Freedom and prosperity throughout history suffered when *man* created, interpreted, and executed the law. On the other hand, freedom and prosperity throughout history soared when man was removed from the political and bureaucratic controls. Our own country soared when we mostly removed the rule of man (i.e., removed a monarchy with our U.S. Constitution).

To complete the evolution into universal prosperity, the powers of the legislative, judicial, and executive branches must be taken away from the opinions and agendas of flaw-filled man and put into a flawless Prime Law.

If you take a hundred well-educated men and women and ask them their thoughts on important issues of law and politics, they will bombard you with many different opinions and agendas — as exemplified by the U.S. Senate. Moreover, once in positions of political power, surrounded by the trappings of irresistible power and wealth, their answers become directed for their own benefits, for their own political clout.

Man is an easily influenced, easily corrupted creature. Therefore, the laws that govern man (i.e., protect man) must be free of man.

The only way to be free of man is to reduce law to its essence. Once at the fundamental nature of something there is no going deeper. All the opinions, agendas, illusions, dishonesties and corruption — all man's faults — no longer matter. The fundamental nature stands unchanged, unscathed, unconditional, uncorrupted...plain for all to forever see and know, which is the nature of the Prime Law.

The Twelve Visions (a Mark Hamilton Publication) demonstrates why protection of citizens is the **only** legitimate purpose of government and is the essence of law. The fundamental of protection is captured in the Prime Law, which supersedes all law. The Prime Law removes man — including all the smart law-school graduates — from the decision-making process of law. Law leaps to another level altogether, for the first time completely free of man.

The Prime Law determines the creation or lack of creation of new laws, not man with his endless opinions and agendas and faults. The fundamental of protection — the Prime Law — determines the interpretation of laws, not man with his endless egos, selfish ambitions, and many human flaws. The Prime Law determines the execution and enforcement of laws, not man who is drawn to intoxicating power, rampant dishonesties, and a capacity for evil.

When the Prime Law removes man from creating, interpreting, and executing law, something amazing happens: the heavy and corrupt ruling-class of man comes off society. In that new freedom, as you will learn throughout this platform, society and technology soar. A Great Technological Revolution takes off and causes our buying power to multiply a hundredfold, maybe a thousandfold, making everyone rich, *including the poor!* We already saw the forerunner with the uninhibited computer revolution in which buying power multiplied a thousandfold in a few years.

Let us now introduce a new grassroots political party with the sole objective to remove man from creating, interpreting, and executing law in order to make all people wealthy, including the poor.[1]

The name of that new political party that removes **man** from governing — removes the corrupt ruling class — is the Twelve Visions Party (TVP). Let us next see how the TVP will do that.

---

[1]A point of confusion among a few readers has been expressed, as follows: "You say the Prime Law will remove man from creating, interpreting, and executing the law...but even with the Prime Law **man** would still create, interpret, and execute the law."

Let me alleviate that confusion: The Prime Law as an amendment to the U.S. Constitution would take *complete control* of governing and remove man from being *in control* of governing. The Prime-Law Amendment would prevent man from creating, interpreting, or executing law based on any decision *beyond* the Prime Law, bound by the Prime Law, the fundamental of protection. Our government will go into another dimension never known on Earth: a pure protection-only government with no initiatory force in the governing body. Man will be prohibited from agenda-law, agenda-regulations, agenda-"justice" that always requires initiatory force. Rule of man will be over. Yes, man will create, interpret, and execute law *within the Prime Law's parameters* of self-defense protection from initiatory force, threat of force, fraud, or coercion. Yet man — our politicians and bureaucrats included — will be prohibited from initiatory force, from ruling via agendas; therefore there can be no rule of man, just rule of flawless law — the Prime Law. Indeed, the Prime Law governs, not rule of man. Man simply carries out the Prime Law of Protection as it applies to society. That complete control over man and complete removal of the rule of man is why I use the expression: *remove man from governing, for the Prime Law takes over governing*. Man must still create, interpret, and execute the law...but will do so as dictated by the Prime Law, void of his own wishes and desires, void of initiatory force necessary for rule of man. Rule of man can never again create, interpret, and execute the law, for without initiatory force, there is no more "rule". There is just man bound by the Prime Law to initiatory-force-free protection only — the only proper purpose of government. The Prime Law will finally deliver a purely free civilization free of the rule of man and will be the unbridled launch of our human potential.

Secret Teachings to My Exclusive Inner Circle

Forbidden Chapter Two
Presenting the Prime Law
for
Universal Wealth, Health, Safety & Peace

The Visionaries envision a profoundly free, wealthy, healthy, and safe society protected by rule of flawless law. Man — even the most educated man or woman — is by nature a flaw-filled creature. Any idea or thought put before man generates endless opinions, arguments, and agendas. Moreover, man is vulnerable to ego, temptations, and irresistible power. Man by nature tends to satisfy his own appetite first. In other words, he puts his own gain before society. At the expense of society, politicians build political clout and re-election power.

Historically, the more successful a political system is at removing man from making, interpreting, and executing law, the freer the nation and the wealthier and healthier the people.

Looking back: throughout the first millennium, the majority of people suffered, even starved under the rule of man.

The Magna Carta in 1215 AD **began a trend** of restricting the rule of man. Prosperity eventually began climbing; the people began living in better conditions.

The U.S. Constitution in 1787 **continued the trend** by *dramatically* restricting the rule of man. Consequently, Americans enjoyed unrivaled prosperity. The majority eventually joined the middle class.

The Prime Law coming with the success of the Twelve Visions Party, will **complete the trend** by *fully* removing the rule of man. All people will become wealthy, including the poor.

America dramatically advanced the evolution from the rule of man (a monarch) to the rule of law (the U.S. Constitution). And America can complete that evolution from the rule of flaw-filled man to the rule of flawless law by *fully* removing man from making, interpreting, and executing law. That final evolution is the Prime Law, which will lift society into unprecedented freedom and its people into never-before-seen wealth, health, and peace.

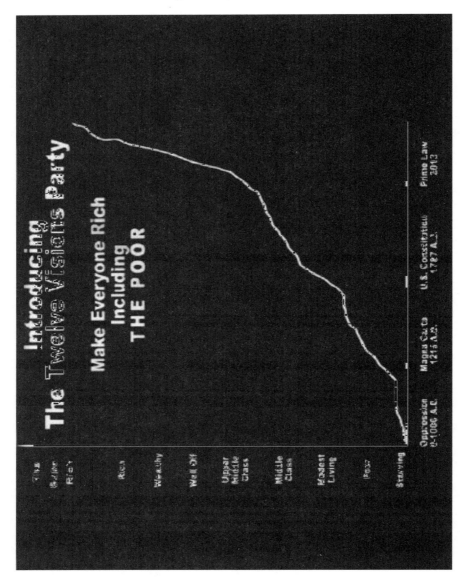

Crossroads of History

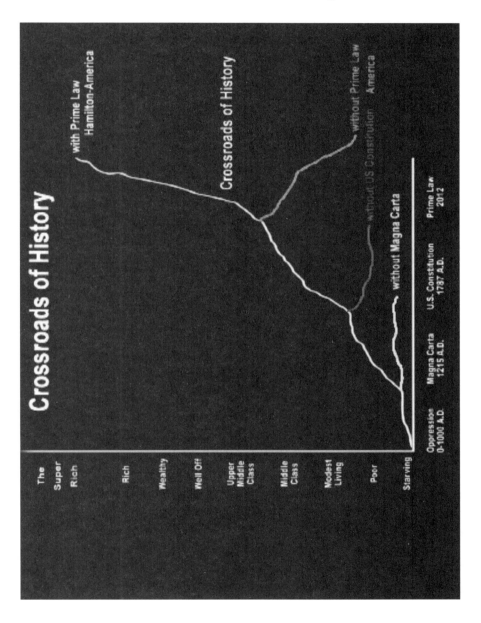

The Prime Law

In recognition of man's inherent shortcomings, the Visionaries aspire to lift the rule of law to a whole new level not yet seen on Earth. The Prime Law completes the millennia-long evolution of removing flaw-filled man from creating, interpreting, and executing law and will lead us to the wealthiest, healthiest, and safest nation to ever exist on Earth.

For the first time, law will be completely free from the faulty motivations of man. The lawmakers, judges, and regulatory bureaucrats will no longer control law. Instead, the Prime Law will control the lawmakers, judges, and regulatory bureaucrats. Instead of man governing our country, the Prime Law — the fundamental of protection — will govern.

The Prime Law
(The Fundamental of Protection)

Preamble

*The *purpose* of human life is to prosper and live happily.

*The function of government is to **provide the conditions** that let individuals fulfill that *purpose*.

*The Prime Law **guarantees those conditions** by forbidding the use of initiatory force, fraud, or coercion by any person or group against any individual, property, or contract.

Article 1

No person, group of persons, or government shall initiate force, threat of force, or fraud against any individual's self, property, or contract.

Article 2

Force is morally-and-legally justified only for protection from those who violate Article 1.

Article 3

No exceptions shall exist for Articles 1 and 2.

Wealthiest, Healthiest, Safest Society on Earth

Politicians, lawyers, judges, and bureaucrats (i.e., flaw-filled man) controlling our laws have eroded our beloved freedom and prosperity. The flawless Prime Law permanently removes flaw-filled man from subjectively creating, interpreting, and executing agenda-law. Law and justice must now adhere to the Prime Law — to protection only — the one and only proper purpose of government.

No longer will flaw-filled politicians, lawyers, judges, and bureaucrats control our laws. Instead, the Prime Law will control our flaw-filled politicians, lawyers, judges and bureaucrats. Perfection will control imperfection.

A protection-only government will spawn a new freedom that will set free a Great Technological Revolution that will bring universal wealth and health to America. Furthermore, with full government resources focused on protection only, Americans will enjoy the safest society on Earth.

The Prime Law was the one missing ingredient our forefathers needed to forever preserve the beautiful country they created. (This fact is elaborated on in the coming section titled "The Prime Law Will Bring Undreamt of Wealth, Health, Safety to All Including the Poor, the Elderly, the Underprivileged.")

Every Twelve Visions Party candidate, every elected or appointed Visionary will sign the Twelve Visions Party (TVP) Contract. That TVP Contract binds every Visionary's decision in any local, state, or federal office or position in all branches of government; the TVP Contract binds every Visionary — yes, flaw-filled man — to the Prime Law. (See the TVP Contract, Chapter Four.)

The results of removing flaw-filled man from controlling government will be universal wealth, health, and peace. We will instead have a flawless Prime Law of Protection controlling a government of protection and controlling its flaw-filled elected and appointed men and women. Law creation, law interpretation, law execution will be held to protection only. Political agenda-law, agenda-justice, and agenda-regulations will vanish, setting free business and technology to do to all industries what they did to the relatively unregulated computer industry. Americans will become wealthy as their buying power multiplies a hundredfold, a thousandfold or more.

That scenario is not a hypothesis; prosperity explosions have occurred among civilizations throughout history by somewhat pulling back flaw-filled man from the controls of government, reducing political agenda-law, agenda-justice, and agenda-regulations. In fact, our country is the shining example of an evolutionary leap from a man-controlled monarchy to the nearly flawless law-controlled republic. Of course, a great prosperity-explosion followed the creation of our country.

Over two centuries later, the Twelve Visions Party gives us an opportunity at the next and final evolutionary leap away from flaw-filled man-controlled government to flawless law-controlled government. The Prime Law is the missing integration our forefathers did not pull together, the should-be capstone to the U.S. Constitution. The Prime Law is the missing link to *pure* freedom and soaring standards of living, forever. Indeed, that missing integration makes the U.S. Constitution flawless and *fully* removes flaw-filled man. The U.S. Constitution was the stepping stone to freedom; the Prime Law is the capstone to freedom. A great prosperity-explosion will follow once again.

The Twelve Visions Party recognizes and captures this opportunity for all people alike...including the poor and the elderly. The Prime Law results in universal wealth for the first time ever on our planet: the next evolution of freedom will bring *all* Americans a wealthy, healthy, and safe life.

Forbidden Chapter Three
Actualizing Universal Wealth & Health

The Visionaries do have a great vision: we see soaring standards of living; we see all the people becoming wealthy, including the poor. We see all the people gaining good health, including the elderly.

Universal Wealth and Health

In this age of rapidly advancing technologies, in a time when buying power can rapidly soar as we have seen with the computers, Visionaries realize that all citizens can soon experience multiplying buying power and great wealth if the government returns to its one proper purpose of *protection only* and removes itself from its improper purpose of promoting the "social good". The *full* dynamics of this return to a protection-only government and the resulting explosion of freedom and wealth for the people in this age of rapidly advancing technologies can be clearly seen later in this platform. You will witness why we are *the* political party to make *all* the people wealthy and healthy, including the poor and the elderly. Universal wealth and health is now actually possible. The Twelve Visions Party exists to actualize that possibility.

Unprecedented Wealth, Health, and Safety

The Visionaries envision a profoundly free, wealthy, healthy, and safe society protected by rule of flawless law. That Prime Law of Protection — no initiatory force — applies to and restricts government itself. Therefore, a government unable to use initiatory force on its people ends all power-building, force-backed, political-policy legislation and regulations for the "social good". Without force-backed political-agenda-law, without force-backed political-policy regulations, without force-backed political-agenda-"justice", then entrepreneurs, businesses, and their super technologies are held back no longer. What we witnessed during the relatively unregulated computer revolution will occur across all industries (including the medical industry) to bring us a Great Technological Revolution. For the first time on our planet, a government would set free a Great Technological Revolution not just in the computer industry, but in *all* industries, quickly bringing unprecedented wealth, health, and safety to all citizens.

The Millionaire-Phenomenon

The flawless Prime Law, not flaw-filled men and women, not agenda-and-ego-driven lawmakers, will direct all political decisions and actions and restrict them to protection from initiatory force. At that fundamental essence of legitimate law and government (i.e., protect the people from initiatory force) not only politicians and bureaucrats, but all people can easily determine the proper protection-only laws. Who is in office becomes irrelevant; political and personal agendas and endless opinions become irrelevant; party affiliation becomes irrelevant; what party holds power becomes irrelevant. The Prime Law of Protection and nothing more remains relevant. Flaw-filled man no longer controls government. The consequences of decisions and actions locked down to the Prime Law will be staggering as *fully* demonstrated in the following chapters.

Without political agendas, policies, and egos controlling legislation and regulations, the geniuses of society will finally be free to accelerate the Technological Revolution and drive our buying power higher than we have ever seen. This millionaire-phenomenon will come to all people, including the poor, as demonstrated in the following pages. Other spectacular consequences are shown in the following pages as well, such as unprecedented health, happiness, love, peace, security, and safety. At the state level, popular planks listed by the Republicans and popular planks listed by the Democrats will either be moved eventually to the private sector if they have nothing to do with the one proper purpose of government — physical protection of the people — or will fall under the Prime Law of Protection.

TVP Planks & Consequences
Rule of Flawless Law to Replace Rule of Flaw-Filled Man:
Throughout history, the more that societies moved away from rule

of man to rule of rational law, the more prosperity the people enjoyed. The Twelve Visions Party presents and supports the Prime Law. All party members will sign the TVP Contract that binds all decision-making to the Prime Law. The Prime Law completes the long evolution from rule of flaw-filled man to rule of flawless law. The result will be an unprecedented prosperity-explosion for the people.

Protection-Only Budget: Imagine all taxpayers' dollars and government's efforts going toward protection, which includes the military, protection-only legislation, police, courts, and prisons. Crime would decrease dramatically. Taxes would decrease dramatically. The geniuses of society, without the bogus government-on-the-offense holding them back, would cause our wealth and health to soar. (The following chapters give a better understanding of the unprecedented wealth that will result from the Protection-Only Budget and its government-on-the-defense. The principle applies at both the federal and state levels.)

Depoliticize and Deregulate: End politicization and regulation of our lives and businesses via the Prime Law of Protection and the Protection-Only Budget. Get down to the one proper purpose of any government: protection from initiatory force, threat of force, or fraud. By removing the bogus purpose of government, particularly regulatory programs for the "social good", the Twelve Visions Party removes the massive and improper government control over our lives and businesses. By getting government out of our lives and out of our businesses altogether, we free the geniuses of society to do wonderful things for us, as follows:

Unprecedented Security: The people will be well taken care of by the geniuses of society, rising by the many millions as the Twelve Visions Party ends political-policy regulations that have nothing to do with protection from initiatory force. The millions of freed geniuses will drive technologies into new dimensions that bring undreamt of values to the people...remarkable values that meet and surpass people's needs and solve their problems.

Universal Wealth: The costs for those new technologies will keep falling toward zero, similar to the personal computers during the computer revolution. The Great Technological Revolution will happen in all industries and make ordinary people more and more wealthy as costs in all industries keep falling.

Universal Health: The new technologies, racing ahead in all industries, will especially race ahead in the medical industry without the destructive cost-prohibitive FDA regulations holding the geniuses back. The geniuses will eradicate disease after disease, and their soaring new technologies will drive down medical costs. People will live with increasingly better health for increasingly longer lives.

Job Explosion & Evolution: Businesses will strive to keep up in the rapid progress of the Great Technological Revolution; everything will change as businesses, to stay competitive, concentrate on bringing out their greatest asset — the unique creativity of their employees. Ordinary people will experience exhilarating entrepreneurial-like jobs at their places of work, and they will love going to work as they discover the creation-driven life, the life they were meant to live.

Extraordinary Marriages & Love: The wonderful falling-in-love feelings in the early weeks of romantic relationships will tend to return. Why? People will rise from a life stuck in stagnation. They will rise into the creation-driven life of their dreams. With that growing source of happiness inside, filling them and overflowing into their romantic relationships, they will forever feel the power of love.

Educating Geniuses: Our children and grandchildren will become "smarter" than today's smartest people. In tomorrow's Twelve-Visions-World education, children will be taught how to integrate knowledge to build success and lead themselves. They will see through illusions and will no longer need or want to be led by "authorities". The need for a ruling class and its regulations will become repulsive to the graduating self-leaders tomorrow. Our children will grow up to live a creation-driven life — the happy and prosperous life they were meant to live. The old structure of education cannot compete against the new mentality and yields to the coming schools of geniuses (more later).

Eradicating Crime & Terrorism: The fear of terrorism will rapidly decline, and crime will nearly cease. The Twelve Visions Party will concentrate every action and every dollar toward *one* purpose: **protect the people from initiatory force**, as declared in the Prime Law. Safer-living statistics will soar.

Conclusion

When 20th-century visionary Henry Ford discovered that the workers should not manage the work, rather the work should manage the workers (via the invention of the assembly line)…society experienced an enormous prosperity-explosion. Mass production began, which accelerated the Industrial Revolution. The people's buying power — their wealth — skyrocketed.

When 21st-century visionary Mark Hamilton discovered that the flaw-filled lawmakers, judges, and bureaucrats should not control the law,[1] rather the flawless Prime Law should control the flaw-filled lawmakers, judges, and bureaucrats…society became poised to experience another enormous prosperity-explosion. Unleashed geniuses of society and non-restricted super technologies will accelerate the Technological Revolution. Once again, the people's buying power — their wealth — will skyrocket.

Indeed, the Twelve Visions Party is *the* Party to make the people rich, including the poor. **That is our Vision!** We have reached a rare moment in time and technology that could literally make all people wealthy. The Twelve Visions Party clearly recognizes and reaches for the switch to ignite the prosperity-explosion.

---

[1] Misinterpretation of the U.S. Constitution, often through ego-driven, political-agenda "justice", steadily opened the way for lawmakers and justices to control the law. The Prime Law forever ends that steady regression from the rule of law back to the disastrous rule of man. Rule of law — the flawless Prime Law of Protection — will permanently reassert itself with the Prime-Law Amendment to the U.S. Constitution.

Secret Teachings to My Exclusive Inner Circle

Forbidden Chapter Four
The Universal-Wealth Movement &
The TVP Contract

The Twelve Visions Party with its Prime Law and Protection-Only Budget understands government's final evolution into providing protection and *only* protection, *the* purpose of government, *without* flaw-filled man in control. As a result, as shown throughout the following pages, removing flaw-filled man from the controls of government means average Americans will live like millionaires without lifting a finger. Everyone will become rich, including the poor.

Indeed, when you get down to the irreducible fundamental of something, a paradigm shift sometimes occurs with almost magical benefits. Consider the following example, an analogy to the Prime Law and the resulting wealth we will enjoy:

In the early 20th century when Henry Ford got down to the fundamental nature of production — down to the *physical movements* of production — the assembly line emerged and caused a paradigm shift from handmade production to mass production. Ford identified, "Do not let the workers manage the work; instead, let the work manage the workers." And that paradigm shift changed EVERYTHING. A national prosperity-explosion followed.

In the early 21st century, when I (the author, Mark Hamilton) got down to the fundamental nature of government — down to the *physical protection* of the individual and his property — the Prime Law emerged, which will cause a paradigm shift from rule of flaw-filled man to rule of flawless law. I identified, "Do not let flaw-filled politicians, judges, bureaucrats manage the law; instead, let the flawless Prime Law manage the politicians, judges, bureaucrats." And that paradigm shift will change EVERYTHING. A national prosperity-explosion will follow, a freedom paradigm accompanied by an *unhindered* Technological Revolution in which buying power will multiply a hundredfold, a thousandfold or more. The computer revolution was a preview of what can come to all industries.

Now let us take a close look at the political party itself. To do so, I must express my thoughts and feelings directly to you. For a long time, I dreaded the idea of launching a political party. I knew that *all* people, *including loyal Visionaries, including myself,* were flaw-filled men and women with all our shortcomings, vulnerabilities, and temptations. We are human, and human beings are not perfect. How could the Twelve Visions Party survive the faults of its members and officials? The answer, I continued to conclude, was: it will **not** survive the faults of man.

How could my new political-party idea ever work? Finally, I realized I needed to take the fundamental decision-making away from party members, yes, away from the Visionaries themselves! In other words, "Do not let the Visionaries (imperfect, flaw-filled man) manage the law; instead, let the unchanging flawless Prime Law manage the Visionaries!" Yes! With the fundamental law of protection — the Prime Law — I could do this! The Twelve Visions Party could now work and truly bring the millionaire-phenomenon to the people!

To control this movement, all Party members who run for office or service in any way must sign the TVP Contract below that assures every decision is made according to the Prime Law.

Now, the Political Party will work beautifully. The Twelve Visions Party can now actualize the unprecedented opportunity to make *all* people rich, including the poor. Indeed, we are at a unique moment in time and technology in which the Twelve Visions Party can ignite a never-before-seen prosperity-explosion.

The TVP Contract

<u>Premise</u>: A Protection-Only Government will lead to the people's greatest prosperity (as demonstrated in *Twelve Visions*, a Mark Hamilton Publication). That is reality. The many opinions and agendas of man cannot alter reality. Yet, while creating, interpreting, and executing law, the attempt to alter reality is continually made: this law...that interpretation...these regulations will improve the people's prosperity...*we promise!* Whether

innocent or not, those sound-good, "social good" government actions beyond protection increasingly control us and slowly kill our freedoms, bit by bit, day after day, steadily aging our country, leading to its eventual death.

The purpose of the TVP Contract is to establish *the* one proper purpose of government, *the* reality of protection. We establish *the* reality of protection through the unchanging Prime Law of no initiatory force, which controls both the selfish and selfless lawmakers, lawyers, judges, and bureaucrats and their endless opinions, biases, agendas, ambitions, egos, desires, delusions and illusions. No longer will those flaw-filled men and women control law and politics!

Contract: I, _____, pledge to subordinate (to the Prime Law) my many preconceived thoughts, despite how strongly I feel, despite whether I believe with certainty or with reservation, for with external and internal confusions and illusions that accompany a power-based government, I honestly acknowledge that always reaching the proper decision is merely impossible. In serving my Party's objective to return to and forever remain a protection-only government in order to unleash an unprecedented prosperity-explosion that will make all the people rich, including the poor, I fully understand the mechanics come down to consistently, always without exception, supporting the biologically irreducible fundamental act of protection — the Prime Law of no initiatory force as spelled out in the National Platform of the Twelve Visions Party. That Prime Law of Protection must control the lawmakers, law interpreters, and law executers, not the other way around. Therefore, every decision I make — even if it goes against the very grain of my mind, heart, and soul — will be made purely on serving the Prime Law. I realize, in the end, that policy will bring forth our vision to make all the people wealthy, healthy, and safe including the poor and elderly, as demonstrated in the TVP National Platform. Again, that policy will bring forth our vision of a profoundly free, wealthy, healthy, and safe society.

If I knowingly go against the Prime Law of *protection*

only for any decision for any reason whatsoever, or if I show a trend of "unknowingly" going against the Prime Law, which is mostly self-evident, the Twelve Visions Party will immediately and publicly disown me and will no longer recognize me as a member.[1]

Lawmakers — *man* — must not control law. Men and women controlling law can lead to anything, can take a country anywhere, even to the point where it becomes law to kill others, as we have seen around the world, throughout history. Man with his many faults of ego, greed, envy, and innocent lack of knowledge and his many vulnerabilities must not control law and interpret the Constitution. Man controlling law, with all his vulnerabilities and faults, has always been a recipe for destruction. No, the flawless Prime Law of protection must control the lawmakers, law interpreters, law executers. If we want to live, for the first time, in a universally wealthy, healthy, happy, peaceful, safe, and truly free society, then the Prime Law of Protection must ultimately become the political point of origin, "the decision maker", not man, not me. Political decisions bound to the Prime Law will effectively minimize crime and eventually end initiatory force including agenda-law, agenda-"justice", and political-policy regulations based on initiatory force, thus unleashing the geniuses of society and their technologies, catapulting our standards of living, buying power, wealth and health for all people, *including the poor*. **That is our Vision**.

All members running for office, appointed to office, or serving

---

[1] Until our force-pay government becomes a voluntary-pay government, all government laws and regulations ultimately sit upon forced tax collection. Therefore, Visionaries understand that all government laws and regulations are ultimately in violation of the Prime Law until the force-pay government becomes a voluntary-pay government. In order for the government to function prior to and through the transition (described in the TVP Platform). Visionaries will legislate, interpret, execute initiatory-force-free protection-only laws, decisions, regulations within our current government knowing that our force-pay government will evolve into a voluntary-pay government with the ratification of the Prime-Law Amendment.

in any way must sign below to abide by the Prime Law for every decision, in quest of our vision. Indeed, we the Visionaries must completely commit ourselves to the Prime Law today via this contract; we must bring the Prime Law to each of the fifty states tomorrow via our State Constitutions; we must bring the Prime Law to our Federal government eventually via an Amendment to the U.S. Constitution, which would act as the overarching, de facto Constitution of America. Visionaries must ultimately bring the Prime Law to the entire world, country by country, forever ending war. The Prime Law brings universal and permanent wealth, health, and peace to all people.

———————————————

Sign here
Member of The Twelve Visions Party

Secret Teachings to My Exclusive Inner Circle

Forbidden Chapter Five
The Prime-Law Amendment
will bring
Undreamt of Wealth, Health, Safety
to all including
The Poor, the Elderly, the Underprivileged

The one proper purpose of government is protection against initiatory force, threat of force, coercion and fraud. Any other purpose ultimately depends upon initiatory force in the hands of a ruling class, the rule of man, which takes away our freedom and, therefore, our prosperity.

Indeed, the more free a country, the more prosperous, as shown throughout history. For the first time with the Prime Law, we are talking about a purely protection-only government and, therefore, a fully free country. There has NEVER been a fully free country on our planet.

Moreover, for the first time, we have reached the technology to experience a *universal* prosperity-explosion as first seen in the computer industry. If technology is set free to rapidly advance, we can ignite that prosperity-explosion in all industries. Prices will begin falling to fractions as happened to the computers. Buying power will soar. People's buying power — *all* people's buying power — will multiply a hundredfold, a thousandfold or more. They will become rich, including the poor.

America originally rose quickly and was so much freer and more prosperous than other countries because it was a country brilliantly controlled by nearly flawless rule of law and not subjected to flaw-filled rule of man as so many other countries.

Yes, man is full of faults, motivated by ego, tugged toward temptations, attracted to easy money, corruption and dishonesty. Man is imperfect, including all Visionaries.

Therefore, the Twelve Visions Party takes America's rule of law one final step further: By going down to the biological fundamental of protection — no initiatory force — the Prime-Law Amendment would end lawmakers from recklessly creating new laws that have nothing to do with protection, and the Prime Law would end justices from recklessly interpreting law and opening the door for government to control us through "social justice" and the "social good", and the Prime Law would stop bureaucrats from establishing regulations based on political policy instead of the one proper fundamental of protection from initiatory force. For, any law or regulation beyond protection against initiatory force *requires* initiatory force; the government regresses to the rule of man.

The Prime Law takes the rule of law *all the way* and ensures a pure, protection-only government. A pure, protection-only government is also a get-out-of-the-way government, which sets free the geniuses of society and ignites the universal prosperity-explosion. The flawless Prime Law was the final rule-of-law integration the founding fathers missed.

The Prime Law has the potential to become an amendment to the Constitution of the United States, where the Prime Law has belonged since the creation of the U.S. Constitution. Let us take a close look at that possibility:

The U.S. Constitution's three main principles of inherent rights, government by the people, and separation of powers provided the basis for the freest and most prosperous nation in history. Just imagine over two centuries ago the new ideas of a nation created to ensure a person's right to life, liberty and the pursuit of happiness as written in the Declaration of Independence, a nation governed by the people, a nation with watchdog checks and balances on political and bureaucratic powers.

The delegates of the Constitutional Convention in 1787 also gave careful consideration to the division of power between the federal government and state governments. The U.S. Constitution, which emerged from the Constitutional Convention in 1787, is called the *supreme law* because the state constitutions and both federal and state laws cannot violate the U.S. Constitution.

The U.S. Constitution does a nearly perfect job setting down the principles and system of government. Things went wrong because of continual *misinterpretation* of the Constitution over generations, which led to repeated violations of the Constitution. What was missing was an overarching constitution, so to speak, the *prime* law of no initiatory force.

Had the Prime Law existed since the beginning, our country would have entered the wealthy/healthy/safe Twelve Visions World generations ago (as seen in *Twelve Visions* and demonstrated in *Superpuzzle*, Hamilton Publications).

If the Prime Law eventually becomes an amendment to the U.S. Constitution — the Prime-Law Amendment — we could again have confidence in the U.S. Constitution, for it brilliantly sets down the system of government and separation of powers, starting with the three main powers of 1) making laws, 2) executing laws, and 3) interpreting laws.

There would be, however, a fundamental change with the Prime-Law Amendment: The whole concept of a government based on *power* — separation of powers, division of powers, checks and balances of powers — would change from a government based on *power* to a government based on *service*. That fundamental change from a power basis to a service basis would evolve a businesslike system — a businesslike protection service — as detailed in Part Three of this platform.

Let us take a closer look at what the Prime-Law Amendment would accomplish. First, as identified in the following chapters, over the past century, our government existed for two purposes:

1) To protect the people

2) To promote the social good

To promote the general welfare of the people has been **misinterpreted** to mean: increase their standards of living or their wealth. Well, as demonstrated in the following pages, politicians *cannot* do that; the government cannot and should not exist to enhance social well-being, not beyond physical protection, which includes justice and proper lawmaking, both criminal and civil. Government merely provides *the conditions* for individuals to pursue their purpose to prosper and live happily. The government guarantees those conditions through the Prime Law, which calls for a protection-only government. Indeed, the Prime Law and its protection-only government guarantee *the conditions* that promote the general welfare of the people. Instead, our politicians spend our money ostensibly for the "social good", but they really want the ruling-class glory and power and importance that goes with spending money (other people's money). The evidence is clear: they do not want anything to do with the deeper effort that goes with soundly spending money. They want control and re-election. The repeated misinterpretations of the U.S. Constitution has led to these blatant violations of the Constitution, such as spending our money beyond protection while bankrupting our future, which could never occur with the Prime Law in place.

So, career politicians with the help of federal justices and regulatory bureaucrats have made a mess of things. Our well-being, standard of living, and wealth can be dramatically lifted by *unhampered* market businessmen and women...by the geniuses of society. But the erroneous second purpose of government must first end.

That bogus purpose of government to so-call "promote the social good" sprang up over the years through career politicians finding ways to spend money and become more and more likable for re-election. The Prime-Law Amendment gets rid of all that, forever.

The one *valid* purpose for our government, as you know, is *to protect the people from initiatory force,* which includes providing justice. The only way to guarantee the protection of *all* people — *equal, unbiased* and *unconditional* protection of all people of all races and all social classes and all career positions in society — is to protect *the individual.* Regardless of race or social status, the Prime Law guarantees everyone his or her unprejudiced rights as an individual, as a minority of one — the smallest of all minorities. Every individual is equally and fully protected.

Now, to provide comprehensive protection of the individual requires going down to and establishing the biologically irreducible fundamental of protection. As an analogy, to capture the comprehensive nature of the cosmos requires going down to and understanding the irreducible, fundamental sub-atomic particles composing the cosmos. The irreducible, thus indivisible, incorruptible fundamental of protection is: elimination of initiatory

432

force, which is the function of the Prime-Law Amendment. There is nothing deeper upon which to argue opinions or agendas. The Prime Law says it all. There is nothing more.

Indeed, comprehensive protection of the individual demands *one prime law* — one overarching, irreducible law: the elimination of initiatory force against the individual and his property. With that *one prime law*, everyone becomes protected from harm caused by man, including harm from government.

Therefore, with the passing of the Prime-Law Amendment, the erroneous purpose of government and its destructive ruling-class of man can never return. Prosperity will soar forever as described throughout this platform. What great news! Indeed, *one prime law* was always needed; *one prime law* eternally guarantees protection and freedom. That one Prime Law could bring about the Twelve Visions World (described in *Twelve Visions*, a Mark Hamilton Publication) if that Prime Law were to become an amendment to the U.S. Constitution, the Prime-Law Amendment.

With that one Prime-Law Amendment in place, it essentially becomes our Supreme Law to which every law must answer. For, the Supreme Law will filter out every law and regulation in violation, namely those that serve the bogus purpose of so-called promoting the "social good", *agenda-law* which requires initiatory force. The Prime Law is the biological fundamental, the point of origin, the beginning of all law. Therefore, no further unhealthy law or misinterpretation of the U.S. Constitution could occur. No more agenda-law, political-policy regulations, or ego-"justice"...no more violations could happen. Government could not tell us how to spend our money or *force* us to pay taxes. As long as we did not commit initiatory force[1], we would be completely free. We would not need ego-and-power-driven lawmakers stirring up legislation...with lawyers and bureaucrats using those laws to control us and drain us. We would no longer need that parasitical ruling-class of man that destroyed our yet-unknown prosperity. Their deceptions could no

---

[1] Threat of force, coercion and fraud are forms of initiatory force.

longer pass through the Prime-Law Amendment — including their forced taxes.

Our government would cease to house a parasitical ruling-class of man as we switched over to the Protection-Only Budget (described in the next chapter) that ends the funds for the bogus second purpose of government — to so-call promote the "social good". The Protection-Only Budget supplies funds to the one proper purpose of government — to protect the country and its citizens from initiatory force, which includes the proper protection-based lawmaking and system of justice, forever unable to violate the Prime Law.

Now, what guarantees our government could never again grow a ruling class? Government can grow a ruling class only through force — pay your taxes or go to prison. With the passing of the Prime-Law Amendment, not even the government could use initiatory force and, therefore, would *forever* cease to be a ruling class. Instead, with the passing of the Prime-Law Amendment, the government would function as a protection *service* you voluntarily pay for. Part Three of this platform explains exactly how that would happen.

Gone would be the days of bogus and destructive government, government on the offense so-called promoting the "social good". Market businesspersons — the geniuses of society — would successfully take over that job of promoting the social good as shown in an upcoming chapter. Then, our new government would forever provide the one specific value of protection, which its citizens — its customers — would voluntarily pay for. People will gladly pay for safety and peace.

Realize, the Protection-Only Budget described in the next chapter would not be enough to permanently end the ruling class. The government could regress into a corrupt ruling class again, eventually, if government could use initiatory force against its citizens with a force-backed IRS. In short, that ugly rise of the ruling class is what happened to our original, beautiful U.S. Government idea meant to exist for protection only. The Prime-Law Amendment would *forever* stop the ruling class from happening again. Indeed, the Prime-Law Amendment pulls out the roots of the ruling class — initiatory force, which includes forced taxes.

Without forced tax collection, government power is not a *ruling* power. Instead, it is an *earned* power, earned from ever-looming, potential competition. Our Twelve Visions Government is nonthreatening to its citizens — to its customers — and is incorruptible.

With initiatory force permanently out of the equation of government due to the Prime-Law Amendment, man can hold no ruling power — no rule-of-man power — and can never again hold ruling power over you whatsoever. For the first time, you will be truly free...you and the many geniuses of society!

The Twelve Visions Government will eventually evolve into a reputable business providing the immense value of protection — peace and safety — a priceless value *citizens will gladly pay for*. If you were unhappy with the protection service, you could withdraw and not pay...and not be a criminal. If enough people did that, a competitive service would rise to guarantee protection — better protection. Those free-market dynamics would force tomorrow's government to provide honest and satisfactory value to you. Those free-market dynamics would guarantee your best protection, including national defense and local police protection as demonstrated in *Superpuzzle* (a Mark Hamilton Publication).

Those free-market dynamics would also free the geniuses of society. With the Prime-Law Amendment to the U.S. Constitution, the prosperity-explosion described in the following chapters would never end. Now, you will read about the wealth, happiness, love, and health you could experience. The following chapters deliver the actual system that will allow *ordinary* people to live the wealthy, healthy, and safe lives they were meant to live.

Secret Teachings to My Exclusive Inner Circle

Forbidden Chapter Six
Multiply Our Buying Power
A Thousandfold

We have reached a special place in time: the idea of real, universal wealth and health can actually happen, and the Twelve Visions Party is highly aware of this unprecedented opportunity. We have identified two paths to universal wealth, health, and security:

Path 1) The ratification of the Prime Law as an amendment to the U.S. Constitution. The Prime-Law Amendment will filter out the bogus second purpose of government. Without initiatory force to pursue the bogus second purpose of government, the dark rule of flaw-filled man — the entire elite ruling class of flaw-filled man — will end in the light of the rule of flawless law, the Prime Law. Geniuses of society would no longer be held back and would be free to multiply our buying power…up to a *thousandfold*, as first seen in the uniquely free computer industry. Multiplying our buying power even a hundredfold would bring Americans universal wealth, health, and security.

Path 2) The process of amending the U.S. Constitution, for all practical purposes, must start with Congress. Therefore, the Prime-Law Amendment will have to wait for the Great Replacement Program to occur first, as described in this chapter. A second, potentially more rapid path to universal wealth, health, and security starts with the Executive Branch, with the President, specifically with his Protection-Only Budget, as described in this chapter. The scenario described in this chapter could happen swiftly (remember Perot's near tipping point in '92). The passing of the President's Protection-Only Budget will effectively cut off the bogus second purpose of government, as described within. Passing the Protection-Only Budget, effectively depoliticizing and deregulating America, will also end the ruling-class of flaw-filled man and free the geniuses of society. The geniuses will do for all industries what they did for the mostly nonpoliticized, mostly unregulated computer industry: they will multiply our buying power a thousandfold, making all Americans wealthy. The Great Replacement Program (replacing ruling-class politicians with Prime-Law politicians) would follow, and the Prime-Law Amendment would then follow, bringing our country, for the first time, rule of flawless law, permanently locking down the conditions of universal wealth, health, and security. The unprecedented wealth for ordinary people is described within. For the first time, what you are reading here about universal wealth, health, and security is not political rhetoric. It is your destiny with the Prime Law.

So, let us view your destiny of wealth, health, and peace. …Just before we do, however, I must take a moment to form the ground for your trek to the viewing point of the life you were meant to live: Starting in the early 1980s, I spent long days developing *Twelve Visions*, a Mark Hamilton Publication that reveals twelve visions of the future — of your destiny. *Twelve Visions* uses a unique blend of past and present facts that snap together like pieces to a puzzle.

Consider that, as with any forming puzzle, a point will come when you can see what the completed puzzle-picture will look like, even before all the pieces are snapped into place. Knowing what the puzzle-picture looks like before it is all there is seeing into the future. You can actually describe the missing portion of the puzzle-picture – describe the future pieces. This ability to show you a puzzle-picture before it is all there — an accurate vision of the future – is called **Neothink®**. I developed and perfected Neothink® over the past thirty years.

I used this Neothink® puzzle-building technique to build *Twelve Visions* — a complete puzzle-picture showing us our future. I reveal a country of wealthy, healthy, and safe citizens (and much more) resulting from very specific psychological and political changes. The pages that follow contain selected portions from four of my Twelve Neothink® Visions; they show us exactly how to bring the people, even the poor, remarkable wealth, health, and peace.

Indeed, the remaining Part Two of this platform consists of the Tenth, Eleventh, and parts of the Ninth and Twelfth Visions from *Twelve Visions* and shows you the puzzle-picture of *your* life tomorrow with the Prime Law.

As you begin, realize there may be a few words and concepts you do not fully understand that were developed in the first eight visions, but just continue reading. We will begin with the Eleventh Vision…

Unstoppable Universal Wealth

"That's the technology paradox: Businesses can thrive at the very moment when their prices are falling the fastest. 'The only thing that matters is if the exponential growth of your market is faster than the exponential decline of your prices,' says George M.C. Fisher, chairman and CEO of Eastman Kodak Co. The challenge is enormous, he says. 'Companies have to project out: How will I be competitive in a world (in which) technology will be virtually free?'

"The new rules require more than ingenuity, agility, and speed. They call for redefining value in an economy where the cost of raw technology is plummeting toward zero. Sooner or later, this plunge will obliterate the worth of almost any specific piece of hardware or software. Then, value will be in establishing a long-term relationship with a customer — even if it means giving the first generation of a product away."

— Business Week "The Technology Paradox: How Companies Thrive As Prices Dive"

Many new technologies bombarded my thoughts as the Eleventh Vision came to me. A great competitive storm of super rapidly evolving new technologies in tomorrow's Twelve Visions World caused consumer prices to fall to fractions.

With the success of the Twelve Visions Party and its Prime Law, the famous free-falling prices of computers and communications spread beyond the computer industry across many old industries and all new industries, reaching nearly all consumer products. Then, even modest paychecks and savings were worth a fortune.

Well, you got rich, without lifting a finger, in that Twelve Visions World. The computer revolution was a forerunner to a Technological Revolution that drove prices toward zero and values toward infinity in most industries.

Today, people wonder where the Technological Revolution will take us. America's richest man and other powerful people predict mind-boggling technological transformations culminating in a *distance-free* world. They are right: the walls of distance have nearly come down as digitized information traveling through broadband fiber-optic cables and between personal satellite dishes let us work, learn, shop, and play anywhere in the world, anytime, regardless where we live. But those visionaries have limited insight into what will *really* happen. They do not predict the *enormous wealth*.

The very large financial benefits of ending the ruling class brings increasing pressure for people to turn to the Twelve Visions Party. The most powerful and fastest moving trends throughout history were economically driven. As this monetarily motivated trend to end the ruling class grows, my Eleventh Vision showed me big government eventually could not hold. My Vision showed me that during the first quarter of the twenty-first century, big government popped off society like a champagne cork. Suddenly, millions of super entrepreneurs spouted forth, out of nowhere. They were the first to jump into the Neothink® mentality. During my Eleventh Vision, those millions of freed super entrepreneurs caused a catalytic progression of tomorrow's super technologies, which caused a catalytic explosion of buying power.

The era of inexpensive super technologies showered upon us. Cost-collapsing telecommunications, fiber optics, digitized information, super-powered personal computers, the Internet, robotics, the Genome Project...those were only a few small clouds at the turn of the millennium before a giant storm of competitive geniuses and their super technologies. With the success of the Twelve Visions Party, the geniuses feverishly competed day and night against each other to bring us breathtaking values for just a few dollars or less. When the technological storm began, more and more affordable super technologies showered upon us day after day, our buying power soared, and it never came back down once lifted by the great technological twister.

Our lifestyles became our previous fantasies as our buying

power kept soaring until we lived like millionaires, including the poor. All along, the only thing that prevented our millionaire-like lifestyles was big government.

Before the success of the Twelve Visions Party, throughout the twentieth century and into the twenty-first century, most industries and their technologies were terribly burdened by big government — by regulation, legislation, litigation, taxes. Most industries and technologies had long been *politicized;* the computer/Internet industry had not (although there was a growing trend, starting with the infamous antitrust lawsuit brought against Microsoft).

Without carrying the same burden, the geniuses in the computer field easily jumped ahead. And that was the difference that allowed prices to miraculously race toward zero.

That was a preview to the Technological Revolution that will happen with the success of the Twelve Visions Party. Over the next three pages are three oversimplified images that flashed before me during my Eleventh Vision: (Author's Note: Although grossly oversimplified, these flash mental images occurred during my Neothinking® process and do make the basic point. The Department of Homeland Security was created after my Eleventh Vision had occurred. Therefore, that executive department does not show up on the following images.)

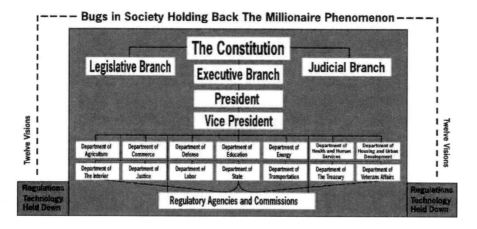

441

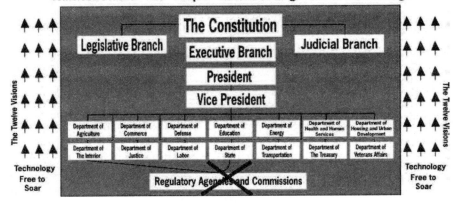

Tomorrow's Make - The - People - Millionares Megatrend To Rid The Bugs

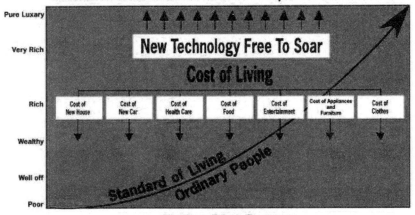

Millionaire Phenomenon Will Make The People Live Like Millionaires

During 21st Century

My Eleventh Vision showed me technologies in *all* areas of life free to race ahead in the way the computers had. In that Twelve Visions Society of rapidly advancing technologies, living costs fell to fractions in the way the computers had. Buying power in *all* areas of life multiplied a hundred times or more. I saw ordinary people living like millionaires in custom homes, driving luxury cars, and vacationing all over the world first class. Even the poor enjoyed the gifts of life.

One man had the power to quickly bring us into that Twelve Visions World where poverty and suffering no longer existed and Americans lived in luxury. That man was the President of the United States. In the twentieth century and early twenty-first century, no President would initiate the millionaire phenomenon because no career politician would slash his own base of power. But now, we have seen a sample of the great prosperity:

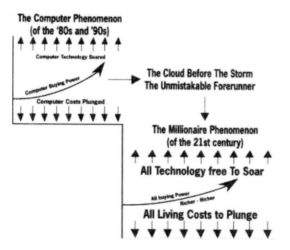

The regulatory seams around society restrict new technologies and hold back the Technological Revolution. Those regulatory seams holding back the Technological Revolution also postpone the job revolution and block a hundred million super entrepreneurs (explained in the Fifth Vision). When big government disintegrated with the success of the Twelve Visions Party, modern technologies burst out everywhere and mixed with millions of unleashed super entrepreneurs using Neothink®. The overwhelming creativity, pumped into the new supersociety, generated prosperity that went off the charts, beyond anything ever contemplated in economic think tanks. Even the poorest Americans experienced enormous wealth.

You Became 100 Times Richer

My Eleventh Vision showed me that by honing in on the national budget alone, our buying power could be catapulted a hundred times or more! We have to do nothing! Let us start with a brief overview of what makes up the national budget:

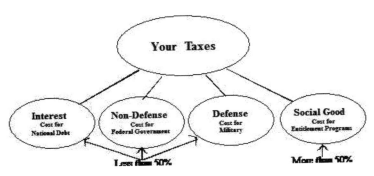

Your taxes break down into mandatory spending programs such as Social Security, Medicare, Medicaid, means-tested entitlements such as Food Stamps, Supplemental Security Income, Child Nutrition, veterans' pensions; and the remaining mandatory spending mainly consists of Federal retirement and insurance programs, unemployment insurance, and payments to farmers. All those Federal entitlement programs, programs ostensibly for the social good, add up to more than half of all federal government spending in the early twenty-first century. The discretionary spending breaks down into defense spending for the military and non-defense discretionary spending, which covers the Legislative Branch, the Judicial Branch, the Executive Branch, including its fifteen executive departments, the EPA, NASA, foreign aid, science…basically whatever it costs to run the Federal government. Then, of course, there is interest on the national debt. Discretionary spending, which is what it costs to run the military and the government, plus the interest on the national debt, add up to less than half of all federal spending in the early twenty-first century.

Finally, federal spending usually creates either a surplus or a deficit, meaning it collects more than it spends in the case of a surplus, or it spends more than it collects, in the case of a deficit. Growing deficits mean growing debt, which means growing interest payments.

Now, let us look at my Eleventh Vision that showed me how to approach the budget to cause our buying power to soar a hundred times or more, without us lifting a finger!

My Eleventh Vision showed me the most sensational creation of wealth the world has ever known. I saw a Twelve Visions President slash government spending by nearly removing the entitlement spending programs and the majority of non-defense discretionary spending. He was very careful that, first, those who had earned entitlements such as social security and veterans' pensions were fully compensated through a spectacular sale of all government assets that had nothing to do with protection. With the trillions of dollars accumulated from the largest sale in mankind's history, social security that was owed was paid off completely, up front and in full, plus interest. Then, the Social Security program ended all together, for the government had no business telling people how to spend or save their money. Veterans' pensions were continued, but managed through a private, third-party service.

The budget to run the government was eventually reduced by over 50% to essential laws, courts, prisons, Federal police, intelligence, defense…everything needed to protect the citizens' peace and safety. The military (including veterans' pensions), courts, prisons, and legitimate lawmaking protected the people from initiatory force. Protecting the people from initiatory force and coercion is, in the long run, the only valid purpose of a federal government. Eventually, all functions of government beyond protection evolved into a businesslike setup, as described in Neothink® trilogy *Superpuzzle* (a Mark Hamilton Publication, 1200-pages). People willingly subscribed to those services.

During this Twelve Visions President's term, there was no

chaos. (The President had a two-year battle with Congress over the budget, but the mid-term elections washed out many of those resisting the President's budget as the people noticed their buying power rising.) Instead, he simplified the Federal Government. The country fell into beautiful order as he led the privatization of many government services. Moreover, great prosperity — the millionaire phenomenon — swept across the country as businesses and entrepreneurs were free to invest in research and development without the burden and risk of an offensive, regulatory government. Big business and garage entrepreneurs both developed new technologies so swiftly, with such rapidly dropping costs, that our buying power began climbing...climbing so rapidly, in fact, poor people previously dependent on government entitlements instead soon lived with the standards of living of millionaires by the end of the Twelve Visions President's term. Soon, *no one* missed big government, not even the most liberal communities. Everyone was too busy enjoying his or her new standard of living...a standard of living only the millionaires enjoyed just one presidential term earlier. A new era had arrived, the Twelve Visions Era.

In the Eleventh Vision, looking back at today's budgets, we knew what defense spending and interest on the national debt were for. But, we had a hard time understanding the spending programs for the "social good" or for much of non-defense government. For one thing, tomorrow we knew the best way to help the people was to set free the geniuses in order to make the people rich: *to make their buying power go so high they lived like millionaires.*

Tomorrow our make-the-people-millionaires program freed technologies and freed super entrepreneurs to drive the new technologies into computerlike revolutions everywhere for everyone. A Twelve Visions President whose career was *not* politics turned inward and slashed his own base of political power — regulatory power — to free the technologies and the super entrepreneurs.

To be the President of the United States before the Twelve Visions World was to be a career politician; the career politician by nature *built* his base of political power, and the President's base of political power was regulatory power — the regulatory

446

bureaucracies, commissions, and agencies beneath him. That was why no president *seriously* wanted to eliminate *most* regulations. Social and regulatory programs supposedly "for the public good" supported the President's and Congress' base of power. Those spending programs, even those entitlement programs such as social welfare, came hand in hand with massive regulations telling us how to spend our money and run our businesses. Unbeknownst to you, but so obvious to me during my Eleventh Vision, those regulations actually blocked the Twelve Visions World in which you would live as a millionaire.

Those so-called "help the people" social and regulatory programs were illusions that actually *hurt the people* while building the Presidents' popularity, ego, and power. In my Eleventh Vision, I was amazed that the "great" presidents of the twentieth century who started "noble" social programs for the "social good" were looked back upon as the worst malefactors of society.

The Biggest Illusion

Today, the massive Federal spending programs on entitlements so-called "for the social good" in turn give the Federal Government absolute power to *regulate* the economy and *rule over* our money. The Federal Government has its regulatory web all throughout our economy — in every business, every consumer product, every job, every profession, including every hospital, every doctor's office, every research and development program, every discovery, every invention, every paycheck, every person's wallet.

In my Eleventh Vision, the people in tomorrow's Twelve Visions World were amazed that politicians and bureaucrats once ruled over our money and our lives. The archaic regulatory web throughout the economy *trapped and paralyzed* new technologies. Without super rapidly advancing technologies, costs did not drop to fractions. Instead, costs went up and up and up for the entire twentieth century. We just could not believe it, looking back: *prices went up for 100 years!* The elderly who lived on set pensions and measly entitlements got trapped in the dungeons of society as long-term inflation ate up everything they had.

Secret Teachings to My Exclusive Inner Circle

Sometime in the twenty-first century, we discovered that the *only* way to truly help the needy and everyone else was to send the economy through a buying-power metamorphosis such as the computer industry's buying-power metamorphosis. The Eleventh Vision showed me the needy and everyone else's limited buying power leapt *a hundred times* when the Twelve Visions President's **Protection-Only Budget** swished away the regulatory web throughout the economy. His budget swished away those so-called "good intentions", such as social welfare and the regulatory bureaucracies that wove regulatory control throughout every nook and cranny of the business world. When that regulatory web was gone, technology was free, and it took off just as the unregulated computer technology had, but in every industry. *Everyone's* buying power quickly rose. (This ended Social Security payments. Moreover, this unique approach miraculously repaid *every penny* of social security to Americans with *full fair-market interest!* That financial miracle meant elderly Americans received a small fortune from the government, all up front, by selling off all government assets that had nothing to do with protection.)

The World's Greatest Irony

The world's greatest irony was: the way to best help the people was to cross out the government's programs to "help the people" and the *massive regulations* that came with those "well intentioned" massive spending programs. Indeed, ending the noble-sounding "higher" causes, those programs for the "social good", ultimately ended the destructive elite class ruling over us, suppressing us. Our Twelve Visions Government shrank to its original and proper purpose of individual protection — *protecting the peace*.

And when that happened, look what happened next: My Eleventh Vision showed me an amazing world without those regulatory webs of "good intentions" so-called "for the social good". The needy and everyone else lived like "kings" as unburdened technology soared, costs plunged, and everyone's buying power multiplied on average a hundred times. *Everyone* became rich...yes, including the poor. It was the *only* program that could ever make *the poor* live like millionaires.

Forbidden Revelation

The "social good" was just a clever way of saying "politicize society, rule over the people, and play God with their money, morals, and lives." The "social good" was the career politicians' and regulatory bureaucrats' prime illusion that manipulated our century-old mental programming for "higher" causes (Vision Prologue).

Sometime in the twenty-first century, we deprogrammed our minds with Neothink® and, like coming out of a spell, we shook our heads and said "enough" to spending more than half of the Federal Budget on the "social good".

Ending The Spell

The first Twelve Visions President ended politicization of our lives and ended government on the offense — ended entitlement and regulatory programs. The Twelve Visions President reduced government to self-defense protection only, a government of defense without an active ruling class telling us how to live. That paradigm shift freed the geniuses of society.

They, in turn, whirled into an aggressive storm of Neothink® competition to serve up our every need. In doing so, they lifted technology into new dimensions, which drove down living and health costs to fractions and brought us spectacular new values and entertainment. The computer revolution of the twentieth century seemed like a little white cloud compared to the storm of new technologies raining on us in the twenty-first century.

As you know, after World War II, we looked back in disbelief at the holocaust. In tomorrow's Twelve Visions World, our children and grandchildren looked back in disbelief at today's politicians and bureaucrats ruling over us. In both cases, millions of innocent people died at the hands of politicians and bureaucrats ruling over us. Everyone, everywhere, in my Eleventh Vision knew the *only* reason the disease-free, wealthy Twelve Visions World never happened in the twentieth century was because, simply put, no politicians wanted to slash their base of political power. They cared only about building their base of power — regulatory, legislative, and spending power. (Indeed, spending money they did not earn

449

brought them enormous, easy power and prestige.) Therefore, we did not have the slightest clue of the phenomenal wealth and health available to us by reducing government to a protection-only government of defense...not until the "Solar Eclipse":

The "Solar Eclipse"

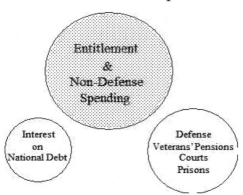

Consider that Einstein's Theory of Relativity (E=mc²) went years unrecognized. Then, a natural phenomenon occurred — a solar eclipse — that demonstrated his theory. Instantly, Einstein and his Theory of General Relativity were a world sensation accepted by nearly everyone. With that solar-eclipse demonstration, the world quickly moved beyond Newtonian physics to Einsteinian physics.

During my Eleventh Vision, I saw a similar phenomenon in politics: The Twelve Visions President's first budget was that "solar eclipse" as he eclipsed many of the solar-high spending programs for the "social good" and most of the non-defense spending. Although Congress did everything possible to undo his budget for their own survival, the unmistakable demonstration of falling taxes and rising buying power still occurred, no matter how diluted. Similar to Einstein's Relativity, instantly the make-the-people-millionaires program of slashing regulations and offensive government was a world sensation.

With that "solar-eclipse" demonstration, world politics quickly moved beyond career politicians and regulatory bureaucrats...into the new political paradigm, the unprecedented get-the-people-rich government.

Needless to say, the Twelve Visions President's Protection-Only Budget was a shock to Congress as he tried to cut the budget *in half* his first year. He wanted no more deceptions — no more politicians and bureaucrats politicizing our lives and ruling over us in the name of "higher" causes. He knew that only the James J. Hills (next chapter) — the geniuses of society — could boost the people's standards of living. Congress did not accept his budget at all. They did not want to give up their ruling class with all its spending and glory.

Yet, Congress had no choice but to give in to some degree because once the people elected a Twelve Visions President, they sensed good things about his route to the millionaire-phenomenon and stood behind him. So the legislative ruling-class, 435 Congressmen and 100 Senators, had to abandon their first thoughts of impeachment. With their very own constituents cheering for the make-the-people-millionaires program, Congress was not able to completely undo his budget. Of course, Congress radically changed the budget, but the President vigorously pointed his finger at the culprits for the whole country to see. Thus, Congress backed off and some of what he submitted took hold.

Bingo. People's taxes dropped immediately. But more importantly, their buying power started going up almost immediately. For the first time, exciting practical results outperformed political rhetoric. After that "solar-eclipse" demonstration, the Twelve Visions President then told America, loud and clear: "Imagine what could happen to your buying power if my Protection-Only Budget passed in its entirety. You could all be rich before my term is over!"

With that realization, the people almost unanimously implemented a nationwide change called **The Great Replacement Program**: Like a big wave at high tide due to the "solar-eclipse" demonstration, the Great Replacement Program washed over the country; it washed away the career politicians and their ruling class. Voters nominated and voted into Congress business owners and genuine, market-driven businessmen and women, knowing they would pass the Twelve Visions President's Protection-Only Budget in its entirety.

Those market-driven businesspeople — the James J. Hills (next chapter) — never cared about building political power. Such as the Twelve Visions President, they were not politicians. Instead, they wanted a free and booming economy. So, to that end, they were more than happy to eclipse their own structures of political power. They were more than happy to eclipse all government "good intentions" — that is, all those social and regulatory programs "for the social good" that were really Trojan Horses carrying massive, suppressive regulations. Those market businesspeople passed the Twelve Visions President's budget in its entirety. The ruling class soon vanished.[1]

Taxes immediately fell by more than half. But far more important, the regulatory/legislative web throughout the economy simply got swished away, which immediately set free the aggressive entrepreneurs who leapt into Neothink® (society's geniuses) and immediately set free the advancing new technologies. The Neothink® geniuses — the miracle makers — drove forth the new technologies. Industry after industry went through unprecedented buying-power miracles. Computer-like revolutions were happening everywhere, in every industry, even in the housing industry, bringing us inexpensive beautiful new homes and ending the real-estate crisis with a building boom.

Indeed, removing the many regulations on the construction industry and its many suppliers and support industries, not to mention removing the bulk of taxes, immediately allowed general contractors to build bigger, better, and more beautiful homes for a lot less money. And that improvement was immediate, before the technological breakthroughs kicked in!

Under the government of offense, your buying power decreased for a hundred years. After the Great Replacement Program led by a Twelve Visions President and his Protection-Only Budget, your buying power increased a hundred times or more *during a decade*.

---

[1] Although only one-third of the Senate could have been replaced during the mid-term election, the public pressure to vote for the Protection-Only Budget overwhelmed the majority of senators.

Indeed, the Protection-Only Budget *quickly* freed the geniuses and launched the wealthy Twelve Visions World. The Prime Law ultimately became an amendment to the Constitution of the United States and *permanently* freed the geniuses and *forever* guaranteed your wealthy Twelve Visions World.

Everyone Will Be Taken Care Of

Tomorrow's get-the-people-rich (by getting out of the way) government physically *protected us* only. The Federal Government was reduced to protection against physical aggression (or an imminent threat). A budget less than half previous budgets was needed to protect our country. The other half to three-quarters of previous budgets was no longer needed. We realized up to three-quarters of the Federal Budget had been wrongly used to *rule over* society through politicizing our lives and our businesses.

The people saw the double negative of money taxed and spent for the "social good". In fact, the whole idea of a government on the offensive for the "social good" became a bizarre thought. The government had one purpose — a government of defense to protect its citizens from physical attack, coercion, or fraud. All the other money taxed straight out of our lives — up to three dollars for every four that we earned, taken from us in taxes for spending other than physical protection and interest on the debt — simply sucked that enormous portion of money out of the economy, particularly out of those hard-working geniuses who liked to reinvest their money into growth to generate more wealth and jobs. The government then redistributed over half of that money to a government-created class of people who "inherited" a living and generated nothing for society.

But even worse than the huge mandatory spending programs was the discretionary spending to regulatory bureaucracies. They ruled over us with regulations that suppressed geniuses and new technologies. So, the negative effect of a government on the offense was painfully double: big government drained our money out of our lives *and then used it to specifically block us from rising into a wealthy paradise on Earth!*

The happy, wealthy people in tomorrow's Twelve Visions

World looked through history books while scratching their heads, wondering why we did not see this obvious double negative a lot, lot sooner. We disastrously accepted the deceptions called "the social good". The destructive ruling class of career politicians and regulatory bureaucrats was well camouflaged as existing for the "social good".

The Elderly Benefitted the Most

What about the elderly and the genuinely needy? Before tomorrow's Twelve Visions World, the elderly were stuck in the poverty-trap caused by the social-welfare illusion. In my Eleventh Vision, the elderly and needy gained the most in the Twelve Visions World, for they *more than anyone* needed a monetary metamorphosis in which their savings and pensions suddenly could buy a hundred times more. And that is exactly what they got. Unburdened, free-to-soar technology began driving down costs to fractions immediately after the Solar-Eclipse Budget passed.

Looking back from tomorrow's Twelve Visions World, when government had regulatory dominance over the economy, prices did not go down. They went up. Inflation was a slow torture for the elderly and the needy on set incomes. Inflation, even slow inflation, eventually trapped many of the elderly and the needy in the dungeons of society as poverty-ridden, dependent "slaves" — "slaves" to big government, forever dependent on their measly entitlement money. That slave class meant guaranteed votes for an ever-increasing regulatory government.

But in the Twelve Visions World, all that changed. Ironically, that change most benefited the huge American slave class — the elderly and the needy. The make-the-people-millionaires program lifted everyone into financial independence and then financial prosperity.

What about health, education, and everyone's welfare? What about all those spending programs that got blacked out? The resulting millionaire phenomenon made *everyone* rich; those previously dependent on entitlements benefited the most. Those previously trapped "slaves", dependent on suppressive big

454

government in order to survive in poverty, for the first time lived like *healthy and wealthy kings* as buying power and jobs began multiplying.

Healthy Kings

Now, I said *healthy* kings because unhampered, soaring technologies not only drove health-care costs to fractions, but eradicated serious diseases. Consider that the FDA, looking out for the "public good", killed many promising low-cost cures with cost-prohibitive regulations. In my Eleventh Vision, I witnessed that unburdened geniuses of society got the public good done and done quickly. Through the help of unburdened super technologies, the Neothink® geniuses quickly, among other things, eradicated diseases (Vision Twelve, later).

Unprecedented Prosperity

I saw the end result of **The Great Displacement Program**: Government assets and programs not part of protecting its citizens from physical force were sold to the private sector. Geniuses of society, not career politicians, took over programs for the social good to finally achieve social good.

The Great Replacement/Great Displacement Program led by a Twelve Visions President and his Protection-Only Budget ushered in the new Twelve Visions Era with no ruling class and no government programs for the "social good". Super technologies and super entrepreneurs, finally free of political pollution, free of even the smallest regulatory impurities, gave the world an unprecedented "power-reactor" explosion of prosperity beyond comprehension in today's terms.

The New Prosperity

The new prosperity made it difficult to look back at the former government programs "for the social good":

- Education: Among lowest standard of industrialized nations.
- Social Security: A greater and greater strain on the economy.
- Welfare: Left the poor in deeper and deeper poverty-traps. Stressing the economy.
- Health Care: Less and less effective.
- Social Programs: Deteriorating results.
- Regulatory Programs: Handicapped America in global competition while driving up costs, suppressing progress, and shrinking our job base...all while arming more and more teams of bureaucrats with guns and legislative-like power.

In the Twelve Visions World, the above programs "for the social good" fell out of the hands of a few hundred politically driven politicians and bureaucrats...into the hands of millions of sharp geniuses who finally did those programs right.

The Eleventh Vision answered my own two questions:

1) How will people take care of their parents with no more government aid and Medicare?

2) How will people educate their children with no more public schools?

First of all, the Great Displacement Program and the sale of trillions of dollars of government assets to private businesses easily repaid Social Security *with full, fair-market interest*. A lot of people suddenly got back small fortunes, especially the elderly who spent their lives paying the taxes that paid for those government assets sold. That sale of government assets ended the flawed Social Security era with everyone being repaid his or her money with interest. Working people no longer poured their money down the Social Security drain; most adults received a big check from the Federal Government, and retirees suddenly got back a small fortune.

We discovered — even those on entitlements discovered — that social-welfare programs of all kinds, including the Medicare and Medicaid programs, were clever illusions that hurt, not helped, the elderly and needy. Those social-welfare programs let the government regulate our economy and politicize our health, blocking computer-like revolutions and free-falling prices for breakthrough cures. Tomorrow, we rescued our parents by freeing

456

the economy and medical industry from those regulatory webs. Soon, health and living costs fell to fractions. Quality of life soared. The Twelve Visions President's "solar-eclipse" demonstration during his first year in office led to the inevitable millionaire phenomenon that made *everyone* wealthy and healthy, including the poor and the elderly.

Now, for our children: In the Eleventh Vision, I witnessed superior private education become the affordable norm and not the unaffordable exception. Today, only the privileged can, in a sense, pay twice for their children's education — once to the government (via taxes) and once to a private school. But tomorrow, everyone paid only once, but for superior private education.

Private schools became very inexpensive as open competition delivered the highest value for the lowest cost once the government's monopoly on education ended. Our children grew increasingly knowledgeable, creative, and motivated. They grew up to become successful, happy, and rich value creators. An upcoming chapter goes into details. (My Neothink® trilogy *Superpuzzle* provides a complete picture of tomorrow's Twelve Visions World, including the political and educational structures and results.)

Money Talks, Abuse Walks

During this Eleventh Vision into the Twelve Visions World, I noticed that the Protection-Only Budget, ending the nearly three out of four dollars spent on entitlement programs and regulatory bureaucracies, collecting only the money needed to protect us…this radically different budget did something else besides set free super entrepreneurs and super technologies that made ordinary people rich. The Protection-Only Budget also eliminated powerful forces of big government that were steadily taking away our freedom and individual rights.

Once the Protection-Only Budget passed in its entirety in the Twelve Visions President's third year in office after the mid-term Great Replacement Program, no more money was available to go to regulatory bureaucracies, all of which had quietly armed their agents over the decades — a dangerous step in America toward secret police and fascism. Those armed armies of bureaucrats ultimately answered to our President as part of his growing structure of power and ego.

The people in the Twelve Visions World simply asked: why should any regulatory bureaucrat be armed? If he confronts a potentially hostile situation, then he should call the local police as any other citizen.

For the previous century, however, the government had been quietly building armies of armed bureaucrats. The IRS, FTC, FDA, EPA, SEC, DEA, FBI, INS, ATF, CIA — every regulatory bureaucracy and beyond had armed agents... *even the postal service came complete with armed bureaucrats!* As the people in my Eleventh Vision looked back, they were amazed at how obvious this abuse of power was, which before went right over their heads.

Those armies of armed bureaucrats, all under the command of the President, grew increasingly aggressive while steadily subtracting our freedom and individual rights. Caught up in the illusions of "social good", we let them rule over us.

The Protection-Only Budget, once in full force with the success of the Great Replacement Program, simply cut off the funds to those growing armies of fascism. The Protection-Only Budget, simply put, *just said no!*

So, while making everyone rich, the Protection-Only Budget saved us from deteriorating freedom and growing government abuse.

Jobs, Wealth, Security

Once in office, the Twelve Visions President's fiscal policy was simple: eliminate from the annual budget up to three of four dollars previously spent.

Looking back over the twentieth century, America got in trouble regarding the currency. In 1933, Franklin D. Roosevelt took us off the gold standard. With no more accountability or disciplines, the government pumped more and more money into our economy. That caused inflation to eat up our parents' retirement savings and pensions, leaving them poor and financially dependent on us and the government.

Pumping un-backed currency into the economy had a short-term stimulating effect on the economy, but a long-term deadly effect. Of course, politicians sold out our futures for short-term re-election gimmicks. The people in tomorrow's Twelve Visions World were amazed, looking back, that fiscal policy had become an exclusive power-and-ego manipulating game for the powers that be. The ordinary working man was the victim. ...After decades of un-backed currency pumped into the economy — forever followed by inflation and increasing poverty for each new generation of elderly and needy Americans — what did we do? In my Eleventh Vision, here was the Twelve Visions President's immediate course of action — a quick one, two punch:

One: He eliminated spending programs for the "social good" and steadily paid off the debt. That cut our taxes in half or more and cut out any need to print more money.

Two: The Twelve Visions President eliminated corporate income taxes altogether (which accounted for less than one-tenth of the Federal Government's revenues). That caused an explosion of business, employment, opportunities, and rising incomes for the people as companies reinvested large sums of money back into their businesses, including cash incentives for employee performance. The money that normally went toward taxes and the "social good" instead went toward expansion, job creation, and employee incentive. The economy boomed. ...This concept was first demonstrated in the early '60s during John F. Kennedy's presidency and reinforced in the '80s during Ronald W. Reagan's presidency.

In the Twelve Visions World, students shook their heads in disbelief at the illusions used by big government that tricked their parents and grandparents into sending a major portion of our wealth down the drain disguised as the "social good".

In the Twelve Visions World, with no more government programs for the "social good", our taxes a fraction of what they once were, and with no more corporate income taxes, the money once flushed away to the "social good" was now reinvested into economic growth. That same money went instead toward starting and expanding businesses, creating jobs, motivating us as in-house

459

entrepreneurs (Fifth and Sixth Visions), and causing dynamic technological growth...which, like the computers, drove up our buying power a hundred times, a thousand times.

The Twelve Visions World —
Technology, Wealth, and Health

Let me sum up my Eleventh Vision: The freed geniuses of society whom I saw in my Tenth Vision (next) mixed with the freed twenty-first-century super technologies that I saw in my Eleventh Vision. First the impurities of society were removed — i.e., the career politicians and regulatory bureaucrats ruling over our money, morals, and businesses in the name of the "social good" (instead of simply and properly protecting us). Second, with the impurities absent, the super entrepreneurs and super technologies went through a catalytic, "power-reactor" explosion that lifted society into a beautiful new world, the Twelve Visions World. In that new world, the people including the poor lived like millionaires.

Here were our steps into that new world: America's growing damnation of politicians ushered in a nonpolitician Twelve Visions President sometime in the first quarter of the twenty-first century. His "solar-eclipse" demonstration quickly brought about the Great Replacement Program. Then his Protection-Only Budget passed in its entirety and ended government on the offense doing the "social good". Everyone's taxes fell in half...and then *in half again* as market businessmen drove down the remaining government expenses for protection by digging into the details and making them efficient.

As that occurred, geniuses of society rose by the millions and steadily raised our buying power as their breakthrough technologies drove costs toward zero. We became essentially a hundred times wealthier and more. Furthermore, every day and night felt as safe as living in Disneyland, for people became wealthy without lifting a finger. Committing crime was too much work. Moreover, the government's sole focus was your protection: national defense on the federal level and police protection on the local level. For the first time, civilization existed in pure freedom.

The Twelve Visions World is the paradise on Earth in which we were meant to live — a world in which we will be very wealthy with exciting opportunities, even for those who now have little opportunity. In my Eleventh Vision, that Twelve Visions World provided ever-better technology for ever-cheaper prices, no longer the sole possession of the computer industry. Major health breakthroughs and cures occurred at increasing frequency and became affordable to everyone, even to the elderly.

Unsurpassed, quality education became available and affordable to all families. Fears of unemployment were forgotten in the perpetually soaring economy with endless selections of exciting, "living" jobs (Fifth Vision). And finally, the millionaire's life of exotic vacations and first-class luxuries removed every last drop of boredom from our lives. Life was fun and exciting.

Looking back left a heavy sadness in our hearts for the millions who died unnecessarily to disease. We realized how career politicians and regulatory bureaucrats cost many of our loved ones' precious lives.

Big government was on the *offense* politicizing our lives and ruling over us. By contrast, the Twelve Visions World's get-the-people-disease-free-and-rich government was only on the *defense* protecting our lives from any physical threat or attack. After depoliticizing society, thus setting free the geniuses of society, then super rapidly evolving new technologies eradicated infectious disease after disease.

As you might suspect, political leaders resisted the idea of depoliticizing America. But, as Victor Hugo once wrote, "An invasion of armies can be resisted, but not an idea whose time has come."

The Twelve Visions World is the world everyone wants to live in, but has no clue of. Once enough people got exposure to the prosperity and love available in that previously unknown world — once fifty-million people saw the Twelve Visions — the following four steps swiftly occurred:

    1) A politically free Twelve Visions President was elected, vowing to enable the people, including the poor, to live like

healthy millionaires by depoliticizing America.

2) The Protection-Only Budget was submitted to eliminate government on the offense. Congress rejected most of the budget, but business owners and potential entrepreneurs could now sense the coming new code of freedom. Suddenly private funds for researching new technologies multiplied in all industries. The Technological Revolution shifted into a higher gear; prices began to fall, demonstrating the potential Protection-Only Budget's mighty effects on the people's wealth and health.

3) The Great Replacement Program washed over the country in the subsequent midterm election like a big wave, washing away most career politicians. Original business owners and other market-driven businessmen and women replaced career politicians nearly unanimously. For, the voting public knew that market-driven businesspeople would pass the Protection-Only Budget without hesitation. Indeed, the Protection-Only Budget passed in its entirety.

4) The Great Displacement Program naturally followed as the government's spending monopolies vanished; private businesses and entrepreneurs moved in to legitimately serve the people. America quickly became a wonderful place to be! Buying power multiplied a hundred times. Ordinary people began living like millionaires. Medical technology jumped into the lead against every disease.

Those make-the-people-millionaires and make-the-people-disease-free phenomena quickly brought three outstanding benefits to us:

1) Near-perfect health to us and our loved ones as medical technology raced forward and eradicated disease after disease.

2) Millionaire wealth as technologies raced forward in every industry like today's non-politicized computer/information industry, driving prices toward zero and standards of living toward millionaire wealth.

3) Supermen and superwomen selves as businesses, in that

rapidly advancing Twelve Visions World, evolved beyond their routine-rut jobs and instead brought out every worker's potential (Fifth and Sixth Visions). Our stagnant routine ruts were left behind as we discovered our human potential and achieved dreams we could never even fathom before (Ninth Vision). Exhilaration and stimulation replaced boredom and stagnation. The job revolution (described in the Fifth and Sixth Visions) poured a hundred-million geniuses into society. Our jobs became our transmission belts to Neothink®. Such creative energy rushing into society lifted our nation's wealth beyond all economic theories or models prior to the success of the Twelve Visions Party. We lived in a wonderful new world never before known to man.

Secret Teachings to My Exclusive Inner Circle

Forbidden Chapter Seven
The Geniuses of Society Bring You Everything You Ever Wanted

"Another sign of a healthy, competitive industry is lower prices. The statistics show that the cost of computing has decreased ten million fold since 1971. That's the equivalent of getting a Boeing 747 for the price of a pizza."

— Bill Gates

Stepping through the doorway into the Twelve Visions Era in my mind's eye, our geniuses made us rich, made us healthy, made everything good for us. The geniuses of society, who first evolved into Neothink®, led the Technological Revolution that raised our standards of living towards that of millionaires. We loved our geniuses; they brought us the gifts of life.

At first, in the late twentieth century, the geniuses freely rose in the computer world and brought ordinary children inexpensive video games that, just a few years before, only the children of millionaires could enjoy. My Tenth Vision showed me that sometime in the first quarter of the twenty-first century, the geniuses freely rose throughout the rest of the business world and brought us inexpensive products that a few years before only the millionaires could enjoy. Indeed, this computer-like *millionaire phenomenon* came to more and more industries beyond the computer industry, making ordinary people such as you and me essentially millionaires without lifting a finger.

Looking back over the twentieth-century, the millionaire phenomenon had already happened in the computer industry because it was uniquely free of big-government regulations. The computer industry gave us a look ahead at what life would be like in tomorrow's Twelve Visions World.

My Tenth Vision showed me that, to the amazement of the people, the millionaire phenomenon came to more and more industries as we universally removed big-government regulations.

After our get-the-people-rich government removed most big-government regulations, technologies in all industries raced ahead like the computers. As in the computer industry, where buying power multiplied thousands or millions of times, our buying power in more and more industries multiplied hundreds, sometimes thousands of times or more. That was because the geniuses were now free to rise and evolve.

Freeing The Geniuses

Simply put, America's falling out with big government freed the potential geniuses of society to drive our costs toward zero and our buying power towards infinity. Fantastic products and services never before imagined quickly evolved and then became cheap and affordable. What happened in the computer/communication world was a harbinger of what happened in my Neothink® Vision of tomorrow's Twelve Visions World. When our government freed technology and the geniuses beyond the computers, we lived in increasing wealth and luxury. People became economically driven to end big government and to embrace get-the-people-rich government.

The Twelve Visions Party ushered in get-the-people-rich-*including-the-poor* government, a completely new political paradigm of entrepreneurs and market-driven business leaders in which your every need, no matter how extraordinary or how small, was taken care of. You and your problems were never alone; help was always on the way for every need.

To achieve that never-alone, always-taken-care-of state, the get-the-people-rich government shifted the responsibility of taking care of you — i.e., social well-being — from a few hundred phony career politicians interested in ruling over you...to a hundred million geniuses in entrepreneurial jobs (the Fifth Vision) with rapidly evolving creativity, very interested in taking care of all your needs and wishes.

Millions of unrestricted geniuses, aggressively seeking out our needs, very rapidly answered our every cry for help. That was the new code of living in tomorrow's Twelve Visions World. Even your slightest problem had you immediately surrounded by quality people, by geniuses of society, wanting to help you. Just one cry for help sent out from your home over the Internet, for instance, ever so quickly led to its cure.

The job of looking out for your well-being and the social good shifted from impotent government and its corrupt ruling class to the miraculous might of an unrestricted genius-driven society. The unleashed creativity and new technology made us wealthy, healthy, safe and solved our problems. Your problems were the geniuses' problems to solve. In short, geniuses were hard at work taking care of you and raising your standard of living.

Today, big-government career politicians do not care about your problems, no matter how real, unless your problems fall into their self-aggrandizing schemes to rule. That is the old code of living soon to be left behind. All good people now have to fight for their survival. If you contract a rare disease, you are doomed. In tomorrow's Twelve Visions World, however, unhampered geniuses using Neothink® developed a cure *before* the disease destroyed you. I saw it all in my Tenth Vision. Tomorrow, you were always safe. Looking back at today's world, if you are not happy with your job and pay or with the direction of your career and income, you are trapped. In tomorrow's Twelve Visions World, genius-driven businesses brought you exciting opportunities including the lucrative career of your dreams (Vision Five), your passion in life (Vision One). Today if you are poor or just not happy with your wealth, you are rather helpless. Tomorrow, the multiplying wealth of society rescued your plight. Today, if you are not happy with love, you grow more and more apathetic. Tomorrow, the happiness available from living the life you were meant to live (Vision Two) helped you activate a new, superlove (Vision Seven). If you felt lonely, the enhanced networking of society brought you quality friends, especially as your own value to the world soared (Vision Nine). If you were having hard times, the curing nature of society took care of you in every way.

Geniuses were there for you, in minutes. Money was no longer an issue. A hundred million geniuses in this country alone took care of your every need.

467

They Brought Us Fortunes

The Twelve Visions Party simply freed the geniuses of society, who became the first to evolve into Neothink®. We sat back and collected the rewards from society's most gifted people. It was a nice exchange: we gave them freedom, and they gave us fortunes. We certainly were at a unique place in history.

In the late twentieth century when conversations at cocktail parties developed about computers and the Internet and how we could access for free computing power that would have cost millions a few years before, usually some attractive yuppie said something like, "Can you believe that amazing technology!" Everyone then shared looks of astonishment. Little did we stop to realize that *the geniuses of society* brought us that soaring technology and buying power. And those geniuses would do so in every industry if free to do so…making ordinary people rich and healthy.

Sometime in the first quarter of the twenty-first century, after fifty million people were exposed to the Twelve Visions, ordinary people began to admire and love those geniuses who brought them new technologies at lower and lower prices. The love grew despite political rhetoric that traditionally caused Americans to envy and dislike the geniuses of society. As the geniuses improved everyone's life in so many ways, the ordinary person developed a warm fondness for the geniuses of society not unlike one would for a highly competent doctor who saved his child's life, for instance.

Indeed, imagine if your own child or grandchild were terminally ill and the heroic efforts of a highly competent doctor saved your child. You would forever feel a warm affection for that doctor who saved your child's life. Or imagine a wealthy person gave you and your family a cashier's check for a million dollars. You would forever feel a very warm closeness to that person who made your life so rich and wonderful.

Tomorrow, the people felt similar feelings towards the geniuses of society, for those geniuses eradicated diseases and lifted us into a wealthy and wonderful world. The hoodwinking by the media that made us envy and dislike the geniuses of society subsided. The Forces of Neothink® were now too great to be stopped. Sure the geniuses were rich, because they were geniuses! But they made *us* rich, too. Furthermore, they brought us the gifts of life: wealth, health, safety, even happiness and love. The entire population, sometime in the first quarter of the twenty-first century, felt a warm closeness to those geniuses who brought us and our families into an increasingly wealthy and wonderful life.

We also felt growing contempt toward those big-government career politicians who blocked the geniuses and their new technologies. Career politicians blocked the gifts and the wonderful lives we were meant to live. Once the people made the twelve-piece connections and felt love for the geniuses of society, then the Twelve Visions Era irreversibly took off.

We sat back and watched in awe as the geniuses of society took care of our needs, fixed our problems, made our dreams come true, and made us rich, *including the poor*.

Of course, career politicians would not let go of their ruling power as we entered the Twelve Visions Era. They hung on, but they were part of the old world on its way out (Vision Prologue). We, in turn, freed the geniuses of society whose life ambitions were to solve our problems and needs, large or small. With the success of the Twelve Visions Party came *The Great Replacement Program*.
Like an unstoppable wave, the voting public replaced career politicians with the market-driven businesspeople of the Twelve Visions Party. Across the country, then the world, the big wave washed away career politicians and replaced them with the entrepreneurs and market-driven businesspeople of the Twelve Visions Party.

Example of a Genius Evolving
Into Neothink®

Just how effective were those geniuses of society at taking care of our every need or problem? Instead of me impossibly trying to describe what I saw in my Tenth Vision, which overwhelmed me to the point of euphoric collapse, let me take you into the life and times of an obscure genius of society who already lived. That way, I can show you already *proven facts*. Now, since some people say the computer revolution was unique — an anomaly based on the invention of the silicon chip — let us go outside the computer industry. In fact, let us go back in time before high technology altogether to see the universal life-lifting power of the geniuses of society *on their own*, even before their catalytic reaction with modern technologies. So, let us now travel back a hundred years…to the down and dirty railroad industry:

This is a story about James J. Hill, a genius of society one hundred years ago. He was well on his way to multiplying standards of living of entire civilizations of ordinary people — including *the poor*. He was single-handedly taking care of their every need until he got held down by big-government regulations. His story represents all geniuses of society, even outside the computer and hi-tech industries.

He was a railroad pioneer back at the turn of the twentieth century, and his story is brought to light in a book called *Entrepreneurs Versus The State* by Burton Folsom.

Let's travel back in time to the 1860s. America was experiencing its first railroad boom. Railroads were being built all up and down the East Coast. Well, as Mr. Folsom identifies in his book, two classes of entrepreneurs exist: market entrepreneurs and political entrepreneurs. Political entrepreneurs make their money by seeking government subsidies, by getting special government rights of way, and by accessing political clout. They seek their success through political clout with government officials.

Market entrepreneurs make their money by providing more and more values and services to society at lower and lower prices. They also create more and more jobs for us.

During America's railroad building boom in the 1860s, an opportunity arose for big government. The political entrepreneurs seeking easy money got together with career politicians seeking popularity, and together they created a deception. The deception was that only the government could finance the building of America's first transcontinental railroad. That deception over 100 years ago is still promoted today; children read about it in their history text books in school.

But that was a deception created by political entrepreneurs so they could line their pockets with lavish government subsidies and by career politicians so they could boost their self-worth by spending money that they controlled but did not earn. They could parade around and say, "Look how important we are. Look how we benefit the American public. We, the big government, are building this transcontinental railroad and opening up the interior and west coast of America." ...A perfect setup for greedy political entrepreneurs joining hands with power-seeking politicians.

So a deception was created: only the federal government could finance the building of the transcontinental railroad. The public bought it, and with great fanfare, Congress went ahead with it.

There were two companies: Central Pacific started building eastward from the West Coast and the Union Pacific started westward from the East Coast. The government paid those companies by the total miles of track they built. So what did they do? Instead of being bound by the disciplines of a bottom line, they were getting lavish subsidies from the government for the total miles of track they built. So they rushed into the wilderness to collect government subsidies.

But because they were being paid by the mile, these companies purposely built the longest, most circuitous routes they could possibly justify so they could get more government money. And they rushed construction to collect their per-mile subsidies. They rushed into the wilderness with poor construction and poor planning.

Remember, the congressmen were spending money that they did not earn but controlled, and they wanted to reap the glory for spending that money. Those politicians, always trying to justify their jobs, always trying to show that they benefit the American public, got into the railroad business where they had no business being in the first place. Controlling tremendous amounts of money they did not earn, they reaped all this popularity that comes with spending the money. Now they could say, "Look how valuable we are; we're financing the building of a transcontinental railroad across America!"

But those career politicians were part of bogus big government. They gladly spent money with their flashy "good intentions", but they were not interested in exerting the nitty-gritty effort that honest business does when it spends money. They were glad to spend the money, large amounts of money. They were glad to reap the glory, large amounts of glory. But they were not about to get out there and exert the nitty-gritty effort to put controls on spending and to make sure that money was spent right. They were not about to get right down into the details themselves to make sure that they were buying the right quality goods at the right prices and that the railroad was being built over the right routes...not like a market businessman would who is spending that money *out of his own pocket*.

So the whole program was laced with fraud from the beginning. The line managers set up their own supplier companies selling their railroads substandard quality rails and ties at exorbitant prices. For, there was no control over the government money.

In addition, because they were getting paid by the amount of rail they built, each company was racing to build as much track as it could before the other one...to get the most money from the government. So instead of taking the proper time to carefully map out the best routes, especially vital for building over hills at the lowest uphill grade, they instead just raced forward and paid no attention to vital planning and surveying. No time to be wasted on planning and surveying, they built track over uphill grades that were far too steep. They did not take the necessary time to do anything right. When winter came, they just kept on building over the plains, right *over* the ice!

Because they wanted to build as much as possible, they did not wait for the ice to melt — they just kept on laying track. When summer came, they had to tear up thousands of miles of track and rebuild it, before they could open the line! And to get more money, the two railroad companies built the *longest* routes with *under-quality* material. ...You can just imagine what the future operating costs this transcontinental railroad would endure.

Indeed, when the Union Pacific was complete, from day one it could not make a profit because its operating expenses were too high. First of all, thousands of miles of shoddily built, under-quality track had to be constantly replaced. Second, because they took the extra-long route, and it wasn't built over the lowest-grade hills, they had to pay a lot more money in fuel costs, wage costs, and it took a lot more time to haul freight across the country. The operating expenses were so high, from day one the Union Pacific was never able to make a profit.

Therefore, the government had to continue to subsidize the transcontinental line once it was built. Union Pacific had to continue to receive more and more government money or it would have gone out of business and stopped running. Indeed, Congress had just spent a fortune financing the building of the transcontinental line. Now Congress could not let their prize transcontinental line declare bankruptcy and close down. So, the government continued financing it.

After the Union Pacific was built, other political entrepreneurs got together with glory-seeking politicians in their areas of the country and said, "The federal government financed the Union Pacific, therefore they have to finance a transcontinental railroad in our region."

So Congress went ahead and financed the building of a transcontinental up North called the Northern Pacific, and one down South called the Santa Fe. Of course, both of those had the same results. They built extra-long, circuitous routes; they turned into an orgy of fraud: substandard quality material used, inflated prices paid, no planning, no surveying, no time taken to select the lowest-grade hills. So right from day one, the other two trans-continentals lost money, and they had to receive government subsidies just to continue operating.

In the meantime, there was a young man way up North, James J. Hill, going about making a living. He was born in a log cabin in Ontario, Canada to a working-class family. His father died when he was a boy, so Hill got a job to support his mother. At seventeen, he moved to St. Paul and got a job for a shipping company. He started in an entry-level position, but he loved the transportation business. He really applied himself; he began making contacts, and he began moving up. Before long, he began making partnerships in local railroads that were being built in his area. With a sweeping vision, yet always focused on nitty-gritty details, Hill commanded success. Eventually, Hill decided that he was going to build the first privately financed transcontinental railroad way up along the U.S. and Canadian border, which at that time was all wilderness with no settlers!

Well, from the beginning the idea was labeled Hill's Folly, and you can see why. How could someone build a railroad that could possibly compete when he had to pay all the building costs himself, and there were three other transcontinental railroads farther South that had all their building costs paid by the government? Moreover, Hill's railroad was going to be way up North where no one lived. Those other three government-financed railroads were located in the main population areas of the United States. In addition, once Hill did complete his railroad, how could he compete with the other three railroads when they continued to receive government subsidies and Hill had to pay his expenses through his own bottom-line profits — and the three other lines proved that no profits existed!

Well, Hill went ahead with his plan anyway. He had to obey the disciplines of a bottom line. He could not go rushing into the wilderness to collect government subsidies. He had to build his line out West one extension at a time. He would build westward into the wilderness a few hundred miles at a time. Then he would send agents back East to advertise to farmers in the East. Hill offered to move people for free into this western wilderness so they could settle and start their farms. Then Hill would give them free rates to ship their crops back to the markets in the East for a couple of years until they got established. He gave a lot of ordinary low-income people exciting new leases on life and made their dreams come true.

This worked. For each extension West, he brought in enthusiastic hardworking farmers; they'd flourish; he'd build up business on his track, and after a while his extension West made money. From those profits, he'd finance another extension West...a few hundred miles at a time. He never stopped. By turning low-income settlers into land-owning entrepreneurs, among others, he settled the entire northern border of the United States with his railroad. And, lo and behold, in 1890 the first American transcontinental railroad was built without one penny of government money! He reached the Pacific Ocean, and he did it by offering people, some of whom had little chance at much in life, an opportunity of a lifetime to own land and become entrepreneurs.

What an accomplishment. But most amazingly, *one man* did it!

Not the entire might of the U.S. Government — one lone man! One genius of society was raising the prosperity of an entire nation! But, now that he accomplished this amazing feat, could he make it work? Here Hill was with his transcontinental, way up North when the population base was farther South; he was competing against three trans-continentals farther South that had their expenses paid for by the government. So, what would happen to Hill's transcontinental?

During the building of Hill's railroad, since it was his personal money that was being spent, he personally dug into the tough nitty-gritty details. With unyielding disciplines and efforts, he put controls on everything: He personally surveyed the routes; he made sure the shortest, most direct routes were built. When the track had to go over hills, he would spend time with the engineers and make sure they picked out the lowest-grade hills. He personally supervised the buying of materials to make sure they got the highest quality rails and ties for the lowest cost. ...So what happened to Hill's Folly? Well, from day one, when it was completed, he made a profit! He ran circles around the three government-financed lines because his operating expenses were so much lower. In addition, his freight took a lot less time to reach the West Coast. From day one, Hill made money. From day one, the government-subsidized transcontinental railroads never, ever turned a profit.

One man was running circles around the almighty U.S. Government! Of course, the incompetence and greed of career politicians could never bring values to the people. But one market entrepreneur could raise the standard of living of a nation.

This one market entrepreneur's advantages kept building momentum and, with a great irony, left Congress's follies in the dust. Hill built up the whole industry of the Northwest. He built feeder lines. For example, if copper were found a hundred miles north, he would build a feeder line, move in a copper company so they could start mining and shipping the copper over his line. If lumber were discovered up in the mountain, he would feeder line up there, move in a lumber company, and they would start shipping the lumber over his lines. If there was a good clearing for cattle ranching a few miles south, he would build a feeder line. ...Railroads discovered that feeder lines became a main source of profit.

But consider Congress's lines built for politicians' own glory and self-worth. Because those railroads were receiving their money from the government, they would have to get Congress's permission to build a feeder line. Well, of course, everyone knows what happens when the government has to make a decision. A simple black-and-white decision to build a profitable feeder line that should be made overnight would be tied up for months, even for years. All the incompetent congressmen would get up and debate over it to get in the spotlight and appear needed and important. …They cared only about themselves, not about what was best for America.

So Hill's railroad ran circles around the three government-financed railroads from day one. In addition, Hill brought civilization and industry to the Northwest: mining in Montana, lumber along the North, apple farmers in Washington, wheat farmers on the plains. He built up the whole region along his railroad line.

Once Hill completed his line to the West Coast, he did not stop there. He kept reaching out and pushing up standards of living. Integrating more and more widely, into Neothink® itself, Hill started reaching out toward the Orient. What about trade with the Orient? Hill did some calculations: if one major province in China substituted an ounce of rice a day with an ounce of American wheat, that would mean 50 million bushels of American wheat would travel over his railroad to China every year! Think what that would do for his farmers! Now, he would make them rich! American farmers exporting huge shipments of wheat to China — what a possibility! So Hill sent agents to Japan and China to begin promoting American trade, the same way he had done during the building up of his transcontinental railroad.

In the meantime, we had these political entrepreneurs in Washington, D.C. still running around wondering how to get more government subsidies to line their pockets. Yet one market entrepreneur was creating jobs and dreams by the thousands. Indeed, Hill sent his agents to Japan and China to start promoting American products, and he went out and bought his own steamship line. He raced his ships back and forth between Japan and China and America. Hill built up American trade with Asia the same way that he built up business along his line. He would send products for free to the Japanese and Chinese if they would just try them. If they liked them, they would come back for more, and Hill would build up the business.

Every day Hill filled his ships with American grain from the plains, with copper from Montana, lumber from Washington, cotton from the South, textiles from New England, rails from Pittsburgh, apples from Washington. He would send them all free to the Far East. The Asians would try these American goods, and if they liked them, then they would come back for more.

In fact, Hill went to Japan, met with Japanese businessmen, and proposed that he would buy southern cotton, pay for it himself, ship it to the Japanese for free, and *give* it to them free. Hill would buy the southern cotton out of his own money if the Japanese would just try this cotton in place of the cotton they normally got from India. Well, the Japanese took him up on his offer; they liked it, and soon Hill's box cars were full of cotton, travelling from the South to the North to the Pacific Coast and then on to a steamship to Japan.

Hill used this strategy to build up all kinds of business. In 1900, Japan started a railroad building boom. Hill recognized the potential of railroads throughout Asia. At that time, the world's suppliers of rail were England and Belgium. But there were a few American rail makers in Pittsburgh. So Hill went to Japan; he purposely underbid the English and the Belgians, paid the difference out of his own pocket just to get the Japanese to try rails made in Pittsburgh. His strategy worked: Japan started buying all their rail from Pittsburgh, which built up the fledgling rail industry in America.

What happened in the 1890s was nothing short of a miracle: When Hill started his push into Asia, trade with Japan was seven million dollars a year. Nine years later, with Hill in charge of this American mission into Asia, American trade with Japan *alone* was fifty-two million dollars! And he was now pushing into China as well! Hill was causing geometrical increases in American commerce. He was spearheading, a hundred years ago, an American dominance of trade in Asia. In the meantime the political entrepreneurs, Hill's so-called rivals, were still running around

Washington, D.C. trying to figure out how they could get more subsidies. And Hill just kept on reaching out, with Neothink®, taking care of people's needs, and pushing up standards of living while spearheading a geometrical increase of American commerce in Asia. That was one hundred years ago.

As time went by, the other three government-financed transcontinentals continued to lose money. The government kept pouring taxpayers' dollars into financing them. The public started getting fed up with this. In addition, as time went by, the frauds committed by the political entrepreneurs started to surface — things like setting up their own companies to sell substandard material at overcharged prices. The American public had to continue to pay subsidies into this hoax just to keep these other three government railroads running. The public finally had enough. So Congress, those eternal glory-seeking politicians, started self-righteously parading the corrupt political entrepreneurs in front of Congress and the nation, forming special-investigation committees.

Well, once again, Congress created a deception: They presented themselves as protectors of the American public. They would nobly project, "Look how great we are; look how needed and important we are; we're going to protect the American public from those greedy and corrupt railroad executives." Yet, the root cause of the problem was Congress itself. Congress was the culprit! Congress spent other people's money in a railroad business where they had no business being in the first place.

So instead of getting up and confessing, "Look, the problem was us. We now realize the problem was us getting into the railroad business in the first place. We had no business in there, so now we're going to get completely out." They could have been honest, but they were not. No, they did not want to say that because that would have exposed bogus big government. Instead, they saw a chance to enhance big government and to increase their own popularity and political power for re-election. They instead self-righteously projected, "Look how we earn our keep. We're protecting the American public." Congress self-righteously started parading those corrupt railroad executives in front of the nation. Congress made the railroad executives solely to blame for the

478

transcontinental fiascoes. And then, to "protect the public", they proposed to form tough regulatory authorities such as the ICC, the Interstate Commerce Commission, and to pass Sherman Antitrust legislation to further get in there and regulate the railroads.

Well, Hill knew what was going on; he knew what the story was here. So Hill moved to Washington, D.C. He set up residence in the country's Capitol. He personally talked to the congressmen. He testified before their special committees. He told them what was going on: the root cause of the problem was big government getting in there where it had no business being in the first place, financing those railroads, spending other people's money on rails. That caused the corruption. Hill gave the example of his railroad. He did not accept one penny of government money while his railroad built up all the industry in the Northwest. And now his line was promoting an explosion of American trade into Asia while the three government-sponsored lines were sinking in corruption.

Now, the congressmen were intelligent men. They were college educated. They knew what Hill was saying. They knew he made perfect sense. They knew his account was the truth, but they did not care because they wanted to justify their own jobs. So they ignored him. They ignored Hill, and they went on to pass the ICC and the Sherman Antitrust legislation, which enabled them to get in and heavily regulate and punish the railroads.

Hill even wrote a book on this whole ordeal and circulated his book to the congressmen, explaining the situation. He presented all the evidence that showed how Congress was doing the wrong thing. But the big-government ruling class ignored Hill because they wanted to advance their own power. The career politicians went ahead and passed the ICC, passed the Sherman Antitrust legislation. And what did that do? Those regulations "for the public good" made it illegal for railroads to make any special deals with customers. They had to charge the same standard rate to all customers. Therefore, the Neothink® dynamics Hill used to build up his railroad, to move in people for free, to make their dreams come true, to ship their freight for free or for a low cost until they got established...was now illegal! Those same dynamics that he was now using to spearhead an American dominance of trade in Asia were all now illegal! Hill was a genius of society who was pushing up ordinary, even poor Americans into prosperity — and WHAM! Big-government regulations smashed him down. Hill's drive into Asia was over.

The year after the ICC's legislation passed, America's trade with Japan alone dropped by 40%. Now remember, Hill was spearheading a *geometrical increase* in trade. Trade with Japan and China was increasing geometrically. Now Congress passed this legislation and, plop, everything dropped 40%.

Hill was forced to sell his steamship lines, he got out of trade completely with Asia, and he was so frustrated, he retired. Suddenly, the miracle was over. He could no longer make ordinary and poor people wealthy and happy.

Now, this was a hundred years ago. Let us stop and look at the implications of this. Let us stretch this out to see what Congress really cut off a hundred years ago. It was bad enough they cut off Hill's trade with Asia back then and destroyed the wealth, lives and dreams of many entrepreneurs dependent on Hill's dynamics, but let us project that into the future to see what they cut off today:

Throughout the past two decades, you have heard our President and top CEOs and top economists say that America's greatest danger economically is its trade imbalance with Asia and our lack of international competitiveness. But who in the world knows that a hundred years ago Hill was spearheading an American dominance of trade throughout all of Asia? That trade dominance was cut off by big-government regulations. Who even knows that? Nobody mentions that today, but everyone has warned about "the greatest economic danger facing America today". Americans have lost jobs by the thousands, have been outcompeted, factories have closed down. Yet who knows that one hundred years ago this one genius of society, *one man*, learned how to tend to people's needs, make people's dreams come true, and spearhead an American dominance of trade with Asia? Who knows that a hundred years ago a man named James J. Hill started something really magnificent that would have painted an entirely different picture of America's future than that of uncertainty today? Big government destroyed that prosperous future when they destroyed Hill a hundred years ago.

The politicians back then knew what they were doing. They were intelligent men. They were college educated. Hill went and explained the facts to them. Typical of big government, however, they only wanted to increase their political powers. The career politicians wanted to advance their images and egos. So they ignored Hill, and they cut off something magnificent a hundred years ago. No different than today, the ruling class back then stopped our great, great grandparents from rising into a paradise on Earth.

So there you have an example of what just one genius of society can do for everyone. And you can see that the geniuses of society will rise in any industry at any time, not just in the computer or hi-tech industries, if not held down by the big-government regulations. And you can see that, when the geniuses rise tomorrow in all industries, our problems, needs, and dreams will quickly be tended to. In short, the Twelve Visions Society tomorrow — a supersociety with millions of James J. Hills — will take care of us and make our dreams come true.

Now, imagine a hundred-million geniuses of society (Vision Five), a hundred-million James J. Hills all using Neothink®…their progress accelerated by modern technology. You cannot imagine, because the image goes beyond anything we can know today.

Held Down in the Darkness

My Tenth Vision showed me that in tomorrow's Twelve Visions World, looking back at today's world was very frustrating. We saw how career politicians and bureaucrats ruling over us and holding down society today caused the only injustice that no one could see, because no one today could see ahead into the Twelve Visions World tomorrow. One obvious example, America would have been the dominant trade of that huge upswinging in Asia, but we never had a clue. America's problems with the trade deficit and people losing their jobs to international competition would have all been reversed. But no one saw that. Instead, we were held down in the darkness. Looking back, no one except those who read *The Twelve Visions* could see the injustice of government ruling over us and holding us down.

James J. Hill started pushing ordinary and poor people up toward that paradise on Earth, but he was slammed back down by big government. Tomorrow, once we lived in the Twelve Visions World and could see the injustice of former big government, to look back became painfully hard to do. The people in the Twelve Visions World realized that every life lost on the battlefield, all famine and sufferings in America and around the world in the twentieth century and early twenty-first century, including deaths from diseases...all of that was encompassed in the Great Suppression — the ruling class holding down America from soaring into the Twelve Visions World.

The Geniuses Pulled Everyone Up With Them

In this Tenth Vision of tomorrow's Twelve Visions World, the geniuses of society were free to go up, and they pulled everyone up with them, including the poor, just as Hill was doing. All our needs were taken care of. We did not have just one James J. Hill, for we had thousands and then millions of James J. Hills making ordinary people's dreams come true.

Tender youth could rise and rise quickly. Tender youth today, by contrast, cannot rise because they cannot struggle through the big-government regulatory web and risk being eaten alive like Hill.

Unburdened technology in tomorrow's Twelve Visions World, regulated not by glory-seeking politicians and bureaucrats but by objective private services, advanced incredibly fast. Science, business, and medicine, no longer being pushed down by big government, advanced incredibly fast, similar to the nonpoliticized computer industry of the previous two decades.

Upon setting free all industries and launching the mighty Technological Revolution, genius-driven new technologies quickly took care of all our problems. Disease, unemployment, poverty, obesity, insecurity, stagnation, racism, crime, budget deficits, the national debt, government abuse, Social-Security deficiency, illiteracy vanished along with big government. So did our personal problems such as a lousy job, lousy love-life, an uncompetitive body, a stagnant mind, an embarrassing home, car, and overall financial self-worth.

Consider that in 1936, mankind reached a new high with the completion of Hoover Dam to harness the Colorado River. After thousands of years, man reached a level of technology that could control nature on a large scale. But man took only another 33 years to go to the moon. Civilization was *begging* to progress *geometrically,* which occurred in my Tenth Vision sometime in the first quarter of the twenty-first century when the big-government legislative/regulatory web was swished away and super technologies and unrestrained geniuses made us wealthy, healthy, and safe.

Too Painful To Look Back

Some readers of this very page lost their lives to disease or lost a precious loved one. Looking back at our loss was hard. My childhood friend John who, at 12 years old, ran and played with all the other children; but the next year, muscular dystrophy started taking over his tall and handsome body. John first needed crutches, then a wheelchair, then an electric wheelchair…his long, limp body strapped in with a seat belt. In those days, John and I would go around doing things that young men do. John was almost in my world, talking about sports and girls. Yet, John would never experience those things. I could sometimes see in John's eyes his longing to throw off his seat belt, jump out of his wheelchair, and scream, "Here I am world! Here I am!" One day John got a cold, and just a young man, he died. Yet, geniuses in tomorrow's unrestricted Twelve Visions Society would efficiently cure his disease.

Looking back, big government held down the lid on America including cures to diseases, but we could not see the harm caused by big government. Tomorrow, it became almost too painful to look back at what and *who* we lost.

Consider looking back at the following image: Imprisoned by hunger, little children in poverty-stricken third-world countries hoped for a little fish with their rice for dinner. If James J. Hill were not stopped 100 years ago, along with the other market businessmen since Hill, then those poor countries would have been industrialized and prosperous a long time ago.

Instead, those third-world children suffered and died to the bitter end of the twentieth century and into the twenty-first century as the "glorious" big-government "good intentions" flourished and lived. The Great Suppression went on and on.

American children have always felt excitement about their futures. Yet, tomorrow when we looked back we realized that America, the land of opportunity, was also the land of disillusionment and disappointment. The drop from childhood dreams to adulthood reality was a deep letdown. Indeed, American adults carried a subdued sadness every day...to the end. Before the Twelve Visions World, Americans died unfulfilled, without experiencing wealth, romantic love, the life they were meant to live.

In tomorrow's Twelve Visions World, looking back became almost unbearable, for we saw what was lost. We failed at our dreams in the twentieth century and early twenty-first century because we were in a society in which we could not win. My Tenth Vision showed me that the Twelve Visions Society, by contrast, would not let us fail. Instead, it made our dreams come true and made every ordinary person, including the poor, wealthy and healthy.

Looking back, people shook their heads in disbelief. The legal battles, regulations, and legislation made opportunities at success limited, costly, and risky. We glumly looked back at the stagnation that killed our dreams, weakened our marriages, and destroyed the thrill of love we felt only during the first few weeks or months of falling in love. And, most painfully, we saw how our children absorbed from us our hopeless resignation, just as we had from our parents.

The Disgraceful End

In the first quarter of the twenty-first century, with the dissemination of *The Twelve Visions*, the Great Suppression came to a disgraceful end. Neothink® was setting free stagnant minds everywhere. Big government could not continue to hold on and strangle progress and kill our dreams. The success of *The Twelve Visions* ushered in The Twelve Visions Party.

With the success of The Twelve Visions Party, society no longer got pushed down with us being squeezed into stagnation-traps where we had always lived. Career politicians lost. Their big-government regulations and harmful legislation — always in the name of the "social good" — lost. Their bogus purpose for government lost:

> **Promote social "prosperity" and provide social "well-being" through social and regulatory programs "for the social good"..."good intentions" to "serve the people" (a deception, enforcing what is deemed the "social good", "good intentions", or the "national will"...mere men and women playing God with our money, morals, businesses, and our lives).**

With the success of the Twelve Visions Party, the proper purpose for government won:

> **Physically protect the people from force (or threat of force) with protection-only legislation, police, courts, prisons, and national defense (plain reality, defending against and punishing initiatory force).**

Tomorrow we looked back and realized in disgust that, as with the transcontinental railroads, our career politicians spent our money to ostensibly enhance our "well-being" and promote social "prosperity", but they really wanted the glory and "importance" that went with spending *other people's* money and ruling over us. They did not want anything to do with the effort, though, that went into building values, which market businessmen and women put themselves through every day when spending their own money.

Career politicians and regulatory bureaucrats today suppress all industries (the computer industry being the most fortunate, least politicized industry). Career politicians today suppress our entire economy and standard of living as they did a hundred years ago with the railroads. Market businessmen, by contrast, are interested in creating and building values, not in ruling others. They create miracles for the human race, from Hill's transcontinental railroad to Jobs' computer software and beyond.

The Miracle Makers

Tomorrow, the miracle makers, the unburdened market businessmen and women, dramatically improved our well-being and prosperity. A Twelve Visions Society, flourishing with geniuses, handed us the gifts of life, especially wealth, health, and peace.

Prior to the Twelve Visions Society, the erroneous idea in the anticivilization that government could "promote social prosperity" sort of sneaked up over the previous century through career politicians finding ways to self-indulge at spending our money to become more and more likable for re-election. Indeed, spending *other people's* money was a fast way to build favorable illusions in the twentieth century and early twenty-first century. But when the people caught on sometime in the first quarter of the twenty-first century, the career politicians' careers ended with great shame.

In this Tenth Vision, market businessmen and women replaced career politicians. Geniuses of society rose and threw open the lid on society and lifted society toward its destiny of great, great prosperity. Each person was pulled up, our wheelchairs left behind. The whole world was then lifted as the communications revolution obsoleted distance and boundaries.

Paradise On Earth

The Tenth Vision showed me that in the Twelve Visions World, irrationality disappeared. Poverty and crime vanished. In the Twelve Visions World, the motivation for people to do dishonest things reversed. In time, in that world of disappearing irrationality, the idea of crime and eventually war became archaic. We achieved paradise on Earth.

Perhaps this all sounds like Utopia. But my Tenth Vision showed me tomorrow's Twelve Visions World truly reversed the motivation for people to do dishonest things, for most problems disappeared, and a millionaire standard of living was automatic — far easier and more lucrative than any possible crime. With the success of the Twelve Visions Party, the era of wealth and peace was here, finally and forever.

Forbidden Revelation

Before the Twelve Visions, the people never knew about this wonderful world. We only dreamed about it when we were children. We needed to "see" it through these Twelve Visions.

Today, we live in a lucky time. Huge financial rewards beckon us to the Twelve Visions Party. Our get-rich era is coming.

Secret Teachings to My Exclusive Inner Circle

Forbidden Chapter Eight
Real Universal Health

"It is not just new viruses that have doctors worried. Perhaps the most ominous prospect of all is a virulent strain of influenza. Every so often, a highly lethal strain emerges. Unlike HIV, flu moves through the air and is highly contagious. The last killer strain showed up in 1918 and claimed 20 million lives — more than all the combat deaths in World War I. And that was before global air travel; the next outbreak could be even more devastating."
—*Time Magazine*

By now during my Neothink® Visions, the images centered more and more around our health. More than anything else in the twenty-first century, the people cried out for the geniuses, with their groundbreaking technologies, to eradicate virulent diseases.

Devastating new diseases were on the rise and, perhaps even worse, drug-resistant strains of several old killer diseases were back. Those frightening new diseases and new strains tended to break down our acceptance of the FDA that suppressed the rise of Neothink® geniuses in the medical industry and held back the rapid advancement of the medical industry. Our physical survival more and more depended on rapid advancement.

My Twelfth Vision showed me that during the early twenty-first century, doctors were less and less able to handle certain infectious diseases that were gaining resistance to antibiotics. A powerful warning came when only a single remaining antibiotic could stop a popular strain of staph infection that commonly spread throughout hospitals. Once that lone remaining antibiotic ceased to work, hospitals would become risky places to visit. Then, the common strep infection gained resistance to antibiotics. My Twelfth Vision warned me of the increasing danger as we advanced into the new millennium. A killer disease, tuberculosis, returned, this time attacking our children, and this time even a combination of antibiotics could not stop it.

In short, infectious diseases caught up with and began to surpass modern medicine in the twenty-first century. The FDA worked against a major medical revolution that was just waiting to explode with greater force than the computer revolution. In fact, the inherent force of a medical/biotech explosion was so great that even with the FDA, genetic engineering such as the Human Genome Project and other biomedical projects were advancing at an all-time pace. But the mighty biomedical explosion could not ignite with the FDA smothering progress. As with computers, the technology needed quick access to the marketplace, which the FDA blocked. Indeed, the marketplace is the oxygen needed to ignite the biomedical explosion, which the FDA smothered.

Here is a brief review of a *Time Magazine* warning.

Killers All Around
New Viruses and Drug-Resistant Bacteria
Are Reversing
Human Victories Over Infectious Disease
(A Review of *Time Magazine* Cover Story)

The *Time Magazine* cover story begins by reminding us how, not long ago, humanity thought that infectious diseases were rapidly becoming a thing of the past. In the 1970s, the medical world started boasting its imminent victory. And why not? Previously deadly illnesses such as polio, small pox, malaria, diphtheria, pertussis, tetanus "seemed like quaint reminders of a bygone era, like Model T Fords or silent movies". And antibiotics transformed the most terrifying diseases known to mankind such as tuberculosis, syphilis, pneumonia, bacterial meningitis, and even bubonic plague into "mere inconveniences that if caught could be cured with pills or shots". Medical students were being told not to go into infectious disease, a "declining speciality". Instead, they were advised to concentrate on "real problems" such as cancer and heart disease.

But, unfortunately, today the era of great medical success and confidence has been giving way to a new era of unnerving medical defeats...and fear. The *Time* cover story states, "The question ceased to be, When will infectious disease be wiped out? and became, Where will the next deadly new plague break out?" The article goes on to tell us about new lethal agents emerging in Africa and South America. As population grows and man settles new parts of the world, such as a new part of the Brazilian rain forest, for example, new deadly diseases spread from other animals such as monkeys to humans. As those deadly agents adapt to humans, they gain the potential for large-scale deadly pandemics. In a world of extensive air travel, those deadly agents become just a plane ride from America.

And it could get worse, the *Time* article claims. Antibiotics are our main defense that stand between us and some of the most deadly bacterial diseases. But bacteria have been evolving and steadily adapting for survival, and now they are well adapting to antibiotics. In fact, the article warns us that every disease known to man is already resistant to antibiotics of one form or another. Several devastating diseases once thought to be nearly eradicated are back and on the rise: malaria, cholera, measles, tuberculosis, even bubonic plague. Perhaps even more threatening are the "seemingly prosaic but once deadly infections" staph and strep. They have become much harder to treat. Both spread through the cleanest of hospitals, routinely cured with antibiotics. But as those two infections develop universal resistance, the article questions, what will happen to our hospitals?

"One of medicine's worst nightmares is the development of a drug-resistant strain of severe invasive strep A," the article states. Severe, invasive strep A killed Muppeteer Jim Henson in 1990; this vicious killer is on the rise.

Bacteria adapt to antibiotics because, while rapidly multiplying, bacteria mutate and change slightly, just enough to outwit their combatant drugs.

Viruses, on the other hand, are usually tamed and sometimes even eradicated by the preventive vaccine. But the article points out that new viruses keep emerging. Viruses that have gone undetected, inhabiting animal populations, can and sometimes do make the jump to humans. The *Time* article tells us that was the case with some very lethal African viruses such as Ebola, which made the jump from monkeys to humans.

Still, the biggest fear of all, as explained in that *Time Magazine* article, would be another killer flu, which usually makes the jump from another animal to humans. Humans have little defense against such a flu, and if it took hold, then it would wreak deadly havoc. The 1997-1998 Hong Kong "chicken flu" introduced such a killer flu that, tragically, killed a few people in Hong Kong but, fortunately, did not take hold and go into a widespread outbreak. Now, each year that avian flu attempts to jump to and spread among humans. When a global outbreak does happen, the world will never be the same.

The *Time Magazine* article was a warning. Today's biomedical progress is impressive, but is it moving fast enough? The answer is: no, not until the technology has quick access to the marketplace, as do the computers. And that means no regulatory FDA.

The definitive antidote is "begging" to happen now, in the early twenty-first century, to rescue the human race from the threatening plagues. That antidote to the threatening human catastrophes is: **super rapidly evolving technologies**. Only rapidly evolving new

Killer Flu: Seattle police wore protective masks during the pandemic of 1918. That killer flu infected 1 billion people and killed more than 20 million in 10 months. The population in 1918 was less than half of today.

492

technologies can win the race against rapidly evolving infectious diseases. But those new technologies will not evolve quickly enough until they can swiftly reach the marketplace.

Starting in the late twentieth century, continuing into the twenty-first century, the national media such as *Time Magazine* repeatedly warned us we were suddenly losing the race against infectious diseases, with mutant strains of old diseases returning after decades of "absence" and new diseases invading us with devastating results. The media warned that a medical defeat to microbes could bring with it human catastrophes such as those experienced in the time of bubonic plague, polio, and killer flus. The Superflu of 1918 infected over one billion people, *half* the world's population in 1918, and killed over 20 million people in just 10 months. Never in the history of the world had there been so many deaths in such a short period of time. Man has not experienced anything close to that catastrophic pandemic since, but in the early twenty-first century, scientists fear a repeat is not far away.

The 1918 Spanish Flu, as it was often called, actually started right here in the United States and infected 25% of our population. Doctors have warned in the early twenty-first century that logistically "we are due" for another killer strain. In fact, in 1976, we survived a great scare — a false alarm, or perhaps more apropos, a fair warning: A soldier at Fort Dix, New Jersey got the flu and died. The medical world was stunned when the virus taken from the dead soldier was a descendent of the 1918 killer flu. The medical world braced itself for another catastrophe of unthinkable proportions. But the deadly virus that made the jump from birds to humans was an isolated case unable, this time, of passing among humans. This time, we were lucky. Next time…

Only super rapidly advancing new technology can prevent a "next time". The race is on. Every year a handful of people die from avian flu. It is only a matter of time before it will pass freely from human to human. The new technology of genetic engineering has the potential to permanently and universally stop deadly viruses and bacteria. The problem with this promising new technology in the early twenty-first century, however, is that it is not *super rapidly advancing*, not fast enough…not until the removal of the FDA.

Remember, *super rapidly advancing* new technology demands rapid access to the marketplace. Breakthrough technologies and drugs must freely reach the marketplace. Private regulatory services with risk-rating systems would be in place, but simply put, the way things are now with the FDA, we will lose the race. For a computerlike medical revolution to happen, the FDA will have to come to an end in order to spring loose the geniuses of society and their new technologies.

The following brief review from the same issue of *Time Magazine* reveals new technologies pursued by doctors, scientists, and businessmen (but again, missing the key ingredient of **market-accessible** *super rapidly advancing new technologies*):

Counterattack:
How Drugmakers Are Fighting Back
(A Review of *Time Magazine* Article)

"Doctors and the public were not alone in feeling cocky about infectious disease a decade ago. The drug companies did too," so began the article. "More than 100 antibiotics were on the market, and they had most bacterial diseases on the run, if not on the verge of eradication."

The pharmaceutical industry simply modified existing antibiotics to stay one step ahead of the bacteria. But that approach no longer works. So, researchers are turning to new technologies to get back in the lead against disease.

One dynamic approach is called "rational" drug design. Scientists study the molecular structure of a bacterium, particularly the active site of the enzyme used by the bacterium to fight off the antibiotic. Next, scientists attempt to design a molecule to "plug up" the active site of that enzyme. Without the effect of that enzyme, the bacterium would once again be killed by the original drug.

A similar concept is being pursued against viruses. You see, viruses cause their damage by invading our bodies' living cells. To invade a living cell involves receptor sites, like little hooks, where the virus joins the cell. Similarly, a molecule can be designed to block the receptor sites so the virus never attaches to our cells thus remains harmless to our bodies. ...So goes the search for such

494

defendant molecules through combinatorial chemistry.

Again, the problem with such new medical technologies is that they are not *super rapidly advancing* ...not as they should be, not like, say, computer technology. How, then, did our country finally get medical technology to *super rapidly advance* to prevent the coming human catastrophes? My Twelfth Vision showed me:

The Great Rescue

I witnessed during the Twelfth Vision that the looming medical catastrophes helped us see reality and depoliticize the medical industry. Two things happened at once by depoliticizing medicine: 1) record amounts of private research funds went toward medical research, and 2) a record number of entrepreneurial geniuses went into medical research. Those unhindered geniuses of society drove medical technology into unimaginable new dimensions that eradicated the most complex diseases. In short, the Neothink® geniuses drove forth those new technologies to save our lives.

Depoliticizing the medical industry, depoliticizing everything about it from regulations on health insurance to regulations on medical research, saved many tens of millions of lives.

Today, each added increment of politicizing the medical industry further bureaucratizes and slows advancing new medical technology, which in turn dramatically drives away private research funds. Medical projects become too inefficient and cost-prohibitive for businesses to invest. Moreover, the lone entrepreneurs, those aggressive geniuses of society, could never function in such a cost-prohibitive, risky environment. The force of their creativity and endless energy that so propelled the free computer/Internet industry is but a fraction of what it could be in the medical industry. They are needed to unlock the cures to the most complex diseases.

In the Twelfth Vision, those geniuses, once they were free to flourish and leap into Neothink®, rapidly unlocked otherwise impossible combinations.

Politicization ravages our health and costs us millions of precious lives. Each incremental step the other way — depoliticizing the medical industry — dramatically frees up thus speeds up advancing technology, which in turn dramatically attracts private research funds and opens up the medical industry to the entrepreneurs and their endless energy and creativity, their speed and ability to ferret out brilliant advances.

In the Twelfth Vision, I witnessed that we outgrew our desire to be ruled over. As people began dying in increasing numbers, at a faster rate than the bio-tech advancements started saving people, we chose to depoliticized the medical industry to make it as free as the computer industry. Survival pressures changed our toleration levels for debilitating big government. Without it, the geniuses did to medicine what they did to computers. Our country won this race against the microbes. In the Twelve Visions World, after depoliticizing the medical industry, more and more geniuses rose up and saved us from worldwide human catastrophes. That medical revolution became known as the Great Rescue. But the human losses were never forgotten.

Two Forces That Brought Us the Twelve Visions World

My Twelfth Vision showed me two forces at work: Rising within us, we felt disillusioned with politicians and regulatory bureaucracies. A steady rebellion against a ruling class started spontaneously rising throughout civilizations around the world, from China and the Orient, through Russia and Eastern Europe, Asia Minor and down through Africa, to the relatively free United States and throughout Central and South America. Those early signs of the new Neothink® mentality, spontaneously rising throughout different civilizations around the globe, affected us at home.

Tomorrow, we started resisting the ruling class and its politicization over our lives just as we would resist a religious cult trying to tell us how to live. A shrinking number of people tolerated big government legislating and regulating our money, morals, and businesses.

That anti-authority trend gained momentum as medical catastrophes loomed. Under growing survival pressures, the people saw more clearly and ended the ruling class.

There was also another, more specific force at work: the inevitable Twelve Visions Party with the underlying mission to

496

prevent the coming medical catastrophes. The Twelve Visions Party, upon its success, set free the geniuses of society. They brought the Technological Revolution beyond the computer industry to the medical industry and to all American industries — the only antidote to the looming medical and economic catastrophes.

The Twelve Visions Party quickly depoliticized the medical industry and set free the drug companies and especially the aggressive entrepreneurs, the geniuses of society. The Twelve Visions Party represented medical technology versus medical catastrophe...the new world of freed geniuses using Neothink® versus the old world of career politicians and bureaucrats suppressing progress. The Twelve Visions Party brought in the new world and unleashed the technologies and geniuses in *all* industries.

When America embraced the Twelve Visions Party, the party for depoliticizing America, then three benefits surfaced:

1. Near-perfect health for the young, the old, and for those in their prime.
2. Millionaire-like wealth for ordinary people, including the poor.
3. Exciting creative jobs *for nearly everyone,* which released nearly everyone's human potential (the Fifth and Sixth Visions).

Young Again

My Twelfth Vision showed me that as the ordinary person got swept into a stimulating life of nearly perfect health and millionaire wealth, he passionately sought life over death. Death at mid-70 simply became unacceptable. Science, medicine, business, and entrepreneurs focused on an epic event: eradicate diseases and illnesses to enable ordinary people to live healthily well into their hundreds, and then beyond.

Technology-blocking "higher authorities" such as the FDA that burdened progress were scorned out of existence by the people.

Today, most people feel the unacceptability of the ultimate disease, *aging*. But few people can relate to their own greatest tragedy of dying in their 70s because:

• The thought of living healthily and prosperously for 130 years

497

or more seems like science fiction.

• One's wealth, health, love and happiness are stagnant or shrinking. At 75 years, life is no longer very stimulating, and the desire to live longer in "old age" is gone.

In tomorrow's rapidly progressing Twelve Visions World, I saw (in my Twelfth Neothink® Vision) that the idea of living longer did not seem so futuristic. What before seemed technologically impossible was in wide use. Without disease, we lived well into our hundreds. Moreover, the idea of extending human life by slowing the disease of cellular degeneration or aging, and slowing the effects of gravity and entropy, became a mass appeal, especially as ordinary people became wealthy, healthy, and in love with life…the young and romantic life. The geniuses were hard at work learning how to extend our lives!

Today, by contrast, people eventually lose the desire to live. Sinking in stagnation, most good people experience limited financial and emotional success. Physically, emotionally, and financially burned out, most older people do not care to live too much longer. Quality of elderly life is far below what it would be in tomorrow's Twelve Visions World. Thus, today the desire to live longer is not in wide demand.

In tomorrow's nonpoliticized wealthy/healthy/exhilarating Twelve Visions World, I saw people regain a childlike desire to live longer. Rich and in love with life, the desire to live longer was in wide demand.

Death Under 100 Became Unacceptable

A strong sense of tragedy grew in us as we got older and closed in on death. We emotionally grasped the unacceptability of dying in our 70s. In fact, the thought of dying at all, not to mention *so young*, grew increasingly intolerable. That unacceptability of dying was a direct result of our deep and permanent happiness as value creators (Vision Two). Tomorrow, the freed geniuses of society raced forward to answer our cries for life as we discovered the persons we were meant to be, forever ending the burden of life (Visions One and Two).

Forbidden Revelation

Most of us today do not grasp the tragedy of dying so young because, as we grow older, we steadily lose our enthusiasm for life. The burden of life comes to the surface as we use up our happy experiences of life (Vision Two). We cannot blame ourselves, for in today's suppressed world, life offers limited mortal doses of wealth and happiness.

My Twelfth Vision showed me that tomorrow's Twelve Visions World actually *reversed* the trend: enthusiasm actually *intensified* as we grew older. As Neothink® value creators, we built larger and larger puzzles of creation, which became very exhilarating. Instead of withering in our ruts, we blossomed in our creations.

In tomorrow's Twelve Visions World, our brief seven-and-a-half decades of life was considered much too brief for the wealthy and happy ordinary person. The demand for living longer grew enormous. First, disease was eradicated to give us healthy life well into our hundreds. Then, major businesses, financial institutions, scientists, research doctors and entrepreneurs embraced the growing demand for longer life. Money, minds, technology, science, medicine came together through entrepreneurial business. Their superpuzzle soon pieced together the ultimate demand of slowing down and eventually curing the disease of aging. (See my Neothink® trilogy *Superpuzzle,* 1200-pages).

The geniuses awakened the sleeping-giant consumer product of all time: life extension. For suddenly, happy people's *brief* time in all eternity became unacceptable. Too brief. Within *your* lifetime, the new Twelve Visions World doubled your journey through life...and eventually more.

The Life We Were Meant To Live

Tomorrow's Twelve Visions World saved us from emotional diminishment and lifted us to the next level of happiness. We lived each and every day with four new frontiers of happiness, described in *Twelve Visions* (a Mark Hamilton Publication).

Today's world brings us uneventful years for the time we have left...for our one short experience of life in all eternity. In the Twelve Visions World, by contrast, my Twelfth Vision showed me

499

we were like children with so much yet to experience. As value creators, we had no limits…always another adventure to create and experience. We finally lived the lives human beings were meant to live. Before the Twelve Neothink® Visions, we had no clue of that life.

Tomorrow, life was bigger than life again, like when we were children. Every new day filled us with exhilaration. Creating exciting new values was how we played as adults. Yes, *play* …like children. We enjoyed the love from our fellow man for creating important values for society. The burden of life was gone. We achieved both the technology and the desire to live a lot, lot longer (Vision Four). We enjoyed nearly perfect physical and mental health for a long, extended life of happiness.

Today, the regulatory and entitlement programs for the "social good" are illusions that politicize our lives and rule over us — over our money, morals, and businesses. The career politicians and regulatory bureaucrats get enormous power, prestige, and they control enormous wealth. On the other hand, we get suppressed and stuck with physical diseases, mental stagnation, and short burdensome lives.

Looking forward into the Twelve Visions World, career politicians and regulatory bureaucrats were left behind. The geniuses jumped ahead into Neothink® and brought us enormous buying power and nearly perfect health. Thereafter, we too jumped into Neothink®. As described in the full Twelfth Vision (in *Twelve Visions,* a Mark Hamilton Publication), four new frontiers of happiness appeared before our eyes and brought us back to our child of the past and a beautiful, long-lost world in which we permanently rediscovered the thrill of life.

Forbidden Chapter Nine
Educating Geniuses

Upon entering first grade at six years of age, the natural motivational drive in the child is gradually lost. You see, the premise of public schools today is: *Prepare children to effectively integrate into society*. Now, imagine that the eager child dreams about growing up and becoming a famous person who does wonderful things...a great value creator. "I'll do great things for the world and become a millionaire!" But those dreams gradually dissipate as the child blends into today's suppressed civilization.

In my Ninth Vision, I witnessed the premise of Twelve-Visions-World schools: *Prepare children to create values that many people need and are excited to buy*. My Vision showed me that on the child's first day of school, the teacher would walk in and say, "I'm going to prepare you to create great things for the world, and as a result you will become famous and rich!" Wow, the child sat up and took notice — his dreams confirmed! His motivation grew with compounding momentum as he steadily gained the ability to achieve his dreams throughout his Twelve-Visions-World education.

The Old School

In today's suppressed civilization, children have little chance to grow up and become rich with a public education. Consider the trend in public schools today concerning the three fundamentals of education. (The three fundamentals of structure, motivation, and thinking as identified by renowned educator, Professor Leonard Peikoff):

Structure: Increasing trend toward class discussions, free-flowing thoughts from kids and teachers, random facts about events and dates pragmatically "structured" to bring the child into "what's happening in today's social environment". The child hears all those unintegrated points (i.e., percepts), but later he forgets much of what he saw and heard in school.

Thinking: The child is not taught to *integrate*. He is not taught to integrate the many random percepts into common denominators

— into a few timeless, unforgettable concepts. He never knows the power of his mind to integrate random percepts into structured concepts for everlasting knowledge. Knowledge is power, but he retains little knowledge. Instead, he absorbs then forgets unintegrated, pragmatic percepts, many regarding what's germane to the politically correct times. When he graduates, his mind is quite impotent as he settles into our suppressed society.

Motivation: He has little certainty, just a go-with-the-flow "education". The child learns to "fit in". He is trapped, at the mercy of our society, economy, national standard of living. There is nothing to be motivated over, for the child implicitly feels less and less power to rise above the suppressed state of things, above the burden of life he sees in his parents, to create new values for society and enjoy the emotional and financial rewards as an adult. Dreams become blurry and fade.

The New School

In tomorrow's Twelve Visions World, by comparison, dreams not only came true for schoolchildren and for adults, too, but those initial dreams were just the beginning. I saw it all in my Ninth Vision:

Structure: Twelve-Visions-World schools had a highly ordered presentation of knowledge, via class lectures, starting with bare percepts and integrating those many percepts by common denominators into a few timeless concepts for rapid absorption and permanent retention of knowledge. Knowledge was power. Through building timeless concepts, the child retained all that he learned in school. Moreover, he observed and learned *how to integrate* to build, piece by piece, onto his base of concepts — to build more and more knowledge and power throughout his life in order to someday *create great values for society*.

Thinking: The child was taught to integrate. He discovered why his mind was infinitely superior to all other animals. He integrated knowledge through common denominators from random percepts into structured concepts. He learned to form a few large concepts, not memorize many specific percepts. Thus, that child

502

retained magnitudes more knowledge through integrated thinking. Soon, he learned how to snap a few of those concepts together into simple puzzles. Integrated, puzzle-building thinking sent thrills through the child, and it would eventually take him to great heights. The child quickly rose beyond the reach of all stagnation traps. Instead of heading toward a routine rut, he was heading toward exhilarating value creation...and a creation-driven life.

Motivation: The child knew with certainty that he could make a difference, for knowledge was power. The child felt certainty and power. He naturally became motivated for more, for superchild would now grow up to become superman or superwoman. The child felt like dynamite! The thrill for life, for expanding awareness and control, gained momentum. He felt more and more power to someday do great things for society and make great wealth for himself — every child's dream. Dreams became focussed and closer. The child became highly motivated.

Our Children Lifted the World

In today's civilization, our education does not properly teach children how *to think, to integrate and build mental puzzles* of new knowledge. In the Twelve Visions World, education and children's minds will exist at a whole different level.

The Ninth Vision showed me that toddlers' rapid learning curves did not slow down. With the same thrill for life and expanding awareness nurtured by proper education, our children and grandchildren evolved straight into Neothink® and soared beyond even the smartest and richest people alive today.

Tomorrow's superchild became a genius of society who, with his peers, made us all rich through brilliant technological breakthroughs that drove prices toward zero and buying power toward infinity, a similar phenomenon to what we have already seen in the computer industry. For the most part, our children and grandchildren lifted the world after the collapse of the ruling class.

Secret Teachings to My Exclusive Inner Circle

On the Prosperous Path in the Twelve Visions World

Obviously, tomorrow's superchild needed a lot of knowledge. The discussion method that dominated public schools in the late twentieth century and early twenty-first century vanished. The original idea behind that popular discussion method was that children taught each other in order to help develop their social and communication skills — to better integrate into society. However, *tomorrow's superchild needed knowledge*. Twelve-Visions-World education used the old-fashioned lecture method in which the teacher did the teaching and filled the child with knowledge.

Now, the superchild rapidly built upon that base of knowledge as he grew up. Unlike us, he was taught conceptual thinking and integrated thinking. To perceive surroundings — see, hear, feel, smell, taste — was automatic and present in most animals. Man's superiority came from his ability *to integrate*. Tomorrow, our children and grandchildren integrated percepts by common denominators into concepts to generate reason and knowledge. That process was called conceptual thinking. Soon thereafter, their minds could build concept upon concept into puzzles of knowledge. That process was called integrated thinking. Tomorrow, without today's education blocking our children's integrated thinking, they reached out more and more widely and onto Neothink®.

Leaving Behind the Old Way

As researched by renowned Professor Leonard Peikoff and detailed in his *Philosophy of Education,* public schools (and most private schools) in the latter twentieth century and early twenty-first century did not teach children how to integrate the endless percepts into a few simplified concepts. For example, instead of teaching children the simple concepts of phonetics (e.g., a "p" makes a "pa" sound), public schools in the late twentieth century taught the look-say or whole-language method. Phonetics required understanding 44 simple concepts (i.e., sounds); look-say required memorizing how to read *every single word* the child ever saw (i.e., perceived) with no simplifying common denominators such as phonics (i.e., no

504

concepts).

Indeed, children in *all* subjects — history, math, science, literature — were taught impotent perceptual thinking and not potent conceptual thinking. History, for example, was taught by unintegrated specific events (i.e., by percepts) and not grouped together by common denominators into concepts. For example, the wrath of human destruction over the centuries was touched on fact by fact (i.e., percept by percept) but not grouped into the basic underlying concept of tyranny, of rule of man — a ruling class. Thus, children did not make connections of logic and, instead, lived their lives in a somewhat helpless "airhead state". They retained very little knowledge since they never learned how to *integrate* percepts by common denominators into interlocked concepts of logic — the very capacity that separated man from the other animals. In short, children never learned *to think*. ...Was it not to be expected that essentially all children in the anticivilization grew up to a life of stagnation? Was it any surprise that smart politicians ran things the way *they* wanted to?

In the Twelve Visions World, as I saw in my Ninth Vision, children grew up to be geniuses with powerful motivational drives. They were intensely happy, for they did not experience the tragedy of their dreams fading as we did. Moreover, as those children tomorrow grew up, they used Neothink® to not only make their own dreams come true, but ours as well.

To get a metaphorical sense of the power of integrated thinking, imagine, for a moment, a large boulder sits near the edge of a cliff. We find the strongest man in the world and ask him to push that boulder over the cliff. He braces his shoulder against the boulder and pushes with all his might. The boulder does not even budge. Well, we could find the next thousand strongest men in the world, line them up, and watch them one by one push the boulder with all their might. But the boulder never budges. ...That is a metaphor for how we are taught to use our minds in school, thus later at work — to helplessly push our thoughts one by one against the big boulder to success. The big boulder to success never budges.

Now, imagine this: you and I and ten average guys brace our shoulders against the big boulder and, all together, give it one big heave. That boulder would roll right over the cliff! ...That is a metaphor for how our children's minds will work tomorrow with a Twelve-Visions-World education — continually bringing together many thoughts into one powerful force to easily push over the big boulder to success. With this powerful *integrated thinking* tomorrow, our children grew up to push through all the money-making barriers that even the thousand smartest men today could never move through.

More Creative Than Today's Smartest People

My Ninth Vision clearly showed me that integrated thinking gave our children more creative power tomorrow than the smartest men and women in the world today. That was why our children and grandchildren actually became creative geniuses, even with average IQs!

Our education today in our suppressed civilization gives us powerless perceptual or specialized thinking that leaves us stranded as adults in routine-rut jobs with specialized tasks. Even if someone today is very good at what he does, he is usually powerless at fulfilling his deepest dreams, sort of like those world's strongest men powerless at pushing over the big boulder.

In tomorrow's Twelve Visions World, however, our children grew up learning how to snap thoughts together into an integrated force that easily pushed over the big boulder to major success.

In today's civilization, the same forces that hold back super entrepreneurs and super technologies also hold back our children's development. You see, career politicians and regulatory bureaucrats increasingly control our educational system. The ordinary person graduates from our public schools with severe short circuits; he or she cannot put together the connections needed to be creative. He or she, in short, cannot integrate.

Make A Change

Knock out of your mind the passive acceptance of your children and grandchildren settling into a specialized routine rut. They can escape the stagnation-trap you perhaps endured.

Imagine their most ambitious dreams, and daydream about them for a few minutes. In your mind's eye, block out the obstacles that will hold them down in a stagnant routine rut. Instead, see your children and grandchildren leading the way to exhilarating success.

With all that you know now, that daydream strikingly demonstrates to you (as it did for me) that, in today's suppressed civilization, they will grow up, trapped in a terminal rut. As simple as it may seem, that striking snapshot of their lifelong stagnation-trap can set off an act of self-preservation: as happened to me, you might start seeking the Twelve-Visions-Party agenda.

With a Twelve-Visions-World education, as seen in my Ninth Vision, our children and grandchildren frequently came up with major marketing ideas, for marketing ideas were simply an exercise of the mind: of finding common denominators that served a lot of people's needs. They then built success upon those structured concepts, say those great marketing ideas, through forward-movement integrated thinking.

Their creativity and energy went toward identifying then servicing society's needs. Indeed, those geniuses — our children and grandchildren — solved people's problems and needs. As a result, enormous creativity and energy rushed into society. Prosperity reigned throughout America, then across our planet. Exhilaration and wealth filled our children's and grandchildren's lives.

Knowledge is power. But creating *new knowledge* is *super power*. The richest people today *created* something new. Through forward-movement integrated thinking, they integrated lots of existing knowledge. While steadily putting together existing knowledge, they hit critical points that broke through into new knowledge. While steadily building their success-puzzles piece by piece, they reached a point when they had snapped together a creative new puzzle-picture. At that point, they experienced Neothink®. Tomorrow, our children evolved into the Neothink® mentality.

Realize, our graduating geniuses were not necessarily gifted with creativity. Not until they built a certain size success-puzzle did they begin springing into creativity. You see, as they built their success-puzzles piece by piece, they began to see puzzle-pictures gradually forming. As they saw their puzzle-pictures coming together, they broke into new knowledge while seeing how their unique pictures and their missing pieces must look like. Then they began *creating* by completing those unique puzzle-pictures.

Forming The Bridge to Money and Power

Sometimes we wonder how a money/power giant got from point A in school to point B on top of the world. Building success-puzzles, piece by piece, formed his bridges to money and power. To build those success-puzzles, piece by piece, though, requires integrated thinking. Tomorrow, under the new code of education, that happened automatically to ordinary people. Today, under the old code of education, that seldom happens to even extraordinary people.

I observed in my Ninth Vision that it was integrated thinking that eventually enabled the entire human race to mentally cross the bridges to a whole new way of orchestrating our minds in the Twelve Visions World, something we called the *Neothink® Mentality*. Neothink® was so superior that once it got started, its natural advantages quickly engaged people everywhere.

Neothink® comes from compilations of complex concepts that, when pulled together, reveal startling, synergistic advancements of human knowledge. (*Twelve Visions*, a Mark Hamilton Publication, is an example of Neothink®.)

Very rare today, Neothink® became our children's and grandchildren's normal mentality in tomorrow's Twelve Visions World. We, too, eventually evolved into Neothink®. With Neothink®, ordinary people routinely contributed life-lifting values to mankind. Ordinary people became extraordinary.

Becoming Geniuses

When that happened, we discovered our unknown selves: our

buried genius within. The measurement for mental power changed from intelligence tests for IQ to the efficacy of one's integrated thinking. IQ no longer mattered (save for subnormal, mental retardation, of course). In time, the superior Neothink® mentality swept across our planet. Babies naturally grew into and children naturally stayed in the Neothink® mentality.

Tomorrow's schools, as seen in my Ninth Vision, taught our children and grandchildren how to Neothink®. As they grew up, they joined the geniuses. Indeed, living exhilarating creation-driven lives instead of boring routine ruts, they joined the entrepreneurial geniuses and created wonderful values for the world.

Your children and grandchildren built larger and larger puzzles of knowledge through integrated thinking. With that integrated, puzzle-building thinking, surpassing their best dreams became natural and fun. They lived the way man is supposed to live. Highly motivated and making more and more conceptual advancements, they learned how to pull the integration string. That was when they saw their first puzzle-pictures. Pulling together their conceptual advancements into one interlocked, synergistic advancement of knowledge, one clear puzzle-picture of new knowledge, they experienced the euphoria of Neothink®. Soon, they crossed over to the Neothink® mentality and continued to pull together those synergistic advancements of knowledge in their lines of work or interests. Of course, they were greatly rewarded with prestige, wealth, happiness, and love.

My Ninth Vision showed me that sometime in the twenty-first century, snapping together synergistic advancements of knowledge became the norm for ordinary people graduating in the Twelve Visions World.

Recommended Reading:

Inside Secrets, Mark Hamilton (nonfiction) teaches adults integrated thinking in their careers.

Twelve Visions, Mark Hamilton (nonfiction) discloses the turnkey advantages of tomorrows Twelve-Visions World.

Superpuzzle, Mark Hamilton (faction) lets us experience living in tomorrow's Twelve-Visions World.

Notes

Notes

Notes

Notes

Notes

Notes

Notes

Notes

Notes